# Edmund Spenser

## Twayne's English Authors Series

Arthur Kinney, Editor

*University of Massachusetts, Amherst*

TEAS 535

SAINT GEORGE AND THE DRAGON. FROM THE 1590 EDITION OF
*THE FAERIE QUEENE.*
*Reproduced by permission of the Huntington Library, San Marino, California.*

# Edmund Spenser

## William Allan Oram

*Smith College*

Twayne Publishers
An Imprint of Simon & Schuster Macmillan
New York

Prentice Hall International
London • Mexico City • New Delhi • Singapore • Sydney • Toronto

Twayne's English Authors Series No. 535

*Edmund Spenser*
William Allan Oram

Twayne Publishers
An Imprint of Simon & Schuster Macmillan
1633 Broadway
New York, New York 10019

**Library of Congress Cataloging-in-Publication Data**

Oram, William A.
    Edmund Spenser / William Allan Oram.
        p.    cm. — (Twayne's English authors series ; TEAS 535)
    Includes bibliographical references and index.
    ISBN 0-8057-8622-8 (alk. paper)
    1. Spenser, Edmund, 1552?-1599—Criticism and interpretation.
    I. Title.    II. Series.
    PR2364.O78    1997
    821'.3—dc21                                                                    96-44377
                                                                                          CIP

10   9   8   7   6   5   4   3   2   1
Printed in the United States of America

*For Micala*

# Contents

# Editor's Note

Edmund Spenser was the greatest poet in the golden age of the Elizabethan Renaissance. William Allan Oram, the coordinating editor of *The Yale Edition of the Shorter Poems of Edmund Spenser,* has written an extraordinarily comprehensive study of the poet and all of his poetry—the first such study to appear in more than a generation. With a shrewd sense of the genres that Spenser studied and transformed in each of his works and an equally acute sense of the current state of criticism, Oram shows how the poet was at once deliberately public and intensely private in what he thought and wrote. This examination will replace that of William Nelson, published in 1963, as the primary resource for understanding all of the poetic works, from *The Shepheardes Calender* to the last great poems. What is especially welcome here is the placement of *The Faerie Queene* where it best belongs, sequentially and thematically with all the works of Spenser, long and short. Oram's readings are exemplary: at once lucid and inviting, enriching and resonant, and yet never final, showing readers where to begin, telling them what they should know, and leaving room for continuing reinterpretation. This is a book of considerable insight, sensitivity, and commitment.

Arthur F. Kinney

# Preface

This book aims to give an overview of Spenser's work, dwelling most importantly on how his poems develop the generic traditions he inherited and changed. I have organized it chronologically because it seems to me that he changed significantly in method and emphasis over the twenty-odd years of his poetic career. While he showed himself capable from the first, in *The Shepheardes Calender*, of dazzling generic experimentation, that experimentation continued and deepened during his life, especially in his returns to the two genres of pastoral and complaint. In his later work he also experiments with an ongoing fictive biography, staging himself in various roles and creating fictional versions of his biographical experience. A final concern of the book is Spenser's uneasy relation to the court world he hoped first as a courtier to rise in, needed later as an Irish landowner to depend on, and distrusted.

To emphasize Spenser's ongoing development, I have separated the two installments of *The Faerie Queene,* placing them among Spenser's other works in order of publication. I have also placed the *Mutabilitie Cantos* as a separate poem at the end. While we do not know for certain when most of *The Faerie Queene* was written, and some late sections may have been drafted early, there is, nonetheless, a difference of emphasis between the two halves of the poem. Although splitting the epic in this way diminishes the sense of continuity between them, it will, I hope, help to set the second installment in the context of the later poetry.

Because there are already many distinguished introductions to *The Faerie Queene,* from C. S. Lewis's luminous chapter in *The Allegory of Love* to Humphrey Tonkin's recent book on the poem, and few attempts at a comprehensive look at the shorter poems, I've reversed the normal proportions for a study of Spenser's work. Two-thirds of these pages go to the shorter poems, and one-third to the epic. While this means that my treatment of *The Faerie Queene* is at best an outline, to be supplemented by the studies listed in the notes and the bibliography, it has been possible to treat the shorter poems in somewhat greater detail. I have chosen to treat several works, most notably the translations in the *Theatre for Worldlings* and *A View on the Present State of Ireland*, in the biographical chapter that opens the book.

I have the great good luck to have many debts to account for, far more than can be mentioned here or in the notes. It was my good fortune to be taught by Harry Berger, Jr., and Thomas Greene: to me (and probably to my readers) their influence is everywhere obvious. Many friends provided expert knowledge—Harold Garrett-Goodyear, Ronald R. MacDonald, Howard Nenner, Thalia Pandiri, Nancy Shumate, Betty von Klemperer among them, while others read and commented on chapters—often several chapters: Nancy Bradbury, Luc Gilleman, Betsey Harries, Douglas Patey, Sharon Seelig, Lauren Silberman. With their usual acuity, learning, and generosity, Harold Skulsky annotated much, and Anne Lake Prescott most, of the total manuscript, correcting my errors and suggesting new ways to see what I thought I saw perfectly well already. Their aid was manifold, but I want in particular to thank Harold for deepening my understanding of the various ways in which Spenser returns to the problem of despair, and Anne for forcing me to consider what Mrs. Spenser would have thought of certain charged passages of the *Epithalamion*. The mistakes remaining are, of course, my own. From the time that he offered me the opportunity to write an introduction to Spenser's large corpus, Arthur Kinney has been the kind of editor one hopes for and rarely finds—encouraging, helpful, and willing at necessary times to give the necessary push. A sabbatical year from Smith College in 1991–92 enabled me to begin serious work on this book. My student assistants Laura Baumeister, Rosemary Brown, and Coral Davenport helped me in many ways and saved me much grief. I owe much the most to Micala Sidore, to whom this book is dedicated.

In all quotations from *The Faerie Queene* I follow the edition of Thomas P. Roche (Harmondsworth: Penguin, 1978), referred to in the notes as *FQ*; for all other poems I use *The Yale Edition of the Shorter Poems of Edmund Spenser*, ed. William A. Oram, Einar Bjorvand, Ronald Bond, Thomas H. Cain, Alexander Dunlop, and Richard Schell (New Haven: Yale University Press, 1989), referred to in the notes as *YESP*. The source for the Five Letters and *A View of the Present State of Ireland* is Rudolf Gottfried's edition of *Spenser's Prose Works* (Baltimore: Johns Hopkins Press, 1949), hereafter cited as *VP*. This edition is volume 9 of the *The Works of Edmund Spenser: A Variorum Edition,* ed. Edwin Greenlaw, Charles Grosvenor Osgood, Frederick Morgan Padelford, and Ray Heffner (Baltimore: Johns Hopkins Press, 1949), hereafter cited as *VE*. Biblical quotations follow the facsimile edition of the 1560 Geneva Bible with an introduction by Lloyd E. Berry (Madison: University of Wisconsin Press, 1969). When necessary *u* and *v*, *i* and *j* have been normalized according to modern usage.

# Chronology

and purchases various properties and eventually (1588; formal grant 1590) acquires Kilcolman Castle, with an estate of 3,000 acres in Munster, which he undertakes to "plant" with English immigrants.

1582    Lord Grey recalled to England in August.

1585    English Expedition to the Low Countries, under the earl of Leicester.

1586    Death of Sir Philip Sidney at Zutphen.

1587    Mary, Queen of Scots beheaded.

1588    Defeat of the Spanish Armada; death of the earl of Leicester.

1589    Beginning of Spenser's lengthy legal quarrel with the Anglo-Irish Lord Roche, his neighbor in Munster. In October Spenser accompanies Sir Walter Ralegh to England.

        1 December    Ponsonby enters *The Faerie Queene* (books 1–3) on the Stationer's Register.

1590    May    Spenser may have returned briefly to Ireland to pursue suit against Lord Roche. Publication of Sir Phillip Sidney's *Arcadia*.

        29 December    *Complaints* entered on Stationers' Register.

1591–?  Publication of *Daphnaïda* (dedication dated 1 January 1591).

        25 February    Spenser receives an annual life pension of £50.

        Publication of Sidney's *Astrophil and Stella*.

        27 December    Dedicatory epistle of *Colin Clouts Come Home Againe*, addressed to Sir Walter Ralegh.

1592    In June the queen discovers Ralegh's secret marriage to Elizabeth Throckmorton and imprisons him. Ralegh is eventually barred from court. Publication of an English translation of the pseudo-platonic dialog *Axiochus*, by Edw. [*sic*] Spenser, possibly the poet.

1593    The Protestant Henri IV becomes Roman Catholic in order to gain French Catholic support for his rule.

?1594   Spenser marries Elizabeth Boyle 11 June, the summer
        solstice.

        19 November   *Amoretti and Epithalamion* entered on
        the Stationer's Register

1595    Publication of *Colin Clouts Come Home Againe* and *Astro-
        phel*. An English fleet sent to attack the Spanish in the
        West Indies fails to take either Puerto Rico or Panama
        City.

1596    Publication of *The Faerie Queene* (books 4–6); Spenser
        probably in London.

        July   English fleet commanded in part by the earl of
        Essex sacks Cadiz. *Prothalamion* most likely written in
        September.

        1 September   *Fowre Hymnes*.

        17 November   Spanish fleet sent against England
        wrecked in a storm off the Bay of Biscay.

1597    Spenser purchases land in Cork for his son Peregrine;
        also rents Buttevant Abbey. English fleet sent to
        destroy ships in northern Spanish ports and to attack
        the Azores fails largely because of bad weather. Span-
        ish fleet sent to attack England also dispersed by
        storms.

1598    Death of Phillip II; death of Burleigh 14 April. *A View
        of the Present State of Ireland* entered on Stationer's Reg-
        ister. Dialogue not published but circulates in manu-
        script copies.

        30 September   Privy Council recommends Spenser for
        sheriff of Cork.

        October   Irish rebellion in Leinster spreads to Munster.
        Kilcolman burned.

        24 December   Spenser returns to England with dis-
        patches for the Privy Council from Sir John Norris. At
        this time may have written and presented the council
        with *A Briefe Note of Ireland* condensing the argument
        of the *View*.

1599    13 January   Spenser dies. Essex pays the cost of the
        funeral.

1603    Death of Elizabeth I.

1609    Publication of *The Faerie Queene* with the *Cantos of Mutabilitie*, in folio edition.

1611    Publication of *The Faerie Queene: The Shepheardes Calender; Together with the other Works of England's Arch-Poet, Edm. Spencer.*

1633    Publication of *A View of the State of Ireland,* ed. by Sir James Ware.

1679    Publication of *The Works of that Famous English Poet, Mr. Edmond Spenser.*

# Chapter One

# Spenser's Career

Until its disastrous last year the outline of Edmund Spenser's career might seem to embody the best hopes of Renaissance humanism. Rising from obscurity (we know nothing certain about his parents except for his mother's name, Elizabeth), he served his prince and became a gentleman, joining the English administration in Ireland and gaining an estate of more than 3,000 acres. As a poet he had, like Milton, an exalted conception of his public role as seer and teacher: he saw himself as a national figure celebrating the glory of the English commonwealth, as Virgil had Rome's. In any event, he did become the most famous poet of his generation and was rewarded for his work with a pension from the queen. His biography would seem in most respects to be what William Nelson has called it—"a success story."[1]

Yet the voices of his work—searching, ambivalent, and at times deeply frustrated—articulate a less happy view of his career. While he regarded the worth of his poetry with serene confidence, he worried increasingly about its reception. His elevated—or inflated—vision of a poet as the court's moral center conflicted with the common view that a poet was an entertainer whose business was "to please." In *The Shepheardes Calender* at the start of Spenser's career, Piers asks disconsolately: "O pierlesse Poesye, where is then thy place?"[2] and in *Prothalamion,* at its end, Spenser speaks of his "long fruitlesse stay / In Princes Court, and expectation vayne / Of idle hopes, which still doe fly away, / Like empty shaddowes" (6–9). The unsuccessful search for patronage is a constant theme of his biography and his poetry. Poets, he says in *Colin Clout,* cannot find fit patrons: "single Truth and simple honestie / Do wander up and downe despys'd of all" (727–28). None of the great men he looked to would long afford him the security he sought, and none of them enabled him to become an insider in the court world.

In addition to some casual allusion and gossip, such as Ben Jonson's offhand comment that Spenser "died for lake [lack] of bread in King Street,"[3] two kinds of evidence bridge this difference in perspective. On the one hand are many external documents—entries in the records of the Merchant Taylor's School or Pembroke College, leases of property, the

1

payments of his pension, legal briefs, state correspondence in his hand. As with Shakespeare, this evidence tells us something about Spenser's gradual rise in prosperity but little about the kind of man he was. On the other hand is his writing—writing that often makes use of his biography for its own ends. As Spenser developed as a poet, he made reference to his own life and career increasingly central to his meaning, but the life was always given fictional patterning: we are shown a version of his life, an aspect of himself. While we do not know much of what we want to about Spenser's life, taking these different kinds of evidence together we can begin to get a sense of both Spenser's great successes and the limits that so constantly frustrated him. If Spenser was England's Virgil, he became a Virgil speaking from the margins rather than the center. For all its successes, his life is the biography of an outsider.

## Early Years: 1552–1569

We calculate from a reference in one of the sonnets of the *Amoretti* that Spenser was born between 1552 and 1554; elsewhere he says that London was his "kyndly Nurse." He claimed connection with the wealthy gentry family of the Spencers of Althorp in Northamptonshire and Wormleighton in Warwickshire, three of whose daughters he praises in *Colin Clouts Come Home Againe.* As a child he attended the Merchant Taylors' School in London; his father (possibly John Spenser, a Lancashire cloth weaver who moved to London) may have been connected with the Merchant Taylors' Company. The school had 250 boys (100 of whom came from poor families and paid no tuition), a high master, and three ushers (subordinate teachers). The school met from seven to eleven o'clock in the morning and from one to five in the afternoon. Although Spenser probably studied music and some arithmetic, he would have devoted most of his time to the mastery of Latin language and rhetoric—Erasmus's dialogues and Latin versions of Aesop's fables in the lower forms, and Horace, Cicero, Virgil, Lucan, and Caesar in the upper forms. In these upper forms the Merchant Taylors' School also offered Greek and some Hebrew: we have records of one examination that included Homer and the Hebrew Psalms. There would have been extensive practice in the writing of Latin rhetorical exercises following Erasmus's *Copia*—phrasing the same idea in various ways.

While we cannot document the effect of the school's headmaster on Spenser, he could hardly have been better chosen as the teacher of England's future epic poet. Richard Mulcaster was a humanist scholar who directed and taught in the school from its founding in 1561 until 1586; eventually he became headmaster of St. Paul's. He was an unusually able man, a northerner educated at Oxford and Cambridge, who later became important in London intellectual circles. From the evidence of his two books on education, *Positions* (1581) and *The First Part of the Elementerie* (1582), he was a born teacher who wrote about educational reform with understanding and passion. He stresses the need to adapt one's instruction to the capacities of the student, and his books come alive with a shrewd sense of how students and teachers think and act. He advocates spelling reform, education for women, physical education, and uniformity of instruction from school to school. Throughout his books he returns to the idea that education prepares one for a public life—that it looks toward virtuous action in the world. This sense of the importance of public service is the kind of lesson a student would internalize and remember long after his Greek was gone; it may have strengthened Spenser's sense of his own poetic calling. Mulcaster wrote a demandingly dense and pithy prose and stressed the potential power and richness of the English language. "I do not think that anie language be it whatsoever, is better able to utter all arguments, either with more pith, or greater planesse, than our *English* tung is." Or again: "I love *Rome* but *London* better, I favor *Italie* but England more, I honor the Latin but I worship the *English*."[4] These sentiments cannot have been lost on a student who would try in his own tongue to surpass or "overgo" the lyrics and the epics of other languages.

Mulcaster's connections with the group of Dutch Protestant refugees in London may have enabled Spenser's first published work. In 1569 one of the exiles, Jan Van der Noodt, published a translation of his own book, which had appeared the year before in Dutch and French editions, *A Theatre wherein be represented as wel the miseries & calamities that follow the voluptuous Worldings, As also the greate joyes and plesures which the faithful do enjoy.* The book consists of three sets of visionary poems, illustrated by woodcuts, followed by 200 pages of commentary, the bulk of the book. Spenser translated the poetry.

The book is an extended meditation on transience, and it brings together the works of three authors who would be central to Spenser's poetry. It begins with six "epigrams," the stanzas of Francesco Petrarca's *Rime 323* that meditate on the death of his lady, Laura. The speaker sees her in six different allegorical guises—as, for instance, a doe, a ship, a laurel tree—and in each case the vision ends in destruction: the doe is hunted to death by hounds, the ship is wrecked, the tree is struck by lightning. Van der Noodt follows the epigrams with 11 sonnets from the short sequence of Joachim Du Bellay entitled *Songe* or *Dream.* In this, too, the speaker has emblematic visions of mutability, but mutability in the public world: it is the city of Rome that appears as a crystal temple, a spire, an oak, only to be destroyed. The moral of *Songe* appears in the opening sonnet when the ghost of Rome appears to the poet and cries out: "Loe all is nought but flying vanitie," and the speaker concludes: "So I knowing the worldes unstedfastnesse. . . . In God alone do stay my confidence." But Van der Noodt goes further, suppressing four of the sonnets in *Songe* to add four others at the end that paraphrase the Book of Revelation. These four place the largely secular concern with earthly mutability in the context of Christian history; the vision of all earthly things passing away yields to a vision of God's final judgment of mankind.

Hindsight makes it hard not to see the *Theatre* as a seedbed of Spenserian concerns and techniques, and not only in its attention to mutability. Translation was a common path for any Renaissance poets who began as schoolboys by imitating others, but this beginning is particularly significant for Spenser. As he developed, his translations—journeyman's work here—would become free imitation, and the poems would engage in an increasingly complex response to the earlier poetry: he would rewrite Virgil's *Eclogues,* Petrarch's *Rime,* and Du Bellay's *Antiquités de Rome* in his own way. He would indeed, like the author of the *Theatre,* set different poets against one another as representative of different attitudes of mind. This first book thus reminds us of how much Spenser, from the start, was a European poet. Despite England's physical separation from the Continent, the cultures of Italy, France, and Spain crossed the Channel easily, aided by the movement of Protestant refugees from France and the Low Countries. Finally, the *Theatre* furnished Spenser with his initial conception of the poet's visionary role. Impersonal and public, the poet is a prophetic voice or a visionary eye: he teaches by presenting the reader with a symbolic vision and explaining it. As he developed, both the poet and the visions he saw would change. The visions grew increasingly complex and opaque, and the poet will become a version of the historic Edmund Spenser.

## Cambridge and London, 1569–1580

In the fall of 1569 Spenser enrolled as a sizer, or scholarship student, at Pembroke College, Cambridge. He received a B.A. in 1573 and an M.A. in 1576, but aside from that there are few references to him in the college records, and we do not know where he was between 1573, when he received his B.A., and 1578, when his friend Gabriel Harvey referred to him as secretary to John Young, the bishop of Rochester and a former master of Pembroke. Cambridge would have been the first step for a prospective minister or academic, but its rhetorical and linguistic training was also a road to preferment at court, and the gentry and nobility were increasingly sending their sons there. As an undergraduate Spenser would have done work in logic, arithmetic, and geometry, but he would have focused again on Greek and Latin authors, especially Virgil, Horace, and Cicero. Of Greek authors he would probably have read some Plato, Aristotle (the *Nichomachean Ethics* and *Politics*), and the Greek orators. Greek authors were studied in parallel texts with Latin translations; we do not know how much Greek Spenser knew, but he seems never to have used a Greek text for which a Latin translation was not available. (If he was the translator of the pseudo-platonic dialogue *Axiochus* [1592], he worked from a Latin version, not from the original Greek.)[5] He would have heard lectures on grammar and rhetoric and been present at and participated in the frequent rhetorical debates by students of the college.

As a center of Protestant learning, Cambridge felt the religious controversies that were increasingly to unsettle England. During Spenser's first years as an undergraduate, Thomas Cartwright, Professor of Divinity, argued against the special vestments that symbolically set priests apart from the people and, more largely, criticized the power of the bishops, advocating the model of a "primitive" church controlled by local congregations. Cartwright was eventually deprived of his professorship, but what later came to be known as the "Puritan" movement continued to trouble the established church. Spenser's own relation to that movement is complex, partly because, unlike Milton, he never seems to have been deeply interested in theological debate. His poetry is nationalistic and hence strongly anti-Catholic, and it seems to accept the largely Calvinist theology enunciated by the Elizabethan church. It joins the Puritans in emphasizing the need for a "learned" clergy. Echoes of Cartwright's criticism recur in *The Shepheardes Calender* and *Mother Hubberds Tale*. Yet on at least one occasion Spenser attacks the desecration of images encouraged by some Puritan leaders.

It was at Cambridge that Spenser met his friend Gabriel Harvey, gifted, ambitious, and several years older than himself. Harvey was learned in several disciplines and tried unsuccessfully for a brilliant career as an academic, at court, and in the law. His vanity and tactless-

ness tended to alienate his supporters, and he later had the additional
bad luck to cross verbal swords with Thomas Nashe, whose portrait of
him as a pedantic fool has stuck to the present day. Nashe attacked Harvey with exultant malice as an "indigested Chaos of Doctourship, and
greedy pothunter after applause . . . a self-love surfetted sot . . . a scholer
in nothing but the scum of schollership, a stale soker at Tullies *Offices,*
the droane of droanes, and master drumble-bee of non proficients."[6]
Harvey was not without a certain ironic humor, but he was at a loss in
this kind of contest.

Spenser saw Harvey differently; in a poem written years later he idealized him for fearless independence.

> Harvey, the happy above happiest men
> I read: that sitting like a Looker-on
> Of this worldes Stage, doest note with critique pen
> The sharpe dislikes of each condition:
> And as one carelesse of suspition,
> Ne fawnest for the favour of the great:
> Ne fearest foolish reprehension
> Of faulty men, which daunger to thee threat.
> But freely doest, of what thee list, entreat,
> Like a great Lord of peerelesse liberty:
> Lifting the Good up to high Honours seat,
> And the Evill damning evermore to dy.
> For Life, and Death is in thy doomefull writing:
> So thy renowme lives ever by endighting. (*YESP*, 773)

This sonnet, with its vision of the humanist writer sitting above and at a
godlike distance from the world, fearlessly proclaiming his opinions and
winning eternal fame in the process, may say less about Harvey than it
does about Spenser's own hopes and values. Harvey embodies here one
image of the profession that Spenser must have cherished, however
much in everyday life he was forced to abandon it.

Worldly success has its pleasures, however, and our next extended
record of Spenser comes in an exchange of five letters with Harvey in
October 1579 and April 1580. Spenser wrote from the house of the earl
of Leicester, the longtime favorite of the queen and a leader of the militantly Protestant faction at court. Spenser was impressed with his new

contacts, especially with Philip Sidney, the earl's nephew and heir, and eager to show them off. "Your desire to heare of my late beeing with hir Majestie, muste dye in it selfe. As for the twoo worthy Gentlemen, Master *Sidney,* and master *Dyer,* they have me, I thanke them in some use of familiarity."[7] The precise degree of familiarity between the two major Elizabethan nondramatic poets has been a matter of debate; the evidence for extensive contact is thin. We do not know what position Spenser held in the earl's household (there is reference to a forthcoming trip to France in the earl's service, but the journey was never undertaken), and, indeed, we have no record except the letters of Spenser's ever having met Sidney. Sidney's only extant reference to Spenser is his cool acknowledgment in the *Apology for Poetry* that "The Sheepheardes Kallender hath much *Poetrie* in his Egloges, indeed worthie the reading, if I be not deceived," along with some doubts about Spenser's employment of "old rustick language."[8] The correspondence with Harvey was published in 1580, when Harvey was trying to gain the position of public orator at Cambridge; it may have been part of an attempt to advertise Harvey's talents and connections.

At the same time it would not have done to antagonize Sidney by claiming what was patently false. Sidney and his friend Edward Dyer, Spenser said, were concerned with the reformation of English versification:

> Nowe they have proclaimed in their *areioi pagoi* a generall surceasing and silence of balde Rymers, and also of the verie best to: in steade wherof they have by authoritie of their whole Senate, prescribed certaine Lawes and rules of Quantitites of English sillables, for English Verse: having had thereof already greate practise, and drawen mee to their faction. (*VP*, 6, ll. 44–49)

The playful reference to *areioi pagoi*—senates or councils—may refer to a loose group interested in experimentation with quantitative meter in English; the Greek term is echoed in other contemporary references to Sidney. Harvey (whose satirical verses, Spenser says, Sidney's courtier friend Dyer likes very well) might hope to be one of such a group. It is unlikely, however, that it ever had a formal or even a very extensive existence. His letters testify to Spenser's wish to become part of this aristocratic set rather than to an achieved position.

The Spenser-Harvey correspondence, published as *Familiar Letters* in 1580, and the notes to *The Shepheardes Calender* give us some information about Spenser's poetic career, although its accuracy is sometimes dubious. The letters mention a series of works that were either lost or remained unwritten, including a *Stemmata Dudleiana,* an *Epithalamion Thamesis* (possibly recycled in *The Faerie Queene,* IV.11), a *dying Pellicane, My Slomber, Dreames, The Court of Cupid, Nine Comoedies, Legendes,* and *The English Poete.* Whether these works existed—it is hard to imagine Spenser writing drama, even closet-drama—we cannot know. Harvey commented that the comedies were closer to Ariosto's comedies than Spenser's "*Elvish Queene*" was to his *Orlando Furioso,* and that if Spenser preferred his epic to the plays, "*Hobgoblin* [has] runne away with the Garland from *Apollo*" (*VE,* 471–72). Spenser had begun work on his epic, and Harvey seems to have found it indecorous.

Harvey addressed Spenser as "Immerito," his pen name in *The Shepheardes Calender,* and in a Latin farewell to one of his letters he sent his greetings to "My Lady Immerita" (*mea Domina Immerita*). This is one of several pieces of evidence suggesting that Spenser (now in his late twenties) had married. His bride may have been the strangely named 19-year-old Machabyas Chylde, who married an Edmounde Spenser on 27 October 1579 at Saint Margaret's, Westminster;[9] we have no other record of the existence of Spenser's first wife. Two children survived from his first marriage, a son, Sylvanus, and a daughter, Katherine.

In 1579, a year before *Familiar Letters* was published, Spenser published *The Shepheardes Calender,* his first great effort to establish himself as a poet. What is most striking about the publication is its elaborateness. This book of eclogues appeared in an edition modeled in part on the enormously influential *Arcadia* of Jacopo Sannazaro, with woodcuts, commentary, and glosses of unfamiliar words.[10] This attention—the kind given to classical texts—suggests that Spenser's poem was advertising itself as a modern classic. As such, it begged comparison with the most famous eclogue-book of antiquity, Virgil's, and recalled the familiar tradition that the career of a heroic poet was modeled on Virgil's, beginning with pastoral, moving on to georgic, and ending with epic. Spenser was presenting himself as Virgil's heir and in doing so was attempting to raise the dignity of the poet's role. He was dissociating himself from both the well-born courtier poet whose poems were circulated in manuscript and from the humble professionals who gained their bread by writing for the press. Instead he was attempting to become what Richard Helgerson has aptly called a "Laureate" poet—a national figure whose poetry was serious cultural work, "a means of making a contribution to the order and improvement of the state."[11]

At the same time Spenser hesitated to strike a fully assertive stance. For all the elaborateness of the book's publication, Spenser's name is not on the title page, and the introductory poem bidding farewell to his book is signed only "Immerito." The equivocation about the name (none of his later poems are unsigned) suggests that Spenser may not yet have been entirely secure in his vocation. The pen name was no secret (as we have seen, Harvey refers to Spenser as "Mister Immerito"), but the absence of Spenser's real name suggests a drawing-back from the full notoriety attendant on authorial status. An aspiring courtier—and Spenser certainly was that in 1579—might have been flouting the conventions of the court in publishing his own work.

Spenser's anonymity may also stem from prudence, given the *Calender*'s tendency to comment on public matters. It has become increasingly clear that the *Calender* is a poem full of references to contemporary issues, both religious and political, perhaps fuller than was quite wise for a fledgling poet. Throughout his life Spenser would continue to insist on his own view of public events, and at times that dogged insistence would make trouble for him. Artistically *The Shepheardes Calender* was a turning point in English verse—a demonstration of what the language could do. In its technical virtuosity (the metrical ease and variety of verse forms in the work, including the first sestina in the language, were unparalleled in earlier English poetry), range of styles, and variety of subject matter, the *Calender* set a new standard for English poetry. The book went through five editions in Spenser's lifetime and was of all his poems the one that contemporaries were most likely to single out for praise. There is, however, no evidence that its success gained Spenser substantial rewards from Leicester's patronage.

## Ireland: 1580–1591

*Familiar Letters* shows Spenser caught up in his literary career, comparing verses with Harvey, wondering whether to dedicate *The Shepheardes Calender* to Leicester (at the last minute he dedicated it to Sidney). Yet just when his work would seem to have established Spenser as "our newe Poet," as E.K., the *Calender*'s mysterious commentator, calls him, his career took what looks to us like an unexpected direction. In August 1580 he sailed to Ireland as the secretary of Arthur Grey, Lord Deputy of Ireland. We do not know why Spenser seems suddenly to have changed his plans and abandoned the possibility of a career at court—or if indeed he had. The influential hypothesis put forth long ago by Edwin

Greenlaw—that Lord Burleigh resented Spenser's attack on him in an early version of *Mother Hubberds Tale* and forced him to leave England under a cloud—lacks conclusive evidence, as do all other explanations. Perhaps the decision to go to Ireland was simply a thoughtful career move. Ireland was also being advertised as a land of opportunity where Englishmen could settle and grow rich. One man deeply involved in settlement schemes was Harvey's patron, Sir Thomas Smith; another, less involved, was the earl of Leicester, who might have aided Spenser in his suit to Lord Grey.

Whatever its cause, the decision to move to Ireland turned out to be the most important of Spenser's life. For when Lord Grey left Ireland in 1582, Spenser stayed behind, a householder with a post in the Irish administration. We have glimpses of his public and financial life over the next ten years as he gradually became a man of some substance. Around 1584 his friend and superior in the Irish administration, Lodowick Bryskett, made him his deputy as clerk to the Council of Munster, so that during the 1580s Spenser handled much of the administrative correspondence for the English bureaucracy in the Munster Plantation.

Equally important, he began to purchase a series of leases in parts of the Pale, and in 1588 he took possession of 3,028 acres in Munster, including the castle of Kilcolman (in 1590 he was granted full perpetual lease). The land was part of the vast estate forfeited by the earl of Desmond when he revolted in 1579, and Spenser undertook to "plant" it with 24 English families. Finding such families was not easy for Spenser, or for the other undertakers. On 8 May 1589 he responded to a government questionnaire that he had managed to install six families; he did not answer a later inquiry.

If the move made Spenser a man of substance, it also removed him from the center of power and culture that was the English court. The distance may have benefited Spenser as a poet, however, allowing him to develop in his own deeply original fashion. *The Faerie Queene* is in many ways a remarkably old-fashioned and idiosyncratic work, with its allegories, archaisms, and fondness for Chaucer and Arthurian romance. While Spenser may sometimes have felt starved for news of the latest in London's literary culture, he did not have to write for it. In becoming a provincial, he may have been freed to make his poem out of the wealth of European culture—the ancient past of Virgil and Ovid, the medieval past of Dante, and the recent work of Ariosto, Tasso, Ronsard, and Du Bellay. Eventually the move gave him a new literary persona as he reshaped the principal figure of *The Shepheardes Calender* into the Irish outsider Colin Clout.

Other aspects of the move were deeply problematic. Spenser went to Ireland during the last phase of the slow sixteenth-century extension of English control over the island. He came as a member of what was in effect a conquering force: the "New English," comprising Elizabethan administrators and settlers, were distinct from both the Anglo-Norman families who had ruled parts of Ireland for generations and the Irish, who had ruled in most of the rest. The fictional dialogue of Bryskett's *A Discourse of Civill Life,* addressed to Lord Grey and set in the early 1580s, includes a number of these colleagues—"Doctor *Long* Primate of *Ardmagh,* Sir *Robert Dillon* Knight, M. *Dormer* the Queenes Sollicitor, Capt. *Christopher Carleil,* Capt. *Thomas Norreis,* Capt. *Warham, St. Leger,* Capt. *Nicholas Dawtry,*" as well as "M *Edmond Spenser* late your Lordships Secretary."[12] As a member of this new ruling elite, Spenser had a profoundly ambivalent vision of Ireland and the Irish. Both his poetry and his prose dialogue on Irish affairs, *A View of the Present State of Ireland,* testify to his appreciation of the beauty and utility of the countryside:

> And sure . . . it is a moste bewtifull and swete Countrie as anye is under heaven, seamed throughe out with manye goodlye rivers replenished with all sortes of fishe moste aboundantlye sprinckled with manye swete Ilandes and goodlye lakes like little Inlande seas, that will carye even shipps uppon theire waters, adorned with goodly woodes fitt for buildinge of howsses and shipps. (*VP,* 559–65)

Spenser's interest in Irish culture in *A View* is unusual in English discussions of Ireland. The book is full of detail about Irish customs and history, and for all its stress on the need to supplant Irish culture with English, it ends with the two speakers looking forward to a time when they can meet to hear Irenius's "observacions . . . of the Antiquities of Ireland" (231).[13]

At the same time the Irish were—potentially at least—the enemy. The Elizabethan government, which dreaded Ireland's use as a launching place for an invasion by the French or Spanish, believed English control of the island to be critical. The threat was a real one, and early in his Irish career Spenser had firsthand experience of both the reality of the Spanish threat and the brutality with which it was countered. Shortly after Lord Grey's arrival as lord deputy, the Spanish sent 600 Spanish and Italian troops to aid the earl of Desmond, who was leading a revolt in Munster. The troops landed at Smerwick and occupied the massive Fort del Oro. Grey marched there with 800 men and laid siege to the fort, battering it with artillery. The defenders had flown the pope's banner, and when they sued for terms, Grey, a resolute Protestant, demanded an unconditional surrender. That given and the soldiers disarmed, Grey had almost all of them slaughtered. He did so partly to set an example, and partly because he dared not with his own limited forces escort so many prisoners through territory ready to revolt.

At the time Grey's ruthlessness was applauded by the queen, and writing in *A View* long after the event, Spenser would passionately justify Grey's conduct. For the poet, as for the other New English, Ireland was a powder keg ready to explode. The other inhabitants of the island, including the Anglo-Normans, were Catholic, uncivilized, and secretly disloyal. Bryskett called the Irish "the most Barbarous people of the world," a view generally held by the New English.[14] Indeed, it has recently been argued that the vision of the Irish as savages became increasingly marked in the last third of the sixteenth century as the occupying English were forced to justify to themselves their appropriation of the country from its inhabitants.[15] Spenser had day-to-day experience of enmity between the New English and Ireland's older inhabitants. Once he had acceded to Kilcolman, he and other New English landowners engaged in continual legal battles with their Anglo-Norman neighbors, who argued that the new settlers had encroached on their lands. Alexander Judson, Spenser's biographer, quotes part of the accusation of Lord Roche, Spenser's principal opponent:

> Also the said Spenser, by threatening and menacing of the said Lord Roche's tenants, and by taking their cattle pasturing upon his lordship's own inheritance, and by refusing and beating of his lordship's servants and bailiffs, hath made waste six other ploughlands of his lordship's lawful inheritance to his so small undoing.

In response, Spenser and his allies asserted that Roche was disloyal and that

> he hath imprisoned in his house sundry persons, viz., a man of Mr. Verdon's, a man of Mr. Spenser's, and other of the freeholders of this country. . . . He made proclamation in his country that none of his people should have any trade or conference with Mr. Spenser or Mr. Piers or any of their tenants. He killed a fat beef of Teig O'Lyne's because Mr. Spenser lay in his house one night as he came from the sessions at Limerick. He killed a beef of his smith's for mending Mr. Peere's plough-iron.

As Judson remarks wryly, while the particular rights and wrongs of these conflicts are hard to decide at this remove, "this litigation does not appear to reflect credit on Spenser: seeing matters from the point of view of an opponent could hardly be called one of his virtues."[16]

Spenser's views were exacerbated by the sense of helplessness about English policy shared by most of Elizabeth's administrators in Ireland. Our own age of telephones and beepers makes it hard to remember just how much in the sixteenth century influence with the queen and her council was dependent on personal *presence*. The administrators of Elizabeth's Irish government were desperately hindered by their inability to make their case from afar. Elizabeth was horrified by the sums her Irish policy was costing her and refused to give her lord deputies the funds necessary to carry it out. (In 1590 the soldiers of Sir Thomas Norris, President of Munster, revolted and marched to Dublin demanding their back pay.) She was also willing to temporize with the Irish and the Anglo-Irish who would make trips to London to argue their case and undercut the work of the administration.

## A *View of the Present State of Ireland*

This is the context for Spenser's *View on the Present State of Ireland*, the long dialogue he probably began in the 1580s, worked on extensively in the 1590s, and in all likelihood never finished.[17] A copy (without Spenser's name) was entered for the printer Matthew Lownes in the Stationer's Register on 14 April 1598 pending "further authoritie" to publish, but that authority seems not to have been forthcoming.[18] The *View* remained unpublished during Spenser's lifetime; we do not know why. Critics have suggested that the manuscript was suppressed by the government, but there is no other evidence for this hypothesis. Perhaps, as has been recently argued, there was a disagreement over publication rights: Lownes was not Spenser's usual printer (Brink 1990, 207). Its nearly 70,000 words represent, in any case, a major and troubling labor, for it advocates the violent suppression of the Irish and their culture.[19]

Irenius is the dialogue's dominant speaker (his name, like Irene's in *FQ* V, combines the Greek for "peace" with the *Ierne*, the classical name for Ireland). He is an authority on Irish history, geography, and culture, and has witnessed Grey's dispatching of the Spanish forces: accordingly he analyzes the Irish problem for his companion Eudoxus and proposes solutions. After a brief initial discussion, his argument divides into two halves, a first section (64–2898), which shows where English policy in

Ireland has gone wrong, and a second section detailing remedies
(2899–end). The first half itself divides into three parts: a section showing why English common law will not work in Ireland as it now is
(64–1124); a long central section on the Irish customs that make English attempts to civilize the Irish futile (1125–2604); and a brief
account of how religion has failed in Ireland (2605–2998—Irenius's
arguments are largely secular: governmental and cultural change must
precede religious reform).

Irenius insists that a policy of gradual reform must fail because Irish
laws, customs, and values oppose those of the English in fundamental
ways. They are, as Irenius says in the first sentence of the dialogue,
aspects of a "salvage nacion" that must be "reduced" [brought] to "better government and Cyvilitye" (6–7). (The association of the Irish with
savagery and the English with civilization is insisted on throughout the
dialogue.) If Irish customs persist they will undermine English "civility."
For instance, the policy backed by many Old English of "surrender and
regrant," by which Irish magnates would give up their claims to independent sovereignty in return for lordship bestowed by the queen, will
not work in an Irish environment. By Irish law the leaders of the various
clans or "septs" hold their land during their lifetime only, and successive
leaders may repudiate their predecessors' acts (128–201). The Irish custom of "bollying," or herding cattle from place to place, creates a popu-
lation of armed herders whose movements are hard to control, who
engage in robbery and pillage, and who provide troops for sept leaders
(1515–50). Irish conditions pervert the English common law: the practice of trial by jury of one's peers, for instance, is corrupted when juries
consist largely of Irish swayed in their verdicts by sept leaders
(666–734). Over time the English who come to Ireland will "degener-
ate," by exposure to the Irish, sinking to their level. Irenius argues that
the Old English, who have intermarried and who allow their children to
be nursed by the Irish, have already undergone such cultural degenera-
tion. Now both the Irish and the Old English bide their time, ready to
rebel against the queen and her New English settlers.

Accordingly, Irenius argues that the English must suppress Irish culture. First, a strong and well-supplied force of English soldiers must
attack the rebels, waste their lands (as well as those of Irish in English-
controlled areas to keep them from supplying their rebel kin), and
starve them into submission. After destroying the rebels, the English
government must force the rest of the Irish to conform to English ways.
It will relocate Irish populations (Munster Irish to Leinster, and Leinster

Irish to Munster) to separate them from their former roots, intermixing the resettled Irish with English immigrants. Healthy adults must become farmers or craftsmen; only the young and the infirm will be allowed to herd cattle. Significantly Irish names, with their clan associations, will be changed for English names denoting particular trades. Although Irenius argues that the military part of the reformation will take no more than a year and a half, a significant military presence will continue indefinitely. The government will establish semi-permanent garrisons throughout Ireland, paying for them with Irish taxes, and each province will have a "provoste marshall" who will arrest and discipline (and in the case of repeated offenses, execute) "such lose [loose] persons as they should finde . . . wandering" (4980–83) about the roads.

What is one to make of this plan? While Spenser was never a particularly gentle poet, the *View* suggests a profound difference between his sensibility and those of his modern liberal critics. Our knowledge of the terrible subsequent history of the English in Ireland adds to the impulse to condemn him ("when he wrote of Ireland," C. S. Lewis wrote, "Spenser was a bad poet because he was in some respects a bad man"[20]) or to distance him from the brutality that Irenius advocates. Attempting to situate the pamphlet historically, Nicholas Canny argued that it is a representative effort: Spenser voices the common position of the New English in Ireland. As such he advocates a common program of radical reform and criticizes the gradualist approach of the Old English and their backers at court.[21] Yet recent work has tended in various ways to dispute this view, dwelling on signs of uneasiness or self-contradiction in the text.[22] Ciaran Brady argues that the New English had no unified vision of what should be done in Ireland, and that Irenius's suggestions are considerabley more extreme than those in comparable pamphlets. Further, on his reading, the *View* is so self-divided that it is hardly coherent as a plan of action.[23] On the one hand it gives lip-service to the stress on assimilation of the Irish associated with the gradualist position; on the other it insists on a campaign of starvation and repression that goes well beyond what most of his New English colleagues advocated. Brady argues that Spenser's frustration with the colonial effort makes him insist that nothing will serve short of violent reform. Yet his commitment to the humanist ideals of *The Faerie Queene* and his anxiety to persuade his audience make him equivocate about the numbers of Irish to be killed and the role that the royal "sword" must continue to play in forcing the Irish to change their ways (Brady 1986, 39–40).

Other work on the *View* takes these signs of uneasiness as deliberate, insisting that Irenius is not the mouthpiece—or not the sole mouthpiece—for Spenser. Such a view highlights the dialogal form Spenser chose for his pamphlet: on occasion, Renaissance dialogues could present opposing views of a genuinely intractable question, leaving the audience to decide. Thus, for instance, More's *Utopia* (1516) considers without reaching a final conclusion whether or not a reform-minded humanist should serve his king. (Dialogues could also, of course, simply dramatize the thinking-through of a single position, as More's *A Dialogue of Comfort Against Tribulation* [1534] develops reasons for refusing to compromise one's religious beliefs.) Annabelle Patterson has made the most persuasive argument for the book's dialogal nature, arguing that though it advocates the repression of the Irish on grounds of political necessity, it also suggests that the English have no monopoly on righteousness.[24] She argues that while Eudoxus ("Of Good Repute") is usually persuaded, he sometimes questions Irenius' solutions, and Irenius himself allows that some aspects of the Irish—including their poetry, their concealing cloaks, and even some of their legal customs—have some value. Here Spenser would seem to allow a subversive second perspective.

Spenser's poetry often balances opposing views of a complex issue without unequivocally authorizing any position. Here his dialogal form allows him to voice a number of counter-thoughts—notably appreciations of Irish culture and uncertainty about the length of the continuing conflict. This last is perhaps Eudoxus's most telling objection ". . . Me semes" he says toward the end of the work "I do see rather a Countrye of warr then of peace and quiet which yee earst pretended, to worke in Irelande, for if youe bringe all thinges to that quietnes, which ye saide[,] what then nedethe to mayntaine so great forces as you have Chardged uppon it?" (4367–70). While Irenius satisfies Eudoxus on this point, the issue has been raised, troublingly, for the audience.

Yet I think that Spenser's ambivalence—or even in the context of this long work his willingness occasionally to voice several opinions—can be overstressed. I find it hard to imagine that Spenser did not write the dialogue to influence public debate about Ireland in the direction that Irenius suggests. That plan, brutal as it is, Irenius justifies as necessary: here, as in book 5 of *The Faerie Queene*, Spenser argues that the use of violence is the lesser of evils. The alternative, so far as Irenius is concerned, is the probability of a massive Irish revolt. The belief that violence is necessary appears when Irenius develops his plan to destroy the rebels by starvation and instances the success of a similar strategy Lord North had used in his Munster campaign against the Geraldines:

> The profe wheareof I sawe sufficientlye ensampled in Those late warrs of mounster, for notwithstandinge that the same was a moste ritche and plentifull Countrye full of Corne and Cattell that ye woulde have thoughte they Coulde have bene able to stande longe[,] yeat ere one yeare and a haulfe they weare broughte to soe wonderfull wretchednes as that anie stonie harte would have rewed the same. Out of everie Corner of the woods and glinnes they Came Crepinge forthe uppon theire handes for theire Leggs Coulde not beare them, they loked like anatomies of deathe, they spake like ghostes Cryinge out of theire graves, they did eate the dead Carrions, happie wheare they Coulde finde them, Yea and one another sone after, in so muche as the verye carkasses they spared not to scrape out of theire graves. (3253–64)

The main impression of the passage is awed horror at the effect of these methods, and some pity. But there is no sign of remorse—of the thought that perhaps Grey should have done otherwise. These tactics, like Grey's slaughter of Spanish soldiers, which Spenser probably witnessed and Irenius defends, are simply necessary. By picturing their horror24 Spenser also pictures their efficacy. The *View* demonstrates in the starkest way how far Spenser was prepared to go to ensure the English regime in Ireland, and with it his own position.

## Spenser in England: 1589–1591

During his nine years in Ireland Spenser had gradually lost many of his supporters in England. Sir Philip Sidney, to whom he had dedicated *The Shepheardes Calender,* died fighting the Spanish in the Low Countries in 1586, followed two years later by his uncle, the earl of Leicester. In *The Ruines of Time* (1591) Spenser mourns Leicester's death as part of a larger pattern of change. "He now is gone, the whiles the Foxe is crept / Into the hole, the which the Badger swept" (*YESP,* 216–17). The "Foxe" is the one councilor we know Spenser counted as an enemy, William Cecil, Lord Burleigh, who had come to hold a position of increasing power. *The Ruines of Time* also laments Sir Frances Walsingham, another activist Protestant and Sidney's father-in-law, who would retire from office and die in April 1590.

Spenser nevertheless returned to England in the fall of 1589; he probably stayed 15 months, making one or more trips back to Ireland.

He arrived with the first three books of *The Faerie Queene* and a new patron, Sir Walter Ralegh. The two may have met in 1580 when Ralegh held a command under Lord Grey, but they certainly deepened their acquaintance in the summer of 1589, when Ralegh, looking over his own vast estates in Munster, met again with his fellow poet and fellow landholder. Like Spenser's earlier patrons Leicester, Sidney, and Grey, Ralegh was militantly anti-Spanish. He was now one of the queen's favorites, brilliant, proud, much admired, and much hated; in the early 1590s he stood at the height of his power. According to the fictionalized account of his visit in *Colin Clouts Come Home Againe,* Ralegh encouraged Spenser to come to England and introduced him to Elizabeth, who heard him read his work. In the dedication to *Colin Clout* Spenser thanks Ralegh for his aid and protection *"against the malice of evill mouthes, which are alwaies wide open to carpe at and misconstrue my simple meaning"* (YESP, 525–26). The epic was published in 1590 with two admiring sonnets from Ralegh. It was dedicated to the queen.

*The Faerie Queene,* Spenser's major bid for royal favor, was his proof that he was a "laureate" poet. It presents England as the heir to the Roman empire, just as Elizabeth's line ultimately derives from that of Aeneas. The first book celebrates the English church, attacking the false church of Rome in a way reminiscent of the *Theatre.* The first installment of the epic repeatedly celebrates the queen, praising her as a model of virtue and a quasi-divine source of inspiration. *The Faerie Queene* embodies an artistic patriotism too, for it was Spenser's attempt to put England on the literary map of Europe, "overgoing" all previous writers of epic, whether classical or Italian. Spenser brought together the materials of Arthurian romance with those of classical epic, displaying the superiority of his own work to all those it includes. While in many ways the praise in the first installment of *The Faerie Queene* is qualified, and its optimism limited, its affirmations are explicit and exuberant.

Spenser's efforts seem eventually to have borne fruit: in February 1591 he was rewarded with an annual pension of £50. But 15 months was a long time to wait for reward, and our very limited record of the time he spent in England suggests that much of it may have been unhappy. One reference in *Daphnaïda,* published in 1591, suggests that Spenser's wife may recently have died.[25] It is out of his experience of this time that Spenser wrote his elaborate pastoral eclogue *Colin Clouts Come Home Againe,* which sharply modifies the picture of England implicit in the opening books of *The Faerie Queene.* What is most striking about

*Colin Clout* for Spenser's biography are not the fictionalized details of the journey but Spenser's satiric independence. For all its hyperbolic praise of Elizabeth, the poem presents her court as corrupt, self-centered, and shortsighted. Most courtiers "fare amis / And yet their own misfaring will not see" (757–58).

Spenser's discontent certainly appears in the volume published at the end of this London stay, a gathering of early and recent pieces entitled *Complaints*. There is disagreement about the degree of Spenser's involvement in arranging and publishing these pieces, but they do share, despite a wide range of genres and moods, a thematic coherence: they deal with loss, mutability, and worldly injustice.[26] The first poems in the book, *The Ruines of Time* and *The Teares of the Muses,* focus on the neglect of the learning that should guide the actions of the present age, and in particular on the loss of Spenser's patrons. Other poems in the volume deal directly or by implication with fraud and deceptiveness at court. If the first installment of *The Faerie Queene* tends with some hesitations to glorify England and her queen, the *Complaints* presents a satiric countervoice. To what degree could Elizabeth's court—or any earthly court—live up to its ideal? How long can any greatness last, individual or national? Is not all worldly hope finally complacent blindness? These are, of course, concerns that go back to Spenser's translations of the verse in Van der Noodt's *Theatre,* some of which appear in the *Complaints* in revised form. Such a volume does not, as has recently been noticed, fit easily into the Virgilian progression from pastoral to epic; Spenser speaks here with a different and more skeptical inflection.[27]

Spenser's tone may have been too acid for comfort. There is evidence that in the spring of 1591 the *Complaints* was "called in"—that is, unsold copies were impounded by the government. The particular source of displeasure was Spenser's thinly veiled attack on Burleigh in *Mother Hubberds Tale,* another instance of his aggressive outspokenness. This satire also contains Spenser's most powerful diatribe against the frustrations and humiliations of the system of patronage.

> Full little knowest thou that hast not tride,
> What hell it is in suing long to bide:
> To loose good dayes, that might be better spent;
> To wast long nights in pensive discontent;

To speed to day, to be put back to morrow;
To feed on hope, to pine with feare and sorrow;
To have thy Princes grace, yet want her Peeres;
To have thy asking, yet waite manie yeeres;
To fret thy soule with crosses and with cares;
To eate thy heart through comfortlesse dispaires;
To fawne, to crowche, to waite, to ride, to ronne,
To spend, to give, to want, to be undonne. (895–906)

## Last Work: 1591–1599

On 26 October 1590, two years after he had moved to Kilcolman, Spenser gained official possession of his plantation; his pension was finally granted the following spring. His apparent delegation of his duties as Bryskett's deputy to the Council of Munster may have given him somewhat more time for writing or for his work in managing his Irish estate. He certainly wrote or finished a great deal of his best poetry over the next years: the second three books of *The Faerie Queene* seem to have been done by 1595. It was probably on 11 June 1594 that he married Elizabeth Boyle, who may have come to Ireland at the urging of her cousin Richard (later to become the fabulously successful earl of Cork). Another son, Peregrine, was born of the marriage. The courtship gave rise to some of the happiest and most playful sonnets in the English language and to its richest marriage poem. In 1595 he published *Amoretti and Epithalamion* and in the same year a book containing *Colin Clouts Come Home Againe* with a series of elegies for Sir Philip Sidney, including his own *Astrophel.* He journeyed to England again in 1595–96, when he published the second installment of *The Faerie Queene,* his *Fowre Hymnes,* and the lovely betrothal poem *Prothalamion.*

These years of fruition may also have been years of increasing anxiety. In England, Ralegh, the patron of Spenser's 1590 visit, secretly married Elizabeth Throckmorton, one of the queen's ladies-in-waiting, who was pregnant with his child. She left court to give birth and returned as if nothing had happened. When the facts were discovered by the enraged queen, Ralegh and his new wife were imprisoned for a short time and then banished from the court.[28] Ralegh's fall was a spectacular example of fortune's instability in the court life Spenser had left behind, and Ralegh figures repeatedly in Spenser's later poetry as an instance of the vulnerability of the courtier's situation. He refrained from publishing *Colin Clouts Come Home Againe,* in which Ralegh plays a prominent part, until 1595, when some of the queen's anger had dissipated, and in *The Faerie Queene* he attempts loyally to defend Ralegh's reputation. But he would have to look elsewhere for a patron.

In Ireland the New English felt increasingly at risk. The victory over the Spanish Armada of 1588 did not look decisive to either the Spanish or the English, and during the final years of Elizabeth's reign there was general expectation of another invasion. Such an invasion might begin in Ireland. Irish anger at English control had been growing during the preceding 25 years of increased English encroachment and was ready to break out in open revolt. In *A View* Irenius comments: "everye daie we perceave the trowbles growinge more uppon us and one evill growinge on another, in soe muche as theare is no parte now sounde or ascerteined but all have theire eares uprighte waytinge when the watchewode shall Come That they shoulde all rise generallye into Rebellion and Caste aweye the Englishe subjeccion" (*VP,* 2937–41). The northern territory of Ulster (never subdued by the English) was in turmoil and in 1596 would become the center of the most effective and powerful rebellion of the century.

The sense of frustration that shapes the proposals of the *View,* much of which was written in the mid-1590s, appears also in the second installment of *The Faerie Queene,* which, from the evidence of Sonnet 80 of the *Amoretti,* Spenser seems to have been finishing in 1594. If the first half of the epic deals largely with the tensions within the individual soul, the second half deals with the resistant world in which the soul must make its temporal home. This second half of the epic, as many critics have noticed, is less resolved and more problematic than the first installment of the poem. It continues with its praise of Elizabeth, but there is an increasing skepticism about the possibility of bridging the gap between the ideal values the poem celebrates and the actual world in which they need to work. The narrator of book 5 laments the loss of the golden age in the proem to that book; it is now an age of crime. Perhaps in reaction to this acute sense of moral compromise, most of the rest of Spenser's later work tends to turn away from the political to the personal, and in particular to problems of love. *Colin Clout* ends by rejecting Elizabeth's court for love's court, and the last works all turn in different ways to the concerns of love and marriage.[29]

These poems also become personal in a way distinctively Spenserian. Where the speakers of Spenser's earlier work are, by and large, choric and impersonal voices, the speakers of the later poems are identified in one way or another with Spenser himself. Where the Colin of *The Shepheardes Calender* is a character very different from the voice of the poet at the end of that poem, the Colin of *Colin Clout* is just as clearly identified with the poet: he makes the journey Spenser made and praises the people Spenser met. He is, of course, not *all* of Spenser, but he develops for the reader a kind of shadow-biography, a way of seeing and understanding Spenser's journey. All of Spenser's later poems similarly turn inward to follow the thoughts of a highly particularized speaker under circumstances that recall Spenser's own. Narrative genres gradually yield to lyric ones, and in the case of Spenser's epic the poet's voice becomes increasingly prominent.

After his return, Spenser seems to have remained in Ireland, cultivating his estate and acquiring property for his second son, Peregrine (Sylvanus was eventually to inherit Kilcolman) (Judson, 174–75, 195). It should be remembered that, however much Spenser's late poetry turns away from the court, Spenser the Irish landowner was deeply dependent on it. His connection with the court was, indeed, strengthened in the last year of his life. In September 1598 he was recommended by the Privy Council to the Irish lord justices for the important office of sheriff of Cork. He was, the council wrote, "a gentleman dwelling in the County of Cork, who is so well known unto your lordships for his good and commendable parts (being a man endowed with good knowledge in learning and not unskillful or without experience in the service of the wars) as we need not use many words in his behalf."[30]

This post was far more prestigious than any Spenser had held, but it came too late. In June 1598 the earl of Tyrone began a rebellion that would involve all of Ireland, and in October the uprising against the English spread to Munster. Kilcolman was overrun and burned, and Spenser, like most of the rest of the New English who could escape, made his way with his family to Cork. In December 1598 he left for London with papers from Sir Thomas Norris for the Privy Council. At this time he may have written "Certaine pointes to be considered of in the recovery of the Realme of Ireland" (part of a group of three papers known collectively as *A Brief Note of Ireland*), a state paper often attributed to him, which urges the argument of the *View* that the Irish must be met with overwhelming force and starved into submission.[31] On arrival he was paid eight pounds for his troubles; shortly thereafter he died in Westminster, on 13 January 1599. His contemporary William Camden records:

> By a fate peculiar to Poets hee alwaies strugled with poverty, though he were Secretary to the Lord Grey, Lord Deputy of Ireland. For scarce had hee there gotten a solitary place and leasure to write, when hee was by the Rebels cast out of his dwelling, despoyled of his goods, and returned into England a poore man, where shortly after he died.[32]

Camden also says that Spenser was buried at Westminster Abbey, "his herse being attended by poets, and mournful elegies and poems, with the pens that wrote them thrown into his tomb."

The funeral was paid for by the earl of Essex, whom Spenser had turned to as a possible patron in 1596 when he wrote *Prothalamion*. This last of his occasional poems celebrates the betrothals of two of Essex's followers. In it time appears as both destructive and creative, and at its climax Spenser turns to congratulate the earl on his victory over the Spanish at Cadiz and to make him an embodiment of England's heroic future:

> Faire branch of Honor, flower of Chevalrie,
> That fillest *England* with thy triumphes fame,
> Joy have thou of thy noble victorie
> And endlesse happinesse of thine owne name
> That promeseth the same:
> That through thy prowesse and victorious armes
> Thy country may be freed from forraine harmes:
> And great *Elisaes* glorious name may ring
> Through al the world, fil'd with thy wide Alarmes,
> Which some brave muse may sing
> To ages following. (150–60)

The idealizing chivalric rhetoric here develops for the last time the grand political vision of a laureate poet. It also places Essex in the line of military Protestant patrons whom Spenser had looked to from the start of his career. Spenser was perhaps looking to start over again.

*Two Cantos of Mutabilitie* was published posthumously in 1609 in a folio reprint of *The Faerie Queene*. It remains unclear when the poem was written or how it relates to the epic, although it reads like a final afterthought on the themes of the epic. A collected works (without *Mother Hubberds Tale,* to avoid the displeasure of Robert Cecil, Burleigh's son) was published in 1611, and a second edition, with *Mother Hubberds Tale* restored, in 1617. In 1633 Sir James Ware published *A View on the Present State of Ireland,* and a more complete *Works* appeared in 1679.

# Chapter Two
# 1579: *The Shepheardes Calender*

When at 27 Spenser published his first major work, a group of pastoral eclogues, he was following a familiar European model. "So flew Virgile," wrote E.K. in the "epistle" prefixed to the poem, "as not yet well feeling his winges. So flew Mantuane, as being not yet full somd. So Petrarque. So Boccace; So Marot, Sanazarus, and also divers other excellent both Italian and French Poetes, whose foting this Author every where followeth, yet so as few, but they be wel sented, can trace him out" (*YESP*, 18–19).[1] The model of Virgil's career suggested that young poets began by writing pastoral and ended with epic. *The Shepheardes Calender* announced the high ambitions of what E.K. was to call "this our new Poete" (*YESP*, 19), and its form accorded with its ambitions. E.K.'s learned—at times pedantic—dedication and introduction preface the book, while the individual eclogues are each headed by a woodcut and a short synopsis and followed by one or more riddling "emblems," almost all in Latin, Greek, or Italian, and an apparatus of notes and glosses appropriate to a classical text.[2] Despite the conventional humility of the short "Envoy" with which Spenser prefaces the book, it makes the claim that "Immerito" will become an Elizabethan Virgil.

At once traditional and daringly experimental, the book brought together a mixture of conventions to demonstrate that this English poet had mastered what the Continent had to offer. The mixture appears most obviously in the *Calender*'s prosody. Like Jacopo Sannazaro's *Arcadia,* the poem contains an anthology of verse forms (thirteen in the eclogues and two more in the introductory "To His Booke" and the coda), most of which Spenser was never to use again. Some of them, like the sestina in "August" (the first published in English) or the elaborate stanzas of "Aprill" and "November," are recognizably Continental; others, like the humble sixain (*ababcc*) that Colin employs in "Januarye" and "December," are common English stanzas; and still others, like the rough four-beat meters of "February," "Maye," and "September" or the rhymes of "March," look back to native fourteenth- and fifteenth-century practice.

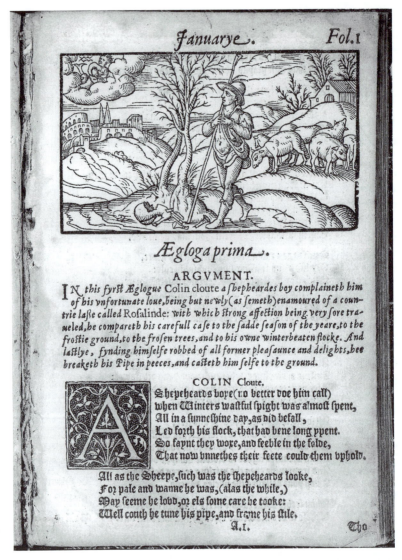

COLIN APPEARS BY TWO LEAFLESS TREES; HIS BROKEN BAGPIPE LIES ON
THE GROUND BESIDE THEM. THE ASTROLOGICAL SIGN FOR AQUARIUS
APPEARS IN THE CORNER. THE ARGUMENT HERE APPEARS IN ITALIC
PRINT; THE TEXT OF THE ECLOGUE ITSELF IS IN BLACK-LETTER TYPE.
FROM *THE SHEPHEARDES CALENDER* (1579).

*Reproduced by permission of the Huntington Library, San Marino, California.*

## Aprill.     *fol.*14

Now ryse vp *Elisa*,decked as thou art,
      in royall aray :
And now ye daintie Damsells may depart
      echeone her way,
I feare,I haue troubled your troupes to longe:
Let dame *Eliza* thanke you for her song.
      And if you come hether,
      When Damsines I gether,
I will part them all you among.

#### Thenot
And was thilk same song of *Colins* owne making?
Ah foolish boy, that is with loue yblent:
Great pittie is,he be in such taking,
For naught caren,that bene so letwoly bent.

#### Hobbinol.
Sicker I hold him,for a greater son,
That loues the thing,he cannot purchase.
But let vs homeward: for night draweth on,
And twincling starres the daylight hence chase.

### Thenots Embleme.

## *O quam te memorem virgo?*

### Hobbinols Embleme.

## *O dea certe.*

### GLOSSE.

Gars thee greete] causeth thee vveepe and complain.      Forlorne] left & forsaken.
Attempred to the yeare] agreeable to the season of the yeare,that is Aprill,vvhich mo-
    neth is most bent to shoures and seasonable rayne:to quench, that is, to delaye
    the drought,caused through dryneffe of March vvyndes.
The Ladde] Colin Clout]    The Lasse] Rosalinda.    Tressed locks) wrethed & curled
Is he for a ladde] A straunge manner of speaking .s. vvhat maner of Ladde is he ?
To make] to rime and versifye.For in this vvord making,our olde Englishe Poetes were
    vvont to comprehend all the skil of Poetrye , according to the Greeke vvoorde *τοιη*,
to make,whence commeth the name of Poetes.

         D ij.            Colin

THE END OF "APRILL" AND THE BEGINNING OF E.K.'S NOTES. FROM *THE
SHEPHEARDES CALENDER* (1579).
*Reproduced by permission of the Huntington Library, San Marino, California.*

As with the verse forms, so with the rest of the *Calender:* its originality lies partly in its inclusiveness. The poem recalls and criticizes many
versions of pastoral—classical and Christian, native and Continental—
and sets them against one another. Further, since pastoral, like epic, is a
hungry mode, the *Calender* incorporates a variety of kinds: complaint,
debate, singing match, satire, encomium, fable, anacreontic myth, elegy.
Spenser refers in passing to many poems, while three eclogues take
inspiration from the neo-Latin poet Mantuan, two from the French Clément Marot, one from the Greek Bion and his French imitator Pierre de
Ronsard, and several more from the Roman Virgil, the primary exemplar of pastoral in the Renaissance. But most of Spenser's herdsmen have
English names; that of his principal character, Colin Clout, comes from a
poem by the English laureate John Skelton, while Chaucer and to a
lesser degree William Langland inform the *Calender* as well.[3] The shape
of the book derives from the sixteenth-century almanac, the *Kalender of
Shepherdes,* itself an English translation of a French original, as well as
from literary calendars like Ovid's *Fasti.*

The *Calender* has few great lines and, unlike his later poetry, contains
few passages that, taken out of context, strike a contemporary reader as
particularly compelling. Its brilliance comes from a Chaucerian density
of context as passages play against others in the book and deepen further in relation to the larger literary traditions that Spenser evokes.
Most of the eclogues imitating specific texts make their departures from
their originals part of their meaning: the new poet reforms the old models in accord with a new vision. His inclusiveness enables Spenser to take
a range of conflicting and mutually illuminating perspectives on various
themes. Interpreters have accurately described it in many ways: as a picture of cosmic order; as a first step toward a Virgilian poetic career; as a
reformist contribution to the national debate on the monarchy and the
English church; and as a self-conscious criticism of its own mode.[4] While
these approaches to the *Calender* are not mutually exclusive, they point
to the book's characteristic voicing of radically differing perspectives.[5]
This chapter approaches its polyphony by considering first the book's
mode and shape, and then its unfolding, eclogue by eclogue.

## Pastoral Traditions

The pastoral mode that Spenser chose and returned to repeatedly
through his career is a varied and at times paradoxical form. Its humble
language and subject matter can announce great aspiration, and the

poems may abruptly shift into high-style eloquence. An elaborately artful, urban form, it professes to describe "simple" country folk. Of all
genres it is the most playfully self-referential, interrogating the nature of
its own art. The first pastoral poet, Theocritus (fl. 270 B.C.) lived in the
great Egyptian city of Alexandria and wrote a series of idylls, or "small
pictures," the first seven of which he set on the rural island of Cos. Five
of these concern herdsmen; in another a village woman tries to attract
her lover by spells; the last recounts the journey of an urban poet (a version of Theocritus himself) to a country harvest festival. The poems present a city-dweller's view of country life. They dramatize the world of
the rustics with an appreciative mixture of attitudes—sometimes admiring, sometimes nostalgic, sometimes amused. The country world is a
sunlit version of what "modern" citified man has lost.

Theocritus's Coan pastorals were only a subset of a larger group of
idylls, many of which dealt with Alexandrian life. When the young Virgil imitated Theocritus, however, he chose the pastoral idylls. Virgil's
*Eclogues* ("selections") are short poems: the longest is only 111 lines.
They consist of alternate dialogues and monologues, concerned mostly
with shepherds and goatherds. But Virgil's pastorals consider other subjects as well. They refer to current political and literary figures so that
the world of the herdsmen comments on the larger world of Roman politics. In his first eclogue, probably the most influential poem in the history of pastoral, the goatherd Meleboeus, who has been dispossessed by
Augustus's recent resettlement of soldiers on previously existing farms,
meets the shepherd Tityrus, who has gone to Rome and received his
freedom. Rome thus appears at once a source of generosity and oppression: Tityrus worships as a god the man who set him free, while Meleboeus sees only the bitterness of his loss. As in most eclogues, very little
happens beyond this exchange: the poem presents a dialogue of visions.
Neither herdsman can fully understand the other's point of view, and
the poem leaves the reader to come to a fuller understanding of the contradiction than either of its protagonists is able to achieve.[6]

Virgil expands the pastoral mode in other ways. Theocritus's *Idylls*
already claimed a kinship with epic: they use dactylic hexameter, the
meter of epic verse, and the dying hero of the first idyll, Daphnis, seems
a figure of near-heroic proportions. In several of the *Eclogues,* especially
the fourth, sixth, and tenth, Virgil transcends the "humble" rustic material of the other pastorals. He begins the fourth eclogue with *Paulo
maiora canamus* (Let us sing of somewhat greater matters) and announces
the birth of a child who will bring back a golden age of goodness and

innocence. His playful vision of a world renewed became for subsequent Christian commentators a prophecy of Christ's birth. It is the single most important model for Spenser's "Aprill" eclogue.

If the fourth eclogue presents a version of prophecy, the sixth plays with the stuff of Hellenistic epic, presenting a vision of mythic history, and the tenth is an essay in love-elegy. Virgilian pastoral is already a mixed genre, setting one kind of poetic vision against another. This generic complexity is reemphasized by the mode's hospitality to allegory. The very simplicity of pastoral figures—herdsmen with conventional Greek names—makes them apt to stand for something else. They can stand for the representatively *human* or, alternatively, for particular historical persons.[7] In his fifth eclogue Virgil laments the death of a "Daphnis" who may be Julius Caesar, while in the Renaissance Petrarch's Latin eclogues further elaborate a political allegory. By Spenser's time the allegorical dimension of pastoral has become commonplace. George Puttenham comments that poets make eclogues "under the vaile of homely persons, and in rude speeches to insinuate and glaunce at greater matters, and such as perchance had not bene safe to have beene disclosed in any other sort, which may be perceived by the Eglogues of *Vergill*, in which are treated by figure matters of greater importance then the loves of *Titirus* and *Corydon*."[8]

Virgil's quotations of other genres and his transformations of Theocritus point to a central concern in his eclogues and those of subsequent writers—their attention to their own art. Eclogues are mostly built around singing—solo complaints, singing contests, elaborate compositions of grief or praise. Accordingly, they develop an ongoing inquiry into the powers and limits of art—and especially the art of pastoral poetry. What is it good for? Recreation? Instruction? Propaganda? Relief? What attitudes are implicit in the poetic language the writer has inherited? Do these traditions evade actual truths? This scrutiny leads to one of the characteristic endings of the eclogue-book, a decision to abandon the pastoral mode for fresh fields and pastures new. Virgil's final eclogue ends: "Arise. The shade [which has been identified with pastoral singing] weighs heavily on singers."[9] Here the author turns away from pastoral song. The eclogue-book marks a stage in his career, one that must naturally give way to larger challenges.

Yet Renaissance pastoral poets embraced more traditions than those inherent in the Virgilian model. Medieval vernacular poets wrote more particularized accounts of how actual shepherds lived their lives, and developed the convention of the *conflictus,* in which opposing characters debate a question. In the playful Latin *Conflictus Veris et Hiemis* (The Debate of Spring and Winter), for instance, the allegorical figures Spring and Winter begin by arguing over the goodness of the Cuckoo's return, heralding spring. The profoundest transformation of the tradition, however, occurs when it assimilates the biblical metaphor of God (and by implication, the good priest) as the good shepherd leading his flock of the faithful to salvation. While Virgil's pastoral welcomes allegory, his stylized, literary shepherds nonetheless root themselves in actual rustic life. By contrast, the shepherding of Christian pastoral is largely metaphorical: the poems concern themselves with the relation between God and the church, or the priest and his flock.

The most famous Renaissance writer of Christian pastoral was the Italian Baptista Spagnuoli, known (for the town of his birth) as Mantuan. The ten eclogues of his *Adulescentia* differ sharply from the Virgilian model. While the first eight eclogues do treat literal shepherds, their ethic throughout is emphatically Christian. Patrick Cullen has usefully distinguished what he calls the "Arcadian" pastoral of Virgil from this "Mantuanesque" Christian tradition.[10] While in some respects the two traditions are similar (both, for instance, show an awareness of the actual physical life of country-dwellers), they differ in essentials. Where Virgilian pastoral often leaves the reader with an awareness of incompatible values (city versus country, nature versus art), Mantuan's eclogues dramatize a conflict between right and wrong. Mantuan develops these conflicts with satiric force, but his absolute oppositions do not lend themselves to complex oppositions of value. Love in Virgil is sometimes pleasant, often destructive, but it is not a moral matter; for Mantuan earthly love is insanity and often the work of the devil. Virgil concerns himself with life in this world, and his pastoral makes much of its values—sweet apples and chestnuts, pleasant song, cool shade on a hot day. By contrast, Christian pastoral looks toward transcendence: this world is at best an inferior good, and more usually a snare, holding us back from the next. The organization of Mantuan's ten eclogues suggests, accordingly, a spiritual maturation as they move from matters of this world to concerns of the religious life.[11] Mantuan's eclogues became an essential part of the grammar school curriculum. They furnished, with Virgil, a crucial model for Spenser, who, when he wrote his own eclogue-book, characteristically chose to incorporate various pastoral traditions and to make his meaning out of the tensions between them.

## The Form of *The Shepheardes Calender*

Spenser's fundamental invention in reworking eclogue tradition was his combination of the calendar form with that of the eclogue-book, associating particular eclogues with the twelve months of the year. The model for this form was a sixteenth-century almanac called the *Kalender of Shepherdes;* the "humble" associations of the book reemphasized the low genre of Spenser's poem. But the calendar shape had two effects: it gave Spenser an inclusive form to embrace the radical variety of the eclogues, and it made a structure out of the poem's concern with time.

Virgil's eclogues deal with time in treating contemporary issues and, in the fourth and sixth eclogues, setting them in the context of a mythic past and future. But Spenser's poem concerns many kinds of time, relating history to the unfolding of individual human lives and to an eternity beyond process. Most largely the poem asks what we are to *make* of time: how are we to envision it, to withstand it, and to render it fruitful? Different characters view it differently. Most obvious is the model of recurrent cycle embodied in the *Calender* itself and in the pattern of death and renewal in the landscape. The second line of "Januarye"—"When Winters wastful spight was almost spent"—stresses the year's turning, and speakers mention this natural cycle in ten out of twelve eclogues. This cyclical emphasis provides the cool reassurance of stability: like the poem, the world has a pattern, even if that pattern includes misery and death. Spenser emphasizes the cycle in the quietly pervasive images of human beings as plants—buds, flowers, branches, trees—all subject to a cycle of growth and decay. "November," like many pastoral elegies, reverses the pattern: the death and regeneration of species contrasts with the mortality of the individual. Out of that contrast comes Colin's Christian vision of eternity beyond temporal pattern, "grasse ay greene" (189).

An alternative model is linear, presenting a vision of progress or (more often) of decline. In "Aprill" Colin's song imagines in its praise of Elisa a new golden age in which peace and poetry flourish together. More often the characters of the poem envision a world irrevocably tainted by the Fall and in decline. The fundamental fact of the *Calender* is the Fall, which is referred to directly and kept constantly before us in its consequences—most insistently in the weather that has resulted from Adam's sin.[12] The characters in the "moral" eclogues like "Maye" and "September" lament the decline of religious institutions; Colin in "June" and Cuddie in "October" lament the decline of poetry and the chivalric institutions it celebrates; and Colin announces that his life has withered from the force of love. Eclogues, from Theocritus on, are static poems in which nothing happens, but Spenser makes this stasis thematic by dramatizing his characters' failure to make their time fruitful.

The book develops the effects of the Fall in its concern with *waste.* The word appears first in "Januarye," when Colin, seeing a dreary landscape, laments: "Thou barrein ground, whome winters wrath hath wasted / Art made a myrrhour, to behold my plight" (19–20). The quiet combination of contexts associates the fallen physical world (at once a mirror and an audience) with Colin's state of mind. He will later say that his "timely buds with wayling all are wasted" (38): the talents time has given have already, at the start of the *Calender,* been squandered in unproductive lament. The word appears in all Colin's eclogues and in other contexts: in "September" Diggon's sheep have been wasted by his mistaken journey, and in "Maye" Piers imagines the child of the bad priest wasting his father's inheritance. Lamenting Dido's death in "November," Colin asks his fellow shepherds to bewail "this wofull waste of natures warke" (64)—waste here, as in Shakespeare's sonnets, involves the loss of what is most valuable in human existence. The vision of waste extends to poetry itself: in "October" Cuddie insists that his art will gain him nothing: "Sike words bene wynd, and wasten soone in vayne" (36).

In their dismay, Cuddie's words suggest a connection between the *Calender*'s treatment of time and its treatment of poetry. For he feels that his words have had no effect: if they had, he would have been able to make a better living. One vision of the poet familiar to Renaissance writers was the magician-singer able to affect the world directly by the power of his words. The classical example is the mythic poet Orpheus, who, Ovid says, could make the trees and the wild animals gather around him to hear his song. According to Renaissance interpreters, this power imaged the poet's ability to civilize barbarous men with his harmonious teaching. Piers touches on this humbler version of the Orphic function when he advises Cuddie to "restraine / The lust of lawlesse youth with good advice" (21–22): given the Fall, the poet may still make the world better through his music. The *Calender* engages in a skeptical examination of this poetic ambition. It asks what pastoral poetry can accomplish, and its conclusions are, at best, mixed. In one of the most searching treatments of the *Calender,* Louis Montrose argues that it dramatizes the failure of poetic persuasion: its stalemates suggest the difficulties Spenser anticipated at court. "The failures of rhetorical efficacy within *The Shepheardes Calender* are projections of the frustrations that a poet with Orphic pretensions must experience in a world not moved by his song."[13]

The second advantage of the calendar form, its inclusiveness, enables Spenser to vary the kind of materials he includes, making his poem into a miniature world. The eclogue-book was, from Virgil on, an anthology in which a young poet could show his skill at various kinds of poetry, but Spenser makes this variation thematic. He sets one kind of eclogue against another, the native against the Continental, the sophisticated against the seemingly crude. The variations of pastoral kinds have the effect of commenting on one another, exposing the limitations of any one version's claim to truth. At the same time, by returning repeatedly to the Colin story and by linking the disparate eclogues thematically, he gives the *Calender* coherence.

In "August" Willye offers to wager a bowl that stands in a long tradition of elaborately carved pastoral artifacts. Like many objects in pastoral poems, it suggests the nature of the book in which it occurs.

> Then loe *Perigot* the Pledge which I plight:
> A mazer ywrought of the Maple warre:
> Wherein is enchased many a fayre sight
> Of Beres and Tygres, that maken fiers warre:
> And over them spred a goodly wild vine,
> Entrailed with a wanton Yvie twine.
>
> Thereby is a Lambe in the Wolves jawes:
> But see, how fast renneth the shepheard swayne,
> To save the innocent from the beastes pawes:
> And here with his shepehooke hath him slayne.
> Tell me, such a cup hast thou ever sene?
> Well moght it beseme any harvest Queene. (25–36)

The art of the first verse pictures the savagery of fallen beings, the "fiers warre" of the animals resulting from the Fall, but makes them into a "fayre sight," distanced and beautiful. The wild vine may be wanton (ivy is linked with Dionysus), but it is also "goodly" and exuberant. The second verse, however, turns away from the purely "natural" subjects of the first and focuses on the relation between the sheep and the shepherd— and metaphorically between the pastor and his flock. The description of the bowl thus opposes two kinds of subject matter—that of nature and grace. The final couplet possesses—if one extends it to the poem as a whole—a certain triumph. This is a new kind of eclogue-book, worthy of a "harvest Queene" such as Elizabeth.[14]

In his "generall argument of the whole booke," E.K. divides the eclogues into three kinds—plaintive, moral, and recreative. These divisions do not appear before Spenser, although his audience would have found the first two familiar.[15] The divisions are hardly airtight ("August" and "October," for instance, might each fall under two categories). But they have influenced subsequent criticism deeply because they suggest what the singers are trying to do. *The Shepheardes Calender* concerns itself above all with how poets and poetry function in this fallen world—with the attempts to make something out of the waste we inherit from Adam. Each of E.K.'s eclogue types examines impulses that give rise to poetry, and to fiction-making. It is often a skeptical examination dramatizing why certain kinds of fiction-making fail.

## The Plaintive Eclogues

E.K. enumerates the "plaintive" eclogues but does not define them any further. Elizabethan readers would, however, have been familiar with two kinds of literary complaints.[16] The first is the grieving speech of a rejected lover; the second is an accusatory account of the world's corruptions, such as Alan de Lisle's medieval Latin poem *The Complaint of Nature.* Colin's complaints in "Januarye," "August," and "December" are the first kind of poem; his elegy for Dido in "November" partakes of the second, as it sees Dido's death as evidence of a world gone radically wrong.

When Spenser began "Januarye" with Colin's complaint about the absent Rosalind, he was starting with the most familiar cliché of pastoral poetry. Shepherds are always falling unhappily in love, and in Arcadian pastoral they sing their woes. Spenser uses the cliché to examine a danger presenting itself to the young poet, the impulse to focus exclusively on oneself. Easily the most accomplished artist of the book, Colin dramatizes this tendency (Johnson, 104–14). Excessive sorrow would interest Spenser throughout his career, but Colin's complaints hardly seem the product of intense grief.

> I love thilke lasse, (alas why doe I love?)
> And am forlorne, (alas why am I lorne?)

> Shee deignes not my good will, but doth reprove,
> And of my rurall musick holdeth scorne.
> Shepheards devise she hateth as the snake,
> And laughes the songes, that *Colin Clout* doth make. (61–66)

The graceful, tepid wordplay of the first two lines undercuts one's sense that Colin is passionately in love. He seems rather, as Harry Berger Jr. has pointed out, to engage himself in the role of rejected lover as a way of making music (1988, 325–46). The emotion displayed in the second half of the verse is less love than pique. Colin is fascinated by a familiar, literary image of himself as a despairing lover; he has lost himself in a pastoral convention.

He is capable of greater things. The fiction of *Calender* makes him the author of its two highest flights, "April" and "November." In each he goes beyond his concern with self to use his art for larger, public purposes. But these flights do not last (the "Aprill" eclogue was composed, we hear, before Colin fell in love), and they show only what his art might accomplish. Spenser makes Colin the central figure of the *Calender* to dramatize the attraction of narcissistic self-display and the resulting stasis. Colin leaves the eclogue-book where he started it, locked into a self-concern that ignores the world his poetry might embrace and affect. Spenser thus makes the lynchpin of his eclogue-book a poet whose refusal to transcend his own role as desolate lover renders him useless. Despite the *Calender*'s attention to the problems of the world at large, Spenser's deepest interest is personal and psychological.

E.K. identifies Colin with the author of the *Calender* in his epistle and reiterates the connection in his notes. The text itself connects Colin with Spenser when in "April" he dedicates himself to Eliza, and when in "September" Hobbinol mentions that Colin was "Roffy's" boy (176). Roffy is certainly John Young, Bishop of Rochester, whom Spenser served as secretary in 1578. At the same time the book distinguishes Spenser from the shepherd boy. It brackets Colin's two monologues with the utterances of the narrator—at the start and finish of "Januarye," and at the beginning of "December" and coda to the whole book, "Loe I have made a Calender for every yeare." The narrator's perceptions differ from Colin's, who remains one character among many in the work. Spenser's ironic distance appears also in Colin's name. *Colin Clout* is one of John Skelton's poems, in which Colin, the outraged speaker, attacks the corrupt institutions of the church. *The Shepheardes Calender* also attacks clerical corruption, but not with Colin's voice. Colin's self-concerned poetry contrasts with that of English satirists reaching back through Skelton to Chaucer and Langland. His name thus reminds us of what he does *not* do: it has what Berger called in another context a "conspicuous irrelevance," the evocation of a value missing from the present context in order to call attention to its absence.[17]

Spenser may have embodied in Colin a potential he felt in himself. The attraction of a poetry of melancholy, if not love-melancholy, is evident in a poet whose first collection after the publication of *The Faerie Queene* was called *Complaints* and who repeatedly concerned himself with the danger of yielding to excessive grief. When he introduces Colin in "Januarye," he does so as "A shepheards boye (no better doe him call)," and the teasing aside plays with Colin's identity. On the one hand, Colin remains an immature rustic, clearly distinguishable from the narrator who describes him. But in inviting the reader to "call" Colin something, Spenser also suggests that Colin is a role, one voice of the ventriloquist-author.

## The Moral Eclogues

Unlike the plaintive eclogues, the moral eclogues concern themselves with more public matters, being, E.K. says, "for the most part mixed with some Satyrical bitternesse" (*YESP,* 23). They contrast with the first group in several ways. Colin's singing is a refined, melodious, and usually solo performance: he speaks, significantly, the book's only monologues. The moral eclogues are dialogues, usually debates, typically longer than the others, and written in a rough, dialect-studded rustic speech recalling the alliterative lines of Langland's *Piers Plowman*—a poem Renaissance writers associated with reform.[18] Where Colin's speeches are typically private, concerned only with self, most of the moral eclogues concern the larger community, at least by implication. The plaintive eclogues are timeless—pure quotation of Arcadian song going back to Virgil and Theocritus. By contrast, the moral eclogues deal with unmistakably timely issues, particularly with the Elizabethan church.

The speakers of "Maye," "Julye," and "September" all consider the church, which the Reformation of the 1530s had left both poorer and less powerful. Many priests still held multiple livings (often by necessity, since such livings frequently yielded less than would sustain their incumbents), paying a pittance to underlings to administer the parishes they never visited. Appointment to many church posts lay in secular hands, and livings were often sold to unqualified incumbents. Many commentators in the 1570s felt that clergymen were insufficiently educated for their tasks as preachers of the gospel, and many Protestants besides those who in the 1590s would become known as Puritans felt that it was necessary to improve the standard of preaching. In addition, more extreme Protestants advocated the dismantling of the church hierarchy and the institution of a presbyterian system of church government, controlled by local congregations. Such views infuriated the queen, who was less concerned with religious reform than with civil order and who saw attempts to tamper with the church as bound to destabilize her government. To raise the level of preaching throughout the country was to encourage unorthodox, if educated, opinion; it was safer to have the *Homilies*—sermons written largely by the government and published with the approval of the church establishment—read aloud on Sundays.

The uneasy relation between the queen and the reformers came to a head with the battle over "prophesyings," gatherings of reform-minded clergy meant to raise the general level of knowledge. A group of clergy and interested laymen would meet to hear several sermons on a particular passage of Scripture, and the clergy would then retire to debate what had been said. The queen, alarmed perhaps by the name given to these gatherings, ordered her archbishop of Canterbury, Edward Grindal, to suppress the practice. Grindal refused to pass the order on as his own, and the enraged queen suspended him from his post for the remaining six years of his life.

Spenser's criticisms in the *Calender* come from the Protestant center. He mentions the greed of certain higher clergy, the ignorance of others, and the danger from Roman Catholic priests, referred to in the eclogues as Wolves and sometimes as Foxes.[19] As Lynn Staley Johnson points out, the *Kalender of Shepherdes* from which Spenser takes the name of his book had a long association with Lollardry and later with Protestant reform (34, 181–84). But while Spenser's shepherds recall nostalgically the purer morals of the early priesthood, they do not consider reforming church government. The hero of the moral eclogues is Grindal, who goes by the obvious anagram "Algrind" in "Maye" and "Julye," a pillar of the Anglican church. E.K., admittedly quick to avoid the imputation of unorthodoxy, comments in "Maye": "Nought here spoken, as of purpose to deny fatherly rule and godly governaunce (as some malitiously of late have done to the great unreste and hinderaunce of the Churche) but to display the pride and disorder of such, as in steede of feeding their sheepe, indeede feede of[f] theyr sheepe" (*YESP,* 101–2).

Yet while Spenser raises important issues—the proper Christian life, the need for an educated clergy, and the danger of Rome—they remain unresolved. *The Shepheardes Calender* is unusual among eclogue-books in that fully half its poems are debates. But in these debates both sides of the argument are developed, with neither achieving a decisive victory. The lack of clear resolution comes partly, as Cullen points out (29–34), from the way in which the speakers of each eclogue tend to embody Arcadian and Mantuanesque points of view—voicing genuine and often irreconcilable differences of value.[20]

These unresolved dialogues also develop the *Calender*'s concern with poetry, for the herdsmen who debate are naive and inadequate speakers. The idea that poetry should be "moral" and should, as Piers says, "restraine / the lust of lawlesse youth with good advice" ("October," 21–22) is a commonplace in the Elizabethan period, and in these eclogues good advice is offered in copious quantities. Yet the failure of the advice to have any effect also suggests the weakness of the theory that poetry is simply advice in pleasing dress. Berger pointed out long ago that the speakers of these eclogues are at best crude rhetoricians, never fully in control of the stories they tell.[21] These eclogues by and large dramatize failures of rhetoric, not, as with Colin, because of a narcissistic concern with self, but because the would-be teachers lack a rhetorician's awareness of their audience.

## The Recreative Eclogues

E.K.'s most capacious category is the recreative, "such as all those be, which conceive matter of love, or commendation of special personages" (*YESP,* 23). This category is partly a catchall, including such diverse poems as "March," "Aprill," and "August" while excluding the love poetry labeled "plaintive." But they share a sense of sudden and at times comic freedom, an awareness of poetic and sexual energy, and a celebration of that energy. In "March" the awareness comes partly from the characters' perceptions of the spring, but equally from our sense of the poet's playing with various poetic traditions. Similarly, in "August," the sole singing match of the *Calender,* the sheer playful engagement in singing turns out to have an energizing and curative power. The most important of the recreative eclogues, however, is "Aprill," in which Colin's song rises above its normal humility to "re-create" Elizabeth,

giving her a pastoral coronation. The poem envisions a joyful renewal
for the state as well as for the individual. And in this eclogue the poetry
also triumphs, suggesting the possibilities for England's future Virgil.

## E.K.

The "E.K." who offers these categories has been a subject of intense and
unresolved speculation. He might be Spenser's otherwise little-known
fellow student at Cambridge, Edward Kirke, or a pen name for his
friend Gabriel Harvey; indeed, Spenser might himself have written the
notes and the elaborate discussions of the poem.[22] Whoever he was,
E.K. plays an important part in interpreting the book's meaning. In his
introduction, he stresses the patriotic ambitiousness of Spenser's poem
and associates the new poet with his European predecessors. He thus
directs the audience's attention to some of what Spenser means to do.
His notes give genuine help in glossing dialect words and identifying
learned references. Occasionally he blurs Spenser's meanings when they
might cause trouble: he glosses Algrind, who is clearly Archbishop
Grindal, as simply "the name of a shepheard." He interprets the religious satire as an attack on Roman Catholicism rather than the English
church establishment. His seeming lack of comprehension would allow
an author to deny he had attacked the church in the face of possible
royal anger.

At times, however, E.K. has a curiously comic voice, reminiscent of
Pope's fictional commentator on the *Dunciad.* His readings of the
eclogues are often one-sided and simplistic, comically misguided
attempts to simplify Spenser's meaning. E.K. identifies Colin unequivocally with the author of the *Calender,* and his love for Rosalind as the
author's love for a particular gentlewoman. He seems at times a parody
of humanist pedantry, as when he glosses "neighbour towne" as "the
next towne: expressing the Latine Vicina" (33). Siding with the Protestant and moralizing censors of the *Calender,* he consistently imposes an
anti-erotic interpretation on the book, as when he comments on the
proverbial emblems of "March" and waxes eloquent on the viciousness
of love: "Hereby is meant, that all the delights of Love, wherein wanton youth walloweth, be but follye mixt with bitternesse, and sorow
sawced with repentaunce" (65). His nervously pompous assertion that
the relation between Colin and Hobbinol has no "savour of disorderly
love, which the learned call pæderastice" (34) has the feel of an in-joke,
as if a particular person is being satirized.[23] If the *Calender* plays with

clichés of literature, refusing to be reduced to the simpler moralizing of a Mantuan, E.K. often presents a comic picture of an interpreter going wrong.

## The Progression of the Book

**Prefatory Material**  The *Calender* begins with several pages of material giving contexts and raising expectations for the eclogues that follow. First the poet speaks a brief lyric dramatizing his relation to the world. It is a strikingly self-protective poem. Instead of addressing the reader or a patron directly, the poet speaks to his book (showing himself to us, so to speak, in profile), instructing it to seek Sir Philip Sidney, to whom the *Calender* is dedicated, and ask his protection.[24] The book's self-display runs the risk of envy and may indeed put the poet in "jeopardee," and so the poet engages in elaborate self-humiliation. He calls the *Calender* an illegitimate child (1–2, 13–15), sung by a lowly "shepheardes swaine" (9) and signs it "Immerito"—"the Unworthy One." Such humility is conventional in dedications, but here it suggests the poet's risk not only in putting himself forward as the new Virgil but in daring to comment on matters of state. Spenser's ultimate model for addressing his book at its beginning rather than its end is the first poem of Ovid's *Tristia*—an address written by a poet suffering exile because of his ruler's wrath at what he has written. Yet the poem ends with a change in tone: "And when thou art past jeopardee, / Come tell me, what was sayd of mee: / And I will send more after thee" (16–18). With the sudden assertion of the first-person pronouns, the poet seems to step forward to promise more. This address to the book is only the first of two: it will recur, changed, in the final envoy.

E.K.'s epistle to Gabriel Harvey follows the lyric. Whether or not Spenser and/or Harvey wrote it, the letter recalls the self-advertisement of the Spenser-Harvey letters published six months later. Spenser's other works are promoted, as are Harvey's in a postscript. The body of the epistle contains a defense of the new poet and an assertion of his place in European literature. If Spenser's initial lyric has been self-effacing, E.K. trumpets Spenser's achievement. "A man can scarce allege his own merits with modesty," Sir Francis Bacon was later to write, but "these things are graceful in a friend's mouth which are blushing in a man's own."[25] While the epistle shifts from topic to topic, its center remains the new poet: he is defended and praised for what he has done, he is identified with Colin Clout, and his further works are listed.

E.K. realizes that the *Calender* may appear strange to its audience, especially in its language. He defends Spenser's use of "auncient solemne wordes" (14–15) on several grounds—that they result naturally from his reading in earlier poetry, that archaic diction is "fittest for such rusticall rudenesse of shepheards," and that (citing classical precedents) they bring "great grace" and "auctoritie" to the verse (14). E.K.'s defense of Spenser's vocabulary fits into the sixteenth-century debate on the proper way to make English an illustrious—or "cultured"—language. E.K. takes a nativist position, attacking the use of "peces and rags of other languages" and praising the goodness of the "our Mother tonge" (16). As Lynn Staley Johnson points out, he thus stresses the poem's Englishness and its implicit patriotism (32–35).

E.K.'s defense of the *Calender* touches on many of the familiar Elizabethan assumptions about love poetry and pastoral. He suggests that the "generall dryft and purpose" of the eclogues is partly biographical. During his "unstayed yougth" the author "had long time wandred in the common Labyrinth of Love, in which time to mitigate and allay the heate of his passion, or els to warne (as he sayth) the young shepheards [that is to say] his equalls and companions of his unfortunate folly, he compiled these xii Æglogues" (19). The fiction that a book of love poetry represents the long-repented work of one's youth occurs often in Elizabethan literature, and while E.K.'s account seems naive, it sets Spenser's work in a familiar generic frame.[26] He further argues that choosing a pastoral persona is an act of self-protective humility, "rather to unfold great matter of argument covertly, then professing it, not suffice thereto accordingly" (18). Despite its stress on humility, the sentence underlines the ambitiousness of Spenser's program, and E.K. goes on to place him in the line of Virgilian poets who write pastoral when young and epic when they mature.

E.K. praises Spenser for many things, but two deserve special attention. The first is his "dewe observing of Decorum everye where, in personages, in seasons, in matter, in speech, and generally in al seemely simplycitie of handeling his matter, and framing his words" (13–14). For E.K., Spenser's art appears in the fit he creates between his matter and the apparent simplicity of the pastoral mode. Related to this stress on decorum is Spenser's structural flair: after praising his syntax, E.K. goes on to comment on "al the compasse of the speach." "For what in most English wryters useth to be loose, and as it were ungyrt, in this Authour is well grounded, finely framed, and strongly trussed up together" (17). Spenser's capacity for "framing" and connecting the various parts of his poem—by the calendar device, by repeated words and images, by thematic variation—makes his first book stand out from earlier sixteenth-century poetry.

The epistle is followed by the *"generall argument of* the whole booke" in which E.K.'s eccentricities are more clearly on display. Much of the "argument" seems a parody of humanist pedantry. It begins by defending at some length a false derivation of "eclogues" (*pace* E.K., the term means "selections" and has nothing to do with goats) and continues with a labored if learned defense of Spenser's decision to begin the *Calender* in January, not 25 March, as was the common custom in sixteenth-century England. The passage recalls the mock-pedantry of Thomas More's letter to Peter Giles at the beginning of his *Utopia.* The argument also brings up the division of the eclogues into plaintive, recreative, and moral, categories that E.K. seems almost to toss off, providing no further elaboration. The effect here, as in much of the *Calender,* is to place the burden of further interpretation on the reader.

**"Januarye"**   The deeply political emphasis of Virgil's eclogue-book is announced in the opening dialogue between Meleboeus and Tityrus about their respective situations and by implication the condition of Rome. By contrast, Spenser begins with the psychology of a particular pastoral type, the shepherd boy Colin Clout. Although *The Shepheardes Calender* concerns itself with contemporary issues, it begins with the mind: knowledge starts with an awareness of fallen human nature. Spenser only gradually extends his analysis to the political and religious institutions resulting from the Fall.

Yet in its quiet way "Januarye" announces many themes of Spenser's eclogue-book, most noticeably its concern with time, love, and pastoral song. The *Calender* opens with an image of frustrated stasis, which Spenser will vary throughout the book as a whole. Pastoral shepherds are forever falling unhappily in love, and in Mantuan and his imitators earthly love is mostly a ruinous insanity. What distinguishes Colin from other pastoral lovers is his skill as a poet, which Spenser juxtaposes with his love-melancholy. "May seeme he lovd, or els some care he tooke: / Well couth he tune his pipe, and frame his stile" (8–9). The paratactic syntax here leaves the relation between loving and singing unclear. Perhaps Colin's skill is evidence of his love or sorrow, or perhaps there is no connection between them. But Colin will insist that the inability of his song to gain his love makes his art worthless: the emotional dead end leads to an artistic one.

Colin's complaint stresses his likeness to the blighted landscape. "Thou barrein ground, whome winters wrath hath wasted, / Art made a myrrhour, to behold my plight" (19–20). What Ruskin called the pathetic fallacy—the idea that the landscape sympathizes with its human inhabitants—is familiar in pastoral literature. But in this poem Nature does not sympathize: Colin merely imagines it does as he projects his own mood onto his environment. The narrator places the scene on a "sunneshine day" (3), and he reemphasizes the actual conditions at the end by mentioning the "sonned sheepe, / Whose hanging heads did seeme his carefull case to weepe" (77–78). The landscape may be winter, but it is not altogether cold, and even the sheep, which Colin compares to himself, only "seem" to weep—seem so to Colin presumably. The elaborate parallelism of Colin's complaint stresses the narrowness of his imagination, which projects its own condition onto everything it considers.

In fact, the hanging heads of the sheep derive from their physical condition, for which Colin is partly responsible. In pastoral poems love often distracts shepherds from their duties: "Never knewe I lovers sheepe in good plight" (20) says Willye in "August." Colin, however, seems to take pride in his distraction.

> Thou feeble flocke, whose fleece is rough and rent,
> Whose knees are weake through fast and evill fare:
> Mayst witnesse well by thy ill governement,
> Thy maysters mind is overcome with care.
> Thou weake, I wanne: thou leane, I quite forlorne:
> With mourning pyne I, you with pyning mourne. (43–48)

Colin's tone here is gloomily triumphant as he reassures himself that he *is* in love and shows all the conventional symptoms. The "care" that afflicts Colin has a particularly important resonance in the *Calender* as a whole, for it has two distinct meanings. Whereas Colin's care is the supposed grief of his love, a shepherd's care is also his duty: shepherds care for their sheep, ministers for their congregations. As Thenot will say in "Februarie," "ever my flocke was my chiefe care" (23). The word suggests the degree to which Colin has substituted his private care for his public duty.

Colin is not, finally, a large enough character to make his situation tragic—"no better doe him call." Why, then, make him the central figure of the book? *The Shepheardes Calender* concerns itself with the working of

the imagination and the capacities of song. Pastoral shepherds sometimes manage to gain new sanity by singing, working through the
obsessions that blind them. Other shepherds may persuade their ladies
with their songs. But Colin's music, proficient as it is, becomes a narcissistic end in itself, an enjoyment of misery. The *Calender* examines the
capacity of the imagination not only to teach and to improve but to
limit, and it makes thematic the stasis so common in pastoral: Colin's
imagination stunts his growth. He sees himself as old already in "Januarye," and he will not change his view of himself between this eclogue
and "December."

Nothing much happens in pastoral eclogues. There is an exchange of
songs or of views, but the closest that an eclogue normally comes to
action is a singing match. Nonetheless, this first eclogue ends with an
act striking for its force: Colin breaks his pipe. He does so out of pique:
the muse has not helped him, nor has his song relieved the passion, and
so he "broke his oaten pype, and downe dyd lye" (72). The picture that
precedes "Januarye" shows the pipe as a bagpipe, an instrument associated iconographically with sexuality. Neither love nor music has helped
Colin, and he attacks both, ending the first eclogue of the *Calender* with
a picture of frustrated stalemate.

**"Februarie"**   "Februarie" begins with the same wintry weather that
provides the background for Colin's complaint. But where in "Januarye"
Colin makes the weather into a metaphor for his own wasted condition,
in "Februarie" it is a metonym, one physical result of the Fall. The
eclogue begins by asking, how should one respond to the weather? And
by implication, how should one respond to a fallen world? This question, however, is obscured by the slanging match between Thenot and
Cuddie in which neither listens to the other. If "Januarye" shows Colin
lost in his monologue, "Februarie" (like many of the moral eclogues)
stages a comedy of mutual incomprehension. It also dramatizes the
fallen passions—among them, anger, envy, and pride—that interfere
with rational debate and limit the effectiveness of poetic fictions.

The opposition of a young man and an old one is a familiar medieval
topic, but here the *Calender*'s concern with time gives it peculiar resonance. Cuddie and Thenot embody opposite ends of life's spectrum.
They are flint and steel, made to quarrel, and their different ages result
in radically different values. Cuddie, an Arcadian sensibility, invests
himself in the delights and pains of the present, praising the one and
cursing the other. He stresses his animal nature, identifying with the

physical shivering of his sheep and with the sexual prowess of his "brag bullock." Thenot, by contrast, is a severe Mantuanesque shepherd whose attitude toward worldly delight is suspicion and whose concern is primarily with duty: "ever my flocke was my chiefe care." His counsel is to invest nothing in the world or its goods; in particular, "All that is lent to love, wyll be lost" (70). His view would seem to include everything that Cuddie omits but to admit nothing of what Cuddie feels.

Yet Thenot's moral stance hides other, less admirable, traits. He leaps to attack Cuddie with suspicious quickness, as if Cuddie were voicing an impulse that he has silenced in himself. When he asserts in passing that he has spent his years "Some in much joy, many in many teares" (18), neither response suggests the unflappably stoical stance he advocates in principle. Both responses suggest that his present bleak picture of life ("Must not the world wend in his commun course / From good to badd, from badde to worse" [11–12]) is partly sour grapes, based on disappointed expectations (Berger 1988, 422–36). Cuddie certainly sees him as envious: "Now thy selfe hast lost both lopp and topp, / Als my budding braunch thou wouldest cropp" (57–58). Like many of the eclogues of *The Shepheardes Calender,* "Februarie" presents a dialogue between speakers who will not listen to one another and who thus cannot begin to resolve their differences.

The fable Thenot tells Cuddie of the Oak and the Briar provides a model of how not to tell a story. It is one of those, Thenot says, that he has heard Tityrus tell in his youth, "But none fitter then this to applie" (100). The stress is on application—on the hearer seeing how it illuminates his own situation. Thenot reemphasizes this point when he tells Cuddie to "listen a while and hearken the end" (101). Presumably Cuddie will see the folly of the Briar, realize the error of his ways, and treat his elders with more respect. But the story that follows is driven by rage, and the melodramatic portraits of the "goodly Oake" and the "bragging Brere" make it impossible for Cuddie to recognize himself in the latter. Thenot's retelling of the story outlines only his vision of a world in which there can be but one truth: "Ambitious folke" (161) slander you in order to do you in. His mild paranoia leaves no room for sympathy and less for fruitful action.

His story is itself out of control, an impression suggested by his miscalculated rhetoric as he imagines the farmer's attack on the tree:

> His harmefull Hatchet he hent in hand,
> (Alas that it so ready should stand)

> And to the field alone he speedeth.
> (Ay little helpe to harme there needeth). . . .
> The Axes edge did oft turne againe,
> As halfe unwilling to cutte the graine:
> Semed, the sencelesse yron dyd feare,
> Or to wrong holy eld did forbeare.
> For it had bene an auncient tree,
> Sacred with many a mysteree,
> And often crost with the priestes crewe,
> And often halowed with holy water dewe.
> But sike fancies weren foolerie,
> And broughten this Oake to this miserye.
>                                    (195–98, 203–12)

The beginning of this passage, with its melodramatically scrupulous ax, its heavy-handed alliteration, and its bathetic moralizing, exemplifies Thenot's clumsiness, but the rest suggests how far he is carried away. For "eld" becomes momentarily not only goodly but "holy," and he imagines the tree being blessed by a priest in an "auncient" magico-Catholic rite. Remembering too late that the old religion is "foolerie," Thenot backtracks and finds he has made the oak responsible for its own death. While the passage may make a glancing historical reference,[27] it chiefly foregrounds Thenot's lack of control.

The anger returns with the gloating lines describing the Briar's eventual downfall ("being downe, is trodde in the durt / Of cattell, and brouzed, and sorely hurt") and the triumphant moral: "Such was thend of this Ambitious brere, / For scorning Eld—" (335–38). But the end, long attended, only prompts Cuddie's rude interruption. Cuddie refuses to recognize himself in the Briar, and so the whole story passes him by. His final line, "Hye thee home shepheard, the day is nigh wasted" (246), suggests that in Thenot's fictions as well as Colin's laments, time can be "wasted."

**"March"** What first strikes the reader about "March" is its ridiculous, bouncy verse form, a borrowing from medieval verse romances and especially from Chaucer's parody of them in "Sir Thopas." The melodious rhetoric of "Januarye" and the rough accentual meter of "Februarie" yield to a stanza that makes it difficult to take anything that goes on very seriously. Similarly, themes we have seen in "Januarye" and "Februarie"—love, grief, the Fall—recur in an unmistakably slapstick mode. This is a wonderfully silly eclogue, and the silliness enables Spenser to develop a new account of human ignorance.

Poems about Eros, god of love, appear in Greek literature and form a considerable part of the body of playful lyric that was revived in the Renaissance as part of the "Greek Anthology." They are imitated by Latin and neo-Latin writers and by others (including Marot, whose work Spenser knew well) in the vernacular languages. Spenser would later write several such "anacreontics" as a bridge between his sonnet-sequence and the *Epithalamion* with which it ends. These poems often tell short, playful stories about Eros (or Cupid) and his mother, Venus, demonstrating metaphorically love's nature. They are marked by a lightness of touch which is sometimes superficial and sometimes playfully subtle. The original model for Thomalin's story of the hunt for Cupid appears in a short poem by the Greek poet Bion, a poem that Spenser may have known and that was previously imitated in French by Ronsard and others. In Bion's poem a young bird-catcher attempts to snare Eros, whom he perceives as a large bird; when he fails, he goes to an old farmer, who advises him to stay away: soon enough the creature will attack him in turn. The boy never really knows what he has confronted; we as readers watch him with superior amusement. Ronsard presents a more saturnine version of the story: although beautiful, Eros is a bird of evil omen (8), and the poem stresses his dangerousness.[28]

Both Bion's poem and Ronsard's are epigrammatic narratives; Spenser sets the story into a dialogue between Willye and Thomalin, two adolescents. The formal change develops both speakers' comic ignorance of the adult sexual world they will soon enter. The opening speeches on the coming of spring set up a new relation between the boys and the seasons. Where Colin makes the weather into a reflection of his inner landscape, and Thenot and Cuddie agree in treating the literal weather as hostile, Willye makes it into a beneficent imperative. As the seasons awaken the plants and animals, so it should awaken them. "Tho [then] shall we sporten in delight, / And learne with Lettice to wexe light, / That scornefully lookes askaunce" (19–21). This is the unproblematic, "hey nonny no" vision of love by which pastoral figures are no more than creatures driven by physical appetites, and the scornful Lettice ("Let us"?) will, contrary to appearances, turn out to be a willing instructress. The rather general phrase for lovemaking ("waxing light") suggests considerable vagueness about just what they are supposed to learn.

Their ignorance is underscored by the literariness of their language. When Willye speaks of "Flora" and "Maias bowre," the classical references contrast with the homely dialect of the rest of his speech, and the opening vision of spring itself has a classical "source" in Lucretius's hymn to Venus at the opening of *De Natura Rerum,* as well as the openings of scores of medieval love poems. The contrast suggests a language and tradition of love that the two children inherit but whose implications they do not fully understand. This ignorance reappears when Thomalin tells of hunting Cupid. The god Eros is, after all, a metaphor for the force of desire, but to Thomalin it appears a literal quarry, a strange quarry with which he can prove his manhood. "But were it faerie, feend, or snake, / My courage earnd it to awake, / And manfully thereat shotte" (76–78). As one might expect, arrows do not do much good, and Thomalin is reduced to throwing stones. Eventually the god returns fire:

> Therewith affrayd I ranne away:
> But he, that earst seemd but to playe,
>     A shaft in earnest snatched,
> And hit me running in the heele:
> For then I little smart did feele:
>     But soone it sore encreased.
> And now it ranckleth more and more,
> And inwardly it festreth sore,
>     Ne wote I, how to cease it. (94–102)

This is, of course, the same "sore" that afflicts Colin, and like him, Thomalin has no idea what to do with it. Willye agrees that this must be Cupid because he knows him by a "token"—the story his father has told of catching him in a fowling net. Spenser presents us again with a picture of two boys discoursing learnedly about Cupid without knowing what their words really mean.

When Cupid does shoot, he hits Thomalin in the heel; E.K. reminds the reader that the wound recalls the arrow that slew Achilles. The allusion has a double effect. On the one hand, it adds to the scene's silliness: Thomalin is nothing like Homer's warrior. But the detail also gestures toward what the boys' limited vision excludes. The experience of war and death exists outside their knowledge, as does the fact of the Fall, which appears elliptically in the literal fall of one of Thomalin's sheep when he was asleep (49–57). The poems remind us of the realities happily beyond the ken of the protagonists as they try to orient themselves in a world of confusing impulses.

**"Aprill"**    There is a stylistic gap between Virgil's third eclogue, which presents a traditional singing contest imitating Theocritus, and the fourth, which playfully envisions the birth of a child who will begin a new golden age. A similar gap occurs between "March" and "Aprill," Spenser's third and fourth eclogues. After the personal and seasonal emphasis of earlier eclogues, "Aprill" turns to public matters, creating a politically charged myth. Like Virgil's fourth eclogue, it celebrates a ruler and, half playfully, half ritualistically, announces the coming of an age of peace. Colin's song describes the pastoral coronation of "Elisa" by her shepherd, and it decks her as a bride in preparation for her marriage to her people (Johnson, 164). The two acts are ultimately one: Elisa's "marriage" to England is also her coronation. This stress on Elizabeth's marriage has, as Johnson and others have argued, a political point: it reinforces the Protestant voices urging the queen to refuse the match with the French and Catholic Duc D'Alençon (Johnson, 144–66).[29] Virgil's golden age will occur in the future, as the child matures; Eliza's golden age has arrived with her marriage/coronation: she alone is necessary for it to continue.

The speaker here resembles the speaker of an epithalamion or marriage-poem, invoking and organizing his representative figures, commenting on their meaning, addressing himself to the participants. The imagined double ritual resembles many later Spenserian processions which unfold an event's meaning. The first stanza invokes the water-spirits and the Muses in singing the song—pairing classical and local deities, representations of art and nature. The second announces the subject, Elisa, "*Syrinx* daughter without spotte" (50), and the third presents a secular epiphany as the poet comes upon Elisa with an admiring cry, like a devotee in the presence of a goddess: "See, where she sits upon the grassie greene, / (O seemly sight)" (55–56).[30] The next three stanzas develop an elaborate praise of Elisa, and in the seventh and central stanza Colin himself proffers his service. The next four stanzas assemble the participants for the coronation, pairing, as in the first stanza, classical and English figures: the Muses, the Graces, the Ladies of the Lake, and the "shepheards daughters, that dwell on the greene" (127). In the twelfth stanza the poet invokes a multitude of flowers to crown the new

Queen—flowers that, in their variety, suggest the variousness of her realm. In the last stanza Colin turns to address the Queen directly.

> Now ryse up *Elisa,* decked as thou art,
>     in royall aray:
> And now ye daintie Damsells may depart
>     echeone her way.
> I feare, I have troubled your troupes to longe:
> Let dame *Eliza* thanke you for her song. (145–50)

Elisa is now "dame Eliza"—*domina,* the lady in charge. The poet can retire, offering to share with his imagined celebrants the "Damsines" or plums he gathers in future: the poet moves from flowers to the promise of fruit.

This outline Spenser fills with symbolic detail that describes the attendants and pictures Elisa herself.[31] The detail suggests the meaning of the coronation and the Queen's relation to her subjects. In his commentary on the eclogue E.K. stresses Spenser's lowering of the Queen in treating her within the pastoral fiction—the praise is not "what the worthinesse of her Majestie deserveth" (78)—but it is hard to imagine what form could offer a richer or more varied source of symbolic materials. The Muses and the Graces surrounding her make Elisa a center of culture and indeed of all civilized behavior. The water-spirits embody the land itself, and the generic "shepheards daughters" suggest Elisa's English subjects. "*Chloris,* that is the chiefest Nymph of al" (122), bears Elisa's crown of olive branches: "Olives bene for peace, / When wars doe surcease: / Such for a Princesse bene principall" (124–26). The play on the root *prince* here reemphasizes the centrality of Elizabeth's role as a bringer of peace; as some of Elizabeth's subjects were aware, the Hebrew meaning of her name could be understood as "Peace of the Lord."

The description of Elisa herself brings opposites together in harmony. She is praised for "Her modest eye, / Her Majestie" (71–72)—humble and proud at once. The red and white roses in her complexion (69) suggest that she unites in herself the warring houses of Lancaster and York. When she appears as "*Syrinx* daughter without spotte" (50), E.K. glosses Pan as Henry VIII and Syrinx as Anne Boleyn; as commentators have pointed out, the image goes beyond that to make Elisa the embodiment of music itself. When Pan attempted to rape the nymph Syrinx, she turned herself into reeds to avoid him; in response he cut the reeds, joining them with wax to form panpipes. The "child," or offspring, of this union would be the melody of the pipes themselves, and hence the harmony—political as well as artistic—that restores the world (Cullen, 113–14; Montrose, 39–42).

Throughout Spenser treats this poem with an extraordinarily light hand; its central stanza, in which Colin swears fealty, epitomizes his method:

> *Pan* may be proud, that ever he begot
> 　　such a Bellibone,
> And *Syrinx* rejoyse, that ever was her lot
> 　　To beare such an one.
> Soone as my younglings cryen for the dam,
> To her will I offer a milkwhite Lamb:
> 　　Shee is my goddessse plaine,
> 　　And I her shepherds swayne,
> Albee forswonck and forswatt I am. (91–99)

The stanza combines opposites, high and low, classical mythology and homely dialect ("forswonck and forswatt"), shepherd-poet and queen. The linguistic play of the stanza is particularly notable: "bellibone" sounds like a dialect term (as it does in "August"), but it anglicizes "Belle et Bonne"—the beautiful and the good, making Elisa into an earthly image of a platonic form. The song's central line, "Soone as my younglings cryen for the dam," creates an image of nurture, for Elisa is a metaphoric center of England's fertility.

The song is propaganda of a high order. Yet, as Louis Montrose has pointed out, this vision of the queen as a nurturing shepherdess ruling by love and not by power is perilously ideal (41–42). The playful pastoral veil covers the actual strains of the queen's court with an image of harmonious fruitfulness. Some strains appear even here as the emphasis on Elizabeth's ties with her people implicitly argues against the threat of a French match. The idealizing vision is further limited by its frame. Colin is absent, and his obsessive grief causes Thenot to ask: "And hath he skill to make [to compose poetry] so excellent, / Yet hath so little skill to brydle love?" (19–20). The poet's capacity for vision does not guarantee his sanity. Though the song praises the present as a golden age, avoiding the vision of waste so apparent elsewhere, its frame insists on the actuality of the Fall.

**"Maye"**    If the praise of "Aprill" envisions a harmonious England with an ideal ruler, "Maye" insists on the problematic actuality of religious conflict. In doing so it implicitly criticizes the golden-world picture of the earlier eclogue, pointing to the strains the earlier vision omits. Against the intricate stanzas of Colin's song and the easy metrics of Hobbinol and Thenot, "Maye" returns to the rough, four-beat measure of "Februarie," and its dialogue is sprinkled with dialect words—northernisms like "kirke" (church), "gate" (goat), "blonket" (gray), and "queme" (to please). This eclogue is the first of three to touch on the state of the church, drawing on the Mantuanesque tradition of pastoral. But the opposition between Piers and Palinode differs from that between Mantuan's speakers in his ninth and tenth eclogues. Instead of a simple right and wrong, there are several sides to the issues, and as in "Februarie," the speakers approach the problem with radically different values. As in "Februarie," the opposition results in another inadequate fiction.

The eclogue begins by recalling the themes of "Februarie" as two older men watch a group of younger shepherds celebrate May Day. Palinode wants nostalgically to join the holiday-makers, while Piers reproves him for such a wish. As in "Februarie," the argument concerns the value of worldly delight, with an Arcadian shepherd opposing a Mantuanesque shepherd, but this version has an explicitly religious dimension. Many Protestants condemned May Day, a holiday held over from medieval times, as a papist and indeed a pagan rite. Piers—whose name recalls Langland's Piers Plowman, associated with church reform—embodies a strongly Protestant point of view, while Palinode—whose name suggests a tendency to recant spiritual truth—leans, with his talk of the celebration pleasing "holy Saints" (15), in a Catholic direction. The ceremonial materials of "Aprill" reappear here with new meaning: the references to Lady Flora and the "flock of Nymphs" (31–33) now appear suspiciously pagan.

The eclogue presents a dialogue of mutually incompatible visions. Like Cuddie in "Februarie," Palinode is a "worldes childe" (73) who comments that shepherds who refuse the goods God offers now are foolish, because "when they bene dead, their good is ygoe, / They sleepen in rest, well as other moe" (67–68). "Good" here is material, and Palinode's sense of the afterlife seems minimal. Characteristically he sees literal

shepherds in front of him and defends his wish to be one of them, at least
in imagination. For Piers, by contrast, "shepherd" is a metaphor for the
Christian pastor. He is less concerned with the merrymakers before his
eyes than with the church, which has deteriorated as its clergy, now
grown rich and powerful, have lost their divine vocation. Palinode's exas-
peration with Piers's strictures (131–47) comes partly from incomprehension: to him there is no reason why the shepherds he sees should "hasten" (152) the sorrow that is part of worldly mutability. The two differ in
temperament. Palinode is a peaceable fellow who thinks it does harm for
pastors to criticize one another. By contrast, Piers feels that friendship
with the enemy can only lead to corruption: "what concord han light and
darke sam?" (168). Palinode wishes accommodation; Piers prefers purity.

Piers's fable accordingly warns Palinode against the goods of this
world. The young kid is a typical fallen soul (we hear that as he reaches
adolescence, the "blossomes of lust to bud did beginne, / And spring
forth ranckly under his chinne" [187–88]), and the Fox who tempts
him is the devil's emissary, who seems associated with Catholic or
Catholic-leaning forces. He tempts the Kid with a bag of trinkets—
worldly toys—the most important of which are a mirror and a bell. The
bell has associations with Catholic rituals, and the mirror, which fasci-
nates the Kid, suggests a narcissistic concern with self. The tale ultimately warns against trusting the devil (the Fox) and his seeming goods.

Yet the tale fails to convey this message to Palinode—and fails in a
way reminiscent of "Februarie." "Satire is a Sort of Glass," wrote Swift a
century later, "wherein Beholders do generally discover every body's
Face but their Own."[32] Palinode does not see himself in the Kid any more
than Cuddie saw himself in the Briar. This happens not because Piers's
tale is driven, like Thenot's, by uncontrolled anger, but because allegorical fables depend on shared conventions—on a common understanding
of what "Fox" and "Kid" represent. It remains unclear whether Palinode
takes the Fox literally or whether it has some other significance to him.
But he clearly does not see the fable's Protestant meaning, since he asks
permission to tell it to "our sir John" because "well he meanes, but little
can say" (309–11). While the ignorant Sir John is just the kind of cler-
gyman concerned Protestants complained of, Palinode sees the fable as
enlivening his sermon. The eclogue ends with the shepherds friendly but
still mutually uncomprehending.

**"June"**   "Maye," "June," and "Julye" are all dialogues, but "June"
contrasts markedly with the ecclesiastical eclogues framing it. Whereas

"Maye" and "Julye" look outward to the problems of religious community, "June" focuses on Colin's willed isolation. Spenser reworks the familiar model of Virgil's first eclogue, in which the dispossessed and wandering Meleboeus meets Tityrus happily reclining under his shady beech. Here, too, an "exile"—Colin—converses with another shepherd comfortably at home in his pastoral environment. But the differences are crucial. Virgil's Meleboeus has been dispossessed by political forces: he is a casualty of Augustus's resettlement of Roman soldiers after the civil wars and would like nothing better than to return home. Colin is self-exiled: his decision to leave the valleys for the hills derives from inner dissatisfaction.

Many critics have pointed to the initial opposition of Hobbinol and Colin (Bernard, 54–59; Nelson, 49). Hobbinol is identified with a formulaic ideal pastoral landscape complete with a "gentle warbling wynde, / So calme, so coole, as no where else I fynde" (4–5), and with birds whose songs harmonize with the sound of the water. Colin sees him as "happy *Hobbinoll* . . . That Paradise hast found, whych *Adam* lost" (9–10)—an image of pastoral content. By contrast, Colin sees himself as an outcast: "But I unhappy man, whom cruell fate, / And angry Gods pursue from coste to coste, / Can nowhere fynd, to shroude my lucklesse pate" (14–16). The echo of the *Aeneid,* whose hero is forced to wander by fate and the wrath of the Gods, has a complex effect. Most immediately it is comic (an effect reemphasized by the bathetic "pate"): Colin sees himself as an epic hero as he dramatizes his grief. He has, after all, been sent to wander not by Troy's burning but by Rosalind's snub. But the reference also brings the memory of a larger world into the pastoral, and with it the traditional connection between pastoral and epic. It reminds us of what Colin might attempt even while stressing how poetically and emotionally immature he is.

The disagreement between Colin and Hobbinol concerns place. Colin has left the "dales" where the shepherds live for the "wastfull hylls" (50), where he can sing alone. The hills are wasteful in being uninhabited, but they also waste Colin's talent. Colin recalls his progression from a youthful poet of pastoral delights (33–40) to a poet of love (41–48), but his development stops there. Maturity and Rosalind's loss "Those weary wanton toyes away dyd wype" (48), and no other poetry has taken their place. Having renounced the shepherd community, Colin might become more than a shepherd-singer but instead he becomes less: when Hobbinol praises his Orphic powers, Colin counters that he has little skill and plays "to please my selfe, all be it ill. . . . Enough is me to paint out my

unrest, / And poore my piteous plaints out in the same" (72, 79–80).
Poetry appears to be no more than therapy, a temporary means of
unburdening oneself.

In condemning the world, Colin invokes the death of Tityrus—
probably Chaucer in this case, as E.K. points out. Tityrus's death is sufficient proof that the world is beyond hope and that poetry itself has
deteriorated; it reinforces Colin's argument for silence. But in fact the
reference to Tityrus has a second effect, suggesting a different function
for poetry.

> Well couth he wayle hys Woes, and lightly slake
> The flames, which love within his heart had bredd,
> And tell us mery tales, to keepe us wake,
> The while our sheepe about us safely fedde. (85–88)

While Tityrus is a love poet, his tales also enable his audience to stay
awake while guarding their sheep. *The Shepheardes Calender* portrays various kinds of waking—not least, bodily awakening in the spring. But
waking also figures heightened spiritual awareness: poetry (or preaching) makes human beings see themselves anew. Since Christian pastors
feed their flocks with their words, the reference to sheep eating safely
may also have a metaphorical resonance: certainly the poet declares in
the coda to the *Calender* that he has taught *"the ruder shepheard how to
feede his sheepe"* (5). Colin's speech, of course, recalls the ideal only to discard it, but it remains applicable to the book as a whole. Lapsing into
monologue toward the end of "June," Colin imagines himself an Orphic
poet, able to pierce Rosalind's heart and show up his rival Menalcas. The
fantasy embodies a self-centered version of the divine capacity to
awaken one's hearers. Yet Colin's skill, evident in "June"'s showily difficult stanza form, continues to operate in a vacuum.

**"Julye"**    Both "June" and "Julye" oppose hills to dales, but the meaning of the opposition differs sharply. In "June" Colin retires to literal hills
to waste his talents. But in the dizzy argument of "Julye," hills lurch
from being physical places where goats graze to metaphors for ambition.
Colin gives up ambition in retiring to the hills, but Thomalin calls Morrell a "goteheard prowde" (1) for preferring to dwell in high places. As
the eclogue progresses, the hill-valley debate grows less important;
indeed, it seems largely an excuse for Spenser's attack on ambition

within the church hierarchy. As with "Februarie" and "Maye," the narrative in the final part of the eclogue—in this case, Algrind's mishap—illuminates what has come before. The eclogue thus contrasts with "June" by returning to the urgent problems of the world beyond the poem, on which Colin has turned his back.

This is the first of the eclogues that Spenser adapted from Mantuan's *Adulescentia,* and here, as in each of his adaptations, he changes his original radically. Mantuan's eighth eclogue, "On the Religion of the Rustics," begins when Candidus urges Alphus to drive their flocks up the hills; when Alphus voices uncertainty, Candidus unleashes a flood of reasons why hills are better than valleys. He receives no argument from Alphus, and Candidus eventually leaves that subject to discuss Pollux's vision of the Virgin Mary and his subsequent teachings.

By contrast, Spenser's "Julye" is a debate—or at least presents itself as a debate—on the relative merits of hills and valleys. The allegorical dimension of hills would seem to derive from the familiar Judeo-Christian call to humility: "Every valleie shalbe exalted, and everie mountaine and hill shalbe made lowe" (Isaiah 40:4). That Thomalin is a shepherd and the hill-dwelling Morrell a goatherd enhances the symbolic opposition. Yet the Christian significance of hill and valley seems unrelated to the character of the debaters. Morrell shows no signs of overweening pride (in his first speech he invites Thomalin to join him), and he likes hills, among other reasons, because they furnish good herbs for goats. He does make the typical mistakes of the pastoral literalist: he believes, for instance, that the higher you are above sea level, the better your chances of getting to heaven. E.K.'s gloss—"Note the shepheards simplenesse, which supposeth that from the hylls is nearer waye to heaven" (132)—is for once on the mark.[33] But simplemindedness is not pride, and Thomalin himself hardly seems a model of Protestant zeal. He chooses the valleys primarily because they are safe, and he manages in his exposition of the early church to mention Moses who "sawe hys makers face, / His face more cleare, than Christall glasse, / and spake to him in place" (158–60) without recalling that he saw God (though not his face) on a mountain (Exodus 33:18–23). His example quietly undercuts his crusade against literal high places.

The bouncy comedy of two herdsmen arguing about hills serves largely to open up the eclogue's primary concern, church corruption. Thomalin attacks shepherds who have become rich and proud at the expense of their flocks, carefully directing his criticism at "Rome":

> For Palinode (if thou him ken)
> yode late on Pilgrimage
> To Rome, (if such be Rome) and then
> He saw thilke misusage. (181–84)

The parenthetical "if such be Rome" looks like a characteristic instance of rustic ignorance, but it also manages to leave the door open for the possibility that what Palinode saw was closer to home. A similarly self-protective irony occurs at the end of his attack: "Sike syrlye shepheards han we none, / they keepen all the path" (203–4). The lengthy attack on church discipline was risky enough to need cover.

The dangers of speaking out are made explicit by the complex example of Grindal, which closes the eclogue. Algrind, an obvious anagram of Elizabeth's embattled archbishop of Canterbury, has already been referred to approvingly in "Maye," and in "Julye" Thomalin speaks of him, with reverence, as a source of wisdom. Thomalin attributes to him the vision of the early church, in which there was no great difference between rich shepherds and impoverished flocks. Spenser's circumspection is worth remarking: his criticism of the ecclesiastical establishment comes from the mouth of a fictional shepherd who quotes another fictional shepherd associated allegorically with the head of the ecclesiastical establishment being criticized. (Grindal was in fact quite clear on the necessity for a church hierarchy.) And with regard to ambition, the example of Grindal is profoundly ambiguous. He has chosen a high place, has stood up for his principles, and has been made to suffer for them by the queen. High places are indeed dangerous. But his example also shows the need for good ministers to uphold their cases of conscience: although Morrell finds riches "a signe of helth" (212), neither shepherd criticizes Algrind. E.K. associates Algrind's accident—a bird has dropped a shellfish on his head—with its source in the biography of Aeschylus. Is Grindal a poet of the kind necessary to the flock—unlike either of the shepherds in this eclogue? One of Grindal's most passionately held convictions was the need for a learned clergy, for preachers who would know what they spoke about. His example certainly dwarfs the limited if good-hearted speakers of "Julye."

**"August"**     One of the firmest conventions of Arcadian pastoral poetry is the singing contest. It occupies two of Theocritus's seven pastoral idylls and two of Virgil's ten eclogues. Spenser has only one contest in twelve eclogues, but he gives it special thematic importance. It contrasts triumphantly with the two "moral" eclogues that surround it: with their bouncy rustic music Perigot and Willye, unlike the moral shepherds, are able to make their language work for them. Their roundelay, an explosion of recreative energy, celebrates the world and their own drives despite the Fall. In this recreation it also reimagines the clichés of Colin's lovelorn singing and undercuts the solipsistic Petrarchism embodied in his sestina.

Willye's initial question, "Tell me *Perigot,* what shalbe the game" (1), suggests that this will be a recreative eclogue. This "game" of love poetry contrasts with Colin's plaintive rhetoric. Perigot, who has the mopes because, like Colin, he has fallen in love, nonetheless joins in the contest, singing a song about the moment of his falling in love. Amaboean song, in which two poets speak alternate lines or stanzas, each trying to outdo the other, is the most common form of the singing match. Here Spenser gives it peculiar force, for Willye's thumping refrains reenergize the Petrarchan clichés of Perigot's remembered experience and give them comic vitality. It is as if Colin's record, recorded at 33 rpm, were played at 45 rpm, an effect of joyfully energetic and vital silliness:

> But whether in paynefull love I pyne,
>> hey ho pinching payne,
> Or thrive in welth, she shalbe mine.
>> but if thou can her obteine. (109–12)

As Shakespeare does in his romantic comedies, Spenser sets Petrarchan clichés against the sturdy "hey ho's," which insist that life goes on anyway and that the sufferings of romantic love are less important than the lover thinks.

Perigot indeed takes the clichés of inherited love rhetoric in new directions. His vision of the lady is more active, more sensual, and more full of joyful movement than that of the tradition.

> As the bonilasse passed bye,
>> hey ho bonilasse,
> She rovde at me with glauncing eye,
>> as cleare as the christall glasse:
> All as the Sunnye beame so bright,

> hey ho the Sunne beame,
>> Glaunceth from *Phœbus* face forthright,
>> so love into thy hart did streame. (77–84)

Normally Cupid shoots an arrow through the lady's eye without the
lady on her pedestal having much to do with it. Here she all but winks,
"roving" like an archer at his heart. The clichéd sunbeam comparison
gains new vitality from Willye's "Hey ho the Sunne beame" and the
sudden shift from the lady's *look* to the *love* that streams into Perigot's
heart. This simile, however, is only the first of three (the look becomes a
thunderbolt and then "dame *Cynthias* silver raye"), and the song suggests brilliantly the delight of poetic improvisation. The singing here
seems to have a therapeutic effect: Perigot comments later, wanting to
hear Colin's song, that "With mery thing its good to medle sadde"
(144). He now seems able to see his poor spirits in the light of Perigot's
laughter.

Colin's sestina (perhaps added late, for there is no reference to it in
E.K.'s subsequent glosses) further develops the contrast. It is, as has
often been pointed out, another tour de force, along with Sidney's "Ye
Goatheard Gods," the first sestina in English. The Italian form, in which
the same six words repeat in rotating order at the ends of the six-line
stanzas, is ready-made for the exploration of an obsessive sensibility. Just
as the end words go round in a circle, Colin's thoughts return to his
longing, his gloom, and his resentment. Where the communal effort of
Willye and Perigot's song effects a change for the better, Colin's solitary
performance insists on his unremitting gloom.

> More meete to wayle my woe,
> Bene the wild woddes my sorrowes to resound,
> Then bedde, or bowre, both which I fill with cryes
> When I them see so waist, and fynd no part
> Of pleasure past. Here will I dwell apart
> In gastfull grove therefore, till my last sleepe
> Doe close mine eyes. (165–171)

It is no accident that this parody of a Petrarchan lament harps on the word
*waste,* for Colin wastes himself in ways he does not fully understand.

**"September"**    The games of "August" yield to the public concerns of "September," the bleakest of the moral eclogues. After the summer expansiveness of "August," the many references to cold weather signal a new movement in the *Calender* as the bounds of pastoral song become increasingly clear and increasingly confining. Spenser adapted "September" from Mantuan's ninth eclogue, in which two shepherds meet in the Roman countryside and one confesses that reports of good pasturage have caused him to leave his home—only to find the Roman fields dry and unfit for life. The eclogue implicitly condemns Rome, thus recalling Virgil's first eclogue with its ambivalence toward the capital city. Spenser changes Mantuan's work to make it more like Virgil's in that Diggon Davie has returned to Hobbinoll's countryside from the city world; the city remains at a distance. Unlike "Maye" and "Julye," the eclogue focuses on what to do, looking beyond pastoral boundaries to activity in the real world. But the prospects for action are grim.

This eclogue differs from the other moral eclogues in the comparative unity of the shepherds: their disagreements take second place to their need to share experiences. Diggon Davie has left for vaguely indicated foreign parts and lost most of what he had. What sheep he has left have been starved by their journey, reminding one of Colin's sheep in "Januarye." Here, however, the sheep starve because of actual political and social conditions, not because of the melancholy of their shepherd. The familiar topics of "Maye" and "Julye" recur: where Diggon has been, greedy and powerful shepherds control others and feed off their charges. But Diggon adds that it is useless to seek redress: doing so will only make matters worse: "Yet better leave of [off] with a little losse, / Then by much wrestling to leese the grosse" (134–35).

The major difference between the two shepherds lies in Hobbinol's comparative quietism. He has already appeared as an innocent in "June" interrogating another wanderer; now his innocence seems a little shopworn. When Diggon makes his criticism explicit, Hobbinol is alarmed:

> Nowe Diggon, I see thou speakest to plaine:
> Better it were, a little to feyne,
> And cleanly cover, that cannot be cured.
> Such il, as is forced, mought nedes be endured. (136–39)

Diggon is committed to protecting his sheep against wolves, where Hobbinol finds it hard to muster the necessary sustained alertness. It is perhaps no accident that this is the eclogue in which the protagonists are almost gratuitously clumsy in speech. Diggon Davie sprinkles his speeches with Welsh dialect words, and at times it is not clear whether he is obscure out of self-protectiveness or incompetence (see lines 74–101). This clumsiness again suggests the inadequacy of these shepherds to the tasks at hand.

The story of Roffy and his dog Lowder, which ends the eclogue, may refer to a particular incident in the diocese of John Young ("Episcopus Roffensis"), whose secretary Spenser had been. As such it may not be fully interpretable. But more largely, it suggests the need for constant wariness: wolves (Roman Catholic clergy) are deceptive, and if one tale shows Roffy triumphant, the other shows Lowder beaten. The burdens of the good shepherd seem—at least to Hobbinol's mind—almost insupportable (236–41). At the end of the eclogue Hobbinol offers the desperate Diggon the comfort of his cottage, reiterating the pastoral virtues of friendship and hospitality, but his kindness leaves obviously unanswered the threats of the larger world that the dialogue has presented.

**"October"**    While poetry forms an implicit or explicit subject in all the *Calender*'s eclogues, "October" focuses on the relation between poet and patron. Spenser adapted the poem from Mantuan's fifth eclogue, in which the needy poet-shepherd Candidus asks for aid from the rich and miserly Sylvanus, only to be put off with excuses. (Sylvanus asserts repeatedly that he is not rich enough to fund the arts.) Spenser transformed the miserly, hypocritical Sylvanus into Piers, not a possible patron but a genuinely sympathetic friend. The change avoids Mantuan's satirical opposition and substitutes a dialogue between an idealist (Piers) and a materialist (Cuddie), another variation of the contrast between Mantuanesque and Arcadian points of view. As in the other moral eclogues, neither understands the other. Spenser has his poetic cake and eats it too: he dramatizes the plight of a poet without patrons, but he suggests as well the limitations of a poet whose primary concern is with patronage.

It is surprising to find not Colin but Cuddie in the book's dialogue about poetry. But Colin and Cuddie seem to represent two aspects of the poet's nature—and two kinds of failure. Where Colin limits his art to his own complaints, Cuddie refuses to sing because it pays badly. E.K. calls Cuddie "the perfecte paterne of a Poete, which finding no maintenaunce of his state and studies, complayneth of the contempte of Poetrie, and the causes thereof" (*YESP,* 170). The language suggests that Cuddie is not a perfect poet but the perfect image of a particular *kind* of poet—one without patrons.[34] Colin and Cuddie agree in their unwillingness to transcend their present conditions as pastoral poets singing the humble songs at which they excel ("June," 65–80; "October," 85–90, 115–19). It is tempting to see them as exaggerating different aspects of the historical Spenser. Cuddie certainly voices a desire for patronage shared by the Spenser of the Harvey correspondence. The parodic treatment of Cuddie and, to a lesser extent, of Colin looks like Spenser's attempt to examine and criticize his own impulses. Piers presents Cuddie with a long list of future careers, but Cuddie can only lament the rewards he has not gained. The friendly dialogue of "October" dramatizes another stalemate even while suggesting poetic options that go well beyond the *Calender*'s limits.

The stalemate appears in the familiar images of sleep and waking, now applied to the relation between poet and community. Piers exhorts Cuddie to hold up his "heavye head" (1); where before he has led the shepherds in their recreations, now "They in thee, and thou in sleepe art dead" (6). Cuddie's sloth is a death to the shepherds, who look to him (as to Tityrus in "June") as a source of vitality. His failure to sing is potentially catastrophic for the culture (an idea Spenser will insist on in *The Teares of the Muses*). Yet Cuddie will not listen. When Piers insists that poetry is a civilizing art, restraining "the lust of lawlesse youth with good advice" (22), Cuddie's refusal dismisses his suggestion.

> . . . who rewards [the poet] ere the more for thy?
> Or feedes him once the fuller by a graine?
> Sike prayse is smoke, that sheddeth in the skye,
> Sike words bene wynd and wasten soone in vayne. (33–36)

For Cuddie—as for many pastoral shepherds—things of the spirit are transient: what is real is what one can eat and touch.

Piers then suggests the Virgilian career that *The Shepheardes Calender* as a whole announces, urging Cuddie to write epic poetry and to celebrate the court (36–54). Cuddie, however, counters with his version of the decline-argument: Virgil ("the Romish *Tityrus*") left pastoral for epic because he lived in an age of warlike virtue, when great men rewarded poets who memorialized their deeds. Now, however, chivalric virtue has declined, and with it patronage; all that men want is "rymes of

rybaudrye" (76). There is, by implication, no place for a new Virgil.
Piers is temporarily stumped:

> O pierlesse Poesye, where is then thy place?
> If nor in Princes pallace thou doe sitt:
> (And yet is Princes pallace the most fitt)
> Ne brest of baser birth doth thee embrace.
> Then make thee winges of thine aspyring wit,
> And, whence thou camst, flye backe to heaven apace. (79–84)

Piers's doubt undermines the Virgilian progression that the *Calender* as a
whole announces: if there is no "place" for the poet at court, the gradua-
tion from pastoral to epic becomes problematic (Montrose, 45–49).

   Accordingly, the next exchange looks beyond epic. Piers first counsels
Cuddie to turn away from worldly subjects and write religious verse, but
Cuddie disqualifies himself. Such poetry is for Colin, who, if he were not
lovesick, would "mount as high, and sing as soote as Swanne" (90).
Piers's contradiction suggests that love transcends the world of the *Cal-
ender:*

> Ah fon, for love does teach him climbe so hie,
> And lyftes him up out of the loathsome myre:
> Such immortall mirrhor, as he doth admire,
> Would rayse ones mynd above the starry skie.
> And cause a caytive corage to aspire,
> For lofty love doth loath a lowly eye. (91–96)

Love is neither the limiting obsession of Colin's eclogues nor simply the
natural sexual awakening of "Februarie" and "March." It is the platonic
force that drives the lover toward the absolutes of the Good and the
Beautiful. As an "immortall mirrhor," it shows the lover what is inner-
most and best in him—what is closest to God. It becomes a means of
divine aspiration.

   Along with this vision of love came, in Renaissance platonism, a
model of inspiration, *enthusiasmos,* as E.K. calls it in his introduction to
the eclogue. A divine power fills the poet, enabling him to speak almost
without conscious effort. Cuddie denies that love enables such inspiration: it fills the head, not permitting the "vacancy" needful for inspired

verse. In its place he offers a comically materialist account of how inspiration works:

> Who ever casts to compasse weightye prise,
> And thinks to throwe out thondring words of threate:
> Let powre in lavish cups and thriftie bitts of meate,
> For *Bacchus* fruite is frend to *Phœbus* wise.
> And when with Wine the braine begins to sweate,
> The nombers flowe as fast as spring doth ryse. (103–8)

This is the kitchen blender theory of inspiration. Cuddie's materialism borders on farce here, and it once again suggests the limitations of his pastoral sensibility. It is no accident that this stanza is succeeded by a fantasy of what Cuddie *might* do if he had the wine he wishes: the passage recalls Colin's closing fantasy in "June" of how sorry he would make Rosalind if he had Orphic poetical powers. In both cases the poets settle for fantasy and for pastoral music; the limits of merely pastoral song become increasingly clear. "November" tests those limits.

**"November"**　"November" is the climax of *The Shepheardes Calender.* Problems of time and poetry, images of sleep and waking, vegetative growth and decay, all appear with the urgency that death gives them. The fact of death—the first effect of the Fall—raises in its most radical form the significance of life. It drives the poet beyond the *Calender*'s usual stalemate to see its issues from a divine perspective. "November" and "Aprill" form the poles of the book. In both Spenser employs a particularly intricate verse form, demonstrating his art, and in both Colin rises temporarily above the humble limits of pastoral song. Yet the frequent echoes of "Aprill" in "November" stress their differences. When Colin recalls the "water Nymphs, that wont with her to sing and daunce, / And for her girlond Olive braunches beare" (143–44), he echoes the celebrations of "Aprill" in order to undo them.[35] "Aprill," born out of the energies of the rising year, looks toward all the world can give; "November" faces the fact that nothing celebrated in "Aprill" can last.

In treating Dido's death Spenser drew on the French poet Clément Marot's pastoral elegy for Louise de Savoie, mother of François I, and on a tradition of pastoral elegy nearly 2,000 years old. Pastoral elegies are usually monologues in which a poet playing the part of a shepherd laments the death of another in pastoral terms. The poet acts as spokesman for an imagined pastoral community, which he calls on and organizes in response to the death: he imagines that the pastoral gods weep in vain, that shepherds and shepherdesses mourn, and that the woods and fields wither in sympathy and the birds and beasts grieve. Yet the poet also faces the limits of his art: although he can conjure up images, he cannot revive the dead shepherd. Accordingly, Moschus's elegy for Bion, written in the second century B.C., imagines not only a sympathy between men and the natural world but an essential difference: where species of plants and beasts die and revive, the individual human being dies forever.

Virgil's fifth eclogue develops the elegy in a new direction. Where one shepherd mourns for the dead Daphnis, a second envisions him transformed into a guardian god: ritual joy balances ritual sorrow. Christian poets often build a similar dynamic into their monologues in which the speaker ceases to mourn as he is granted a vision of the dead shepherd in heaven. This turn from sorrow to consolation is crucial, and great Renaissance Christian elegies like Milton's *Lycidas* (1638) or his *Epitaphium Damonis* (1639) develop particular insight into the psychology of conversion.

While Spenser does not imitate Marot's rather prettified elegy closely, the deepest difference between the two poems lies in the context of "November." Marot's poem stands alone, whereas the traditional themes of Spenser's elegy gain resonance from their earlier appearance in the *Calender*. For the first time Colin sings in person, but only about matters of grief in tune with the season: his mood coincides with the darkening year. The weather, which has marked the Fall earlier, here underscores the fact of death, Adam's legacy. Colin's lament refers back to the problems that appear earlier in the *Calender:*

> Waile ye this wofull waste of natures warke:
> Waile we the wight, whose presence was our pryde:
> Waile we the wight, whose absence is our carke.
> The sonne of all the world is dimme and darke:
>     The earth now lacks her wonted light,
>     And all we dwell in deadly night,
>         O heavie herse.
> Breake we our pypes, that shrild as lowde as Larke,
>         O carefull verse. (64–72)

Colin's command here recalls the peevish breaking of his pipe in "Januarye," but his cause is now a larger despair. As he says later in one of the elegy's great lines—"All Musick sleepes, where death doth leade the daunce" (105)—faced by the dance of death, the Orphic harmonies that awaken human spirits can do nothing. Accordingly, Colin gains a stature that he has lacked earlier. His pipe-breaking assumes new force in part from his calling on all shepherds to end their music: he acts for a time as the head of a pastoral community, not as a self-created exile.

Moreover, Colin sees Dido's death as a "wofull waste of natures warke." "Waste" here encompasses many earlier meanings but further suggests that her death is senseless. As often in Christian elegy, the mourner begins with what one might call a "pagan" view of death—an absence of faith in a providential scheme that will give death meaning. As he says later, "happy cheere is turnd to heavie chaunce" (103): like her life, Dido's death is fortuitous. The "care" of "O carefull verse" is not the love-melancholy he has celebrated elsewhere but a loss of faith in "Dame natures kindly [i.e., natural] course" (124) and, with it, a loss of faith in a moral order.

In Spenser's poem, as in most Christian pastoral elegies, the business of the second half is to find psychological justification for the speaker's transcendence of his grief in a new vision of Christian truth. The crucial stanza in "November" is the eleventh, when Colin stands back to generalize about the "trustlesse state of earthly things" (153) and concludes:

> Now have I learnd (a lesson derely bought)
> That nys on earth assuraunce to be sought:
> > For what might be in earthlie mould,
> > That did her buried body hould.
> > > O heavie herse,
> > Yet saw I on the beare when it was brought,
> > O carefull verse. (156–62)

The literal vision of the body ("Yet *saw* I on the beare") becomes proof that the best of this world ("For what might be in earthlie mould") is only transient; this grim acceptance of mutability allows the revelation that reverses the poem's central terms. Earth now appears a hindrance, and concern with this life yields to Christian hope for the next. Colin now imagines Dido's soul "unbodied of the burdenous corpse" (166), for the body that held it is no longer a container but a weight: Dido's cherished earthly part becomes a prison.

From here it is only a step to Colin's epiphany of the soul in heaven: "I see thee blessed soule, I see, / Walke in *Elisian* fieldes so free" (178–79). This new sight recalls both his vision of Dido's bier and his earlier vision of Elisa in "Aprill." Here, however, Colin goes beyond the political mythmaking of "Aprill" to a vision grounded in divine truth: he yields his own voice to that of revelation. The "Fayre fieldes and pleas-aunt layes . . . / The fieldes ay fresh, the grasse ay greene" (188–89) makes the language of pastoral into Christian metaphor for the delights of heaven beyond language. He ends: "Ceasse now my song, my woe now wasted is," reversing the *Calender*'s key term. Woe exhausts itself through the process of mourning, but it also dissipates in the light of the new truth. Along with this turn in the vision of the world comes an implicit shift in the conception of poetry. For a moment Colin follows Piers's advice and "flyes apace" toward heaven, using his art to bring divine truth to his hearers. The revelation he receives makes him a prophet, not a mourner, and his song ends as a homily. He has tem-porarily taken on the role of teacher to his fellows, acting as an inspired mediator between human and divine.

"November" ends, however, with the weather: "Now gynnes to miz-zle, hye we homeward fast." Many eclogues close by referring to the coming of night or foul conditions and the need to drive the flocks homeward; nine of Spenser's twelve end so. But here the weather is par-ticularly English, and particularly emblematic: "mizzle" suggests the cloudiness and lack of clarity in everyday life. We have, with typical Spenserian realism, returned from the unearthly light of poetic vision to the murkiness of ordinary sight.

**"December"**    If "November" forms the climax of the *Calender*, rising above the fallen world to a vision of eternity, "December" provides a denouement in which Colin shrinks again to the "Shepeheards boye" of "Januarye," "June," and (implicitly) "August." Whereas he breaks his pipe in "Januarye," here he hangs it permanently on a tree. Spenser emphasizes the circularity with other returns: he reverts to monologue for the first time since "Januarye" and employs its simple six-line stanza, making "December" exactly twice the length of the first eclogue. Even the eclogue's structure, a retrospective of Colin's life in terms of the four seasons, recalls his speeches in "Januarye" and reemphasizes his place as a natural creature, confined to the temporal round. In the context of the large vision of "November," Colin's pastoral now seems fatally limiting—to this world, to these griefs.

Spenser takes the poem's controlling metaphor from another of Marot's pastorals, his "Eglogue au Roy, soubz les noms de Pan & Robin." At times he imitates closely the verbal details of Marot's poem (much more closely than "November" imitates its original), but as usual, he transforms the whole. In part, as in "November," the difference comes from the larger work's pressure on the individual eclogue: Colin can hardly say, "Thus is my sommer worne away and wasted" (97), without the permutations of that word coming to bear on this instance. But the difference also stems from the central intention of its speaker. Marot's Robin looks back on his life from its end as he addresses his king, François I, under the name of Pan, asking him for aid in his old age; a final four lines joyfully announce that the aid has been given.[36] Colin's Pan is simply the god of shepherds, and he asks for nothing but a hearing. His is an extended complaint, a vision of a life that has gone by without fruition, ending in an expectation of death.

Colin's account of his life reviews the frustration and limitation so much a part of the *Calender* as a whole. After a period of thoughtless "libertee" in youth, he comes to love, which effectively changes his view of the world.

> Where I was wont to seeke the honey Bee,
> Working her formall rowmes in Wexen frame:
> The grieslie Todestoole growne there mought I se
> And loathed Paddocks lording on the same.
>> And where the chaunting birds luld me a sleepe,
>> The ghastlie Owle her grievous ynne doth keepe. (67–72)

The Bee image traditionally embodies natural order; Colin's alternative vision of Toads "lording" themselves on their toadstool thrones creates a kingdom of blight. While his account follows Marot in mentioning what he learns in his maturity, none of the learning serves any purpose.

> My boughes with bloosmes that crowned were at firste,
> And promised of timely fruite such store,
> Are left both bare and barrein now at erst:
> The flattring fruite is fallen to grownd before,

> And rotted, ere they were halfe mellow ripe:
> My harvest wast, my hope away dyd wipe. (103–8)

The vision of decay merely confirms Colin's earlier expectations. His love has wasted his life, and he looks to death with a melancholy appetite. His elaborate adieus to delights, to his sheep, to Hobbinol, and to Rosalind show him exiting with a certain panache. It is the moment he has been waiting for.

The difficulty in judging Colin's farewell arises from the structural metaphor Spenser borrows from his source. Marot writes of Robin as he ages; the seasonal metaphor is a natural one to choose. But Colin has appeared twelve months previously as a shepherd's boy, and Spenser is under thirty. Are we to think that Colin has aged with the year? Or is this simply another melodramatic exaggeration of an adolescent sensibility? While the text does not resolve the question, I think it does not need to. For Spenser's point is finally that the poet's pastoral Colin-stage ends here: the particular sensibility Colin embodies goes nowhere (it may not be an accident that no "emblem" appears after this monologue) and needs to be transcended.

This transcendence occurs at the end of the book. From Virgil on, pastoral is a mode that seems inherently unstable, ready to lead to something else. Now Immerito takes over from Colin (he is given an emblem after the coda) and speaks in a tone of ringing achievement:

> *Loe I have made a Calender for every yeare,*
> *That steele in strength, and time in durance shall outweare:*
> *And if I marked well the starres revolution,*
>     *It shall continewe till the worlds dissolution.*
> *To teach the ruder shepeard how to feede his sheepe,*
> *And from the falsers fraud his folded flocke to keepe.* (1–6)

There is a new "I" here, one speaking in triumphant tones, and the language recalls that of Ovid at the end of the *Metamorphoses,* or Horace at the end of the second and third books of the *Odes.* Our new poet has arrived, and he challenges comparison with the great Latin classics. Yet this coda differs from these classical models in its didactic stress. Not only will the *Calender* last as long as the world, but it will teach shepherds how to keep their flocks. The poem itself offers an answer to the vision of life as waste, and it will remain a source of enlightenment to all shepherds.

The second half of the envoy turns from the reader to the book. He thus returns to the address, "To His Booke," with which the *Calender* began.

> *Goe lyttle Calender, thou hast a free passeporte,*
> *Goe but a lowly gate emongste the meaner sorte.*
> *Dare not to match thy pype with Tityrus hys style,*
> *Nor with the Pilgrim that the Ploughman playde a whyle:*
> *But followe them farre off, and their high steppes adore,*
> *The better please, the worse despise, I aske nomore.* (7–12)

While Spenser couches the comparison with Chaucer and Langland in humble terms, he nonetheless compares himself to England's greatest poets—and in the minds of sixteenth-century readers, to early Protestant reformers.[37] Immerito here claims his English ancestors, and his final line suggests that the book's "free passeporte" gives it the right, not simply to flee hostile readers, but to judge them.

# Chapter Three
# 1590: *The Faerie Queene*

## General Overview

Spenser published the first installment of *The Faerie Queene* in 1590 when he had returned from Ireland to England with Sir Walter Ralegh. In *Colin Clouts Come Home Againe* he portrays Colin reading his poem to Cynthia, and there is no reason to doubt that Spenser read sections aloud to the queen. The poem reemphasizes Spenser's Virgilian identity. It fulfills the promise of *The Shepheardes Calender,* and its first lines, "Lo I the man, whose Muse whilome did maske, / As time her taught in lowly Shepheards weeds," echo a passage that opens Renaissance editions of Virgil's *Aeneid:* "I am that poet who in times past made the light melody of pastoral poetry. . . . now I turn to the terrible strife of Mars."[1] Like Virgil, Spenser had moved from pastoral to epic, and he was now presenting his own ruler with a poem that, like the *Aeneid,* would celebrate his country's destiny. Although *The Faerie Queene* takes place in Faerie, it remains England's first major, self-consciously patriotic poem.

As such the stanza invokes both a classical and a European context. Its fifth line, "And sing of Knights and Ladies gentle deeds," imitates the opening of the *Orlando Furioso* by the sixteenth-century Italian Ludovico Ariosto: "Le donne, i cavallier, l'arme, gli amori, / le cortesie, l'audaci imprese io canto" (Of ladies, cavaliers, of love and war, / Of courtesies and of brave deeds I sing).[2] The opening stanza thus encompasses the classical Latin writer and the modern Italian. Just as Spenser combined various models of the mode in *The Shepheardes Calender* only to make his own triumphant pastoral, so his epic invokes earlier models in order to overgo them. In blending epic and romance with allegory, the 1590 *Faerie Queene* creates a new synthesis, at once European and English: for all their ritual modesty the opening lines announce that this English epic will be something new—and better.

The stanza Spenser created for *The Faerie Queene* typifies his ambition, combining foreign with native elements and overgoing both. Its clearest predecessor is the Italian ottava rima (*abababcc*), a fast-moving narrative vehicle propelled by the triple repetition of the two rhymes and punctuated with a couplet. Spenser's stanza (*ababbcbcc*) goes beyond this simple form by reorganizing the rhyme scheme to slow the movement, to unify the whole, and by adding an extra line with an extra foot—an alexandrine—at the end. The rhyme scheme owes much to the English rhyme royal (*ababbcc*), a stanza identical to Spenser's for the first six lines and much used by Chaucer and his imitators for higher subjects.[3] But Spenser avoided the separation of the final couplet from the rest of the stanza that characterizes both the Italian and the English verse forms, insisting instead on the unity of the whole and marking the end with the stately movement of the final alexandrine. The result combined the elaborate rhyme scheme of a lyric with the simpler stanza of a narrative—deliberate, ruminative, and profoundly original.

**Epic and Romance**   To say that Spenser had two primary models for his poem, Virgil and Ariosto, is both true and misleading, for Spenser had many models. Epics typically imitate earlier epics and include in themselves other forms as well. Ariosto had already taken the form of the chivalric romance, which he had inherited from his predecessor at the Esté court, Matteo Maria Boiardo, and fused it with the concerns of Virgilian epic. (The Ariostan line Spenser imitates with "And sing of Knights and Ladies gentle deeds" itself revises the *Aeneid*'s first announcement: "I sing of arms and the man.") *The Faerie Queene*'s rather different combination of romance and epic incorporates other traditions as well: it owes much to the humbler genre of popular English romances and makes great use of both the Bible and Ovid. The first book of Spenser's poem alone brings together many genres—allegorical pilgrimage,[4] pastoral, epithalamion, satire, dream-vision, Ovidian metamorphosis, sermon, apocalypse—as well as other cultural forms, including procession, marriage-feast, allegorical tableau. Nonetheless, it is the combination of epic, romance, and allegory that gives Spenser's poem its characteristic variety and density and provides the primary forms that create his meaning.

Epic is originally a classical genre, embodied in Homer's *Iliad,* to a lesser extent in his *Odyssey,* and—most important for Renaissance writers—in the *Aeneid* of Virgil. Latin epics were written after Virgil by Lucan, Statius, and others, but in the Middle Ages the classical form went dormant until Petrarch revived it with his Latin poem *Africa.* Renaissance critics placed the epic alongside tragedy as the highest of the genres, the supreme test of a poet's powers. Romance, by contrast, is a common medieval form that developed during the eleventh and twelfth centuries; the word originally meant simply a poem written in the vernacular.[5] Medieval romance made use of three sets of legends: the "matter of Rome," in which classical stories were reworked in medieval dress; the "matter of Britain," concerning the deeds of King Arthur and the Knights of the Round Table; and the "matter of France," which centered on Charlemagne and his court. Individual romances were written by the eleventh-century French poet Chrétien de Troyes and others; the matter of Britain appeared in many forms and languages, including the long French prose cycles of the twelfth century and their late English reworking in Malory's *Morte D'Arthur*. In the early sixteenth century Ariosto's *Orlando Furioso* (1532) gave brilliant development to the matter of France, and its synthesis of romance and epic was followed by the *Jerusalem Delivered* (1581) of Torquato Tasso, who developed a more severely classical synthesis of romance and epic. Spenser knew most of these, and others.

In the letter to Sir Walter Ralegh that Spenser appended to the 1590 *Faerie Queene* he refers to his epic as a "history" and to himself as a "Poet historicall."[6] This description may seem odd for an obvious fiction set in the land of Faerie, but for Spenser it was central: epics deal with national history, or with historic legend. The history recorded in the epic has a felt connection to the events of the present, most obvious in the *Aeneid*, a poem about the origins of Rome written while the Roman state was undergoing its transformation into an empire. Spenser chose as his central figure the young Prince Arthur, the most famous of English kings and proclaimed as an indirect ancestor of the Tudor dynasty. Like the *Aeneid*, the Italian romance-epics link past and present by genealogies extending from their epic heroes to a modern dynasty; *The Faerie Queene* includes three such genealogies, connecting its heroes backward with the race that founded Rome, and forward to Spenser's Tudor present.

The epic is also distinguished by its scope. It is the longest of the forms inherited from antiquity (the *Aeneid* runs to nearly 10,000 dense hexameter lines, and Spenser's first installment alone was close to 18,000). But scope goes beyond length. Epics deal typically with crucial moments in the life of a civilization—the founding of cities or their fall. The action occupies large spaces—the *Aeneid* covers much of the Mediterranean world—and in classical epic (although rarely in Spenser) the action extends to the heavens as counsels of divine powers look down on mortal actions and consider their significance. One critic has termed epic's subject "cosmic politics"—the relation between human history and the forces behind that history.[7] Epic scenes usually develop in leisurely, detailed, deliberate fashion. Even the most typical figure of speech in the epic, the extended simile, takes time to develop its own small universe in elaborate detail.

The characters of epic are mortal but larger than life, able to lift stones that would take three men today to budge. The epic hero stands forth as the greatest—the bravest and strongest—of his race, a representative of his civilization. He may be, like Aeneas, the founder of his line or simply a supreme instance of its strengths. His greatness and the importance of the battles in which he fights create what Thomas Greene has described as "epic awe": the reader's amazement before the spectacle of supreme human exertion and achievement (14–19). Yet Spenser's poem, with its peculiar inwardness, creates this effect less than most epics. Physical prowess, essential in Homer and Virgil, never interests Spenser much: his most convincing battles are psychomachias, dramatized struggles of the mind. Spenser rarely attempts in epic fashion to describe fighting armies; kingdoms are won or lost within the soul.

Whereas the epics concern the fate of cities, romances focus on the growth of an individual protagonist. (Romances typically mention historical events, but they remain peripheral to the main action; the increased historical content in the later books of Malory's romance moves the work in the direction of epic.) The typical medieval romance-story follows a single knight, often a young knight, who leaves his civilized court for a strange and magical wilderness where he encounters a series of trials, some of which he fails; eventually he returns, somewhat matured, to his court. This hero may display the strengths and weaknesses of the court culture from which he comes, but his weaknesses are individual and important largely because they hinder him from becoming a complete knight. Unlike the hero of an epic, who remains essentially the same from beginning to end, the romance hero can grow. (In this, as in other ways, the heroes of *The Faerie Queene* look to romance.) Whereas the epic hero concerns himself with warfare and city-building, seeing love as at most a dangerous trap, love is often for the romance hero the means by which he matures. Ariosto's adding "le donne" to Virgil's "arms" enlarges his subject in the direction of romance.

Renaissance critics commented on the fact that whereas epic plot structure focuses on a single central story, romances—especially the Italian romances of Boiardo and Ariosto—braid together many different plots in what the French called *entrelacement*. This movement between simultaneously developing stories lends itself to thematic comparisons,

treating the nature of love, faith, loyalty, or betrayal in different contexts. In *The Faerie Queene* Spenser alternates his narrative mode, shifting
from the single unified plot of epic to a romance braiding of stories; on
occasion these modal shifts themselves come to have thematic implications.

The world of romance abounds in what Renaissance critics referred to
as the "marvelous"—instances of magic and prodigies like giants,
dwarves, and monstrous beasts. It is a world of forests and enchanted
places in which the hero loses himself and of marvels whose meaning
puzzles him. (Britomart wandering somewhat bewildered through the
House of Busyrane finds herself in a typical romance situation.) The
hero's perplexity extends to the reader. Whereas in epic we look from
above, privy to the forces directing events, in romance we tend to
remain at ground level, in the dark. Epics typically unfold in the known
world, and it is easy to locate their events on a map, but doing so with a
romance is difficult or impossible. Space in romance is elastic: castles
appear abruptly and without warning, responding to the needs of the
narrative. Time is also flexible: while important deadlines sometimes
occur, time in other respects is vague. Coleridge's famous comment on
the "marvelous independence and true imaginative absence of all particular space and time in the Faerie Queene" points to a characteristic of
medieval romance that Spenser's poem merely exaggerates.[8] This
absence of mappable space in romance makes it hospitable to allegory. If
a knight's arrival at a new place is not determined by external geography, it seems determined by his mental state or the nature of the quest
on which he engages. Places come to have meaning and to embody
moral stages.

After Virgil the language of epic tends toward high style, adapted to
the importance of its subject, while the language of romance varies more
widely, between formal speech and colloquial exchange. Spenser created
for his poem an idiosyncratic language that often gives an impression of
elaborate formality. Its syntax and vocabulary tend to be Latinate, but its
diction also makes frequent use of English archaisms: the "whilome" of
the opening line ("Lo I the man, whose Muse whilome did maske") has an
old-fashioned ring, and the past participles with the enclitic *y-* ("ypight,"
"ydrad") look back to Chaucerian usage. Impatient with the blending,
Ben Jonson said in *Timber, or Discoveries* (1641) that "Spenser, in affecting
the Ancients, writ no Language" (*Works,* 8:618), but Spenser seems to
have wanted to create a linguistic world markedly different from that of
common speech or even of learned humanist speech—a world that would

allow both the mystery of his romance events and the dignity of his epic themes. While it is a language whose initial strangeness bewilders, it moves with surprising ease between the serious and the comic.

**Allegory**    In the letter to Ralegh, Spenser first introduces the work as a "continued Allegory, or darke conceit" (15). A conceit is an extended metaphor, and this is the most common Renaissance definition of allegory. Allegory is a metaphor that develops into a plot. Where a metaphor equates two things—love and fire, life and a journey—Spenser's allegory elaborates the idea in great detail: the romance plot becomes metaphorically charged, a vehicle for presenting a variety of meanings, including (in the first book) an individual's quest for holiness. In reading allegory like Spenser's, one needs to start with the literal story—the plot itself, attending to the fictional action as carefully as possible. Gradually, in the process of reading, the allegorical dimensions of the poem begin to shine *through* the narrative, illuminating it. One of Spenser's early critics, Sir Kenelm Digby, commented that "if one heed him not with great attention, rare and wonderful conceptions will unpercieved slide by him that readeth his works, & he will thinke he hath mett with nothing but familiar and easy discourses but let one dwell a while upon them and he shall feel a straunge fulnesse and roundnesse in all he saith."[9]

For instance, the first episode in book 1 shows Redcrosse lost in the Wood of Error. Typically we do not know at first that it is the Wood of Error. Rather, the poem introduces us—and the young knight—to the process of losing one's way. Redcrosse and Una seek the Wood to avoid a storm, but once inside it they find themselves caught up in the "delight" (I.i.10.1) of their surroundings. The verse emphasizes the sheer pleasure of the place and its variety: the catalog of trees associates them with many of the world's civilized occupations—love, war, agriculture, building, sailing, archery. Indeed, the Wood seems like an image of the world in its delightful multiplicity, and we only gradually notice its sinister potential. The leaves are thick, "not perceable with power of any starre" (I.i.7.6), and this darkness becomes more apparent when Redcrosse and Una try to discover a way out. They find that in yielding to the pleasure of the place they have lost their path and their bearings: they are "Furthest from end then, when they neerest weene, / That makes them doubt, their wits be not their owne" (I.i.10.6–7). Here "end" has a double sense: literally it is the goal of their journey, but if one takes the Wood as an image of the world, and Redcrosse and Una as Christians, the darkness suggests spiritual blindness, and the loss of "end" figures a loss of purpose. Losing one's physical orientation suggests what it feels like to lose one's moral bearings and, indeed, one's trust in one's own faculties. Only then do we hear that this is the "wandring wood" and recall that *errare* in Latin means "to wander": the physical wandering of the knight figures our own erring in the dark Wood of this world.

Spenser here translates the complexities of a moral situation into physical ones, but it is essential to reading the narrative never simply to discard the literal level in apprehending the meanings it infolds. Rather, the allegorical senses shine through the romance narrative, giving it a peculiar radiance of meaning. The Wood in which Redcrosse loses himself is ultimately internal, and we learn much about his—and our—limitations when we find him foolishly braving Error herself and subsequently unable to move in her serpentine coils. Book 1 gives us, in Berger's words, a soul "unfolded into an environment" (1988, 68); while the allegory in other books of *The Faerie Queene* operates somewhat differently, it always forces the reader to stay aware of the literal level of the romance plot.

In the opening books Spenser's repeated images of place embody states of mind—dark woods in which the savage and the uncivilized dwell, caves and dungeons that suggest mental and spiritual limitations, castles and houses that epitomize visions of self. These repeated images vary in meaning from context to context. The Cave of Error yields later in the first canto to the underground House of Morpheus, in which the paralysis created by the serpent Error reappears as careless somnolence: in both, the rational self loses its capacity to act. These caves look toward the frustration and loss of the Cave of Night and the sense of hopeless fatality in the cave where Redcrosse meets Despair. Images repeat from book to book as well: the pagan Cave of Night, set in the middle of the first book, looks toward the pagan Cave of Mammon in the middle of the second, while the second book's seductive, enervating Bower of Bliss opposes the third book's Garden of Adonis, a center of creative energy. Minor characters in the first installment of the poem often embody aspects of the main characters. When Redcrosse fights with Error, he is dealing with his own perplexity; when he encounters Despair, he listens to his own hopelessness.

The allegorical dimension to the poem has a complex effect on the presentation of characters. The romance plots make one read the heroes as psychologically complex, individualized figures, and Spenser's often brilliantly evocative verse reinforces this reading. But the allegorical dimension generalizes the heroes' experience: it makes Redcrosse's

encounter with Error a striking image of a situation that happens to all
of us. In reading such an allegory one shifts continually between apprehending the character as an individual caught up in a particular situation and seeing him as an image of a more general state of mind. Occasionally Spenser makes the shift fully explicit, as he does when Error
immobilizes Redcrosse:

> Tho wrapping up her wrethed sterne arownd,
> Lept fierce upon his shield, and her huge traine
> All suddenly about his body wound,
> That hand or foot to stirre he strove in vaine:
> God helpe the man so wrapt in *Errours* endlesse traine.
>
> (I.i.18.5–9)

The first eight lines of the stanza focus on the literal action, but the final
alexandrine stands back to generalize. Such explicit exegesis occurs
rarely in Spenser, but the oscillation between specific and general is
essential to his mode. This continuous shifting also suggests why, for all
its moving seriousness, Spenserian narrative remains detached from its
characters, who often appear in an ironic or even a comic light.

The poem's allegory determines its major structural innovation, its
division into largely self-contained books. Instead of the single plots of
Virgil or Tasso, or the multiple braided plots of Ariostan narrative,
Spenser develops in these three books three primary narratives, each
independent of the others (although some characters appear in several
books, and Arthur in all of them), and each concerned with the exploration of a particular virtue. In the letter to Ralegh, Spenser plans twelve
books devoted to "private" virtues, possibly followed by a second group
that would consider twelve public virtues—a plan he would modify radically in the 1596 continuation of the poem. This organization gives an
analytical and encyclopedic cast to the narrative and raises the question
of the relation between the main protagonist of each book and the virtues
he or she, in Spenser's word, "expresses." Should each knight be seen as
perfect in his virtue or as only aspiring toward it? Indeed, to what degree
should we interpret Spenser's major characters as psychologically complex figures like their kin in the romances, and to what degree are they
simply transparent images of the concepts they represent?

In fact Spenser's poem draws on both conventions at once, his characters shifting easily between the psychologically verisimilar and the fig-

ural. Minor characters—Sans Joy or Orgoglio in book 1, for instance—
work primarily as images pointing to the meanings they embody, but
even these can on occasion receive independent treatment. In the second
book Pyrocles' squire Atin embodies an impulse toward conflict, urging
both his master and Cymocles into battle. But when he finds Pyrocles
madly drowning himself at the end of canto 6, he grieves and rushes
into the lake to save him. Here, for a moment, Spenser treats him simply as a faithful squire and puts the meaning he bears elsewhere on hold.
Other characters may change in their associations. When Duessa
appears in book 1, Spenser links her with the Roman Catholic Church,
but when she reappears at the opening of book 2, her religious associations have vanished: she has dwindled into a romance sorceress.

On the other hand, the major characters usually have a profound
interiority. Their interiority differs greatly, however, from the freestand-
ing complexity of characters in a nineteenth-century novel. The protagonists of Spenser's epic poem dream, act, and feel ambivalently, and they
change, but their changes are teleologically directed. They may never
fully achieve the book's governing virtue but they move in its *direction*.
The relation between the central figures of the first three books—Redcrosse, Guyon, and Britomart—and their virtues is intensely problematic. In none are the virtues fully achieved at the opening of each book.
Rather, the reader sees the knight growing into or at least toward the
virtue that the book examines. As in romance, the young knight needs
to live up to the ideal he exemplifies.

**Plot as Rhetoric**    In a famous passage of *Areopagitica* (1644) Milton
refers to Spenser as a "better teacher than *Scotus* or *Aquinas*": in other
words, he sees the poem as didactic, a means of teaching.[10] Milton's view
of Spenser is Spenser's own, for in the letter to Ralegh he appended to
the 1590 edition of the poem he speaks of the end of the work as the
fashioning of a gentleman—creating him through the moving disciplines of his art. In an age when poetry was conceived as a branch of
rhetoric, this didactic function was a commonplace, but in practice
Spenser teaches in several ways. First and most obviously, Spenser insists
that he teaches by *example:* the word *example* recurs frequently in the letter, and Spenser sets himself in the line of epic writers who present their
readers with a list of idealized epic heroes—models for emulation in life.

First Homere, who in the Persons of Agamemnon and Ulysses hath
ensampled a good governour and a vertuous man, the one in his Ilias, the

other in his Odysseis: then Virgil, whose like intention was to doe in the person of Aeneas: after him Ariosto comprised them both in his Orlando: and lately Tasso disseuered them againe, and formed both parts in two persons, namely that part which they in Philosophy call Ethice, or vertues of a private man, coloured in his Rinaldo: the other named Politice in his Godfredo. (15)

Spenser argues that his work engages a complex teaching in which the nature of virtue is not "delivered plainly in way of precepts" but embodied in moving examples. Spenser does not develop his thought fully here, but it resembles the argument Sir Philip Sidney makes in his *Defence of Poetry* (1595): the moving examples of literature teach better than those of the philosopher. They do so because they involve the passions: the experience of reading causes us not only to learn what is good but to want to emulate it. The clarified, radiant images we find in poetry make us want to choose virtue and shun vice. While the philosopher may teach us what the good is, the poet makes us want to do it. By this reading, the characters form mirrors in which the readers may fashion themselves. At the same time, here, as elsewhere in the letter, Spenser oversimplifies his actual practice. For Spenser's heroes—even Prince Arthur—are less simple and less idealized than this description might suggest. They falter, make mistakes, and engage in actions embarrassingly distinct from the virtues to which they aspire, and the reader's relation to them is thus more complex than simple emulation. The reader needs to understand them and judge them—a sympathetic experience that is practice for living.

This complex understanding of the poem's characters suggests a second way in which it is didactic. Although the world of the poem remains murkier than the world in which we move, it is nonetheless extraordinarily complex, demanding an alertness of response. The puzzles of the allegory provide us with training in interpretation, the opportunity to make sense of the confusing appearances of language as training for the practice of making sense of the confusing appearances of the world. The Wood of Error is training for a world of error. In a variety of ways, the poem prepares one for an actuality in which one's capacity to make sense of events—to recognize the truth in appearances—is as important as one's capacity for physical bravery.

Critics have pointed to the many parallels between the first three books of *The Faerie Queene,* published in 1590, and the second three, published in 1596; the third book, especially, seems indissolubly connected to the fourth and the fifth.[11] Yet there is evidence that when he published the first three books of the epic Spenser did not have the structure of the second half clearly in mind. Although he speaks in the letter to Ralegh of twelve books treating the private virtues and a possible second twelve treating the public ones, the second installment of the epic shows a radical condensation of that plan: the last two virtues, Justice and Courtesy, are entirely public virtues. The second half of *The Faerie Queene* differs from the first in tone, in outlook, and even in allegorical technique. Accordingly, here I treat the first installment of *The Faerie Queene* as an unfolding work complete in itself and avoid using events in the second half of the poem to gloss earlier ones. This practice has the advantage of keeping the focus on what is most clearly apparent in the epic of 1590 and, later, of enabling one to see more clearly how the poem of 1596 distinguishes itself from the first part of the epic, revising it in retrospect.

## Book 1: Fall and Redemption

Holiness concerns the relation between the individual soul and God; it is prior to other virtues because it ultimately determines one's capacity to engage in them. Holiness as Spenser portrays it in this book, as in the works of Augustine, is a state in which the believer finds in God an *end*—a fully satisfactory object for human love and a purpose for being. As such it involves *wholeness,* a unity of body and spirit, in God's service. The name of Una, Redcrosse's lady, means "One": she embodies, among other meanings, the potential wholeness of the Christian, just as her archrival, Duessa, has a name that means "Two": the number of duplicity and self-division. When Redcrosse travels with Una, he is whole in his allegiance to his lady and his dedication to the quest she has given him; when he wanders with Duessa, he is self-divided. The first book of *The Faerie Queene* focuses with almost unwavering intensity on Redcrosse as he betrays his initial faith and regains a deeper wholeness, coming to know himself and to submit his will to God's.

In the Protestant environment of the first book such wholeness comes entirely as God's gift. No Christian can gain it for himself by his acts, by self-discipline, or by prayer. The narrator comments at the opening of canto 10, glossing Redcrosse's confrontation with Despair:

> What man is he, that boasts of fleshly might,
>     And vaine assurance of mortality,

> Which all so soone, as it doth come to fight,
> Against spirituall foes, yeelds by and by,
> Or from the field most cowardly doth fly?
> Ne let the man ascribe it to his skill,
> That thorough grace hath gained victory.
> If any strength we have, it is to ill,
> But all the good is Gods, both power and eke will. (I.x.1)

This stress on man's inevitable tendency to do evil without God's aid is essential to the book's account of Redcrosse. More than the other heroes of *The Faerie Queene,* the young knight is an Everyman whose weaknesses mirror our own. He may seem to do admirable deeds of arms, but unless they proceed from a good *will,* they result from pride or from another sin, and all human wills were corrupted with Adam's fall. Hence the book recalls at important points the Calvinist doctrine of predestination—the belief that God has already determined before our creation who will be saved and who will be damned. Without God's grace, the will is not free to do good; bound to sin, Christians can do nothing to save themselves.

This is the simplest book of *The Faerie Queene* in outline, a fall followed by redemption. As he appears in the opening tableau of canto 1, Redcrosse is a young knight who has yet to live up to the ideals embodied in the armor he wears. Spenser's letter to Ralegh glosses the armor as the metaphorical "whole armour of God" that Paul describes in the Epistle to the Ephesians as necessary to withstand not only flesh and blood but "spiritual wickednesses, which are in the hie places":

> For this cause take unto you the whole armour of God, that ye
>   may be able to resist in the evil daye, & having finished all
>   things, stand fast.
> Stand therefore, and your loines girde about with veritie, &
>   having on the brest plate of righteousnes,
> And your fete shod with the preparation of the Gospel of
>   peace.
> Above all, take the shield of faith, wherewith ye may quench
>   all the fyrie dartes of the wicked,
> And take the helmet of salvation, and the sworde of the Spirit,
>   which is the worde of God. (Ephesians 6:13–17)

The first stanza mentions that the armor contains "deepe wounds" suggestive of Christ's suffering for mankind, and ultimately Redcrosse will imitate Christ's suffering in canto 11 when he battles the Dragon. But it is not yet clear that he possesses the virtues that would make him a true Knight of Holiness. The stress of the opening stanza on the knight's youth and his restive steed suggests that Redcrosse's immature energies are controlled only with difficulty, and the comment that "nothing did he dread, but ever was ydrad" (I.i.2.9) suggests a naive belief in his own invulnerability. The young knight will have to learn the limitations of his own powers and his need of God's aid; further, he will need to learn to fight not for his own glory but for God's, submitting his will to his maker's.

Redcrosse will not, in fact, "stand fast" during the course of the book. Trusting to his own might, he will fall further and further into sin, and in the seventh canto, having discarded his armor, he will be quite literally blown over by the wind of Orgoglio's club. His fall, complete in his near-fatal confrontation with Despair, will, however, provide the self-knowledge necessary for salvation, and with that a new capacity to undertake his divine mission. The book thus tells the story of a fortunate fall, a humiliation necessary if the knight is to engage in a true imitation of Christ.

Spenser gives this comparatively simple story extraordinary resonance. Without attempting *continuous* allegory, he constantly associates Redcrosse's fall and recovery with other areas of meaning—psychological, political, historical, and theological. As Walter Davis has emphasized, book 1 yields best of all the books of the poem to the traditional fourfold analysis of medieval commentary: literal, moral, tropological, and anagogical.[12] At the *literal* level this is a story about a headstrong young knight and his lady, a knight who falls but is eventually healed to fight a dragon. The *moral* dimension appears in the psychological analysis of Redcrosse's fall and redemption, suggested by the characters he meets. But George is the patron saint of England, and beyond the moral allegory are *tropological* or historical meanings as individual episodes in cantos 4 and 7 suggest moments in the history of the British church. Behind all, and very notable in cantos 7, 8, and 11, is an *anagogical* dimension of meaning: we see the characters as enacting the battles at the end of time described in the Book of Revelation.[13]

The complexity of Spenser's reference appears in Una. She is, on the literal level, a plucky romance heroine, loving her knight and willing to forgive his many failings. Her temporary despair when she learns that Redcrosse is Orgoglio's captive only points up her entire fidelity to him.

But the doggerel tags at the beginning of each canto at times refer to her as Truth, and her fidelity to Redcrosse is an image of the One True Faith, which she embodies. Her presence comments on Redcrosse's moral condition: without Una he is truthless, *un*faithful, *un*directed, and self-divided. Further, the poem associates Una with a particular source of truth, the English church, an identity insisted upon by her contrast with the Roman Catholic Duessa. Her wanderings in the third canto typify the many simultaneous meanings possible in Spenser's allegorical fable. Historically the wanderings may recall the early days of the English church—housed for a time in Roman Catholic institutions (imaged in the blind Corceca) until restored to her rightful place under the auspices of Arthur (Henry VIII?).[14] Yet the picture of her search for Redcrosse in cantos 3 and 6 also recalls the search for her lover of the female speaker of the Song of Songs, allegorized throughout the Middle Ages as the quest of the church for Christ—the Christ whom Redcrosse eventually will imitate. And the search also images the care of the church for her own straying members, unwilling to give up even those unworthy of her love. The final canto, with its happy betrothal, looks toward the final marriage of Christ and his church at the end of time.

The nature of Redcrosse's quest is also complex. We learn from the letter to Ralegh that Redcrosse appears as "a tall clownishe younge man" (17); his rusticity is reemphasized by his being found as a baby in the furrow of a field, by his name, Georgos, which is Greek for "worker of the earth" (farmer). Spenser makes much of the name and of Redcrosse's connection with the earth—the earth that formed Adam. His quest is in part a personal "harrowing"—being cultivated like the earth to become God's saint. As James Nohrnberg has pointed out (278), when Arthur fights Orgoglio to rescue Redcrosse, the giant digs furrows with the blows of his club (I.viii.8).[15] The end of this quest is, in one reading, the Christian's confrontation with death, for all human beings face a final battle with death. This association is reemphasized by the references to the Dragon's jaws, which gape like the mouth of hell, as well as by several biblical references—to the wide shadow underneath the Dragon's waist ("Yea, thogh I shulde walke through the valley of the shadow of death, I wil feare no evil" [Psalm 23:4]) and to the sting at the end of the Dragon's tail ("O death where is thy sting! O grave where is thy victorie!" [1 Corinthians 15:55]). Yet the reference to the Book of Revelation—in which the forces of God overcome those of the Dragon (Satan)—gives the battle a wider dimension. Redcrosse is imitating Christ in a conflict that looks toward the final conflict of the Last Judgment.

It is a successful battle, and so the poem is ultimately comic in its structure, in the same sense that Dante's *Divine Comedy,* whose happy ending reemphasizes the divine order of creation, is comic. The comedy is apparent from the beginning of the poem, when Redcrosse's foolhardy ignorance continually appears in the light of God's loving protection. Error has immobilized Redcrosse in her coils, and Una stirs him to free his hand and continue the battle, crying, "Add faith unto your force, and be not faint" (I.i.19.3). Here Redcrosse is spurred to save himself by an influence beyond himself—by the voice of Truth, which is ultimately God's. The curious pastoral simile occurring immediately after Redcrosse wins reemphasizes the divine element in his success. It compares the knight to a shepherd watching his sheep peacefully feeding, a reference that recalls the familiar psalmic image of God as a shepherd caring for the flock of the faithful. In this case God is looking out for Redcrosse's spiritual welfare. Again and again Redcrosse finds himself in extreme danger—stunned, imprisoned, paralyzed—only to be saved by someone or something beyond himself. Arthur rescues him from Orgoglio, Una moves him to turn away from Despair, and both the Well of Life and the Tree of Life protect and heal him during the fight with the Dragon. Perhaps the most ironic of these divine rescues comes in the fifth canto. When Duessa attempts to encourage Sans Joy, who has almost beaten Redcrosse, she calls out to him, "Thine the shield, and I, and all" (I.v.11.9). Redcrosse hears her words, misinterprets them as meant for himself, and with "quickning faith" (I.v.12.3) revives and attacks once again. God here works though Duessa: his providence uses all means to bring about his ends.

The Calvinist stress on man's incapacity to save himself creates a problem of tone. Is the poem comic, a tale of fall and redemption under God's benevolent care? Or does it portray the nightmare of uncertainty to which a believing Calvinist was subject, never sure of his own salvation? The poem also raises the related issue of how far Redcrosse is responsible for his failures, an issue that appears when Archimago separates Redcrosse from Una. Redcrosse dreams that Venus herself brings Una to his bed in a pagan pastoral celebration and wakes uneasily to find—seemingly—that his dream has taken on flesh: Una is there "before his face" (I.i.49.5), offering to kiss him. His first reaction is murderous fury, the response of one tempted by what he sees, but he restrains himself. When he wakes, however, Archimago shows Redcrosse a second illusion of Una making love with a lustful squire; Redcrosse burns "with gealous fire, / The eye of reason was with rage yblent"

(I.ii.5.6–7), and he leaves angrily. The narrator comments later, "Still flying from his thoughts and gealous feare; / Will was his guide, and griefe led him astray" (I.ii.12.3–4).

Redcrosse's headstrong act raises a problem of judgment. He makes a terrible mistake in trusting to Archimago's proof, but is he to blame for it? The opening stanza of canto 4 asserts that he is: he has taken the evidence of his eyes—which is finally the province of the devil, mere illusion—over his *faith* in Una. By romance convention, Redcrosse should have trusted his lady instead of the ocular proof Archimago supplies. (Una's association with Truth itself makes Redcrosse's doubt a doubly faithless act.) Yet if we take seriously the idea of man's innate depravity, we cannot expect much of Redcrosse. Archimago's hallucinatory powers—like those of the devil—remain absolute, and in the absence of divine prompting, how are we to believe that Redcrosse can do more than follow his fleshly vision? The book supplies evidence for both Redcrosse's guilt and his incapacity to behave well; it leaves us with an uneasy uncertainty about the extent of his culpability.

Archimago's part in Redcrosse's defection exemplifies the allegorical use to which Spenser could put his romance conventions. The magician whose spells blind a young knight is a common figure, but Spenser gives Archimago a significantly close relation to Redcrosse's mind. He takes his dream from the Cave of Morpheus, an underworld characterized by carelessness, the desire to turn away from difficult duties to enjoy a somnolent ease. This desire seems far from the conscious striving of the fiery young knight, but it remains a hidden potential: it will surface in the seventh canto when Redcrosse devotes himself to lovemaking with Duessa, and again when Despair speaks temptingly of death as a state of rest. Archimago (the name hovers between "archi-mage" [the greatest magician] and "arch-imago" [the greatest image or appearance]) is the first of many false artists in Spenser's poem, tempting the will with perverse images. But he also embodies Redcrosse's own untrustworthy and passionate imagination. At times he stands in for Redcrosse as well. When Redcrosse leaves, Archimago promptly dons similar armor and accompanies Una on her travels: the picture of Christian armor concealing the weak and skeletal body of Archimago gives us a moral X-ray of Redcrosse's condition.

With the loss of Una comes a loss of direction; his lady provided Redcrosse with a quest, and without her he has no purpose. This absence of purpose appears in a series of rapid changes. He encounters the first of the Sans brothers, Sans Foy, an image of his own "faithless" mind in repudiating Una, and they instinctively engage in battle. One of the ironies of the poem appears here: as a Christian knight, it is fitting for Redcrosse to do battle with a "faithless Saracen" because they are champions of different faiths. But in fact the simile that compares them to two rams fighting for the rule of the flock (I.ii.16) suggests that the actual motive is not religious duty but sexual drive. It is Duessa they fight for, and Duessa is a compromising prize: her trappings associate her at once with the Catholic Church and with the scarlet woman of Revelation. When Redcrosse acquires her, he becomes the "protector" or the wooer of Una's opposite. One might see the shift from Una to Sans Foy and Duessa as a movement from faith to a faithless embracing of the Catholic Church. Although Redcrosse appears to have beaten Sans Foy, he has simply internalized the pagan's attributes. Leaving, he takes with him his enemy's shield as well as his own: the meaning of the red cross on one shield is compromised by the words "Sans Foy" on the other.

It is the House of Pride, one of the two symbolic centers of the book, that suggests Redcrosse's new state of mind. Spenser imagines the House in part as an English Renaissance court—high, many-windowed, full of persons bent on self-admiration and self-promotion, and ruled over by a virgin queen; it is a satiric portrait that suggests at once what is wrong with Redcrosse and what is wrong with the world in which Spenser lives. The center of the House is Lucifera, who is less a character than an allegorical summary of the fallen human tendency to try to make an *end* of oneself, to see one's own glory as sufficient reason for being. If the Calvinist sees the self as utterly corrupt, unable to rise above its corruption without God's aid, Lucifera embodies a contrary view that insists on an ideal of self-sufficiency—an ideal associated in the early books of *The Faerie Queene* with paganism. Lucifera claims as her parents Jove, "or if that any else did Jove excell: / For to the highest she did still aspyre, / Or if ought higher were than that, did it desyre" (I.iv.11.7–9). Lucifera's ignorance of anything beyond the classical gods here suggests an incapacity to think beyond a world view in which man is all-important and the gods consequently are mere projections of human attributes.

To a Christian, the belief in human self-sufficiency is pitifully mistaken. Lucifera is not Jove's daughter but the offspring of Pluto and "sad *Proserpina,* the Queene of hell" (I.iv.11.2). The inhabitants of the House, aware of weakness and unworthiness (the walls of the House are high, "but nothing strong, nor thick" [I.iv.4.3]), are moved to uneasy competition to prove their superiority. (Lucifera emblematically competes with her throne, fearing it will outshine her [I.iv.8.7–9].) Further, the desire for God built into human nature cannot be satisfied, according to Christian belief, except in God: love for any lesser object, including the self, seen independent of the divine hierarchy necessarily ends in frustration.[16] This frustration appears emblematically at the end of the fifth canto in the Cave of Night, where Aesculapius manifests a painful restlessness, sick with a "heavenly fire, that raged evermore" (I.v.40.9). It appears as well in the House musicians, who play "To drive away the dull melancholy" (I.v.3.5).

A parallel restlessness, created by an unsatisfying "end" for her energies, appears in Lucifera's abrupt departure "to take the solace of the open aire" (I.iv.37.2). The wish for distraction, for the "solace" of a world beyond the confines of the court, is ironically frustrated: the progress takes place in an open graveyard whose reminder of death is hidden by delusive mists (I.iv.36.6–9). Lucifera's six "counselors"—the rest of the seven deadly sins—all provide variations on the idea that sin involves a turning from God to the self. All of them, like Lucifera with her mirror, focus on themselves; when they look at others, they do so only for self-comparison. The procession of the seven sins is a common *topos;* here Spenser gives it a powerful psychological development. All act with the compulsiveness of sin, all have symbolic diseases, and all are incapable of joy.

Spenser develops the theme of melancholy with the meeting of Sans Joy and Redcrosse. Literally the ensuing conflict recalls the battle with Sans Foy, another fight between pagan and Christian—but again Redcrosse is only a titular Christian, since he fights not for Christ but "all for prayse and honour" (I.v.7.6). Indeed, the prizes for victory remain the same dubious trophies Redcrosse won from Sans Foy: the shield with its sinister identification, and Duessa. The simile that compares Redcrosse to a griffin fighting for his "rightful ravine" (I.v.8.5) against a hungry dragon emphasizes and extends this irony. On the one hand, the simile is heavily ironic: the repeated line "So th'one for wrong the other strives for right" (I.v.8.1, I.v.9.1) is undercut by the fact that between the two beasts there is no right and wrong—"ravine" is never "rightful"—but only a question of brute power. On the other hand, the choice of beasts—a dragon for Sans Joy, a griffin for Redcrosse—calls on a traditional identification of the dragon with Satan and the griffin with Christ. At the end of the book Redcrosse does imitate Christ in battling a dragon. Thus, the simile stresses the ideal to which Redcrosse has aspired while suggesting simultaneously how far he is from it.

Psychologically, the battle dramatizes Redcrosse's attempt to sup-press a fit of melancholy, brought on in part by his sense that he is insufficiently appreciated (I.iv.15). But the victory he gains is again pyrrhic. While he renders Sans Joy unconscious, he cannot kill him: the depression the pagan knight embodies can be suppressed but not elim-inated. Further, the victory results in Redcrosse's full acceptance into the House of Pride, where he does homage to Lucifera. At this point in the narrative the alternative to despair is an inflated sense of self-worth; Redcrosse's spiritual sickness grows as he is "beguiled" by the false healing of Lucifera's doctors and distracted from his condition by her musicians (I.v.17).

The confirmation of Redcrosse's pride does not last long. His dwarf—whom critics usually gloss as his limited human reason—discovers that Lucifera's house has a cellar (another of the poem's images of hell) that imprisons those who have gone astray through pride. The image differs from the Cave of Night in its moral specificity: these are not generalized forces of darkness but the result of the spiritual imprison-ment that pride creates. Warned by this knowledge, Redcrosse leaves quietly, and humiliatingly, by a "privie Posterne" (I.v.52.7), riding by "a donghill of dead carkases" (I.v.53.8). Houses in *The Faerie Queene* often suggest the human body, and the scatological imagery here sug-gests the fleshly corruption awaiting the attempt to make the self and this world primary.

Battles with giants occur often in romance tradition. What Spenser does with this common motif in book 1 is to internalize it, making it an essential part of Redcrosse's psychological decline. Orgoglio's name is Italian for "pride," but the context of his appearance suggests that his version of pride differs from Lucifera's. Whereas the House of Pride emphasizes aspiration, the opening of canto 7 depicts premature relax-ation. Redcrosse has removed the armor of God and now distracts him-self with physical pleasure: when he "feedes upon the cooling shade, and bayes / His sweatie forehead in the breathing wind" (I.vii.3.1–2), the emphatic verbs suggest a certain desperation. The dwarf's revelation about Lucifera's cellar has shocked him into abandoning the race for glory and devoting himself instead to physical pleasure. His subsequent seduction by Duessa confirms this new concupiscence, and it is at the moment of consummation that Orgoglio rears his head.

Among other things, Orgoglio is a walking phallic symbol, carrying a club and introduced as a "masse of earthly slime / Puft up with emptie wind, and fild with sinfull crime" (I.vii.9.8–9).[17] According to medieval medicine, male erections were caused by air, and so the wind that fills Orgoglio has an anatomical as well as a metaphorical reference (Schroeder, 150–52). Orgoglio embodies Redcrosse's own unrestrained "pride of the flesh," the carnal impulses that now dominate his rational self. (In terms of the religious allegory, Redcrosse's dalliance with Duessa involves "spiritual fornication" with a figure associated with the whore of Babylon in the Book of Revelation, and hence with the Roman Catholic Church.) When Redcrosse tries to fight Orgoglio and discovers that he cannot, without his armor, "stand" against the wind of Orgoglio's club, the narrative reemphasizes the weakness of human reason without God's aid. Redcrosse subsequently languishes in Orgoglio's dungeon, which turns out to be the castle sewer. Again, the scatological imagery suggests that without God's aid flesh is, like the bodies outside the House of Pride, mere corrupt matter.

With the separation of Redcrosse and Una in canto 2, book 1 splits into two stories, suggesting in a minimal way the *entrelacement* typical of romance plotting. The Una plot of cantos 3 and 6 is less elaborate than the Redcrosse plot, yet Una's patient search for her knight as he blunders from bad to worse suggests that, however blind Redcrosse may be to them, the hidden forces of Truth are still at work in his service. The Una plot also develops a somewhat different view of fallen nature. While the Redcrosse story stresses its fundamental corruption, the sections in which we see Una remind us of the goodness still implicit in creation. First the Lion, then the Satyrs, then Satyrane come to Una's assistance, all of them instinctively recognizing and responding to her goodness. The Lion protects her; the Satyrs save her from Sans Loy; and Satyrane escorts her out of the Wood. Reverence for divine Truth is implanted "naturally" in created beings.

The protected moment in which a hero or heroine resides with pastoral folk is a common motif in the Italian romance-epics. Spenser uses it in canto 6 both to affirm the goodness of the simple and the natural and to suggest its limitations in relation to the realm of the spirit. The Satyrs who rescue Una are half-human, half-goat, and they dwell in the woods: as such they embody human nature at its most primitive and most removed from the light of the Spirit. Like the wood god Sylvanus, who tries vainly to make sense of Una, comparing her to Venus and Diana (I.vi.16), their frame of reference has no room for the transcendent realm she embodies. Much as they love Una, they cannot comprehend her. Their world is a world of material things, and they cannot go beyond them to the Christian Truth she teaches; hence they wish to worship her or—failing that—her ass. The friendly comedy of this canto thus turns at once on the Satyrs' goodness and their limitations.[18]

The second half of the book moves from the complex meandering of a romance double plot to a unified epic narrative; moments like Redcrosse's view of Hierusalem reemphasize the epic stress of this second half. The battles that follow—between Arthur and Orgoglio, and between Redcrosse and the Dragon—draw on the imagery of the Book of Revelation, suggesting that the particular conflict of the romance plot also foreshadows the cosmic opposition at the end of history. The shift quietly suggests a new sense of direction, a gathering momentum corresponding to the gradual healing of Redcrosse himself.

This healing begins with the intervention of Arthur, who, in the poem's psychological allegory, Spenser associates with God's Grace (I.viii.1), freeing the soul imprisoned by the compulsive power of the passions. Arthur stands forth in the seventh canto as everything Redcrosse is not, fully armed, prepared, measured, and even joyous. He engages in careful argument with Una, persuading her to tell her story and stressing the possibility that reason has some part in the containment of Despair: "Flesh may empaire (quoth he) but reason can repaire" (I.vii.42.9). Here, as in many of the Una episodes, the morality seems less Calvinist than Christian humanist. As usual in book 1, even Arthur cannot succeed against Orgoglio without supernatural aid—in this case the light of the diamond shield he bears. But in this light of Grace, Orgoglio suddenly weakens, strikes blindly, and shrivels away.

The Book of Holiness turns repeatedly to the sin of despair, because self-knowledge without sufficient knowledge of God's mercy shows one only how deeply unworthy one is of salvation and how rightfully one is damned. When Arthur finds Redcrosse in Orgoglio's dungeon, he wishes at first only for death, and his appearance later suggests the spiritual starvation he has undergone (I.viii.41). In this weakened condition he meets Despaire, whose description (I.ix.35) echoes that of Redcrosse: the young knight once again looks in a mirror. Despaire sums up the book's image of evil: the minimal "wood" in which he lives consists of dead and broken trees whose only fruits are the corpses of those who have hanged themselves. Like Error, he lives in a cave, and he speaks with a rhetoric whose soothing music recalls the somnolence of the House of Morpheus.

Despaire's message, sweeping aside Redcrosse's initial arrogant intention of avenging the dead Sir Terwin, is precisely what Redcrosse's exacerbated conscience assures him of: his utter unworthiness of salvation.

One common way of understanding Despaire here is to insist on the one-sidedness of his views: he quotes Scripture selectively, repressing any reference to divine mercy. When, for instance, he asks, "Is not his law, Let every sinner die?" (I.ix.47.5), he echoes Romans 6:23—"The wages of sinne is death"—but like Marlowe's Dr. Faustus, he leaves out the second half of the verse: "But the gifte of God is eternal life through Jesus Christ our Lord." Yet Despaire's comments are not so easily dismissed: most believing Protestants accepted that the majority of sinners would indeed die and that a strong conviction of unworthiness might indicate that one was doomed. Further, Despaire plays with the temptation that recurs throughout Spenser's work, the impulse simply to give up: "Is not short paine well borne, that brings long ease, / And layes the soule to sleepe in quiet grave?" (I.ix.40.6–7) In the end Despaire reduces Redcrosse to a state of paralysis recalling his immobilization by Error; Una must once more insist on the possibility of grace and scold him into a rejection of Despaire's temptation.

The allegory of the House of Holiness is flatter than the allegory of the scenes leading up to it. The elaborate schematization of the Dame Celia and her three daughters, Faith, Hope, and Charity, and the seven beadsmen recalls the static tableau of the seven deadly sins in canto 4. The shift in mode quietly reemphasizes the orderliness of God's Truth after the bottomless uncertainties of Despaire. Yet despair remains a crucial issue in this canto, as it is in the larger book. The lessons Redcrosse learns from Faith only exacerbate his sense of sin, and he must undergo penance in the cellar of the house—"Downe in a darkesome lowly place farre in" (I.x.25.7). This basement recalls the caves and dungeons of earlier episodes and transforms them, for this prison has as its end Redcrosse's spiritual healing. When he arises, he is reborn. On arriving at the House, Redcrosse does not meet Charity because she is pregnant, but she does appear, having delivered her child, when he issues from his dark and lowly retreat. Spenser suggests the connection between the birth of Charity's child and the rebirth of the young knight when Mercy helps the baby take his first steps and "firmely did upbeare, / As carefull Nourse her child from falling oft does reare" (I.x.35 8–9).

Redcrosse's ascent of the Mount of Contemplation returns to an epic *topos* in which the hero makes a journey to an otherworldly place and gains a vision of his destiny and that of his race. Spenser uses the moment to suggest Redcrosse's full maturation into a Christian knight. In classical works this vision occurs in the underworld, but Christian epic translated it to a mountaintop. Spenser associates the Mount of

Contemplation triply with Moses's Mount Sinai, Jesus' Mount of Olives, and the classical Mount Parnassus: Redcrosse's experience brings together the wisdom of the classical world with that of the Old and New Testaments. Redcrosse's destiny is the Hierusalem that he sees, where he and the "race" of the elect will end. He also learns his name, "Saint *George* of mery England": he has now matured to the point where he can learn the name—the identity—that he will bear throughout English history. But he responds to the vision by wishing either to remain on the mountain or to die (I.x.63). Redcrosse's wish for release from the world's corruption recalls the desire to avoid *care,* which appears as early as the Cave of Morpheus and recurs often in the book. When Contemplation reminds Redcrosse of his unfulfilled quest, Redcrosse agrees easily to his demand, but the unexpected response to the vision suggests the unchanging power of the desire.

The final battle with the Dragon recalls the initial battle with Error: again Redcrosse nearly loses, this time twice, and each time he is in need of divine rescue. The Dragon has a solidity equal to that of the landscape itself, and the poem compares it with a hill or a cliff: it is an aspect of the nature with which we all contend. Even Redcrosse's armor comes into complex play once more. When he has wounded the Dragon, it breathes fire at him, roasting him in his armor: "That erst him goodly arm'd, now most of all him harm'd" (I.xi.27.9). The armor of God does not give ease: confronting the fear of one's own death may in fact lead again to despair, and so the narrator suggests:

> Faint, wearie, sore, emboyled, grieved, brent
> With heat, toyle, wounds, armes, smart, & inward fire
> That never man such mischiefes did torment;
> Death better were, death did he oft desire,
> But death will never come, when needes require. (I.xi.28.1–5)

Death once more is the wish of the soul tormented by its own "inward fire": the metaphor of the armor brilliantly suggests the simultaneous need for divine aid and the pain of enduring it. Yet divine mercy is forthcoming in the two places—the well of life and the tree of life—from which Redcrosse rises, refreshed and perhaps rebaptized, to vanquish his opponent.

The final canto returns to the pastoral mode of canto 6, but with a difference. The natural and human worlds join to celebrate a betrothal that is at once human and divine. Una appears for the first time unveiled, the radiance of her beauty itself foreshadowing the time of the final marriage between the warfaring Christian and the One True Church. The tone moves between the comic, rustic genre sketches of the countryfolk measuring the Dragon, "To prove how many acres he did spread of land" (I.xii.11.9), and the solemn sound of the angels, who echo the human singing at the wedding. A characteristic moment occurs when Una's maidens bow to her:

> And her ador'd by honorable name,
> Lifting to heaven her everlasting fame:
> Then on her head they set a girland greene,
> And crowned her twixt earnest and twixt game;
> Who in her self-resemblance well beseene,
> Did seeme such, as she was, a goodly maiden Queene.
>
> (I.xii.8.4–9)

This scene once again revises earlier moments in the poem. While the adoring maidens recall the adoring Satyrs, they know Una's "honorable name" and lift her fame to a Christian heaven. Una's seeming such as she is contrasts with Duessa and Lucifera, for whom seeming opposes being. Most important is the lighthearted pastoral crowning of Una with a garland. This has its own history in the poem, including the ill-fated garland of Fradubio's branches that Redcrosse attempts to give Duessa and the olive garland with which the Satyrs deck Una. But the garland image first appears when Redcrosse dreams in Archimago's house of Venus leading Una—crowned with ivy by Flora—to his bed. The libidinous dream now becomes an inadequate foreshadowing of which the present garlanding in its triumphant innocence is the fulfillment.

   Yet the rejoicing is not unmixed. The return of Archimago suggests that, like Despaire, evil will not vanish while the world lives, and while the canto draws on the pastoral imagery at the end of the Book of Revelation, it does not describe the final judgment but only its foreshadowing. Redcrosse and Una meet in betrothal, not marriage, and when at the end of the canto Redcrosse leaves to continue Gloriana's service, Una mourns. Even the music of this final section strives "to drive away the dull Melancholy" (I.xii.38.8): the passage quotes the description of the music in the House of Pride as a reminder that dull melancholy continues as part of the human condition. As many critics have noted, this

is the first of the endings of *The Faerie Queene* that are not endings: final
fruition is deferred.[19]

## Book 2: The Need to Be Wary

The romance quest of the second book is not to kill a dragon but to
catch an enchantress; whereas the Dragon of the first book recalls the
satanic beast of Revelation, the enchantress looks back to the classical
figure of Circe in the *Odyssey,* who tempted her victims and turned them
into swine. In book 1, where Spenser deals with the soul's relation to
God, the divine end of earthly actions makes itself insistently present, as
in the text of the Revelation to John. By contrast, the second book concerns itself with this world and recalls classical texts—the *Aeneid,* the
*Odyssey,* and Aristotle's *Nichomachean Ethics.*[20] Christian concerns do not,
however, vanish from book 2. The second half of the book insists that
Temperance in this world is impossible without God's grace. Yet the
classicizing, this-worldly emphasis of the book enables Spenser to alter
his angle of vision, considering the daily human difficulty of living a
sane life while moved by powerful irrational feeling. Even after the
intrusion of the divine in the eighth canto, the book continues to focus
on this world. Whereas Redcrosse has a vision of heavenly Hierusalem in
canto 10 of book 1, the corresponding section of book 2 gives Arthur
and Guyon an understanding of their bodies, their minds, and secular
history.

Renaissance psychology, following Plato, divided the passions into
two groups, the *irascible* (like grief and anger), concerned with pain, and
the *concupiscible* (like gluttony or sexual desire), concerned with pleasure.[21] The first are "knightly" passions, noble though potentially
destructive if not restrained; the second are simply base. Yet all these
passions appear in the book as dangerous forces, ready to control and at
times to destroy the personality in which they exist. To avoid disaster
one must be wary, and book 2 presents a series of victims who suffer
from their lack of wariness, including Amavia, Mortdant, Huddibras,
Sans Loy, Phedon, Pyrocles, Cymocles, and Verdant. To an unusual
degree the characters of this book appear to be sufferers, not actors, driven by their dominant passions.[22] Guyon and Arthur gain some of their
victories when their passion-driven opponents overthrow themselves.[23]

Spenser inherited a long and somewhat blurred tradition of thinking
about the virtues of rational restraint. In the *Nichomachean Ethics* Aristotle contrasts Temperance and Continence. Temperance, a habitual har-

monizing of reason with appetite, is possible because "the temperate man craves for the things he ought, as he ought, and when he ought; and this is what rational principle directs."[24] Here the passions cooperate with the reason, aiming for what is noble. The allied virtue of Continence, by contrast, assumes passions at war with reason: the continent man needs the willed capacity to check his powerful appetites (*NE,* book 7, esp. 1145–52). During the medieval period the definition of the two virtues shifted: Continence became in some accounts an aspect of Temperance, and Temperance itself was Christianized as one of the four cardinal virtues.[25] Spenser does not distinguish consistently between the two, and his Temperance appears most generally as rational self-control (Evans, 113).

Spenser associates his Temperance with a chivalric purposefulness by making its opposite the sorceress Acrasia. The female temptress who turns her victims into animals goes back to Circe of the *Odyssey,* whom subsequent commentators interpret allegorically. George Sandys paraphrases the sixteenth-century mythographer Natale Conti on Circe as lust that, "getting the dominion," "deformes our soules with all bestial vices; alluring some to inordinate *Venus;* others to anger, cruelty, and every excesse of passion: the Swines, the Lyons, and the Wolves, produced by her sensuall charmes."[26] Comparable figures appear in Ariosto and Tasso, whom Spenser imitates closely in cantos 6 and 12. But Spenser gives his Acrasia an allegorical single-mindedness lacking in his predecessors: whereas Tasso's Armida reforms and converts to Christianity, Acrasia is Intemperance itself. She embodies the impulse to give up knightly striving—an impulse associated in book 1 with despair. Her name means, literally, *powerlessness:* her victims lack the willpower to follow their own better judgment. The lust in her garden is passive: while her victims engage in sex, they appear drugged and slumberous rather than vitally active. Sensuality here involves dissipation rather than rutting—a yielding to slackness, not indulgence in rape. There will be rape aplenty in book 3, but book 2 does not deal with sex as an *interpersonal* force at all, focusing rather on its tendency to relax the moral will. Temperance, by contrast, unites body and spirit in obedience to a higher end.

As a Knight of Temperance, Sir Guyon acts from the start more competently than the young Saint George. Prompted on occasion by his passions, notably by anger, he recovers himself quickly: the first episode of book 2 demonstrates the limits of his straying. In a mistaken surge of anger and pity he launches himself at Redcrosse but stops short of attacking the cross on his shield. If in book 1 Spenser dramatizes the fall and recovery of a fallible Everyman, in book 2 he examines a knight superior to others. Guyon never removes his armor, and even his horse, emblem of his passions, treads "with equall steps" (II.i.7.9). His companion, the Palmer, seems to embody what Renaissance writers refer to as "right reason"—an instinctive knowledge of the good and ultimately of God. The religious associations of a palmer as a pilgrim also suggest his sacred dimension. He manages to catch and correct those passionate impulses to which on occasion even Guyon gives vent.[27]

Yet Guyon exhibits certain limitations during the first half of the book associated with the kind of temperance he demonstrates. The Aristotelian virtue rests on an ideal of moral self-sufficiency—of a man whose passions cooperate with his reason because "the noble is the mark at which they both aim." (NE, 1119b, 373). Yet for a Protestant, as book 1 makes clear, the belief in such self-sufficiency is a delusion. Human beings are corrupt by nature and control their unruly passions only with God's aid. Despite the respect he shows Redcrosse's shield, Guyon does not recognize its implications for his vision of himself, and his comments on other characters rarely suggest an awareness that what happens to them could happen to him. When the Palmer congratulates Redcrosse on his success, Saint George replies:

> His be the praise, that this atchiev'ment wrought,
> Who made my hand the organ of his might;
> More than goodwill to me attribute nought:
> For all I did, I did but as I ought. (II.i.33.2–5)

Whereas Redcrosse looks to God for his virtue, Guyon looks to himself.

Guyon's tendency to underestimate the seriousness of the evil in the world appears in some comically tinny utterances to those beyond his aid: when he asks Amavia to tell her story, he comments, "He oft finds present helpe, who does his griefe impart" (II.i.46.9). Arthur gave Una the same counsel (I.vii.40–41), but Una did not have a dagger protruding from her breast. Later he tells Phedon that all his hurts "may soone through temperance be esed" (II.iv.33.9), consigning the guilty memory of Phedon's murders to comfortable oblivion. For all his difference from Redcrosse, Guyon also tends to see his "end" in terms of his own glory, and his token "fall" and recovery in the central cantos of the poem suggest the limits of what he can do without God's aid.

The second episode of book 2 defines the nature of Guyon's quest. The story of Amavia, Mortdant, and Ruddymane is, as Guyon says to the Palmer, an image of mortality, of fallen human nature driven by its passions. In several ways the episode returns to matters treated in book 1—suicide and ungoverned lust. But whereas in book 1 Redcrosse's lust for Duessa appears primarily as infidelity to Una and the faith she embodies, the treatment here stresses passion's destructive power. The center of the episode is Amavia, half-character, half-emblem, whose punning name ("love of life," "way of love") stresses the paradox by which love of life can move one to embrace death. As a long-suffering, deeply devoted lady, she is willing to disguise herself as a pilgrim in order to rescue her husband Mortdant from Acrasia's garden. But she can see nothing to live for with Mortdant dead. Her rather operatic speeches dramatize her sense that Mortdant is everything, and in dying she consigns her baby to the mercy of the Wood instead of surviving to nurse it. Spenser marks her out as "pagan" in her views: her opening words refer to the heavens as "carelesse" (II.i.36.1), and the Palmer (refusing to judge her suicide) gives her a recognizably pagan burial. The same violence of passion characterizes her husband's death: rescued from a life of sensual luxury, he drinks the water of the pure fountain and dies; the very violence of the shift kills him. The bloody hands of the baby suggest, as the Palmer says, the degree to which the fact of sin (as opposed to its punishment) cannot be washed away: like all of us, Ruddymane is born impure.

The rest of the second canto, however, concerns itself with a very different, and Aristotelian, understanding of virtue and vice. The idea that virtue is a norm from which extremes depart is central to the *Nichomachean Ethics* and appears in Medina (in Greek, "the mean"), whose gracious welcome of Guyon is exaggerated in one direction by the lasciviousness of Perissa (in Greek, "too much") and in the other by the cold self-denial of Elissa (in Greek, "too little"). The sisters embody extremes not only vicious in themselves but hostile to one another, and they egg on their lovers, Sans Loy and Huddibras, to fight. The result is a small chaos always threatening to enlarge. In trying to stop the fight Guyon finds himself joining it, and only Medina, as the mediating figure, can persuade the opposing warriors to make peace. What is most curious about this episode is its distance from the world of the rest of the book, for which the idea of virtue as a self-sufficient, normative *center* is not adequate: it has little to do with the death of Mortdant and Amavia and the fulfillment of Guyon's quest. Several books of *The Faerie Queene* have a flatly schematic early episode that later events complicate.[28] This canto is one of them.

The third canto interrupts Guyon's story to follow Braggadocio, who has stolen Guyon's horse. What is most striking about Braggadocio's meeting with Belphoebe is its absence of connection with the rest of the book: Belphoebe will not reappear until the middle of book 3, and Braggadocio not until late in the same book. Both figures also exist outside the limits of Guyon's world in moral terms. Belphoebe, who is temperate in Aristotle's sense, does not need the self-discipline that Guyon and others must struggle for. Braggadocio, who is absolutely ignoble, also sees no need to struggle: he tries merely to create the impression of nobility in order to enjoy its perks. They have, in Berger's words, a "conspicuous irrelevance" to the issues Spenser explores in the rest of the book (1957, 150–60), and their comic meeting defines the limits within which the other characters move. As always when Braggadocio appears in the poem, Spenser suggests that the ideal of knighthood is very handy for a thoroughgoing opportunist. Braggadocio's meeting with Belphoebe recalls Aeneas's meeting with his mother Venus in the *Aeneid,* but it differs in Braggadocio's comic inability to comprehend the being he addresses.

Phedon returns us to imperfect but struggling humanity. The tale of a bridegroom tricked into believing that he has witnessed the seduction of his bride-to-be occurs often in the Renaissance, appearing, for instance, in the main plot of *Much Ado about Nothing* (1600); Spenser takes his version from the fifth canto of *Orlando Furioso.* But Spenser makes his account much grimmer than Ariosto's and avoids its happy ending. While the story appears to be an instance of the dangers of unchecked anger and overhasty judgment—tendencies to which Guyon is susceptible—it raises deeper problems. Spenser blurs the motivation of the squire who tricks Phedon, making him act like Shakespeare's Don John, who does evil simply because it gives him joy. Both victim and murderer, Phedon continues to blame others for what he has done instead of accusing himself; Furor catches him as he attempts to kill his lady's innocent lady-in-waiting.[29]

Guyon's encounter with Pyrocles and Cymocles and his brief stay with Phaedria repeat common romance motives—the battle with a strange, pagan knight and his brother, and the temptations of a sorceress who distracts a knight from his goal. Spenser reworks these traditional motives by psychologizing them. Pyrocles (whose name includes the Greek root for "fire") is the irascible impulse writ large. His shield proclaims "Burnt I do burne," and the words suggest violent impatience that gives rise to external aggression. Pyrocles is active in relation to others, but passive in relation to his own fury: he is driven as much as he drives. His brother Cymocles (whose name includes the Greek for "wave") also cannot control his passions, shifting without transition from the irascible to the concupiscent. He appears lasciviously inert in Acrasia's garden, but Atin (characteristically unwilling to explain what it is all about) rouses him to a desire for combat until Phaedria distracts him. Roused again to battle with Guyon, he is soothed once more by Phaedria's pleading. He embodies, as Evans has suggested, the tendency of the roused passions to exhaust themselves, losing themselves in the short term with no final, rational goal (127).

Phaedria (the name derives from the Greek for "glittering, cheerful") is a junior Acrasia whose aim is distraction. Her characteristically shallow boat transports knights away from their destinations to her island, a never-never land of singing birds and musical fountains. Her song (II.vi.15–17) recalls Christ's urging of his followers to consider the flowers of the field and take no thought for the morrow, but she turns it into a comic plea for self-indulgence. Significantly, she leaves behind both Guyon's Palmer and Cymocles' Atin: the temptation of careless ease rejects any impulse to action, good or bad. Without his Palmer, Guyon does not know quite what to make of Phaedria, but he does make it clear that he is unhappy on her island; when she sees that he will make her life uncomfortable, she ferries him back to the mainland. The succession of Pyrocles, Cymocles, and Phaedria may, as Evans argues, suggest that Guyon alternately strains too hard and relaxes too much (126–28). Certainly he has lost the Palmer and, with him, his direction.

This loss of direction appears in his descent into Mammon's underground house, the book's turning point. Critics disagree widely about the meaning of this episode—which ends with Guyon's faint—and most important, about his initial decision to enter Mammon's realm.[30] Is it a heroic imitation of Christ or a culpable yielding to the wish to see what does not concern him? Guyon's condition when he agrees to Mammon's offer suggests an answer. Is Guyon to be understood as a character with "motives" at all?

The answer is suggested by the larger context Spenser establishes for Guyon's act. For all his abilities he has accomplished very little in the first seven cantos of the book. He arrives too late to do more than listen to Amavia's dying words and swear revenge; he loses his horse; he holds his own against Sans Foy and Huddibras but cannot end their conflict;

he masters Furor and frees the guilty Phedon only to free Occasion later to torment Pyrocles; he loses the Palmer, delays with Phaedria, and eventually will end up on Mammon's doorstep in a dead faint. The seventh canto begins with a simile comparing him to a mariner whose guiding star has been obscured by "foggy mistes, or cloudy tempests," forced to trust to his experience and his earthly aids of "card and compass" (II.vii.1.4–7). Without the spiritual guidance of the Palmer, Guyon has to use his feeble earthly reasoning powers. As he proceeds, the narrator tells us that he "evermore himselfe with comfort feedes, / Of his owne vertues, and prayse-worthy deedes" (II.vii.2.4–5). This seeming complacency may conceal an anxious whistling in the dark, but the lines surely stress that Guyon looks to himself rather than to God for comfort. He is, so to speak, attempting to live entirely off his own resources; the metaphor of feeding looks toward the lack of food that will cause Guyon to faint later on.

Mammon introduces himself as "God of the world and worldlings" (II.vii.8.1) and offers to show Guyon what he later calls "the fountaine of the worldes good" (II.vii.38.6). Spenser thus associates him not only with riches but with all the temptations of this world as opposed to the next. Mammon's rusty iron coat is "underneath enveloped with gold" (II.vii.4.2), and the image suggests an original golden age that has declined into an iron present—or in Christian terms, an initial state of innocence now lost. The world he embodies may once have been simple and good, but now it is "darkned with filthy dust" (II.vii.4.3). He boasts that his riches will buy anything one could wish, including honor and rule. Guyon does not, finally, yield to any of Mammon's particular temptations. His honor is unpurchasable: he depends on a sense of his own rectitude (his deeds must be "praise-*worthie*"), which he will not trade for the external power and fame that a being like Mammon can offer. Yet he does yield to the impulse to endure temptation, an impulse that shares something with Redcrosse's pride.

The descent into hell is a familiar *topos* in epic, and Spenser uses the tradition to suggest Guyon's strengths as well as his weaknesses. Traditionally the epic hero descends to the underworld because he needs to: there he will gain knowledge to complete his journey. This necessity appears in various ways in the cases of Odysseus, Aeneas, and even the pilgrim Dante of the *Divine Comedy*. But Guyon's adventure differs from these others in that there is nothing in Mammon's cave that he needs to learn. As with many of his earlier adventures, Guyon remains unhurt but accomplishes nothing: his achievement is negative. It has often been argued that Guyon's temptation recalls the temptation of Christ by Satan, but the likenesses make Guyon appear more like Christ's anti-type, an inadequate version of God's son.[31] Once Guyon has entered the underworld, Mammon substitutes himself as a guide for the Palmer—like the Sibyl in the *Aeneid* or Virgil in the *Divine Comedy*—and indeed counsels him to avoid fighting Disdain (II.vii.42). The spectacle of Guyon being *advised* by Mammon—and taking the advice—suggests something wrong about the whole business. In fact, when he comes face to face with Disdain, Guyon is, in a manner familiar from book 1, facing himself. His manner throughout the canto involves variations on disdain, sometimes polite and sometimes less so, and it recalls his attitude toward many of the characters in the book—a slight condescension toward weaknesses he does not realize he shares.

The tour through hell has three parts: an initial display of Mammon's riches; the vision of Philotime; and the Garden of Proserpina. For the first Guyon has only disdain: this could not possibly tempt him. The second is a different matter. Philotime's name means "love of honor," and she embodies an ambitiousness that is deeply appealing to Guyon's nature. She holds a chain that traditionally embodies the love or the harmony binding the world together in hierarchical order. By contrast, this chain aids movement, enabling courtiers to rise and thrust one another down. (The mythographer Natale Conti associated the image with ambition.[32]) But marriage to Philotime is insufficient to tempt Guyon, whose sense of honor goes beyond the public splendor she offers. The third and most obscure temptation is the Garden of Proserpina. According to the traditional myth, Proserpina was forced to remain in the underworld six months of the year because she had eaten the seeds of a pomegranate; were Guyon to relax and rest prematurely on the silver stool Mammon offers, or to eat the food of the underworld, he would be trapped. He refuses, seemingly without difficulty.

The Garden of Proserpina does, however, offer Guyon a sight that suggests a fundamental weakness. In the river of the damned he notices two sinners, Tantalus and Pilate, the one submerged up to, the other above, his head. Tantalus tries vainly to eat and drink, while Pilate tries to wash his hands. The traditions Spenser inherited made Tantalus an image of pride and blasphemy, and Pilate partly responsible for Christ's death. His fiction connects them by stressing that both act *in vain*. Tantalus attempts to eat and drink, but the retreating fruit and water "made him vainely swinke" (II.vii.58.7), and Pilate's attempt to wash the filth from his hands is equally unsuccessful: "Yet nothing cleaner were for such intent, / But rather fowler seemed to the eye; / So lost his labour vaine and idle industry" (II.vii.61.7–9). These paired examples of vain labor, the one to satisfy hunger, the other to wash off filth, combine to suggest the condition of man without grace. The image of endless restless motion looks back to the picture of Aesculapius in the Cave of Night, trying vainly to assuage the inextinguishable divine fire. The image suggests the endlessly unsatisfied restlessness of human nature, driven by the love of the divine and unable to find relief outside God's love. Like Ruddymane, Pilate is unable to cleanse his hands, not because he is a supreme sinner but because he embodies an extreme version of our common guilt.

In responding to these figures, Guyon treats them as absolutely different from himself. He accuses Tantalus of greed, having a "minde intemperate," but he misdiagnoses the sinner. Tantalus is suffering from a hunger that earthly food will not satisfy—and it is no accident that Guyon himself will soon faint for lack of food. For the lack of food and drink that eventually causes Guyon to faint demonstrates his simple mortality. We have already found him "feeding" himself with the memories of his praiseworthy deeds before he goes into the Cave, and throughout the underground journey he "feeds" his eyes, but he necessarily neglects the literal food his human nature needs to stay alive. Thus, unlike Christ, who went underground for three days only to rise again, Guyon emerges from hell in a starved condition and, anticlimactically, faints. He has tried to live too much from himself and needs both literal food to keep body and soul together and the metaphorical food of God.

The battle that follows over Guyon's sleeping body recalls Arthur's battle with Orgoglio in the eighth canto of book 1. Once again the hero of the book lies helpless, in need of Arthur's rescue; again the conflict has an allegorical sense in which Grace overcomes the treacherous forces of the hero's fallen self. Alone, the Palmer as right reason can do nothing; he can only ask Arthur to intercede (as he does) for him. Guyon remains unconscious during the battle because he is, in the familiar metaphor, spiritually asleep or dead (MacLachlan 1983, 93–98); he wakes only when Arthur has won—when Grace has conquered. Here he has come alive to the *need* for divine aid and to his own weakness. Restored to the Palmer, he can now venture on to the Castle of Alma, where he will come to know himself more fully.

The Castle of Alma is, like the House of Holiness, a place of learning; yet instead of learning about God here, Redcrosse learns about his earthly nature. The guided tour through the castle, a model of the human body and the human psyche, has as its function the celebration of God's creation: it has the slightly old-fashioned neatness of the allegory of the House of Holiness. Just as Guyon comes face to face with himself in Shamefastnesse, as Arthur does in Prays-Desire, so the whole canto develops their self-recognition. They come to the books containing their respective genealogies—accounts of where they fit in history.

The account of an epic hero's descendants, usually ending in the poet's patron, has been a regular feature of epic poetry since Virgil; such a genealogy occurs in the third canto of book 3. Less usual here is Spenser's attention to Arthur's—and hence Elizabeth's—ancestors. The canto's backward look connects Rome and Britain and places Arthur at a pivotal point in English history. It also contrasts the fictional world of Faerie with the colder, less shapely world of English history. Spenser took much of his account of English history from Geoffrey of Monmouth's *Historia Regum Britanniae* (c. 1136), and it is a grim affair. The account has three stages: the first (stanzas 1–36) charts the coming of the Roman Brutus to England and follows the reign of his descendants until their extinction; the second (37–49) ends with the Roman conquest; and the final stage (50–68) takes the kings of Wales up to Arthur's father, Uther Pendragon, and breaks off. The account stresses the uncertainty of the world's gains; times of peace and prosperity end abruptly in renewed warfare, civil or foreign, and rivalries between members of the royal family are a chief source of discord. Against this long, brutal chronicle Spenser sets the idealized history of Guyon's Faerie ancestors. These continue in an unbroken, magic-working line for 700 generations until Oberon and his daughter Tanaquil, romance pseudonyms for Henry VIII and Elizabeth. The canto sets what Spenser thought of as actual history against the idealized vision of process imaged in *The Faerie Queene,* acknowledging how uncertain the actual world is in contrast to the comparative neatness of his fiction.

The final cantos of this book further compare Arthur and Guyon. Arthur deals with the more desperate conflict, in which he is taxed to the full; by contrast, Guyon, following the Palmer's reliable advice, proceeds on an odyssey toward the capture of a new Circe. The battle between Arthur and Maleager, with his aids Impatience and Impotence, recalls the battle between Guyon and Furor aided by Occasion, but Maleager threatens Arthur much more seriously. The continued attack on the Castle of Alma emphasizes that, however good its original construction, it finds itself in constant danger from within and without. The senses are not only miraculous means of perception but avenues of inva-

sion. Spenser models Arthur's battle partly on that between Hercules
and King Antaeus, who regained his strength whenever he touched his
mother earth. Renaissance mythographers often allegorized Antaeus as
corrupt desire, and Maleager is often equated with original sin. His
name means "badly sick," or "badly weak": as a state of mind, *aeger*
often designates deep depression, which links the figure with Despair in
the first book.[33] He embodies the natural weakness of fallen human
nature, and his nightmarish inability to die images the impotence of
human beings to put an end to their inherited corruption. Just as
Arthur had to save Guyon, so Timeas must save Arthur in extremity:
one cannot fight these foes unaided. Arthur's final disposal of Maleager
in a "standing lake" (II.xi.46.6) suggests a version of baptism: only
through God's grace can we cast off the earthly "body of this death."

The Bower of Bliss is Guyon's second great challenge after the Cave
of Mammon, and it suggests just how far Guyon—and the virtue of
temperance—will take us. Less desperate than Arthur's conquest of
Maleager, Guyon's victory implies that conquest just as the second book
implies the first: only when the weakness at the heart of fallen man
yields to Grace can Temperance come into play. It also contrasts with
Guyon's descent into the Cave of Mammon. Where Guyon went into
the Cave unaccompanied by the Palmer, he now has the Palmer by his
side, ready to dissuade him from rash actions. And where he went into
the Cave as essentially a sight-seeing tourist unconnected with his quest,
the destruction of the Bower *is* the object of his quest. Guyon is now on
track, performing the service for which he was commissioned.

The model for Guyon in the last book is Odysseus, whom Renaissance mythographers often allegorized as the type of the rational man,
and his conquest of Circe as reason's mastery of the passions.[34] Guyon's
voyage sometimes seems to recall the picture in canto 2 of Temperance
as a mean between opposing vices. For instance, the boat steers between
the Gulf of Greediness and the Rock of Vile Reproach, the one concerned with the unchecked desire to consume, the other with the
unchecked impulse to squander or give away. But these seeming opposites are not extremes in an Aristotelian sense at all. Spendthrifts squander their resources by using them to satisfy the appetites imaged in the
Gulf of Greediness: in both cases one must simply restrain desire.

All the traps of this voyage, real and illusory, attempt to slow or stop
the progress of the boat, and so Guyon relies not only on the Palmer and
his unfailing judgment but on the Boatman with his strong back and
unswerving dedication to his task. In the Boatman Spenser images that

sheer perseverance that, without flinching, continues in the heroic task. The one point of real dismay comes when

> suddeinly a grosse fog overspred
> With his dull vapour all that desert has,
> And heavens chearefull face enveloped,
> That all things one, and one as nothing was,
> And this great Universe seemd one confused mas.
>
> (II.xii.34.5–9)

Here chaos seems to have come again: Acrasia's forces obscure the familiar landmarks, and perhaps the sense of moral certainty by which one guides oneself. Despite the fear this uncertainty creates, the travelers continue on: "whiles th'one did row, and the other stifly steare / Till that at last the weather gan to cleare" (II.xii.37.4–5). This steady continuance is faith in action.

The Bower itself is one of Spenser's superbly evocative set pieces, a place whose melodious verse suggests the temptations it embodies. As a false Eden it draws on a long tradition of earthly paradises, most notably on the work of Ariosto and especially of Tasso, from whom Spenser imitates the song of stanzas 74–75, reworking them in accordance with the emphases of his own book. The narrative insists on the garden being "temperate" in one of the word's root meanings: it is a harmonious *mixture* in which all things work together to a common end. Spenser stresses the weather's idyllic balance, which involves "Nor scorching heat, nor cold intemperate" (II.xii.51.5), while in an emblematic harmony, "Birdes, voyces, instruments, windes, waters, all agree" (II.xii.70–71). Yet the *balance* that creates a paradisiacal setting is calculated to bring about an intemperate end—the loss of self in sensual pleasure. The garden's purpose is quite literally *perversion*—the turning-aside of the self from God.

As such it attempts to destroy the controlled warrior ethic that Guyon upholds. This purpose appears first in Acrasia's transformation of Mortdant from an active knight into a passive voluptuary, and Mortdant reappears in the picture of the enervated Verdant at the other end of the book. Although Verdant seems to have been a youth of promise, he has lost his identity: the name on his shield has been erased (II.xii.80.3–4), and he appears to be asleep, his spirit "quite molten into lust and pleasure lewd" (II.xii.73.8). The stress on greenness in *Ver*dant suggests that in giving up his human duties the young knight has become plantlike, a mere creature of growth and decay. Verdant will eventually turn into Mortdant, dying without ever transcending a purely natural—but less than human—cycle of activity.

C. S. Lewis long ago pointed to the artificiality of the garden, where "Art as halfe in scorne / Of niggard Nature, like a pompous bride / Did decke her, and too lavishly adorne" (II.xii.50.6–8). Here the cooperation of art and nature, a standard *topos* of praise, becomes a rivalry resulting in an aesthetic intensification: "so striving each th'other to undermine, / Each did the others worke more beautifie; / So diff'ring both in willes, agreed in fine" (II.xii.59.5–7). The rivalry suggests the garden's underlying disharmony, which nonetheless brings about a common perverse end. Ideally both art and nature move their viewers to acknowledge God's bounty and to devote themselves to his purposes. Here, however, they exist to distract one from the divine; in this, on Spenser's reading, they undermine each other and themselves. In the tempting attractiveness of the Bower Spenser examines the misuse of the poet's art as well. (It is no accident that the garden has "shady Laurell trees" [II.xii.63.2].) Spenser's sensuous art appeals to the reader as the Bower does to Guyon: both use moving images to appeal to the imagination, and the images of the Bower make the reader feel the force of Guyon's temptation. The gate to the Bower is made, appropriately, of ivory, the material in the *Aeneid* of the underworld gate through which false dreams come to the world (*Aeneid,* VI.895–96).

Spenser plays with this misuse of art in the scene of the two bathing nymphs. Although Guyon has little difficulty dismissing allegorical figures like the Genius and Excess, the two nymphs bathing in the fountain capture his attention. The brilliant stanzas (II.xii.63–67) in which Spenser describes the effect of the nymphs alternately submerging themselves and displaying themselves focus on Guyon's imagination. The half-sight of those who hide beneath the water or within their golden hair stimulates Guyon more than simple nudity. Like a titillated reader, Guyon imagines more than is explicitly revealed, and the sight thus resembles pornographic writing, stimulating the mind's erotic fantasies. It succeeds with Guyon, in whose "sparkling face / The secret signes of kindled lust appeare" (II.xii.68.5–6): it needs the Palmer's rebuke to recall him to his original purpose.

Guyon responds to the temptations of the garden with destructive anger, overthrowing the false Genius's bowl (II.xii.49), "violently" cast ing down the cup of Excess (II.xii.57.3), and destroying the whole Bower in a much-quoted stanza:

> But all those pleasant bowres and Pallace brave,
>   *Guyon* broke downe, with rigour pittilesse;
>   Ne ought their goodly workmanship might save
>   Them from the tempest of his wrathfulnesse,
>   But that their blisse he turn'd to balefulnesse:
>   Their groves he feld, their gardins did deface,
>   Their arbers spoyle, their Cabinets suppresse,
>   Their banket houses burne, their buildings race,
> And of the fairest late, now made the fowlest place. (II.xii.83)

This scene of the hero destroying the garden does not occur in Spenser's main model, Tasso's *Jerusalem Delivered.* Armida, the enchantress of that garden, destroys it along with her own palace, and eventually for love of her Rinaldo turns Christian. By contrast, Acrasia is not an independent character: she embodies what is *in* Guyon, and Guyon deals with her (and himself) ruthlessly. The poem stresses the righteousness of Guyon's "wrathfulnesse," but its very violence suggests a destructive urge that goes beyond the necessary, giving the picture of the garden a kind of posthumous poignancy. Guyon's virtue here appears strikingly negative: confronted with sexuality, he represses it absolutely. But sexuality is more than a temptation to fall: it is a mainspring of human action, and so Spenser turns to book 3, in which sexuality appears a real if danger-ous good.

## Book 3: The Metamorphoses of Love

Spenser's Chastity is a larger virtue than our modern understanding of the word suggests. Its center is the idea not of restraint but of fidelity, and it includes the fruitful use of sexuality in marriage. The concept of "married chastity" occurred often in the period, especially among Protestants; the term was also used to describe the soul's fidelity to God (Tuve, 119). Britomart's chastity is one with her fidelity to Artegal, whom she will not meet until book 4, but for whom she will search with steady persistence. The stress on the use of sexuality rather than its repression distinguishes the third book from the second, where sexuality

appears primarily as a danger and the idealized body of the Castle of
Alma lacks genitals. For all the monstrous variations on sexuality in
book 3, the narrative does present it as a beneficent instinct, a force for
the creation of beauty in the world. Indeed, the book's center, the Garden of Adonis, makes *its* sacred center a mount of Venus.

Chastity also differs from the subjects of the earlier books in being an
interpersonal virtue. Holiness concerns one's relation to God, and Temperance one's relation to one's own body: no second person is needed to
achieve either virtue. But Chastity demands someone to whom one can be
faithful and with whom sexuality can become more than temptation. The
interpersonal stress affects the poem's allegory, making book 3 one of the
hardest to interpret. Whereas books 1 and 2 operate by dramatizing
struggles within the self, developing variations on the psychomachia, book
3 operates in a more varied fashion. On occasion its allegory is internal, as
when in canto 5 Timeas is attacked by three "Forsters" (foresters) who
seem to embody his own lusts. But in other situations the status of crucial
figures remains unclear: is Busyrane an aspect of Amoret's consciousness?
Of Britomart's consciousness? Does he embody cultural traditions that
both heroines can accept or reject? Is he some or all of these or something
else? Certainty is difficult. When in canto 1 Guardante shoots an arrow
that grazes Britomart's skin, does this close encounter suggest Britomart's
vulnerability to love? (In the next canto she will be wounded on looking
into Merlin's glass.) Or is it simply the allegorical equivalent of a lewd
glance at a heroine who has, after all, been surprised in her shift? There is
often a fuzziness about the allegory of book 3 that suggests the difficulty
one often has in disentangling inner from outer, in separating what is
really out there, in the world, from oneself.

The quest of this book shifts as its central virtue shifts. Whereas the
earlier books focus on the destruction or capture of an enemy—the
Dragon, Acrasia—the third follows a quest for a mate.[35] And unlike the
marriage of Redcrosse and Una, postponed to the end of time, this
union will result in a Welsh line issuing eventually in the reign of the
Tudors. In book 3 Britomart becomes the link between two genealogies,
one that connects her line with that of Aeneas, stressing the movement
of empire from Troy to Rome to England (III.ix.38–51), and a second
that makes Britomart the ancestor of Elizabeth herself (III.iii.26–49).
Chastity takes on a political dimension as it contributes to the formation
of a line of British kings.

Yet despite this epic stress on the hero's part in history, the form of
this book differs strikingly from that of the earlier books. Its debt to

Ariostan romance-epic is more overt than in the earlier books;[36] this debt appears not only in specific borrowings but in the *entrelacement* of the plot construction. Whereas books 1 and 2 follow their heroes, departing in Redcrosse's case only to trace Una's wanderings, and in Guyon's only to describe Arthur's battle with Maleager, book 3 follows Britomart into the fourth canto and then drops her; she will not return again until canto 9. Cantos 4–8 develop love's nature in the Garden of Adonis and an intertwined group of romance plots in which characters and half-characters, drives and impulses wandering around the erotic landscape, meet and confront one another.

The third book develops meaning largely by Ariostan theme and variation. The narrator comments that it is wonderful to see how diversely Love plays its pageants in diverse minds (III.v.1), and the book develops this wild variety. Love forms—and deforms—all the characters of book 3, and the metamorphoses they undergo develop a complex, experimental, and at times very funny account of its nature. The several independent plots of the book allow for continual shifting comparison, reemphasized by repeated nodal images—the picture of wounding with Love's arrow,[37] for instance, or the image of a protective woman bending over a recumbent man. These insistent gestures toward comparison force the reader to consider the metamorphoses Love creates.

In classic epic fashion, the third book begins in midstory, with Britomart already on her quest: we will not hear how she has come to wear armor until the retrospective narrative of the second and third cantos. In Spenserian fashion, the effect of the reversal is to give an initial picture of a paradox, a woman in armor, leaving the reader only gradually to come to an understanding of what it means. The female warrior appears often in epics, most notably in the Camilla of Virgil's *Aeneid,* and the Bradamante of the *Orlando Furioso,* on whom Britomart is partly modeled. Spenser reinforces the paradox by presenting Britomart initially as a union of opposites:

> For she was full of amiable grace,
>> And manly terrour mixed therewithall,
>> That as the one stird up affections bace,
>> So th'other did mens rash desires apall,
>> And hold them backe, that would in errour fall;
>> As he, that hath espide a vermeill Rose,
>> To which sharpe thornes and breres the way forstall,

> Dare not for dread his hardy hand expose,
> But wishing it far off, his idle wish doth lose. (III.i.46)

This combination of traditionally female qualities ("amiable grace") and traditionally male ones ("manly terror") creates an image of beauty that is not fragile but sturdily independent, even challenging. Her beauty stirs men, but her manly terror—which *is* in part her chastity, a courageous independent will—repulses those who would mistreat it. The enchanted spear she carries and her willingness to engage in combat (she has been in three battles by the time she vanishes in the fourth canto) reinforces the impression of male aggressiveness. Half of her name is associated with Britain, but the other half with Mars: Britomart is a formidable opponent.

On the other hand, much of the first canto is devoted to the revelation of the comic incompatibility between this formidable exterior and Britomart's actual lack of worldly experience. The comedy of the Malecasta episode lies partly in the mutual incomprehension of the two women. Each takes the other's appearance at face value. A holdover from the world of book 2, Malecasta is hardly conscious of interpersonal relations, viewing others simply as means of pleasure. Her mistake about Britomart's sex suggests the limitation of her awareness: the potential lover she sees is lust-inspired fantasy. Similarly, Britomart projects *her* lovelorn seriousness onto Malecasta, taking her rote expressions of passion for the real thing.

The second and third cantos revert to the beginning of Britomart's quest. Her falling in love with an image—Artegal's—is a common romance motif, but Spenser gives it meaning by setting two different interpretations of the act against one another. Britomart—and to some degree her nurse Glauce—views her love through the lens of Ovid's *Metamorphoses*.[38] While Glauce distinguishes her charge from the unnatural lovers Myrrha, Byblis, and Pasiphae (III.ii.40–41), Britomart sees herself as like Narcissus, loving an image without a body (III.ii.44)—all figures out of Ovid's long poem. The myths of the *Metamorphoses* embody in book 3 a view of love as destructive and purposeless. Whereas the loves of the *Aeneid* always appear in relation to Rome's destiny, those of Ovid's poem disrupt human attempts at order without forming part of any cosmic scheme. Britomart sees her passion as catastrophic happenstance; while Glauce insists that the love is not evil, her futile attempts to banish it by magical mumbo jumbo suggest that she really agrees with her charge.

By contrast, the third canto stresses a heroic view of love. The opening stanza of book 3 stresses that love is a divine fire "ykindled first above, / Emongst th'eternall spheres and lamping sky, / And thence pourd into men," and that it gives rise to "all noble deeds and never dying fame" (III.iii.i.2–4, 9). One of the fruitful false etymologies of the Renaissance was the derivation of *hero* from *eros:* by this understanding, love does not hinder noble deeds but spurs them on. Further, Britomart learns from Merlin in this canto that the cause of her love is not blind passion but providential destiny. The union of Britomart and Artegal will create a line that will rule the British nation, a line ending in Spenser's Queen. For all the ambiguities surrounding him and his origins, Spenser's Merlin here acts as a prophetic artist who encourages Britomart by envisioning the line that marriage with Artegal will create. The long, painful account of her descendants, which stresses the bloodshed and frustration that will accompany their rule, nonetheless ends with a paean of praise to Elizabeth, in whom England will find peace.

Yet, with characteristically Spenserian willingness to allow doubt to enter his vision, Merlin stops abruptly:

> But yet the end is not. There *Merlin* stayd,
> As overcomen of the spirites powre,
> Or other ghastly spectacle dismayd. (III.iii.50.1–3)

Elizabeth's childlessness puts Merlin's triumphant vision at risk; the lack of "end" here stresses the uncertainty haunting all human endeavor.[39] This uncertainty appears again in the story of the wall that Merlin plans to build around Britain—a fantasy of perfect security—only to have the project remain incomplete when he is seduced by Morgan La Fay. Yet, despite these anxieties for the reader, Merlin's vision enables Britomart to place her love in history—to see that her romance quest for a lover possesses epic implications. The final words of canto 3, "Forth rode Britomart" (III.iii.62.9), emphasize her name and with it her place as a new hero.

The men of the first canto—and indeed, of the first half of the book—provide a sense of hapless contrast. Whereas Britomart rises from initial uncertainty to an awareness of her place in history, the male figures tend to wander from their goals. Guyon is knocked off his horse at the opening of the first canto, and his face is saved only by Arthur's tactful excuses about his saddle being too loosely cinched. The encounter suggests that

Guyon, who struggles primarily to control his sexuality, is not cut out for the more complex problem of making it work for him. Accordingly, Britomart, Chastity's representative, overcomes him; when he exits, he will not appear for the rest of the book. Soon after Florimel enters the scene pursued by a villainous forster, the newfound fellowship of Arthur, Guyon, and Britomart dissolves immediately. Arthur and Guyon, "Full of great envie and fell gealousy," rush off after the fleeing Florimel "in hope to win thereby / Most goodly meede, the fairest Dame alive" (III.i.18.2, 7–8). These comically mixed motives, chivalry coexisting with half-perceived lust, separate the men from Britomart, "whose constant mind, / Would not so lightly follow beauties chace" (III.i.19.1–2), and treats Arthur, idealized heretofore, as another male on the prowl.

A different kind of deflection characterizes Marinell, who avoids the love he fears will end his life. He appears at first a powerfully aggressive knight, and Britomart instinctively responds to him with anger. (In his fearful chastity he embodies her worst fear in searching for Artegal—that he will not return her love.) But when Britomart wounds him, the simile of an ox being brought to ritual slaughter (III.iv.17) suggests his inner nature—passively huge and finally helpless. His situation—living on the shore bordering his mother's oceanic world—suggests that he cannot leave that protective mother and his childhood to become a mature self. A life of continual avoidance is, as the narrator comments, "too too hard for living clay, / From love in course of nature to refraine" (III.iv.26.3–4). In love's place he chooses the safe, sterile riches that the sea gives him—riches that Britomart scorns (III.iv.18).

The fourth canto, with its attention to Britomart, Marinell, and Arthur, is a bleak one, elaborating a mood of helpless frustration. As several critics have pointed out, the canto develops three complaints about the world's blind instability.[40] The first is that of Britomart, who, alone after parting with Redcrosse, lapses into melancholy brooding. Her lament (III.iv.8–10) reworks Rime 189 of Petrarch's *Canzoniere,* in which Love appears allegorically as a blind voyage over a rough and dreary sea. Britomart's version makes Love her "lewd Pilot" and Fortune her Boatswain, both being "bold and blind" (III.iv.9.6–9). Despite Merlin's prophecies, she sees herself going nowhere; the grand overviews of epic rarely have a lasting effect on their recipients. The book ends with Arthur, who, having been frustrated by nightfall in his pursuit of Florimel, cannot sleep and imagines night as the nurse of all the world's woes. His complaint develops the insomniac's intense and burdened sense of a world gone wrong. Yet he prefaces the lament with an account of his blurred desire for Florimel and his Faerie Queene, throwing an ironic light on his impatient questioning of God's wisdom.

Between these two complaints comes the deeply felt lament of Marinell's mother Cymoent, who, having attempted to keep her son safe from the women she feared would wound him, finds that her efforts seem only to have brought about his death. Cymoent's perception goes deeper than that of others: recognizing her blindness in attempting to avert what was fated, she also sees her folly in keeping her son from love: "I feared love: but they that love do live, / But they that die do neither love nor hate" (III.iv.37.5–6). Each of these complaints pictures the world as unstable and tricky, if not purposeless, and voices doubt about the possibility of achievement.

One of the most interesting variations on the theme of chastity is that of Belphoebe's relation to Arthur's squire Timeas. In the letter to Ralegh, Spenser associates Belphoebe with the queen in her private person, and Spenser's treatment of her remains respectful. As another variation on the chaste Martial Maid, she differs strikingly from Britomart: if the latter combines Venus and Diana, Belphoebe follows Diana alone. Kathleen Williams has pointed to the way the elaborate, emblematic picture of her rose (III.v.51–55) contrasts with the simile of Britomart-as-rose in canto 1: unlike Britomart's hardy flower, Belphoebe's rose is delicate, hidden, and clearly associated with her virginity and its secrets.[41] Her sylvan enclosure (III.v.39), alone with her nymphs, recalls her foster mother Diana and limits her sphere of action. Yet Spenser insists that, unlike Marinell, who refuses to leave his place, she is truly chaste, faithful to her ideals: she creates not babies but noble deeds.

At the same time her relation to Timeas shows her in a comic light. She displays all the goodwill in the world in attempting to heal the young squire wounded by the lusty Forsters but naively fails to notice his love. Timeas, a parody of the self-abasing lover of Petrarchan tradition, cannot bring himself to speak to Belphoebe about his desire, while Belphoebe's inexperience leaves her utterly unable to understand his decline: the result is simple deadlock. In such a situation, love leads nowhere: Timeas abandons his duty to Prince Arthur, remaining in a static, frustrated posture of Petrarchan anguish. The passage suggests the silliness of a forever-unconsummated Petrarchan longing and comments also on Spenser's queen, Belphoebe's counterpart, who expected her favorites to play Petrarchan roles.[42]

The Garden of Adonis is the book's center, and it offers a response to the vision of blind helplessness voiced by the complaints of the fourth canto, and to the book's depiction of love as random violence. It is not the providential answer of Britomart's historical vision, but one based on a large sense of beneficent cycle—a cycle that, like the steady movement of *The Shepheardes Calender,* reassures with its promise of continuity and its celebration of the world's multiplicity. It is not a specifically Christian answer. The radical eschatology of the first book has no place here: Spenser has chosen to work with different materials.

The mode of the Garden canto separates it from the rest of the book. It is myth, set off from the rest of the narrative and retaining only a tangential connection with it. When Venus finds Amoret, the goddess takes her to the Garden, but the poem never attempts to imagine her—or any other individual—developing there. In interpolating a canto-long myth into his poem, Spenser again widens his epic's generic range to include philosophical and cosmological speculation in the traditions of Lucretius's *On the Nature of Things* or Palingenius's *Zodiac of Life.*

The Garden is largely neoplatonic in conception, although the mingling of Christian and neoplatonic thought in the Middle Ages and Renaissance blurs the boundaries between them. The Garden exists as a realm halfway between the pure and timeless Being of the Platonic One, which Christians identified with God, and our own world of Becoming.[43] As the "first seminarie / Of all things" (III.vi.30.4–5), it is the place of forms that instantiate themselves in matter—the "fleshly weeds" (III.vi.32.5) of bodies—to form the particular beings of our world. The conception of the Garden owes something to Plato's myth of Er, the realm to which those who die return for 1,000 years to be purified before venturing out into the world again, clothed in new bodies; the myth of Er was further developed as Plotinus's *rationes seminales,* or "seminal reasons."[44] The "thousand thousand naked babes" (III.vi.32.3) of the Garden venture through the golden gate, under the protection of the Genius—a Roman god of generation—and return eventually for replanting. Spenser's characteristic blending—or blurring—of neoplatonic and Christian traditions appears in the language that describes this seeding. A "first seminarie" suggests that the Garden is a place of species, not of individuals, and that they become individuals on being clothed in matter. Yet the language of "naked babes" desiring to enter the world insists on the notion of individual souls.

Spenser's discussion of time in the Garden—a place halfway between a timeless realm of being and an endless realm of becoming—attempts to reconcile these opposites. It seems at first as if Time has no part in the Garden, until halfway through his description the narrator calls Time a

"Great enimy" "to all . . . that in the *Gardin* of *Adonis* springs"
(III.vi.39.1–2). In what sense does Time exist in the Garden? The context of the preceding stanza (III.vi.38) suggests that Spenser here speaks
not about the Garden itself but about Time in the world of Becoming,
and that Venus's grief at the deaths of her "deare brood" (III.vi.40.4)
concerns their end in our world. But since the Garden exists to send
souls *into* this world, Time exists potentially there as well.

Spenser makes this potential presence clear by picturing the Garden as
a place containing *all* time, and in doing so he shifts his conception of it:

> There is continuall spring, and harvest there
>> Continuall, both meeting at one time:
>> For both the boughes doe laughing blossomes beare,
>> And with fresh colours decke the wanton Prime,
>> And eke attonce the heavy trees they clime,
>> Which seeme to labour under their fruits lode:
>>> (III.vi.42.1–6)

The Garden includes both spring and fall, and Spenser has quietly
changed Time's associations. For if Time withers, it also gives rise to
fresh individuals of all species, bringing them to fruition. Spenser's version of the myth stresses the goodness of the process itself: the one
unmistakable biblical reference occurs when the narrator mentions that
all things in the Garden "yet remember well the mightie word, / Which
first was spoken by th'Almightie lord, / That bad them to increase and
multiply" (III.vi.34.4–6). What saves the world from chaos is the
blessed variety of life itself, embodied in a recurrent and stable cycle of
generation.

Spenser's account does not possess the exactitude of philosophy but
moves instead into the area of myth, in which what is represented is
imaginatively felt as much as intellectually understood.[45] When the narrator says that he knows the Garden "by tryall" (III.vi.29.5), he seems to
speak of the act of intercourse itself; the Garden is, among other things,
an enclosed place like a womb. Its center is explicitly a "Mount of
Venus":

> Right in the middest of that Paradise,
>> There stood a stately Mount, on whose round top

> A gloomy grove of mirtle trees did rise,
> Whose shadie boughes sharpe steele did never lop,
> Nor wicked beasts their tender buds did crop,
> But like a girlond compassed the hight,
> And from their fruitfull sides sweet gum did drop,
> That all the ground with precious deaw bedight,
> Threw forth most dainty odours, & most sweet delight.
>
> (III.vi.43)

The tone is complex here, joyful praise moderated by awe. The Mount is not only sensuously erotic but "stately," and the myrtle trees form a gloomy grove. Natural pleasures in this place share in something hidden, august, removed from full knowledge. The Garden is fully *natural* in remaining beyond human artifice: it is a beneficent opposite to the Bower of Bliss.

These stanzas create an impression of trespassing on sacred territory, which appears as well in the narrator's ambivalent treatment of chaos:

> For in the wide wombe of the world there lyes,
> In hatefull darkenesse and in deepe horrore,
> An huge eternall *Chaos,* which supplyes
> The substances of natures fruitfull progenyes.
>
> (III.vi.36.6–9)

Here chaos seems frightening—"hatefull darknesse"—yet it is also necessary to "natures fruitfull progenyes." The image of chaos as a womb throws into relief the maleness of the narrator, who sees this female realm as at once dangerous and beneficent.[46] This complex mixture of joy and fear also appears in the treatment of the myth of Venus and Adonis. Unlike the sensual, sentimentalized version of the myth in Malecasta's castle, the two figures here embody in themselves the dialogue of Form and Matter that the Garden as a whole has depicted. Adonis's mortality is a continual metamorphosis. He is "transformed oft, and changed diverslie" (III.vi.47.7) as Form fails to impose itself permanently on Matter. Spenser's language leaves it unclear whether Adonis is Form (as traditional iconography had it) or Matter (as the syntax of the passage suggests); the blurring stresses the interdependence of both. Beneath the Mount is the womblike Cave, which imprisons the boar that will take Adonis's life: like chaos, which is both terrible and fruitful, the womb of the mountain is a source of both life and its dissolution.

After the Garden's calm insistence on the goodness of generation, the second half of the book seems to dissolve into erotic chaos. As critics have pointed out, Arthur does not appear in the eighth canto here, as he has in books 1 and 2, to give the plot a new, regenerative direction. Whereas women tend to dominate in the first half of the book, men dominate in the second, and there is a new stress on rape and seduction. The interlacing of romance plots grows more insistent, and the plots themselves less resolved. Most of the characters of the first half of the book fail to reappear in the second; Spenser creates a multiplicity of new characters, many of them embodied emblems, like the Hyena who chases Florimel, or the giantess Argante, who appears bearing the Squire of Dames.

Florimel is Marinell's love, and she embodies contradictory qualities: an overmastering fear, imaged in the picture of her horse running uncontrollably away, and a constancy that has caused her to search for Marinell in the first place. The fear is more evident. Florimel's name suggests "flower-honey," and she seems irresistibly and unwillingly attractive. Her brief appearance in canto 1 ruptures the fellowship of Britomart, Guyon, and Arthur, suggesting that eros not only creates human bonds but destroys them. Her tendency to run away only increases her attractiveness. Invariably attracting pursuers, she flees through the book—from the Forster, from Arthur, from the Witch and her Son, from the Hyena—and she continues to flee until trapped in the Fisherman's skiff.

Her temporary stay with the Witch and her oafish Son parodies the *topos* of the *intermezzo*: the hero or heroine's recuperation with good country folk. The Son is struck by Florimel's beauty, and his worship of her recalls, comically, Timeas's worship of Belphoebe. But whereas Timeas's love arrests his passage toward knighthood only temporarily, the Witch's Son is a native of the woods whose sloth (III.vii.12) precludes his ever leaving them. Stasis, here as elsewhere in Spenser, is degrading. When Florimel runs away, the revengeful Witch sends the Hyena after her. While the Hyena's meaning is enigmatic[47]—it seems most likely an image of lust as devouring appetite—its ferocity is undeniable, and it forces Florimel to abandon her horse and commit herself to the sea in the old Fisherman's boat. There, in a scene at once pathetic and comic, she finds that she must face first a rapist and then a god. Yet if Marinell's easy fall suggests an inner weakness behind his powerful exterior, Florimel's initial impression of fragile beauty is belied by her constancy under pressure. Proteus's metamorphoses present Florimel with the worldly vicissitudes that might tempt a heroine to give up her love, but she displays a loyalty that Marinell has still to learn.

Against Florimel, defining her chastity by contrast, is the False Florimel created by the Witch for her Son. She is, quite literally, a figure of fantasy. The Witch fashions her out of the materials used for traditional comparison in Petrarchan love poetry—eyes like lamps, hair like golden wire, skin white as snow. The False Florimel behaves like a sonnet lady too, remaining beautiful but unattainable. She wishes not, however, for chastity but for power. Spenser gives the spirit who inhabits the False Florimel a male pronoun (III.viii.8–9), perhaps suggesting that the spirit is a contradictory male fantasy, the pinup exterior concealing an animating spirit of nasty calculation. The idealized figure of Petrarchan rhetoric contrasts with the suspicion that all these chaste graces simply serve a vicious manipulativeness. (A similar opposition appears in Ralegh's brilliant lyric "Nature, That Washed her Hands in Milk.") The False Florimel teases the Witch's Son for a while, entertaining him "with shadowes" (III.viii.10.8), only to pass easily into the possession of Braggadocio, and from thence into the possession of a "stranger knight." The comic smoothness of her transition from one lover to the next, and her capacity to make them all think themselves "in heaven, that [were] in hell" (III.viii.19.9), contrasts with Florimel's awkward constancy.

The False Florimel typifies the later cantos' exploration of sex and power, the association of love with war. Against the romance melodrama of Florimel's mishap in cantos 7–8 Spenser sets the predatory yet hapless male trio of Satyrane, the Squire of Dames, and Paridell. Satyrane, who has been left fighting Sans Loy in book 1, reappears as the noblest of the three, but his arms of "rugged steele unfilde" (III.vii.30.4) suggest a still inadequate moral education. He means well, and his binding of the Hyena with Florimel's girdle appears to be an emblem of restraining lust with chastity, but his lust will not stay restrained forever. He no sooner attempts to do battle with Argante— herself an image of unrestrained female lust—than he loses the battle: presumably a willing lady leaves him "unable to withstand, / Or helpe himselfe" (III.vii.43.3–4). When Argante releases him to flee from the female warrior Palladine, Satyrane finds that the newly tamed beast has escaped.

The Squire of Dames first turns up as Argante's helpless captive; when Satyrane unbinds him, he is covered in mud, an emblem of his moral state. He appears to be the victim of his own seductions. His initial quest to seduce as many women as possible is ordained by his mistress, Columbell; the parody of the romance quest here shows the lady attempting to participate in her lover's male power, making it hers. Yet when the Squire returns to his mistress with the pledges of 300 women, Columbell devises a "punishment" for his successful seductions by sending him on a quest to find an equal number who will refuse him. The central concern of the episode is not with sex but with power—the power exercised by Columbell over both the Squire and his victims. The seductions here, as elsewhere in the book, go nowhere. The locker-room atmosphere of the exchange between Satyrane and the Squire of Dames (cf. III.vii.56–58) dramatizes how easily Satyrane's untrained chivalry degenerates into easy cynicism. Ideals require training.

The third member of the men's club is Paridell, whose shield, with its burning heart, proclaims his vocation as a seducer. In Paridell seduction has been reduced to a habit, a set of programmed responses. When in canto 9 he and Hellenore exchange darts—glances—of lust, Hellenore's arrow passes into his heart but produces "No paine at all: for he so oft had tryde / The powre thereof, and lov'd so ofte in vaine, / That thing of course he counted, love to entertaine" (III.ix.29.7–9). Paridell's seduction of Hellenore parodies Paris's original rape of Helen, and the fall of Troy reappears in the burning of the castle; the meaning of the parody lies partly in the sense that for Paridell everything is repetition. The search for pleasure alone yields nothing new.

In this reenactment Malbecco plays the part of Menelaus, Helen's husband; the account of his obsession and his metamorphosis is one of Spenser's most brilliant achievements. The epic again widens its generic range, reworking the familiar fabliau-plot about an old cuckold and his young wife to explore the crippling nature of jealousy, which turns "love divine / To joylesse dread" (III.xi.1.5–6). Malbecco uses Hellenore and his gold to shore up an inadequate sense of self: in possessing both he is *someone.* Yet his possession is shadowed by fear that he will lose them: his "privie guilt" over his inability to perform sexually (III.ix.3–5) causes him to suspect his wife. The irony of Malbecco's efforts lies in their self-destructiveness: his attempts to lock up Hellenore make her wish to change her lover, while his urge to hide his gold enables Braggadocio to steal it. Despite their obvious differences, he recalls Marinell, another inadequate self haunted by a sense of personal vulnerability. Marinell's false chastity and Malbecco's possessive fidelity both derive from fear, and both figures cling to a state of stasis, refusing to venture beyond their self-imposed boundaries. Spenser's treatment of Malbecco after Hellenore has refused to return with him develops his own version of an Ovidian metamorphosis. Malbecco's obsession shrinks him to an inhuman simplification, jealousy itself, a creature hiding in a cave, plagued with self-hatred and "continuall feare" (III.x.58.3).

Hellenore comes out better than her predecessor: seduced and abandoned by Paridell, she finds a new and satisfying home with the Satyrs. While she seems to have moved down the scale of being—the lady of a castle has become the plaything of half-human creatures—she has risen in one respect. The Satyrs treat her as a sentient being, not as another golden object, and she rightly refuses to return to Malbecco's castle. Hellenore's ending is not particularly edifying, but more of her is engaged in her new home than in her old.

Paridell, Malbecco, and Hellenore all contrast with Britomart in their isolation from the world of history. Britomart reappears in the ninth canto and soon after knocks Paridell off his horse: her victory is most obviously the triumph of Chastity over Seduction, but more interestingly, the epic pits her version of the Trojan War against his. Both are its heirs: Britomart's line derives from Aeneas, as Paridell's does from Paris, but their descents differ significantly. In Spenser's version of the myth, Paris's offspring retreat to the island of Paros, where they stay safely unconnected with the rest of the world during the time when Britomart's ancestors are struggling to gain a bloody toehold in Britain. The similarity of names in the line—Paris, Parias, Paridas, Paridell—suggests a world without change, static and self-involved.

By contrast, Britomart's ancestors have moved from Troy to Alba, from Alba to Rome, and from Rome to England in a restless endeavor to found a new Troy. They have exposed themselves to the danger and suffering implicit in mortal endeavor, and as a consequence, Britomart looks forward to the glory of Troynouvant. The two give very different accounts of the fall of Troy itself. For Britomart it was an instance of worldly mutability, a "lamentable fall of famous towne, / Which raignd so many years victorious" (III.ix.39.2–3). By contrast, Paridell sees it as a particularly spectacular romance in which Paris, "Most famous Worthy of the world" (III.ix.34.1), gained the most famous lady and created a war that caused the deaths of "noble warrioures / Whose fruitlesse lives were under furrow sowne" (III.ix.35.7–8). For Paridell the fruitless deaths glorify Paris; for Britomart the war is an instance of tragic mutability.

Britomart's greatest challenge comes, however, in the next cantos, when she faces the work of Busyrane, whose seductions aim at the mind rather than at the body. Busyrane is, according to the narrative, a wicked enchanter who holds Amoret captive, tormenting her in a vain attempt to gain her love. That he is more appears in the extraordinary attention Spenser gives to his castle, which embodies a distinct view of the world and of love—a view radically different from that implied in the Garden of Adonis.[48] Like Acrasia, whose garden ends book 2, Busyrane is an artist, and in the tapestries of the first room, the sculpture of the second, and the masque of the third, his representation of love stresses very largely its associations with power and pain. Spenser repeatedly stresses the lifelikeness of Busyrane's art (III.ix.35.32, 34, 41), and his praise suggests how dangerous such art can be: its very vitality captures the imagination, persuading the viewer of its truth.

The tapestries Spenser details in canto 11 present a gleaming assortment of stories from Ovid, all treating love in terms of its associations with pain, rape, manipulation. In a few, like the treatment of Leda (III.xi.32), it is unclear who is manipulating whom, god or woman, but in all of them the principles appear driven by the sadistic Cupid, whose statue Britomart sees in the second room, a deity who makes both gods and mortals his victims. Love appears to be the effect of chance: Cupid shoots his arrows "at randon, when him list" (III.xi.48.3), and the sense of providential history that Britomart has come to recognize as guiding her wandering remains absent. Love's capacity not to inspire but to deform appears in the physical transformations the gods undergo and reappears in the second room, where the poem gives a generalized impression of unstable and lying appearances. "A thousand monstrous formes therein were made, / Such as false love doth ofte upon him weare, / For love in thousand monstrous formes doth oft appeare" (III.xi.51.7–9).

If the tapestries are largely classical and Ovidian, the masque of the third room develops out of a tradition of medieval love poetry. It presents the course of a particular love from initial idleness (which medieval love poetry often prescribes as necessary for true loving) through infatuation to tormenting grief and shame and *"Death* with infamie" (III.xii.25.9). What is crucial here is the sense of an inexorable progress, a movement as sterile and deforming psychologically as the previous Ovidian images have been deforming physically. It is not that Busyrane's view of love lacks foundation: as Kathleen Williams said long ago, it builds on the element of hostility always present in sexual relations (109). But it makes that hostility central and unmixed with other feeling and leaves out the possibility of loving fruition, just as in book 1 Despair omits the possibility of Grace.

If the narrative presents Busyrane as an artist working *through* Amoret's imagination, the allegory suggests that he *is* her imagination, conditioned by 2,000 years of literature in which love appears to lead only to misery. As Thomas Roche has pointed out, Spenser's description of the masque's characters links them with Amoret's fears of what may happen to her:[49]

> There were full many moe like maladies,
>> Whose names and natures I note readen well;
>> So many moe, as there be phantasies
>> In wavering wemens wit, that none can tell,
>> Or paines in love, or punishments in hell. (III.xii.26.1–5)

The center of the procession, the captive Amoret with her heart cut out, pierced with Cupid's dart and bleeding in a basin, suggests brilliantly the woman's separation from her own emotional center. Amoret's fear leaves her painfully paralyzed, unwilling to give up her love and unable to follow it.

Busyrane's connection with Amoret appears most clearly in Britomart's inability to kill him without simultaneously killing her: Busyrane forms a part of Amoret that she cannot do without. He must undo his enchantments for Amoret to be freed. The actions suggest a liberation of the imagination, a recognition of what sexuality can mean (DeNeef, 14–18; Quilligan, 197–99). It is signaled by a change in the emblem of the pierced heart:

> The cruell steele, which thrild her dying hart,
>> Fell softly forth, as of his owne accord,
>> And the wyde wound, which lately did dispart
>> Her bleeding brest, and riven bowels gor'd,
>> Was closed up, as it had not bene bor'd,
>> And every part to safety full sound,
>> As she were never hurt, was soone restored
>> Tho when she felt her selfe to be unbound,
> And perfect hole, prostrate she fell unto the ground.
>> (III.xii.38.1–9)

The original image of the heart on the platter is an emblem, stylized, allegorical, vivid with meaning. In this stanza, by contrast, the image is more obviously sexualized, more anatomical, and—surprisingly—more joyful. The dart falling softly forth ceases to be a weapon, and the wound "closed up" is no longer a wound. Amoret becomes "perfect hole" because she sees love differently.[50] Busyrane has, so to speak, been reeducated.

Britomart shares a good deal with Amoret. Like her, she has been wounded by love, and her Ovidian fantasies about the meaning of her experience in the second canto look toward Busyrane's tapestry. Spenser stresses that she is fascinated with the Ovidian pictures and statues (III.xi.49–50, 54; III.xii.5, 29), and her puzzling over the cryptic direction "be bold, be bold, be not too bold" develops her own uncertainty about the proper relation between prudence and aggression. Yet she is also dedicated to an understanding of love that goes beyond Busyrane's, one with historical roots and meaning, one linked with a royal destiny. Unlike Amoret, she is able to act, and she acts in a way impossible for Amoret's lover Scudamour. Scudamour's "greedy will" (III.xi.26.3) makes his wish to free Amoret simultaneously a wish to possess her; accordingly, he cannot cross the moat whose flames image the desire burning within him. Britomart's aiding Amoret, by contrast, is a sisterly act, untainted by the desire to possess, and her freeing Amoret seems obscurely linked with a self-liberation from the fears Busyrane represents.

Yet for all Britomart's success, book 3 ends unresolved. Scudamour and Amoret embrace one another passionately—so passionately indeed as to leave one uncertain whether the hermaphroditic mingling of selves is an ideal or a short circuit in which necessary boundaries between individuals are lost.[51] Britomart appears uncertain, watching the lovers and half envying (original ending, III.xii.56.6) the bliss she sees before her. Her half-envy is partly desire for the complete loss of self that the two lovers display, and partly an awareness that her own destiny marks her out for something greater and more difficult.

The knights of the first two books of *The Faerie Queene* complete their quests, but here for the first time Spenser leaves his hero with her quest unfinished. Too much material may have suggested itself to Spenser for him to confine it within a single book (book 4 on Friendship, which Spenser would publish in 1596, is often read as the other "half" of book 3, and the story of Britomart and Artegal continues through book 5). But there may be a second reason for the lack of closure. The endings of books 1 and 2 are already tentative: Redcrosse must serve Gloriana

before returning to marry Una, and in the final stanzas of book 2 Guyon
is confronted with Grill, who does not *want* to become a man again. In
telling Guyon to "Let *Grill* be *Grill,* and have his hoggish mind"
(II.xii.87.8), the Palmer acknowledges an inability to change fallen
human nature. Spenser's emphasis on the inconclusive grew steadily
while he worked on *The Faerie Queene*. In a mutable world all expectation
of a happy ending must face Arthur's comment that "Nothing is sure,
that growes on earthly ground" (I.ix.11.5), and so Spenser defers the
happy ending of the Britomart story until the next book—and then
ultimately to books that he never wrote.

# Chapter Four
# 1591: The *Complaints*

William Ponsonby entered Spenser's *Complaints. Containing sundrie Small Poems of the World's Vanitie* in the Stationers' Register on 29 December 1590, more than a year after the first installment of *The Faerie Queene*. The volume gathers together poems and translations, some recent, some originating in Spenser's student days. The degree of his involvement in their publication remains unclear. Brink has argued that we should believe Ponsonby when he asserts in his letter to the reader that the book was his own doing (1991, 160–62). The success of *The Faerie Queene*, he says, has caused him to assemble "such smale Poemes of the same Authors; as I heard were disperst abroad in sundrie hands, and not easie to bee come by, by himselfe; some of them having bene diverlie imbeziled and purloyned from him, since his departure over Sea."[1] But printers commonly claimed responsibility for publishing works their authors did not wish to acknowledge, and some evidence suggests that Spenser worked on the book himself. A few changes made while it was in press look like authorial corrections, and he prefaced the four sections of the volume with special dedications to Mary Sidney, Countess of Pembroke, and the three daughters of Sir John Spencer of Althorp, with whom he claimed kinship.[2]

The *Complaints* appeared when Spenser had been waiting more than a year for Elizabeth's reward for his epic, and at least one powerfully angry passage in *Mother Hubberds Tale* (891–914) seems to owe something to his unhappiness as a suitor at court. His aspirations may have been blocked by William Cecil, Lord Burleigh: the only certain political satire in *Mother Hubberds Tale* is an attack on Burleigh under the guise of the Fox (1137–1204). This attack—and possibly others we cannot be sure about—landed Spenser in some trouble. Gabriel Harvey commented in 1592 that "Mother Hubberd in the heat of chollar, forgetting the pure sanguine of her sweete Feary Queene, wilfully over-shott her malcontented selfe," and Nashe in reply confirmed that the poem had kindled "sparkes of displeasure" (quoted in Stein, 81, 82). Other references indicate that the *Complaints* volume was "called in"—that is, unsold copies were impounded by the government (Stein, 84–86). It was not reprinted in Spenser's lifetime, and when his first *Collected Works* was published in 1611, *Mother Hubberds Tale* was omitted, probably for fear of Burleigh's son Robert Cecil, who had succeeded his father as lord chancellor. Copies of *Mother Hubberds Tale* were printed after Cecil's death, and the poem was included in the second *Works* of 1617.

Whoever arranged the volume, its title announces that the poems share a common medievalizing Spenserian mode. The medieval complaint is an umbrella term embracing different forms:[3] it encompasses the laments of forsaken lovers, the religious lyrics in which Christ and Mary lament their sufferings, and a quasi-philosophical genre, the account of the world's fallen condition lamenting man's sinfulness or helplessness. The opening stanza of Chaucer's "Lak of Stedfastnesse" strikes the characteristic tone of the complaint:

> Somtyme the world was so stedfast and stable
> That mannes word was obligacioun,
> And now it is so fals and deceivable
> That word and deed, as in conclusioun,
> Ben nothing lyk, for turned up-so-doun
> Is al this world for mede and wilfulnesse,
> That al is lost for lak of stedfastnesse.[4]

The large generality of Chaucer's vision is typical of a mode given to attacking not individuals but the condition of the world. The complaint thus includes the visionary inquiry into the nature of the human condition that the epic performs in other periods. It was also the vehicle for attacks on social and religious abuses. As Ronald Bond has commented, the tone of the genre spans the spectrum between elegy and satire: stress on the world's wretchedness makes for lament; stress on its sinfulness makes for criticism (*YESP,* 218).

While in the Renaissance a complaint is usually the lament of a lover, the form does not lose its potential for large indictment of the fallen world: Erasmus wrote a *Complaint of Peace* (1516). For Spenser the form's visionary potential and its concern with man's errant condition on earth make it almost as central as pastoral. Complaints appear in the laments of the *Theatre for Worldlings* and the moral eclogues of *The Shepheardes Calender,* and they open and close the *Mutabilitie Cantos,* his last published poem. The *Complaints,* written in midcareer, excludes the love complaint—this is the only book of Spenser's in which sexual love does not figure—and develops the philosophical potential of the mode. While some are lyric and some narrative, all the poems treat earthly "vanitie"—life's emptiness, its uncertainty, its transience. They survey the world to expose its limits.

The emphasis on limitation makes for gloomy reading, and portions of the *Complaints* seem an aggregation of wheezy commonplaces about the world's evils. But despite their variation in quality, the poems are never simply gatherings of clichés. They dramatize human responses to the world's vanity. Occasionally, as in the *Visions* sonnets, Spenser engages in comparatively uncomplicated moralizing, but even these three sequences have different emphases, so that the group moves, in Jan van Dorsten's phrase, "from moral advice to eschatological meditation."[5] Some speakers, like Verlame in *The Ruines of Time,* respond with despair; others, like that poem's narrator, come eventually to place this world's ruins in the context of the next world's rejoicing. Still other figures, like the Fox and the Ape in *Mother Hubberds Tale,* find life's instability a source of opportunity: the change governing their world enables them to abandon their "natural" places for better ones. Indeed, to justify his present-day thievery, the Fox recalls the cliché of a lost golden age in which there was supposedly community of goods (136–53).

In the *Complaints* we can see Spenser experimenting with various voices. One hallmark of his later work is his complex dramatization of the speaker's thinking, and in this book he treats his narrative voices in strikingly different ways. The narrator of *Visions of the Worlds Vanitie* and the primary speaker of *The Ruines of Time* are comparatively simple figures, reductions of the human personality to a visionary eye. They recall the narrator of Du Bellay's *Songe,* translated in the volume as *Visions of Bellay,* while Verlame is a kind of homage to Du Bellay's Roman Genius in *Les Antiquités de Rome* (1558). Although the voices of *The Teares of the Muses* embody Renaissance humanist learning, they also recall the authoritative speakers of medieval complaint. The narrator of *Muiopotmos* derives ultimately from a playful, garrulous Ovidian prototype. In *Mother Hubberds Tale,* as Kent Van den Berg has pointed out, a literate man revises an oral tale and finds himself at times swept away by his own narrative.[6] A surprising number of the other poems also include at least token appearances by a second voice—*The Ruines of Time, The Teares of the Muses,* and *The Ruines of Rome.*

The inclusion of translated poems by Du Bellay, Petrarch, and (so Spenser thought) Virgil in the volume intensifies the impression of competing voices. Humanists often speak of translation as a patriotic act, importing the riches of another literature into one's own culture.[7] Spenser here brings his great progenitors into dialogue with his own work. Du Bellay's *Ruines of Rome,* which meditates on the city's greatness and its loss, is a particularly important sequence for Spenser; the French poet is a pervasive influence on all the lyric sections of the *Complaints.* The volume might be seen as Spenser's response to his great French predecessor, and his attempt to assimilate Du Bellay's vision into his own deeply Protestant view. As in *The Shepheardes Calender,* Spenser's translations make the *Complaints* into a European volume, incorporating past voices in a renewed argument.

This foregrounding of past poetry is one aspect of the book's concern with art. It is a Renaissance commonplace that art opposes fallen time by creating the immortality of poetic fame and by teaching human beings how to rise above their fallen state. Spenser's first volume, *The Shepheardes Calender,* looks skeptically at these claims and concerns itself largely with how the poets of the book come to fail. The *Complaints* volume is often equally skeptical as it focuses on art as the guardian of fame. The account in *The Ruines of Time* of the immortality poets grant (393–406) sounds out as triumphantly as anything in Spenser's work, but it is countered by the gloomy frustration in *The Teares of the Muses,* whose choric speakers lament the world's neglect of learning and the victory of ignorance and oblivion. The book also displays an emphasis (apparent already in *The Faerie Queene*) on the amorality of the imagination. The artists of the two most arresting poems in the volume are its villains—the Spider of *Muiopotmos* and the Fox and the Ape in *Mother Hubberds Tale,* who manipulate fame for their own corrupt ends.

In several ways the volume recalls the first installment of *The Faerie Queene.* Like the epic, the *Complaints* deals with large stretches of time and space and defines the limits (though not the powers) of human beings and human civilizations. It also engages in frequent epic parody. The parody is worth remarking because it is more than mockery: while the book treats its animals and insects with epic formulas, the death that comes to them comes to us as well. Their vulnerability images ours. The poems touch as well on the epic concern that Thomas Greene has called "cosmic politics"—the relation between human events and divine agency (406). Divine justice is at issue in the small cosmos of *Muiopotmos* and recurs in *The Ruines of Time, Prosopopoia,* and the translations of *Virgils Gnat* and *The Ruines of Rome.*

Yet the *Complaints* differs importantly from the epic. The lyric emphasis of the volume stresses suffering over action, meditation on the world's vanities over heroic effort. Two out of its three narratives, *Virgils Gnat* and *Muiopotmos,* have so little action that plot is swallowed by description or lament, and the indefatigable protagonists of the third, *Mother Hubberds Tale,* end where they started. The volume's bleak account of human vanity has ironic implications for the epic's praises. While *The Faerie Queene* shows Spenser fulfilling the promise made by *The Shepheardes Calender* to follow the Virgilian pattern and become England's epic poet, the *Complaints* offers a less optimistic view of her potential greatness.[8] If the world's goods are all ultimately vanity, doomed to fail, then the English commonwealth may fail too.

Like *The Shepheardes Calender,* the *Complaints* experiments with verse forms, including two variations on the sonnet, Surrey's version (*ababcdcdefefgg*) for translations, and Spenser's own (*ababbcbccdcdee*) in most of the original sonnets. The pentameter couplets ("ryding rime," as Gasgoigne calls it) of *Prosopopoia* seem chosen for their association with Chaucerian satire, while *Muiopotmos* and *Virgils Gnat* adopt the ottava rima of Italian narrative poetry. Spenser would never use either again. Sometimes the verse has a numerological significance. *The Teares of the Muses* is composed of 100 six-line stanzas, the perfect number of stanzas somewhat compromised by the number six, which is associated with this world. On the other hand, the seven-line rhyme royal of *The Ruines of Time* plays with a pattern of six-against-seven. The secular first section of the poem is composed of seventy stanzas, which Richard Schell associates with the seventy years the Jews were to be enslaved by Babylon (*YESP,* 229). On the other hand, the second set of visions is composed of two groups of six visions each followed by a final Christian envoy. In William Nelson's words, "Six are the days of this mutable world; on the seventh God rests and change ceases" (69).[9] This pattern recurs at the end of the volume, where the six sonnets of *The Visions of Petrarch,* with their secular grief, are succeeded by a final sonnet calling for rest in God.

## The Ruines of Time

In *The Ruines of Time* Spenser tries to join two quite distinct topics. The poem, he says in his dedication to Mary Sidney, Countess of Pembroke, is "*intituled by the generall name of the* worlds Ruines: *yet speciallie intended to the renowming of that noble race, from which both you and he* [Sir Philip Sidney] *sprong, and to the eternizing of some of the chiefe of them late deceased*" (230–31). The poem pairs the concern with time and decay announced

by the "generall name" with the "special" poetic task of glorifying the
Dudley family, which included Spenser's then-deceased early patron the
earl of Leicester as well as Sir Philip Sidney and his sister Mary. Spenser
wrote surprisingly few eulogies for a Renaissance poet, and he usually
made them part of larger symbolic statements. In this case poetic fame
is not only what the poem gives but what it examines as it considers
responses to the world's ruins. If the result is not fully integrated—the
strain between topics makes the poem disjointed enough for Renwick to
hypothesize that it was "written in fragments and pieced together in
haste"[10]—it still articulates brilliantly the contrasts between the different conceptions of art and different visions of the world that the following poems also develop.

The poem divides into two contrasting visions. In the first (1–476)
the narrator sees the spirit of the Roman British city of Verulamium and
hears her complain of her ruined condition. The lament of Verlame—
Spenser's shortened form of the name—is largely secular and tragic:
only the "moniment" of the poet's or the antiquary's record partly
redeems the ruins of time. In the second section (477–686) the narrator
envisions emblems of transience and transcendence through which
death leads to divine reward. The Christian emphasis of this second section thus extends and corrects the largely secular vision of the first. Yet
this general structure is further complicated by the division of the long
first section into three contrasting parts, the initial appearance and
lament of Verlame (1–175), a central elegiac praise of the Dudleys and
their relations (176–343), and a praise of poetry as a fame-giver
(344–476).

Verlame dominates the first section. A female figure, "sorrowfullie
wailing, / Rending her yeolow locks, like wyrie golde" (9–10), she
recalls the Genius of Rome who appears in the tenth sonnet of the
*Visions of Bellay,* which will appear later in the *Complaints.*

> Hard by a rivers side a virgin faire,
> Folding her armes to heaven with thousand throbs,
> And outraging her cheekes and golden haire,
> To falling rivers sound thus tun'd her sobs.
>   Where is (quoth she) this whilom honoured face?
> Where the great glorie and the auncient praise,
> In which all worlds felicitie had place,
> When Gods and men my honour up did raise? (*VB,* 127–34)

Verlame's appearance, actions, and questions echo those of Du Bellay's Rome, and a couplet addressed to Rome insists on the connection. "And of the whole world as thou wast the Empresse, / So I of this small North-erne world was Princesse" (83–84). The lines make her the English equivalent of the Roman glory and Roman ruin that Du Bellay considers in *The Ruines of Rome* and *Visions of Bellay,* which appear later in the *Complaints.* Yet Verlame's Roman, secular associations are also Catholic ones. Her eminence as a city makes her one in a biblical succession of doomed, ungodly cities, the most recent of which, for English Protestants, was Rome itself. As Schell points out (*YESP,* 226), a crucial biblical text for the poem comes from Hebrews 13:14: "For here have we no continuing citie: but we seke one to come." Catholic religion, for Protestant critics, was ultimately pagan and idolatrous in its reliance on the things of this world and on human church tradition in the place of Scripture.

In her unrelieved despair, Verlame embodies a state of mind common to most fallen human beings, for whom the world's happiness is every-thing and its loss is unrelieved catastrophe. Her powerful complaint dominates the first section of the poem, yet its grieving extremity makes it suspect. She seems ignorant of Christian truth: her only reference to the gods is to accuse them of the envy that has brought about her mis-ery (24–25). Spenser uses her "pagan" complaint to dramatize a reac-tion common to believing Christians overwhelmed with sorrow, and to suggest its inadequacy. The impulse to complain—to wish for a differ-ent lot—must ultimately yield to Christian patience as one submits one-self to God's decrees. Here the genre of the complaint comes in for criti-cism as the voice of the world loved too much.

After Verlame's lament Spenser shifts from his general theme to his particular one, developing the eulogy of the Dudley family. Although Verlame remains the ostensible narrator of this part, her point of view effectively lapses for the next 250 lines. Christian references appear, and several times the speaker is not a city but a poet (e.g., 259, 306–16). The inconsistency seems to me a weakness in the poem, necessitated on the one hand by the large structural opposition of the two visions, and on the other by the need to include the material on the Dudleys. Yet Spenser also shapes this section to repeat the opposition of secular and Christian by contrasting the two extended portraits of the earl of Leices-ter and Sir Philip Sidney, which frame the other praises of the Dudley family. The elegy for the earl of Leicester reiterates in his life the large loss of Verlame: "He now is dead, and all his glorie gone, / And all his greatnes vapoured to nought" (218–19). Spenser stresses the instability of the earl's political career as he dies, deserted by the flatterers who haunted him during his prosperity. This is Verlame's experience in the terms of a particular life at the Elizabethan court. The poem links Sidney, by contrast, with divine reward: in dying, he returns to his "native place" in heaven and remains there, happier than he has been on earth (288–308). The praise of the family thus reworks the theme of earthly vanity and initiates the compensating idea of salvation.

While the function of literature in memorializing the dead appears first in relation to the antiquary William Camden, Spenser's praise of the Dudleys *dramatizes* the poet's role as fame-giver. He calls attention to his act of praising ("Nor may I let thy husbands sister die, / That goodly Ladie" [274–75]), and this demonstration leads into the first movement's final section, which celebrates the Muses as bestowers of a secular immortality.

> The seven fold yron gates of grislie Hell,
> And horrid house of sad *Proserpina,*
> They able are with power of mightie spell
> To breake, and thence the soules to bring awaie
> Out of dread darkenesse, to eternall day,
> And them immortall make, which els would die
> In foule forgetfulnesse, and nameles lie. (372–78)

The rhetoric here opposes the underworld of oblivion to the "eternall day" of poetic fame. The terms are classical, as are the later examples— Hercules, Castor and Pollux, Orpheus and Eurydice—suggesting the essentially secular nature of the immortality fame can give. But the stanza also recalls the Christian paradigm that it omits—the image of Christ's harrowing hell, bringing the souls of the virtuous Hebrews "Out of dread darknesse, to eternall day" (cf. *Amoretti,* 68). The language thus exalts poetry while reminding the reader of a larger immortality granted by faith.

When Verlame breaks off, the narrator remains in sorrowful astonishment, moved by her lament but uncertain of her "doubtfull speach" (485). The second part of the poem clarifies its meaning with two sets of six "tragicke Pageants" (490), which recall the *Visions of Bellay*: they are emblematic hieroglyphs, symbols enfolding divine truths. The first six visions—like Verlame's lament for herself, or the elegy for Leicester— emphasize the world's transience.

> I saw an Image, all of massie gold,
> Placed on high upon an Altare faire,
> That all, which did the same from farre beholde,
> Might worship it, and fall on lowest staire.
> Not that great Idoll might with this compaire,
> To which th'*Assyrian* tyrant would have made
> The holie brethren, falslie to have praid. (491–97)

The vision, like many in this section, conflates several references. The idol explicitly recalls that in the third chapter of the Book of Daniel (495–97), but it suggests also Phidias' statue of Zeus, one of the seven wonders of the ancient world. It is any image that absorbs and constricts earthly efforts to know the divine, and as such it is doomed to ruin. The subsequent emblems each demonstrate the world's fragility in various contexts—a tower, a garden, a giant statue, a bridge, two bears. Each falls to ruin: the speaker is left with the fact of transience, which is all that the unaided secular intelligence can know. The two bears that form the final vision stand apart from the other images, which are all human artifacts: since the emblem of the Dudleys was a bear, it may represent the earl and his brother, Ambrose. As such the bears' ruin contrasts with Sidney's triumph in the second set of emblems, as the Leicester-praise opposes that of Sidney in the Dudley section of the poem.

The speaker is caught between "feare and pitie" (579) at what he sees, until he is instructed by a new voice:

> Behold (said it) and by ensample see,
> That all is vanitie and griefe of minde,
> Ne other comfort in this world can be,
> But hope of heaven, and heart to God inclinde;
> For all the rest must needs be left behinde. (582–86)

The second set of visions focuses on Sidney as an example of Christian patience. In each case the death on earth leads to an image of translation and/or metamorphosis. The swan sings his death-song and wings to heaven, where he becomes a constellation; the harp similarly becomes a heavenly sign; the coffer (Sidney's coffin?) is transformed into a star. On the other hand, the virgin soul comes at the call of the bridegroom, the knight rides to the heavens, while Mercury bears the ark containing Sidney's ashes "above the skie" (668). Most of these images reemphasize the importance of poetry: the swan and the harp both suggest Sidney's capacity as a singer, the knight is mounted on Pegasus, and the Mercury who carries the ark to heaven is associated with eloquence. Yet the nature of the singing has changed: poetry is no longer a secular fame-giver but a divine music. The swan prophesies its own death; the harp gives rise to "most heavenly noyse" (612).

In the final stanzas to the "immortal spirit of Philisides" (Sidney) the narrator himself changes in his stance. He now acknowledges the verses as his own and addresses himself to the countess of Pembroke:

> And ye faire Ladie th'honor of your daies,
> And glorie of the world, your high thoughts scorne;
> Vouchsafe this moniment of his last praise,
> With some few silver dropping teares t'adorne:
> And as ye be of heavenlie off spring borne,
> So unto heaven let your high minde aspire,
> And loath this drosse of sinfull worlds desire. (680–86)

Here the narrator ceases to be simply a fame-giver and becomes a moralist, opposing the decaying world to divine reward.

## The Teares of the Muses

Despite its elegiac tone, *The Ruines of Time* affirms the poet's power to give fame and holds out hope of Christian immortality. By contrast, *The Teares of the Muses* portrays a cultural crisis in which the worth of poetry and of all true learning has been disregarded, and the human community has lost the moral guidance they provide. More directly than any of Spenser's other poems, it laments the absence of the patronage that should support poetry in the present age. *The Teares of the Muses* presents an embattled apology for learned poetry. Parts of it imitate Du Bellay's *La Musagnœmachie* (The Battle of the Muses, 1550), a humanist manifesto in which the forces of the new learning vanquish an old monster, Ignorance, associated with the "darkness" of the medieval past. Characteristically bold in reworking the French poem, Spenser reverses its plot: the Muses' thrones, placed "in th'hearts of men to rule them carefully" (314), have been usurped by Ignorance and her minions. Their tyranny leaves men prey to vanity, sloth, and degraded pleasure-seeking.

Melpomene comments: "he that is of reasons skill bereft, / And wants the staffe of wisedome him to stay, / Is like a ship in midst of tempest left, / Withouten helme or Pilot her to sway" (139–42; cf. 490–91).

The Renaissance Muses embody much more than forms of poetry.[11] They are a classical invention, goddesses associated with a wide range of physical and mental arts; collectively they sum up the civilized life of a culture. During the classical period and the Middle Ages the associations of particular Muses altered, and we are still unsure which Muse Spenser invokes at the opening of the first book of the Faerie Queene— Clio, Muse of history, or Calliope, Muse of epic poetry. But together the nine Muses embody the sum of human learning: beside Clio and Calliope, there are Melpomene, Muse of tragedy; Thalia, Muse of comedy; Euterpe, associated with the flute and hence with pastoral poetry; Terpsichore, Muse of the dance; Erato, associated with the lyre and hence with love poetry; Urania, Muse of astronomy and hence sacred verse; and Polyhymnia, Muse of rhetoric. History and astronomy would not now be associated with poetry any more than would dance, but for Spenser and his predecessors they are all disciplines that imitate the world's essential patterning. Astronomy introduces us to the perfect, mathematical clarities of the heavens, and dance is an earthly image of their orderly motion. By some humanist accounts at least, history records the noble examples of the past. Spenser's term for their collective activity is "learning," which furnishes the moral and intellectual bearings that enable human beings to direct their lives.

These bearings come partly from the self-knowledge the Muses afford. Urania comments that "By knowledge wee do learne our selves to knowe, / And what to man, and what to God wee owe" (503–4), and the different Muses suggest various ways in which this is true. Thalia says that comedy displays man's "likest image" (201), and Calliope argues that memorializing heroic deeds gives men incentive to act nobly (451–56). The Muses also provide *measure,* a term that includes not only proper poetic meter (547) but all instances of proper order in the world and in the human psyche. Erato, Muse of love poetry, rules "in measure moderate / The tempest of that stormie passion" (379–80); she teaches human beings how love leads the soul upward, becoming a spur to virtue, not an incentive to vice. Similarly, Melpomene argues that the misfortunes of tragedy prepare one to bear Fortune's changes "with constant patience" (133), cultivating a contempt for her uncertainty. This stress on measure recalls the poetic theories of *La Pléiade* in France, which attributed to the metrical patterning of verse and music a quasi-magical, calming, and inspiring effect on its audience—a kind of temperance.[12]

In addition, Spenser suggests that the Muses have a part in the perfecting of creation itself. The poem's introduction imagines the world mourning the plight of the Muses, as it would the death of a shepherd in a pastoral elegy, because their absence impoverishes what God has made:

> And all that els was wont to worke delight
> Through the divine infusion of their skill,
> And all that els seemd faire and fresh in sight,
> So made by nature for to serve their will,
> Was turned now to dismall heavinesse,
> Was turned now to dreadfull uglinesse. (37–42)

Nature (the power that carries out God's creation plans) makes all things to serve the Muses' will in the sense that human art provides their final shaping. Their divine "infusion" makes things display the ideal patterns with which they were originally stamped, patterns that have been blurred with the Fall. Without this infusion the world displays only "dreadfull uglinesse."

The poem's shape emphasizes the formal dignity of the Muses' complaint. After the introduction each lament presents the deterioration of the culture from a different perspective. While Erato points to the connections between bad love poetry and degraded lovemaking—a theme Spenser returns to briefly in *Prosopopoia*—Urania laments the loss of religious awareness that her own neglect has brought on, and as Muse of rhetoric, Polyhymnia launches the fullest attack on bad poetry. They employ a common high style with occasional variation: Erato ironically drops her language in calling on Venus: "Faire *Cytharee*, the Mother of delight, / And Queene of beautie, now thou mayst go pack" (397–98). Spenser further emphasizes the poem's formality by the ritualistic refrain-stanza at the end of each lament and by the numerology of the whole. The 100 six-line stanzas divide evenly between the nine Muses and the introduction—except that Euterpe's lament fills ten stanzas and the introduction takes eight. The disparity may imitate the breaking of the ideal pattern that the Muses lament.

The many good poets alive in 1590, as well as the "violent, noisy" style of *The Teares of the Muses,* has led Renwick and others to see the poem as an early work, composed before Spenser left for Ireland in 1580

(181–82). Yet an early date seems unnecessary. All the targets of attack and some of the language appears in *Colin Clouts Come Home Againe,* published in 1595 but written after Spenser's English sojourn of 1589–90. Spenser's taste is not ours. Most of the best English poets in 1590 were dramatists, and we do not know that he ever noticed the astonishing development of the popular theater. Indeed, *The Teares of the Muses* refers contemptuously in good humanist fashion to bad art's appeal to the "vulgar" or common citizen (194, 319, 365–68). The court poet he most admired, Sir Philip Sidney, had died in 1586, leaving no other major figure to take his place.

While this grim series of complaints is limited in its success, it is not the work of a poet bored by his task. Shrill and repetitive, its careful formality stems partly from an attempt to control feelings of angry frustration. It attacks the perversion of art and here as elsewhere associates bad art with the court. Thalia describes bad comedy:

> In stead [of good art] scoffing Scurrilitie,
> And scornfull Follie with Contempt is crept,
> Rolling in rymes of shameles ribaudrie
> Without regard, or due Decorum kept,
> Each idle wit at will presumes to make,
> And doth the Learneds taske upon him take. (211–16)

The invading personifications of Scurrilitie, Follie, Contempt, and Idle Wits all resemble courtiers who, sometimes arrogant, sometimes obsequious, engage in slander and shameless ribaldry "Without regard, or due Decorum kept." Elsewhere bad art is associated with "flattery," which is the *sine qua non* of the courtier's life. The angriest lines accuse Idle Wits of "presum[ing] to make" without acknowledging the skill and learning necessary for poetry. This is the voice of a poet who finds that his high aspirations for his art are not shared by the audience for whom it is intended. Good art, the Muses insist again and again, is attended with true pleasure—with "naturall delight" (552). But the court wishes only for entertainment—pleasure in the most reductive sense (cf. *Faerie Queene,* VI.xii.41). The stanzas praising Elizabeth with which the final lament ends seem to be the wishful thinking demanded by a thin-skinned queen. Spenser's sense of vocation was at risk, and so in disgust at the end of the poem the Muses all, like Colin Clout, break their instruments.

Spenser's formal experiment in speaking through the Muses has its costs. The monologues are static, and the violence Renwick complained of ends by creating an effect of dreary monotony. This kind of poem is easily ridiculed, and the repeated announcement of the next Muse "in rew" about to begin her complaint reminds one uncomfortably of pigeons on a branch. Most important, Spenser leaves no room for irony. Verlame, the principal voice of *The Ruines of Time,* is clearly limited in her understanding of events, and the poem's meaning lies in the opposition between her vision and the speaker's gradual enlightenment. Here, by contrast, Spenser imitates the structure of many medieval complaints in making the speaker an unassailable authority: the Muses, after all, embody learned tradition. In leaving no gap between his own view and that of his speakers, Spenser loses the possibility of ironic juxtaposition so central to his art. Taken straight, his Muses are hard to take seriously. Spenser may have recognized the unsatisfactoriness of the experiment: he would never again abandon his own voice for those of mythological figures, nor build a poem out of their repeated monologues.

## Virgils Gnat

The concern with patronage connects *The Teares of the Muses* with the first translation in the *Complaints, Virgils Gnat.* The obscure, unhappy sonnet to Leicester prefacing the poem suggests that Spenser felt that he had been undeservedly "wrong'd," either by or because of his patron. Although there has been much speculation about this wrong, we do not know enough to begin to establish its circumstances. The dedicatory poem must have been written before Leicester's death in 1588, and it may even date from Spenser's original move to Ireland. The final couplet makes it clear that the poet feels that he, like the gnat of the poem, has acted to help—perhaps to warn—Leicester and has been unjustly punished for his care. The dedication points obscurely to an instance of the willful blindness that the Muses lament.

*Virgils Gnat* is itself a teasing, curious, highly sophisticated work.[13] Attributed during the Renaissance to Virgil, it is more likely by Ovid or by one of Virgil's imitators. The story is small matter: when a gnat wakes a shepherd to save him from a snake, he is killed by the man he has benefited and returns as a ghost to reproach him in a dream. The narrator spins out this incident to almost 700 lines by invoking the world of heroic events that its limited pastoral plot supposedly excludes. As he returns from the dead, the gnat gives an account of the other inhabitants of the underworld and, through them, of the Trojan War and the history of Rome. The poem differs from the others translated in the *Complaints* in its easy playfulness. It proposes well-worn clichés only to undercut them: after insisting on the lack of danger in the shepherd's life, for instance, the poem shows the shepherd menaced by a snake. The distinction between pastoral and epic announced by the poem's opening is insistently blurred by what follows. The whole work is a tour de force, and Spenser's version also demonstrates his prowess. The translation into the ottava rima stanza of the Italian epic poets is on the whole faithful by Elizabethan standards (it expands considerably, especially in description), and Spenser's verse often displays masterly poetic skill.

> And the sweete waves of sounding *Castaly*
> With liquid foote doth slide downe easily. (23–24)

## *Prosopopoia, or Mother Hubberds Tale*

If the complaint form ranges between elegy and satire, *Prosopopoia* stands at the satiric extreme. The formal manner typical of the collection yields to the colloquial plainness that Renaissance critics saw as appropriate to satire: "Base is the style, and matter meane withall" (44). The stylistic informality also stems from Spenser's invocation of a Chaucerian model. Alone of Spenser's works, it employs the pentameter couplets that would recall the dominant verse form of *The Canterbury Tales,*[14] and it pretends, like them, to be the written version of an oral performance. Beginning with an astrological opening that recalls Chaucer or his contemporaries, the first three episodes focus on familiar targets of attack in medieval satire, the three estates of commons, clergy, and nobility. The beast fable looks back to Chaucer's "Nun's Priest's Tale," which itself reworks the verse tales of Renard the Fox composed in French and Dutch in the twelfth and thirteenth centuries.

The poem also differs from the other *Complaints* in its Chaucerian comic energy. Where most of the volume insists on the limits to worldly endeavor—limits imposed by mortal weakness, chance, and time—*Mother Hubberds Tale* dwells almost exuberantly on its rogues' sense of possibility. Although their plots invariably unravel, they return to the attack: each setback leads to a new attempt at metamorphosis. In addition to Chaucer and the cycles of Renard the Fox, *Mother Hubberds Tale* recalls the picaresque narrative of *Lazarillo de Tormes* (one of four books

Spenser gave Harvey in 1578), a narrative in which the protagonist moves from episode to episode with unbounded, amoral energy. Spenser takes more chances in *Mother Hubberds Tale* than he does in the rest of the *Complaints,* and the result is a richer and more deeply troubled poem.

The trouble develops out of the first term of the title. "Prosopopoia," as Van den Berg points out, can mean simply "personification"—for example, the attribution of human characteristics to animals—but in his *Arte of English Poesie* (1589) George Puttenham also calls it "counterfeit in personation"—that is, pretending to be what one is not.[15] Spenser uses the medieval genres of estate satire and beast fable to explore the characteristically Renaissance problem of self-fashioning.[16] Where estate satire, for instance, typically describes the vices of each group, Spenser's poem concerns itself primarily with individuals: it shows how the rogues *become* shepherds, clergymen, and courtiers, highlighting their capacity for self-transformation. The stress on counterfeiting also distinguishes Spenser's fable from the typical stories of Renard the Fox. The medieval Renard is a great nobleman whose burrow is also a castle; he presents his lion-king with the typically medieval problem of the nobleman who will not obey his titular lord. Spenser's protagonists, by contrast, are nobodies who recreate themselves in their various roles.

As such they pose the familiar Renaissance question about the limits of self-fashioning: how far can one determine one's nature by an effort of will? Pico della Mirandola's *Oration on the Dignity of Man* (1486) offers the most famous assertion of human possibility. For Pico, man has no innate nature: he is a Protean creature with the ability to choose his being, sinking to the level of the beasts or rising to that of the angels.[17] The social counterpart of this philosophical formulation appears in Castiglione's *The Book of the Courtier* (1561), which debates how far a man can shape himself to play a part at court. The Fox and Ape display—or parody—this metamorphic ability. They are quite literally beasts, but they gain positions of power by changing their speech and clothing. Their success points to injustices in the Elizabethan political and social system.

The world of the poem fits the rogues who inhabit it. As the poem's opening stresses, it is a fallen world full of "plague, pestilence and death" (8). In the eyes of the Fox and the Ape, it is also a world governed by chance or fortune—a cosmos with no moral structure. To prosper in such a world one must seize the main chance, shifting as conditions shift. As "sonnes of the world so wide" (135), the Fox and the Ape are supremely fitted to take advantage of this instability. Early in the

poem the Ape asks the Fox whether they should follow a particular
trade, and the Fox answers that they should tie themselves to neither
trade nor place nor lord: "For why should he that is at libertie / Make
himselfe bond"? (132–33). The bonds securing the social order here
oppose the "freedom" of a self without ties. Like Edmund in *King Lear*
(1608), the Fox will not "bind" himself to anything but his present self-
interest. The Fox and the Ape repeatedly see themselves as "free" (see
160, 161, 168), and their conception of freedom is Edmund's, an
absence of restrictions on appetite.

Against the two rogues the tale sets the narrator, a character partly
modeled on the intrusive narrators of Chaucer's fictions. As Van den
Berg has pointed out (86–87), the narrator calls attention to his own
part in creating the tale he has heard from Mother Hubberd when he
says that he will write it "in termes, as she the same did say, / So well as
I her words remember may" (41–42).[18] His account of her tale is thus
mediated by his memory, and he often breaks off the narrative with
digressive comment. Neither a fully independent character nor a simple
mouthpiece for Spenser's views, the narrator dramatizes an aspect of his
creator that the poem distances and examines. We learn a good deal
about him. Like many Chaucerian narrators, he cannot sleep, but his
insomnia comes from a sickness that the poem's introduction calls a
"common woe" (14) — perhaps an image of our fallen condition.[19] The
narrator is representative of us all in being sick and potentially erring, in
need of the comfort his friends provide. As he tells the tale he has heard
from Mother Hubberd, he interrupts it with irritable outbursts:

> Shame light on him, that through so false illusion,
> Doth turne the name of Souldiers to abusion,
> And that, which is the noblest mysterie,
> Brings to reproach and common infamie. (219–22)

Here and elsewhere in his comments the narrator is sensitive to the
rogues' implicit degradation of an ideal—here the "noblest mysterie" of
the military life — and his sensitivity suggests an uneasy awareness of
how easily ideals are compromised. The rogues' success in assuming the
external trappings of one profession after another suggests how corruptible these professions are.

The narrator reacts with particular anger to the rogues' compromising of the integrity of art and courtiership. This poem, more than any

other in the *Complaints,* concerns itself with artistry, and the two rogues
are the primary instances of the artist as con-man. They are actors, and
the poem details their various costumes—the worn-out soldier's uni-
form, the elaborate courtier's garments, and the lion's skin. They adopt
verbal costumes as well. The poem is full of verbal performances, from
the ignorant priest's account of how one obtains a benefice to the caustic
descriptions of the Ape's tales and songs at court. The poem provides
examples of the corruption that occupies the Muses in the earlier complaint: the Fox and the Ape pervert language, and with remarkable success. The Ape is finally ostracized by the other courtiers not because of
his villainy but because he cannot buy new clothes.

The poem is most acid in treating the court. While courtiership has a
bad name in Renaissance satire, it is nonetheless an ideal, potentially a
guarantee of the social order. Yet the ideal's precariousness is striking
here, as it is later in the sixth book of *The Faerie Queene,* and prompts the
narrator's most notable digression—his extended praise of the ideal
courtier. When the Fox and the Ape tarnish the ideal by their actions,
the narrator tries to set the record straight.

> Yet the brave Courtier, in whose beauteous thought
> Regard of honour harbours more than ought,
> Doth loath such base condition, to backbite
> Anies good name for envie or despite:
> He stands on tearmes of honourable minde,
> Ne will be carried with the common winde
> Of Courts inconstant mutabilitie,
> Ne after everie tattling fable flie;
> But heares, and sees the follies of the rest,
> And thereof gathers for himselfe the best. (717–26)

The "Yet" with which he opens emphasizes the narrator's defensive need
to insist on the validity of the ideal, and his defensiveness grows increasingly marked in the repeated negatives: the brave courtier does *not*
backbite, shift loyalties, or run after gossip. His first extended positive
assertion undercuts itself. When he claims that the true courtier notices
others' follies and "thereof gathers for himselfe the best," he presumably
means that the courtier separates the wheat from the chaff, but his
words betray him. If the best one can find at court is folly, then the best
one can gather is still folly.

Part of the narrator's difficulty lies in the "honor" that he makes the courtier's cardinal value. Honor is a notoriously flawed virtue, at best the last infirmity of noble mind and at worst a blind concern with one's own importance. Spenser had just published the first book of *The Faerie Queene,* in which Redcrosse finds just how imperfect a value honor is. In *Mother Hubberds Tale* the values of the true courtier, which the narrator tries to distinguish from the practices of the Ape, turn out to have a disquieting similarity. Does the courtier's desire for fame (769) differ in kind from the Ape's ability to manipulate appearances? The uneasiness appears in Castiglione's *The Book of the Courtier,* which contains much of the material of this passage:[20] Spenser lets his well-meaning narrator stumble into contradictions already present in the source.

The same tainting of courtiership appears toward the end of the portrait when we learn that the good courtier is "practiz'd well in policie" (783), a word with negative connotations in Elizabethan parlance. What policy involves grows clearer when the narrator describes what the courtier learns:

> [He] thereto doth his Courting most applie:
> To learne the enterdeale of Princes strange,
> To marke th'intent of Counsells, and the change
> Of states, and eke of private men somewhile,
> Supplanted by fine falshood and faire guile;
> Of all the which he gathereth, what is fit
> T'enrich the storehouse of his powerfull wit. (784–90)

"Supplanted by fine falshood and faire guile" is a problematic line; the oxymorons suggest a troubled conscience. Under what conditions is falsehood fine and guile fair? While the narrator may be speaking with grim realism about a world in which innocence is impossible and one must choose the lesser evil, this realism undercuts the idealization upon which the speaker has insisted. Again the intensely negative vision of the court tends to contaminate the ideal of the courtier who remains in it but not of it.

The quietly corrosive implications of the tale appear again in the final episode. *Prosopopoia* proceeds by a series of separate incidents: as in a picaresque novel, each seems sealed off from its predecessor. In each case the greed of the Fox and the Ape makes them overstep their bounds so that the cheat is discovered. The final case is more problematic: here no villainy the rogues commit leads to their unmasking by earthly authorities; divine intervention is necessary. The passage (1225–70) in which Jove sees what is wrong and sends Mercury to wake the Lion calls attention to itself because the descent of Mercury is, as Thomas Greene has pointed out, an epic *topos*: it does not belong in a satirical poem (Greene 1963, 303). It may be a metaphorical suggestion that God is in his heaven and will intervene when necessary. But it is more likely to draw attention to the fact that the system has not worked. The ruler charged to protect the commonwealth remains asleep, while a dog—or an Ape—is obeyed in office. The rogues are protected by their own guard and by their appearance of legitimacy. Spenser breaks the generic frame to suggest how dangerous—and how successful—these creatures are: only the gods can help.

Yet Mercury, sent by Jove to restore order, compounds the problem, for Mercury is himself an image of the artist as con-man.[21] A shape-changer and a god of thieves (see 1287), he embodies through his long-standing association with eloquence all the skills that the Fox and the Ape have made suspect. Thus his descent to return the world to its natural order reminds us of art's potential for amorality: illusion is a powerful and dangerous instrument. Even the poetic justice meted out to the Ape—the loss of his tail and the clipping of his ears—compounds the uneasiness of the ending. Without his large ears and long tail, the Ape may find it easier to pass himself off as human in the future. It is perhaps significant that the narrator ends with an apology for his tale: "For weake was my remembrance it to hold, / And bad her tongue that it so bluntly tolde" (1387–88). The tale meant to cure restlessness may well make one more restless yet.

## The Ruines of Rome

If the satire of *Prosopopoia* shows Spenser at his most unbuttoned, his translation of Du Bellay's *Antiquités de Rome* presents him working once more in formal high style. The French sonnet sequence is self-consciously grand, abandoning the genre's usual concern with love for epic matter. Du Bellay, in Rome on a diplomatic mission, wrote the *Antiquités* as a meditation on the fragility of human achievement. The city that epitomized the human potential for good and ill and fostered the greatest civilization Renaissance writers knew had come eventually to nothing. The sequence evokes Rome's grandeur with ritualistic intensity and searches for a meaning in its fall.

Spenser's translation, *The Ruines of Rome,* fits into the larger context of the *Complaints* in its concern with time and human limits, and it has par-

ticularly close ties with *The Ruines of Time*. Indeed, it has been argued
that Du Bellay's sonnet sequence—which was followed by the shorter
visionary sonnet sequence *Songe*, translated later in the *Complaints* as
*Visions of Bellay*—furnished a model for the two-part structure of
Spenser's poem.[22] *The Ruines of Rome* also develops the epic scope of the
*Complaints*. Despite the lyric form of this sonnet sequence, it dramatizes
an epic concern with human greatness, even while insisting on its ultimate limits.

One aspect of the Roman achievement is its art, apparent not only in
the ruined buildings that Du Bellay repeatedly evokes but in the poetry
of Horace, Virgil, and Lucan that the sequence echoes. The sequence
invokes the tradition of the *translatio imperii*—the gradual movement of
empire and civilization westward, from Babylon to Greece, from Greece
to Rome, from Rome to France—as Du Bellay attempts to take over
where the Roman poets left off. The first sonnet dramatizes the French
poet's own heroic attempt to confront the Roman ruins and to summon
up the spirit of the earlier civilization. He is thus a link in the chain
tying the Renaissance present to the antique past. Spenser adds a further
link to that chain by translating the sequence and adding a final sonnet
that praises Du Bellay's achievement. Spenser and his country become
the final inheritors of the Rome that the French poet has invoked.

The grand rhetoric of Spenser's translation often creaks a bit, and in
general his version is shriller and less subtle than the original. At times,
however, it gives a sense of Du Bellay's melancholy force:

> Beholde what wreake, what ruine, and what wast,
>
> And how that she, which with her mightie powre
>
> Tam'd all the world, hath tam'd herselfe at last,
>
> The pray of time, which all things doth devowre. (33–36)

As the final line of the passage suggests, Spenser's translation of *The
Ruines of Rome* appealed greatly to Shakespeare, who transformed it
again in his own sequence.[23]

## *Muiopotmos, or The Fate of the Butterflie*

The most brilliantly tantalizing of the *Complaints* is *Muiopotmos, or The
Fate of the Butterflie*, whose story would fit on a postage stamp: its
unwary insect-hero enjoys the delights of a garden only to be trapped

and killed by a spider. From this minimal matter Spenser makes an extraordinary work, resonant and cool and finely polished. The very simplicity of the story suggests that it is about something more than itself; the spider and butterfly are emblematic creatures with a variety of meanings—a long tradition, for instance, associated the butterfly with the human soul.[24] Accordingly, critics have found in it allegories of the fall of man, envy at court, or some more particular topic, and they have generally been able to support their claims by reference to particular parts of the text. Yet even the most persuasive allegories tend to substitute themselves for the poem, replacing its purely *fictive* world with the world we know. The poem glances at several possible meanings, but remains irreducible to any one of them.

Its inconclusiveness is a hallmark of its mode. Where most of the *Complaints* display the high melancholy exemplified in Roman literature by Virgil, this poem associates itself with the trickier and more elusive poetry of Ovid. Practically every major Elizabethan poet produced a short narrative (modern critics have been unable to agree on a name for the kind) marked by Ovid's combination of erotic suggestion, rhetorical finesse, and tonal instability.[25] The narrator of Ovid's *Metamorphoses* strikes his poses and qualifies his opinions with an irony that leaves it unclear how far he means what he says. Ambiguities of meaning are matched by sudden shifts in tone. The *Metamorphoses* describes human viciousness, weakness, and vulnerability with terrible accuracy, yet Ovid limits his pathos by placing his rhetoric, like a sheet of glass, between the action and the reader. When the adolescent Pyramus mistakenly commits suicide, Ovid checks the reader's incipient pity with an obtrusive simile comparing the blood issuing from Pyramus's body to water spurting from a lead pipe. We are distracted from the narrative subject as we attend to the craftsman-narrator. The elusiveness of Ovid's stance and his cool distance from his subject matter show themselves in *Muiopotmos*.

The crucial fact about the poem is that its characters are insects whom the speaker nonetheless treats with mock-heroic gravity. The narrative contains epic similes, epic catalogs, quotations from both Virgil and Ovid, and mock-passionate addresses to the Muses and the gods; it suggests in its description of Clarion's soaring flight the large vistas typically found in epic. The hero's name, Clarion, recalls the trumpet associated with Fame (see *Teares,* 463), and he is described as arming himself in breastplate and helmet with his antennae acting as two spears. Aragnoll, the spider, is a matching villain. The opening, which promises to sing "of deadly dolorous debate, / Stir'd up through wrathfull *Nemesis* despight, / Betwixt two mightie ones of great estate" (1–3), presents the conflict as a matter of heroic importance.

In fact the opening stanza has little to do with the story (Clarion never fights his opponent, remaining oblivious of danger until he is trapped), but it sets up a mock-heroic frame that affects the meaning of the narrative in several ways. Most obviously it is comic: to treat a butterfly grandly is to make it seem all the smaller and slighter. Yet this comic emphasis is muted by the knowledge that Clarion will die: awareness of both his beauty and his fragility limits the laughter evoked at his expense. Further, since Clarion resembles us—and the heroes of epic—in his mortality, the heroic language imports some epic seriousness into his small world. It suggests that the fate of the butterfly may hold meaning for our own.

The effect appears in the ending of Spenser's mock-heroic introduction. After calling on Melpomene, Muse of tragedy, to tell of Clarion's fall "to lowest wretchednes," he asks: "And is there then / Such rancour in the harts of mightie men?" (15–16). The next line makes it clear that Clarion is not a man but one of "the race of silver-winged Flies" (17), and so the question appears comic at first. But the lines also imitate the most famous question of Virgil's *Aeneid*. After blaming Juno's fury for the misery of Aeneas and the Roman state after him, Virgil asks: "tantane animis caelestibus irae" (Can such great anger dwell in heavenly spirits?) (I.11). This troubled line about the nature of the world's guiding powers recurs in Renaissance epic and resonates here, since, despite its miniature size, *Muiopotmos* also concerns itself with the nature of divine powers. The Virgilian quotation complicates the word *men* because it refers at once to heroes and butterflies by superimposing on them a third reference to irrational gods. Is blind fury built into the web of being? Are gods to men as wanton boys (in Gloucester's comparison) are to butterflies? Since the heavenly spirit of Virgil's passage is female, is Spenser criticizing the justice of his easily angered queen? Spenser presents these tantalizing connections without insisting on them.

The emblematic potential of the story appears in its hero. Clarion embodies what E.K. might call a "recreative" spirit. Sensuous, joyful, and greedy, he is a creature of innocent impulse. Spenser's language suggests Clarion's delight in the world he finds, whether it is in flight (41–48) or in food (177–80) or in bathing his "tender feete" in the dew (181–82). Occasionally Spenser also describes him negatively: he is

greedy (177–79, 201–5) and has a "wavering wit" (160), giving himself
over fully to his "unstaid desire" (161) in "riotous excesse" (168). But
these excesses are in fact as natural to him as to any fallen creature;[26] it is
not that they are bad per se so much as that in a fallen world they lead
to disaster.

For the garden in which Clarion perishes is a version of the world.
The narrator gives a two-stanza catalog of the flowers in the garden
(185–200), which, like the catalog of trees in the Wood of Error (*Faerie
Queene*, I.i.8–9), tends in its variety to suggest the larger variety of the
world. Spenser calls it a "Paradise" (186), and that designation, too, suggests how the original Paradise was an incipient world containing all of
nature's variety within it. But the comparison of the garden with Paradise has a second function: reminding one that the original Paradise is
lost, and that the world we have is not entirely beneficent. "What more
felicitie can fall to creature, / Than to enjoy delight with libertie, / And
to be Lord of all the workes of Nature" (209–11), exclaims the narrator,
and his words could describe the situation of the unfallen Adam, who
reigned happily over the unfallen world. But Clarion is *not* Adam, and
the garden is not Paradise. The innocent pleasure that characterizes
Adam's unfallen existence is not possible here.

The two small myths that Spenser sets into the story reemphasize the
world's fallenness. While both of them are explanatory myths of origin,
and both, as Bond has pointed out, deal with envy, they are in other
ways opposites.[27] The first presents an instance of divine injustice. When
Venus's envious nymphs falsely accuse Clarion's ancestor, Astery, of
using Cupid's help to gather flowers, the goddess hotheadedly turns her
into a butterfly. Astery has done nothing to deserve the transformation,
and the episode stresses the world's unexpected viciousness.

The second story, Spenser's account of Arachne's transformation into
a spider, is a psychological myth, an account of *human* malice. Spenser
inherited the story from Ovid's *Metamorphoses,* where the covert sympathies of the poem seem to favor Arachne. Foolhardy as she is in challenging Athena to a weaving contest, Arachne nevertheless wins and is terri-
bly punished by the enraged and powerful goddess. In Spenser's poem,
by contrast, Arachne challenges and loses, and her subsequent transformation is, like Malbecco's metamorphosis, her own doing. Athena's
tapestry depicts her contest with Neptune for the city of Athens, during
which she presents the city with the olive tree. The tapestry presents an
image of harmonious and fruitful order, but she adds a final touch to the
solemnity:

> Emongst those leaves she made a Butterflie,
> With excellent device and wondrous slight,
> Fluttring among the Olives wantonly,
> That seem'd to live, so like it was in sight:
> The velvet nap which on his wings doth lie,
> The silken downe with which his backe is dight,
> His broad outstretched hornes, his hayrie thies,
> His glorious colours, and his glistering eies. (329–36)

The picture celebrated in the verse stresses not only the lifelikeness of the picture but its joyous vitality. It suggests a wantonness that is natural and (to borrow one of Spenser's other adjectives) glorious. Arachne responds with humiliated envy, "That shortly from the shape of womenhed / . . . / She grew to hideous shape of dryrihed, / Pined with griefe of follie late repented" (345, 346–48). The story develops in its own terms a vision of the hatred that beauty inspires in those who lack it.

Aragnoll is the heir of Arachne, and he extends the analysis begun in the Arachne myth. He embodies all that Clarion excludes. Referred to as "The foe of faire things, th'author of confusion" (244), he recalls the devil without being limited to that religious formulation. Like Iago, he hates what is beautiful because it embodies a felt lack within himself, and instead of attempting to attain the beautiful, he tries to destroy it. Unlike Clarion, who is an innocent consumer, he is an artist, but his art differs from that of the Fox and the Ape in *Prosopopoia*. Their art is simply the illusion of the con-man out to satisfy his appetites. Aragnoll's art is more frightening because it means to destroy. Spenser avoids any suggestion of the actual reason spiders kill flies: Aragnoll kills only because he wants revenge. He embodies the fallen viciousness that makes present-day gardens dangerous.

The narrator of the poem—very much an Ovidian narrator, chatty and given to platitudes that may or may not explain the story—offers many reasons for Clarion's death, but it is not clear which, if any, we are to believe. He attributes Clarion's fall to (1) the tendency of good fortune to change to bad (217–20); (2) the "thousand perills" that lie in wait for us and against which without divine guidance we are helpless (221–24); (3) the "secret doome" of the heavens (225–32); and (4) divine vengeance (240). The picture of a narrator trying vainly to make sense of an event whose meaning eludes him is epitomized in the stanza that describes Clarion's final capture and hesitates at length over its cause:

> The luckles *Clarion,* whether cruell Fate,
> Or wicked Fortune faultles him misled,
> Or some ungracious blast out of the gate
> Of *Aeoles* raine perforce him drove on hed. (417–20)

The narrator cannot make up his mind. He blames earthly disasters on the cruel heavens—perhaps—but cannot decide whether they are guided by fate or fortune. Earlier he has apostrophized Clarion whose "cruel fate is woven even now / Of *Joves* own hand, to worke thy miserie" (235–36). The gods, too, are weavers, larger versions of Aragnoll, and mortals are simply doomed.

Are these words, as has been argued, simply an analogue for Calvinist ideas of predestination and human sinfulness?[28] Unlike *The Ruines of Time,* in which Verlame's view yields to the narrator's subsequent illumination, the inadequate formulations of the narrator here result in no authoritative truth. Indeed, the effect of this narrator's uncertainties is to make a final understanding more difficult. The shimmering fable invites interpretation only to frustrate it,[29] and readers, left with a picture of mortal beauty and its vulnerability in the world, must make what they can of that.

### *Visions of the Worlds Vanitie, The Visions of Bellay,* and *The Visions of Petrarch*

The *Complaints* concludes with three sets of sonnets that recall the emblematic visions of *The Ruines of Time.* Two are revised and improved versions of the "Epigrams" and "Sonets" that Spenser had translated for the *Theatre for Worldlings;* the third, *Visions of the Worlds Vanitie,* is an original short sequence in a similar mode. Each sonnet develops a concise exemplum or a mysterious emblem that looks behind earthly appearances to the truth of things. As a group these visions stress the world's mutability and its insecurity. Like the speaker of *The Ruines of Rome,* the speakers in these sonnets are wondering representatives of ourselves, visionaries who report what they only sometimes understand.

Spenser's original sequence comes first. *Visions of the Worlds Vanitie* differs from the others in the plainness of its exempla, which come mostly from natural history, and its insistence on the vulnerability of power. Each sonnet presents an instance of a greatness (a bull, a crocodile, a dragon) dominated by insignificance (a fly, a bird, a spider), and the sequence displays a satiric edge that the other sonnets lack. It concerns itself with the limits of earthly greatness and ends with a warning:

> . . . if that fortune chaunce you up to call
> To honours seat, forget not what you be:
> For he that of himselfe is most secure,
> Shall finde his state most fickle and unsure. (165–68)

The words could be addressed to Lucifera's court in the House of Pride—or to Elizabeth's.

Spenser's translation of Du Bellay's *Songe* as *Visions of Bellay* broadens the insistence on individual insecurity to include the fragility of civilizations. This version of the sequence omits the four sonnets in the *Theatre* that Van der Noodt made from the Book of Revelation but includes four from Du Bellay's sequence that the *Theatre* omits. Images of worldly greatness appear—a temple, a pillar, an ark, an oak—only to crumble. These translated emblems are more complex than those of the *Visions of the Worlds Vanitie,* and in several Rome is an ambivalent figure. In the sixth sonnet, for instance, she is a wolf who not only suckles her whelps, Romulus and Remus, but hunts "roming through the field with greedie rage / T'embrew her teeth and clawes with lukewarm blood" (76–77); eventually she is hunted down and her corpse hanged. The 14 visions are prefaced by a sonnet in which the speaker sees the spirit of the Tiber River—who announces that "all is nought but flying vanitee" (11)—and ends with a generalization: "Sith only God surmounts all times decay, / In God alone my confidence do stay" (13–14). Spenser's treatment rather flattens Du Bellay's resonant French, but the group as a whole develops the vision of worldly insecurity voiced in the first sequence in the context of the final security God affords.

The sonnets translating Petrarch's Rime 323 (they most likely rework Marot's translation of the poem) change its meaning by isolating it from its context in the original sequence. Petrarch's mysterious canzone envisions Laura as a doe, a ship, a laurel tree, a fountain, a phoenix, and a lady, each of which is destroyed, and it ends by longing for death. Its new context depersonalizes the poem, which seems to meditate less on Laura than on earthly beauty: "Alas, on earth so nothing doth endure, /

But bitter griefe and sorrowfull annoy" (81–82). In Petrarch's poem and in Spenser's first six sonnets the speaker does not fully understand what he has seen: the Phoenix, for instance, is associated with Christ's resurrection and hence with Laura's, but this meaning seems to remain beyond his view. Yet Spenser insists on the divine perspective with an original seventh sonnet—just as Petrarch would do in the final poem of his own sequence, and as the final group of visions does in *The Ruines of Time*. Seven is the number of divine rest, and so Spenser's final sonnet completes what is inadequate in the vision of the rest of the sequence. He comments that when he beholds the world's "tickle trustles state":

> I wish I might this wearie life forgoe,
> And shortly turne unto my happie rest,
> Where my free spirite might not anie moe
> Be vext with sights, that doo her peace molest. (89–92)

This looking toward heaven as the only security gives a final perspective to the gloom of Petrarch's series. It also voices the fatigued longing for a final rest that recurs elsewhere, most movingly in the *Mutabilitie Cantos*. The note of longing, however, is temporary, and the poem ends addressing its "Lady" with a grim warning very much of a piece with the rest of the book:

> . . . though ye be fairest of Gods creatures,
> Yet thinke, that death shall spoyle your goodly features.
>
> (93–94)

## Chapter Five

# 1591–1595: Return to Pastoral

Although Colin Clout bids farewell at the end of *The Shepheardes Calender,* Spenser never stopped writing pastoral poetry. Pastoral episodes recur in *The Faerie Queene,* as they do in the *Aeneid* and the Italian romance epics; as we have seen, several of the *Complaints* have a pastoral coloration. But the pastorals Spenser wrote in the early 1590s—*Daphnaïda* (1591), and *Colin Clouts Come Home Againe* and *Astrophel* (published together in 1595)—differ from Spenser's earlier experiments in the mode. The Mantuanesque rustics of "May" and "September" have disappeared and with them their choppy, dialect-studded verse. These later poems are courtly works, employing a graceful and sometimes powerful iambic pentameter in a variety of stanza forms. They are also courtly in being occasional poems written in response to incidents—two deaths and a journey—of interest to Elizabeth's court. Each deals with the traditional pastoral opposition of action and contemplation, to which Spenser gives a characteristic vocational edge, questioning how deeply one should commit oneself to a world at once fruitful and disappointing, beneficent and corrupt.

Different as they are from each other, the poems all push beyond normal pastoral limits. *Daphnaïda* and *Astrophel* depart from traditional elegiac form, while *Colin Clout* expands the eclogue's length and range. In particular they work with a problem central to the second half of *The Faerie Queene*—the fraught relation between the poet's fictions and the actual world. While some eclogues in *The Shepheardes Calender* refer to historical persons (like the Queen in "Aprill") or events (like Grindal's fall in "July"), historical concerns are intermittent, interrupted by the many eclogues purged of history. In these later pastorals, by contrast, historical reference is central: the fictions give actual events generic shape, enabling the poet not only to lament them and to celebrate them but to interrogate them. By giving fictional names to historical figures, treating Elizabeth as Cynthia, Arthur Gorges as Alcyon, and Sidney as Astrophel, Spenser sets them in the moral and aesthetic frame that pastoral supplies. *Daphnaïda,* for instance, places Arthur Gorges in the tradition of lovers and mourners reaching back to Virgil and beyond: we judge him against his predecessors in previous pastoral poetry. Further, the pastoral mode calls up a set of values that, if not necessarily espoused in every pastoral poem, are usually at issue—innocence, simplicity, community, happy recreation, and kindness in its double meaning of "naturalness" and "beneficence." These are the values invoked (although they may not prevail) in the conflicts that the poems explore.

In these poems Spenser experiments further with various voices. The narrator of *Astrophel* is a limited pastoral shepherd whose ignorance recalls that of Verlame or the puzzled speaker of *Muiopotmos*. In the other two pastorals, however, the poet engages in a new experiment—dramatizing moments in his own biography. While the proem to the first book of *The Faerie Queene* displays the poet's progress as he moves like Virgil from pastoral to heroic verse, it makes little attempt to connect this literary figure with the humanist poet-administrator dwelling in Ireland. By contrast, Colin's adventures in Cynthia's court rework Spenser's adventures in Elizabeth's, developing a view of Spenser's life and a vision of his nature. Similarly in *Daphnaïda,* the narrator speaks of a personal, unexplained grief, which probably corresponds to the death of Spenser's first wife, Machabyas Chylde.

## *Daphnaïda*

*Daphnaïda* is the first of Spenser's unconventional elegies, written for Douglas Howard, the wife of Spenser's acquaintance Arthur Gorges. The poem is dated January 1591, which by modern reckoning would place its writing in the five months after her death in August 1590. Spenser seems not to have known Douglas Howard personally—he speaks in the dedication of "the great good fame which I heard of her deceassed"—but he did know Gorges, a good friend and kinsman of his patron Sir Walter Ralegh and a gentleman-courtier a bit younger than himself. Spenser's not knowing Howard may partly account for his saying so little about her, but pastoral elegies tend in any case to focus less on the dead than on the grieving survivors.

In finding a form for his elegy, Spenser adapted Chaucer's *Book of the Duchess,* but as with all his Chaucerian imitations, he changed radically what he used.[1] Both works portray a conversation between the narrator and a man mourning his dead lady, but while Chaucer's poem balances sorrow against happiness, suggesting that both are part of life in a fallen world, Spenser's elegy becomes a study in obsessive grief. Chaucer's poem begins when, unable to sleep, the narrator reads in Ovid's *Meta-*

*morphoses* how Queen Alcione learns in a dream of her husband's death and eventually dies of sorrow.[2] He sleeps and dreams that he wakes, joins a hunt, and comes on the Man in Black (a fictional avatar of Chaucer's patron John of Gaunt, who had lost his first wife Blanche) grieving for his dead love. While the Man in Black refuses at first to name his sorrow directly, saying merely that he has played chess with Fortune, who has taken his queen, the narrator's tactful questions eventually lead him to describe his lady's beauty and goodness, his wooing, and her eventual acceptance of his suit. The radiant memory establishes his past happiness, mitigating by implication his initial account of Fortune's cruelty.

It is just this balance of sorrow and joy that Spenser's poem avoids. The opening stanzas banish the Muses and invoke the Furies in their place, announcing that "here no tunes, save sobs and grones shall ring," and the rest of the poem single-mindedly carries out this program.[3] It is spring, but a spring whose flowers, like Douglas Howard herself, have died in an early frost (27–28). The narrator, stricken with melancholy at the start, is awakened from his own sorrow only by the more formidable grief of the mourning Alcyon—the husband here, not the wife—whose uninterrupted complaint for his loss occupies most of the poem. Unlike the dialogue between Chaucer's narrator and the Man in Black, his lament causes no change in Alcyon's mood: he tears his hair "as one disposed wilfullie to die" (552) and departs rudely.

If Spenser departs from Chaucer's poem, he also omits the most typical conventions of pastoral elegy. Unlike "November," *Daphnaïda* lacks a final Christian vision in which the mourner realizes that the dead shepherdess has gone to a happier place. Yet the hope of heaven appears in the poem when early in his lament Alcyon quotes Daphne's dying speech, only to forget it in what follows. Spenser also avoids the consolatory picture of nature mourning the dead shepherdess, and in its place we have Alcyon's wish that nature itself will collapse in chaos. The absence of a sympathetic nature parallels the absence of a pastoral community—the gathered shepherds and shepherdesses whose sympathies lift the mourners out of isolation. The conversation-frame that Spenser borrows from *The Book of the Duchess* only emphasizes Alcyon's unwillingness to share his grief—or, indeed, to listen. He grieves alone.

What are we to make of this seemingly comfortless elegy? Its unusual features make better sense if we consider Alcyon's function in the poem. His name is a masculine form of Alcyone, the queen who in Chaucer's account of her story in *The Book of the Duchess* quite literally dies of grief. It thus associates him from the start with a character driven by extravagant sorrow. His memory of Daphne (briefly recalled as an idyllic friendship with a white lion, a heraldic sign associated with the Howard family) is a fantasy of unbroken happiness, while the present world appears utterly worthless (Harris and Steffen, 30–31). Unlike Chaucer's mourner, Alcyon is self-centered to the point of boorishness. He introduces himself with large self-pity as the "wretchedst man that treades this day on grounde" (63), refuses to listen to the narrator, and rejects comfort "as stubborne steed, that is with curb restrained, / Becomes more fierce and fervent in his gate" (194–95). The image of the horse refusing to be curbed recalls Redcrosse's mount in book 1 of *The Faerie Queene* and has a history going back to Plato's *Phaedrus*. It is usually associated with unruly passion, often sexual passion,[4] but in this case the passion is grief, which moves Alcyon to think about suicide and to dwell obsessively—and proudly—on his loss.

By making Alcyon a pastoral figure, Spenser invokes a line of grieving shepherds going back to the beginnings of pastoral poetry. Such shepherds fall into two groups. The first is the mourner, lamenting a death and doing so for the whole community; pastoral poetry tends to treat such shepherds with respect and admiration. The second is the unsuccessful lover, grieving over his rejection; from Theocritus on, poets tend to view such shepherds in comic terms. In *The Shepheardes Calender,* Colin grieving for Dido embodies the first tradition; Colin grieving for Rosalind embodies the second. As a shepherd lamenting a death, Alcyon would seem to fit into the first category, but the self-centeredness of his sorrow associates him with the second.

While Alcyon's long speech is a complaint—like those in the volume published the same year—Spenser here treats the form with ironic distance. For the believing Christian the world may be fallen, but it is ultimately guided by God's providence. To protest too much against one's particular fate is to display impatience, a willful refusal to accept God's decrees. Full awareness of this world takes as a given both its beneficence (since God did make it) and its ultimate transience. Although some of the laments in the *Complaints* are presented without irony, Spenser's poetry often dramatizes the complaint's potential for self-centeredness. When in *Daphnaïda* Alcyon attacks the world for not living up to his expectations, his complaint is fully ironized, a dramatization of grief's shortsightedness.

Alcyon's complaint occupies seven groups of seven seven-line stanzas; critics have pointed to the number's association with judgment or penance.⁵ But this numerological perfection contrasts with the angry solipsism of the complaint that concentrates so intensely on *this* world. Perhaps more relevant is the number's Augustinian connection with the seven ages of this world as opposed to the eighth age of the next.⁶ Alcyon begins by accusing the divine powers of injustice in causing Daphne's death: "What man henceforth, that breatheth vitall ayre, / Will honour heaven, or heavenlie powers adore / Which so unjustlie doe their judgments share" (197–99). He ends with a satisfied vision of his death and burial, with mourners weeping at his grave. The complaint dwells on Alcyon's sufferings and the inadequacy of the world that has let them occur. He sees himself as the victim of "importune fates" (387) that have conspired against him to punish him for unnamed misdeeds; eventually he will pacify them with his suffering, and they will permit him to die. Like Verlame in *The Ruines of Time,* Alcyon develops a proto-pagan view of the world—not because he is incapable of recognizing the Christian God, but because the picture of a world driven by vengeful fates agrees with the exaltation of his own heroic suffering.

Against this adolescent intensity Spenser sets two figures. The first is Daphne herself, whose dying words Alcyon recalls early in his complaint. She sees death as a final haven, a cause for rejoicing, and from that point of view asks, "Why should *Alcyon* then so sore lament, / That I from miserie shall be releast, / And freed from wretched long imprisonment?" (271–73). She supplies the explicit Christian perspective lacking elsewhere in the poem, recalling what Alcyon ought to remember. She reminds her grieving husband of their child and asks him to care for her: "My yong *Ambrosia,* in lieu of mee / Love her: so shall our love for ever last" (290–91). The line quietly insists on the commonplace that parents survive in their children. While discounting worldly happiness, she nonetheless stresses Alcyon's worldly duty as the child's father. Alcyon does not, however, refer to the child again, preferring to envision himself a solitary outcast.

The other figure is the narrator, whom we see grieving early in the poem (36–38) and who compares himself to Alcyon (64–66). His resemblance to the mourner, however, is less important than the difference between them. Where Alcyon focuses on his own misery, the narrator from the beginning looks beyond himself to "the miserie / In which men live" (36–37). On discovering Alcyon's grief, the narrator forgets his own in an attempt to comfort him. The self-transcendence that often marks the end of pastoral elegy occurs here for the narrator, but Alcyon vanishes unchanged into the wilderness.

Spenser's poetry often returns to the danger of melancholy, a passion as destructive as lust, and in such a reading Alcyon embodies an impulse in the narrator, and perhaps in Spenser himself. But if one recalls that Alcyon is a fictional version of an actual person, the poem may also present a friendly warning. I have argued elsewhere that the work attempts to remind Alcyon's grieving original, Arthur Gorges, of the potential egocentricity of prolonged mourning.[7] Seeing himself in the boorish Alcyon, Gorges might have been forced to ask himself whether he wished to act as his fictional double acts. A curious moment in the poem reemphasizes this idea. When Daphne bequeaths her child to her husband, she uses her actual name, Ambrosia, and the intrusion of that name into the pastoral fiction momentarily asserts the reality of the actual world. To attend to Ambrosia is to go beyond the absolute, pastoral grief in which Gorges has lost himself; it is to become more than a literary shepherd. Spenser was slightly older than Gorges, and by this time he had probably also lost his wife—quite possibly the reason for the narrator's melancholy at the poem's opening. This unflattering pastoral portrait of his friend would enable him to suggest with unconventional tact that grief itself must be outgrown.

## The Colin Clout Volume

In 1595 Spenser published a book in two roughly equal parts, the first containing *Colin Clouts Come Home Againe* and the second (headed by *Astrophel*) a group of elegies, by various hands, for Sir Philip Sidney. Spenser probably wrote his own poems earlier, although he revised *Colin Clout* before he published it.[8] We do not know why he delayed publishing the elegies for Sidney, whose death had occurred nine years earlier, but he may have had political reasons. In the fall of 1591 Spenser's patron, Sir Walter Ralegh, secretly married the pregnant Elizabeth Throckmorton. On discovering the deception the following spring, the furious queen imprisoned the couple for a time in the Tower of London; afterward she banished them from court. Since Ralegh is singled out for praise in *Colin Clout* and contributed an elegy to the *Astrophel* series, Spenser may have withheld the manuscript from publication until the queen's anger had cooled.

Together *Colin Clout* and *Astrophel* might be called *The Book of the Three Poets,* for they deal with Spenser, Ralegh, and Sidney, all of them noted courtier-writers. Each poet created a different relationship between his court life and his literary art, and the volume as a whole constitutes a meditation on the nature of the poet's allegiances. The poems set the active life in the world (or the court) against a life of pastoral retirement. They examine, directly or by implication, the question Piers raises in "October": "O pierlesse Poesye, where is then thy place?" (79).

***Colin Clouts Come Home Againe*** Like *Daphnaïda*, *Colin Clouts Come Home Againe* stretches the traditional pastoral form, though the urbanity of its tone conceals at first the originality of its experimentation. It is an eclogue like those of *The Shepheardes Calender*, a dialogue between shepherds, but *Colin Clout* is three times longer than any eclogue in the *Calender*, and longer than any other eclogue Spenser would have known. Its ambitiousness is enhanced by its incorporation of other genres—satire, songs of praise, a mythic river-marriage, and, most surprisingly, a mythological hymn in which Colin celebrates the God of Love. The hymn, especially, is a high-style form, and Spenser takes advantage of pastoral's instability—its readiness to transcend its ostensibly humble subject matter—to write an eclogue ending in praise that rises above even the grandeur of Cynthia's court.

The central consciousness of the poem is Colin's, but Colin has changed since his appearance in *The Shepheardes Calender*. Where the earlier shepherd-poet begins and ends his career in isolation, the Colin of this eclogue forms the center of his community. He appears "Charming his oaten pipe unto his peres, / The shepheard swaines that did about him play" (5–6), and throughout the poem their friendly interruptions stress his relationship to his listeners. Indeed, Colin's influence extends beyond the *human* community, for Hobbinol tells him that, when he left, the natural world itself mourned and withered (16–29), while now, on his return, "both woods and fields, and floods revive" (30). The language recalls pastoral elegy, in which nature appears at first to mourn for a dead shepherd and later to rejoice in his immortality.[9] Like the Daphnis of Virgil's fifth eclogue, Colin seems to have become a quasi-magical source of vitality. The suggestion that a divinity hedges the poet appears also when the initial description compares the happy shepherds surrounding Colin to "hartlesse deare, dismayd with thunders sound" (9). The abrupt shift from jollity to dismay suggests the shepherds' awe at a poet whose verse has divine force. His powers appear stylistically in his heightened praises of Elizabeth and Love and his denunciation of the court (680–730), passages that repeatedly echo the Old Testament. Colin has become a poet-priest.[10]

The Colin of this poem is more closely associated with Spenser than the Colin of *The Shepheardes Calender*. E.K.'s identification of Spenser with his poet-protagonist seems to have caught on. Several contemporaries refer to Spenser as "Colin," as he himself does in *The Ruines of Time* and *Daphnaïda,* and Colin's trip to England obviously parallels Spenser's journey of 1589. Further, the marked irony that surrounds Colin's self-pitying appearances in *The Shepheardes Calender* has disappeared: Colin now has a dignity and a breadth of vision largely absent from his character in the earlier poem. Yet Colin is not all of Spenser. His single-minded integrity differs from the complex calculation necessary for someone who, like Spenser, worked for the English government, and where Colin willingly contents himself with praising Rosalind, his maker would later insist on marrying Elizabeth Boyle. Colin thus affords a particular version of Spenser's voyage, informed by his own insistent pastoral values, but his understanding is not Spenser's. He voices one side of his creator's more complex and divided personality.

The difference between Colin and Spenser gives force to the surprising announcement that forms the poem's title: Colin Clout has come home again! A courtly audience might well assume that Spenser's return "home" was his trip to the English court from the barbarous wilds of Munster. But for Colin "home" is Ireland. The ambiguity of the title thus raises the question of where poets belong—at court or away from it. The opposition of city (or court) and country is a pastoral *topos,* but Spenser develops it here with a complexity unmatched in his earlier work. Models for the contrast exist in both pastoral and satire: as we have seen in *The Shepheardes Calender,* the two modes are necessarily related. A satire like Wyatt's "Mine Owne John Poins" (?1536) attacks the court from the perspective of a speaker who has left it for a home in "Kent and Christendom"; it is only a step from this to "September," in which Diggon Davie returns home and relates how he has lost everything in the city. Both poems join in a traditional attack on city and court as places of dishonesty, dissembling, vicious competitiveness, uncertainty, and fear.

Spenser's poem, however, complicates these models by presenting the court as both beneficent and corrupt. Colin's picture of England sometimes changes in midsentence, as it does when he caps an extended praise of England with an account of its graciousness:

> For end, all good, all grace there freely growes,
> Had people grace it gratefully to use:

> For God his gifts there plenteously bestowes,
> But gracelesse men them greatly do abuse. (324–27)

The second and fourth lines undercut what the first and third assert. To use the material and spiritual graces God has given England is to use them *gratefully,* with an awareness of their divine source. "Gracelesse men"—corrupt, ignoble, perhaps damned—pervert these gifts for their own ends. Ireland also appears doubly, as both the home of a loving pastoral community and a place of barbarous violence "where cold and care and penury do dwell" (657). The sudden changes in perspective educate the reader, as Spenser's poetry often does, by forcing him to work out a truth that will embrace both kinds of testimony.

Cynthia is the center of the court considered as an ideal, just as Colin is the center of the Irish shepherds, and she appears a source of divine power and wisdom, mediating between heaven and earth.

> Her words were like a streame of honny fleeting,
> The which doth softly trickle from the hive:
> Hable to melt the hearers heart unweeting,
> And eke to make the dead againe alive. (596–99)

The Old Testament association between honey and the Word of God deepens the otherwise facile compliment that Cynthia's words bring the dead to life.[11] As supreme head of the English church, Elizabeth acted as God's representative, an active channel of divine grace; more specifically, she was the ruler to whom English Protestants owed the restoration of the gospel after Mary's reign. The power of these praises derives partly from their articulation of the humanist dream that learning and power—humanist and prince—could join to impose on the fallen world the patterns of an ideal realm apprehended deep within the mind. The description of Cynthia's words making the dead again alive recalls Colin's effect on the Irish landscape (22–31): ideally both queen and poet mediate between God and the English people, illuminating them and guiding them with sacred wisdom. These are, however, Cynthia's praises, not Elizabeth's. Just as Colin is not Spenser, so Cynthia is not the queen, or not all of her: the idealized icon excludes those aspects of the actual Elizabeth that frustrated and baffled her poet.

The symmetrical pictures of Elizabeth's twelve poets and her twelve ladies are less exalted. With a few exceptions, like the lovely tributes to his relatives, the three Spencer sisters, the praise of the ladies often sounds formulaic, lacking the force of Cynthia's celebrations. Praise of her poets is limited.[12] Of those whom Colin commends most highly, Astrophel and Amyntas are dead, and two more, Alabaster and Daniel, are sufficiently unknown to the court that Colin uses their actual names. While Aetion (probably Drayton) receives unreserved eulogy, Colin is less than enthusiastic about his fellows. "Good Harpalus" is "woxen aged" (380); Corydon, an able wit, is "meanly waged" (382); and Alcyon remains focused on his grief. Alcon should write more ambitious work; Palin envies Colin; and "old Palemon free from spight" (396) is now grown hoarse. Most of the best poets are dead or unrecognized, and the rest are either past their prime, distracted, or competing for limited court favors. As an account of poetry at the royal court, this is not promising.

The twelfth poet, the Shepherd of the Ocean, is the most complex and interesting representative of the court.[13] He is a pastoral version of Sir Walter Ralegh, who accompanied Spenser to England and acted as his patron with Elizabeth. Ralegh embodied all the success a poet-courtier could have wished: a younger son in a Devonshire gentry family, he had made his fortune by his personal brilliance and his extended, playful courtship of the queen. (His association with the ocean may derive from Elizabeth's punning nickname for him as her "Water"; the role appears in his longest poem, "the 11th: and last booke of the Ocean to Scinthia," probably written after his disgrace.[14]) His poetry (as *Colin Clout* suggests [172–75]) was an important means of gaining and keeping the queen's favor: Ralegh was a poet-courtier for whom courtiership came first and poetry second. Spenser had chosen a different path. He had announced himself as an epic poet and lived much of his adult life in Ireland, at a distance from court intrigue. Ralegh's shining success and his subsequent catastrophic fall may have aroused admiration, envy, and wariness.

Ralegh appears early in the poem as a "straunge shepherd," singing and piping with Colin, and graciously offers to take him to court. The interchangeable language of the scene in which they make music ("He pip'd, I sung; and when he sung, I piped, / By chaunge of turnes, each making other mery" [76–77]) suggests a quasi-allegorical relation between them: they are at once brothers and opposites, embodying different views of the world. The strange Shepherd's values appear brilliantly in his invitation:

> He gan to cast great lyking to my lore,
> And great dislyking to my lucklesse lot:

> That banisht had my selfe, like wight forlore,
> Into that waste, where I was quite forgot.
> The which to leave, thenceforth he counseld mee,
> Unmeet for man, in whom was ought regardfull
> And wend with him, his *Cynthia* to see:
> Whose grace was great, and bounty most rewardfull.
>
> (180–87)

The beneficence of the invitation is limited by the unconscious arrogance of its assumptions. The Shepherd dismisses Ireland—which appears at the poem's opening as a harmonious community—as a wasteland for any man "in whom was ought regardfull." "Regardfull" suggests that at court, as in the House of Pride, one must be seen if one is not to be "forgot." The present eye, as Ulysses says in *Troilus and Cressida,* dwells on the present object.

The strange Shepherd gains added ambivalence from his association with the ocean, which, like the court it resembles, appears doubly in the poem. While it appears to him a fruitful field that he keeps for his Queen (240–43), Colin describes it as a place of dangerous instability in which a "thousand wyld beasts" (202) wait to devour voyagers. The account reworks the classical *topos* that treats seafaring as both a civilized advance and a loss of innocent pastoral security.[15] The ocean is a common metaphor for the world governed by Fortune,[16] and Colin triggers this association when describing adventurers like Ralegh:

> And yet as ghastly dreadfull, as it seemes,
> Bold men presuming life for gaine to sell,
> Dare tempt that gulf, and in those wandring stremes
> Seek waies unknowne, waies leading down to hell.
>
> (208–11)

The ambivalent language evokes both the image of an epic hero descending to hell to gain wisdom for his journey and the more sinister image of an adventurer willing to risk his soul for material gain.[17] Colin echoes the passage later when he claims that he left court because he dared not "adventure such unknowen wayes, / Nor trust the guile of fortunes blandishment" (670–71). If the strange Shepherd displays the court's generosity, he also bears its taint.

In the last third of the poem Colin's ambivalent picture of the court stabilizes in satiric attack. While the criticisms appear in many Renaissance satires, Colin molds them into an indictment like that of the proem to the sixth book of *The Faerie Queene*—that the court's glorification of "outward shows" perverts the ideals "deepe within the mynd" (VI.proem.5) that ought to guide it. The indictment has a vocational dimension: poetry, which should teach and illuminate, is misused in slander and flattery or trivialized in pleasing entertainment. "Ne is there place for any gentle wit, / Unlesse to please it selfe it can applie: / But shouldred is, or out of doore quite shit, / As base, or blunt, unmeet for melodie" (707–10). Colin's comment lends to the charges of *The Teares of the Muses* new dramatic force. The poet who claims a role as a national teacher lacks an audience. The court refuses to take his teaching seriously: most courtiers "fare amis, / And yet their owne misfaring *will not see*" (757–58, italics mine). This is the frustration of a Renaissance poet who has labored to make himself into a new Virgil and has succeeded, only to find that his view of his art is not shared by others.

If the court trivializes the divine force of poetry, it also degrades love: Colin's indictment begins not with lust but with self-advertisement.

> . . . Love most aboundeth there.
> For all the walls and windows there are writ,
> All full of love, and love, and love my deare,
> And all their talke and studie is of it.
> Ne any there doth brave or valiant seeme,
> Unlesse that some gay Mistresse badge he beares:
> Ne any one himselfe doth ought esteeme,
> Unlesse he swim in love up to the eares. (775–82)

The names on windows epitomize Love's misuse as "outward show." Divine Eros is reduced to material form, letters scratched on glass (the walls and windows are literally "full of *love,* and *love,* and *love*") to enhance the reputation of the courtier-lover. Mistresses are as useful for the "badges" they give their lovers as for their bodies. Love's practitioners limit its meaning to "courting vaine" (790), and the pun suggests another abuse of God's graces.

In "October" Piers, frustrated by Cuddie's unwillingness to write heroic poetry, suggests that he make wings of his "aspyring wit, / And, whence thou camst, flye backe to heaven apace" (83–84), and the last part of *Colin Clout* follows this suggestion as Colin abandons his political role, turning from Cynthia's court to the court of Love.[18] The generic shift from satire to mythological hymn signals Colin's rejection of a political role. (For Spenser, of course, who needed Elizabeth's favor, such an absolute rejection would have been neither feasible nor desirable.) When in the middle of the hymn his friend Cuddie comments that Colin's words spring from a "celestial rage" (823)—divine inspiration— and continues, "Well may it seeme by this thy deep insight, / That of that God the Priest thou shouldst bee" (831–32), he makes the change of role explicit. Colin has become Love's priest.

Colin's account of Love blends many literary-philosophical traditions, some of which were already combined in the Middle Ages, from the winged Cupid of anacreontic and Petrarchan traditions to the neoplatonic Cupid—the emanation of Venus, source of beauty—to the differing creators of stoic, platonic, and Christian belief.[19] Where later, in the *Fowre Hymnes,* Spenser will insist on the differences between traditions, here he blurs distinctions in playful syncretism. (The playfulness appears in the account of generation in earth, air, and sea, a paraphrase of Genesis: "The Lyon chose his mate, the Turtle Dove / Her deare, the Dolphin his owne Dolphinet" [865–66].) Colin's version of these traditions makes love a fundamental creative force, affecting both the pain and disturbance imaged in his wounding arrows and the concord binding the world together.

Indeed, Colin's Love wounds in order to reveal the lover's divinity:

> For beautie is the bayt which with delight
> Doth man allure, for to enlarge his kynd,
> Beautie the burning lamp of heavens light,
> Darting her beames into each feeble mynd:
> Against whose powre, nor God nor man can fynd
> Defense, ne ward the daunger of the wound,
> But being hurt, seeke to be medicynd
> Of her that first did stir that mortall stownd. (871–78)

This neoplatonizing account of beauty's effect plays on the ambiguities of the phrase "enlarge his kynd." If we look to the account of animals choosing mates, enlarging one's kind involves generation: all God's creatures are moved by beauty to be fruitful and multiply. But in the immediate, human context, enlarging one's kind involves coming to fuller spiritual knowledge of what one is. Human beings, unlike animals, possess "the sparke of reasons might" (867), and so beauty darts her painfully bright beams into each feeble mind, creating new visionary awareness of this world in relation to the world of ideal forms. The only cure for such a wound comes through "her that first did stir that mortall stownd": the feminine pronoun encompasses both the beloved and the ideal beauty in which she participates.

To both the lover responds with "praiers lowd importuning the skie / Whence he them heares, and when he list shew grace, / Does graunt them grace that otherwise would die" (880–82). Here the mention of grace recalls the distance between the lover's worship and Cynthia's. When the Shepherd of the Ocean mentions earlier that Cynthia's "grace was great, and bounty most rewardfull" (187), he connects Cynthia's courtly graces with material gain. By contrast, Love's granting goes beyond material—sexual—reward: the account of his grace recalls the revitalizing force associated briefly with Cynthia-the-ideal and with Colin (29–31, 596–99). Love is the ultimate source of all vitality, and his gifts supersede those of the court. It is in final repudiation of earthly courts that Colin returns at the end of his hymn to those whose "courting vaine" makes them "outlawes" (890) to Love's rules:

> For their desire is base, and doth not merit,
> The name of love, but of disloyall lust:
> Ne mongst true lovers they shall place inherit,
> But as Exuls out of his court be thrust. (891–94)

Here Love's court opposes Cynthia's; those at home in the one will likely become "Exuls" from the other, just as Colin, who seemed to be "forgot" in Ireland, turns out to be Love's priest. There is something here of Augustine's two cities, the City of the World and the City of God: Colin resolutely turns his back on the World.

It is in this context, I think, that we should understand the praise of Rosalind that caps the poem. Where much of the eclogue praises Cynthia, the end of the poem turns from the worldly queen to the lady whom Colin can celebrate privately, and who is for him a key to the knowledge of the divine. "So hie her thoughts as she her selfe have place" (937): it is her spiritual "place" that draws Colin, not her body. Colin does not love Rosalind with any hope of winning her; in that sense the Colin of this poem is no nearer success than the boy of *The Shep-*

*heardes Calender.* But Colin here takes the *form* of the Petrarchan stalemate—the lover adoring, the beloved remaining beyond reach—and
reinterprets it in neoplatonic terms. Colin now sees Rosalind as a divine
emissary, "excelling all that ever ye did see" (934), who has enabled him
to raise himself out of the lowly mire. She gives him the "grace" that will
allow him to "praise her worth, though far my wit above" (942).

> Such grace shall be some guerdon for the griefe,
> And long affliction which I have endured:
> Such grace sometimes shall give me some reliefe,
> And ease of paine which cannot be recured. (943–46)

Again grace is associated with inspiration: the God of Love operates not
by ending pain but by making it fruitful.

The shift from queen to Rosalind, public to private, appears also in the
poem's organization. While *Colin Clout* seems deceptively loose in form,
an extended, meandering conversation among shepherds, it has, as David
Birchmore has shown, a fairly tight, symmetrical structure.[20] At the center is Colin's praise of his love, bracketed by praises of the queen's poets
and her ladies-in-waiting, praises enclosed in turn by twin praises of the
queen. These are surrounded by accounts of mutability on the ocean and
in the court, themselves bracketed by discussions of love, while the whole
is enclosed by praises of Colin's two ladies—Cynthia at the beginning
and Rosalind at the end—and by the picture of Colin with his shepherd
followers. This symmetry, however, emphasizes a progression: where
Colin begins by praising Cynthia, he ends by praising Rosalind, to whom
he returns. The poem's central line contains his ambiguous declaration of
loyalty, "I hers ever onely, ever one" (477), which recalls Elizabeth's
motto, *semper eadem* (always the same). Yet it applies not to Cynthia but
to Rosalind. Like Colin's later vision on Mount Acidale in the sixth book
of *The Faerie Queene,* the substitution asks where Colin's loyalty lies, and
his final praise of Rosalind implies an answer.

The small myth that Colin sings to the Shepherd of the Ocean further treats, in its playful, comic fashion, the relation between love and
power that the larger poem examines. Spenser sets the story in a
renamed version of his own Irish holdings, and it concerns the joining of
two rivers—the Bregog with the Allo (or Mulla, in Spenser's fiction).
Mulla's mountain father, "Old Mole," wants to marry her to another
river, but Bregog, too slippery for him, splits himself into many chan-

nels and goes underground to join secretly with his love. When Old
Mole discovers the deception, he hurls down huge stones to block Bregog's streams. Colin concludes:

> So of a River, which he was of old,
> He none was made, but scattred all to nought,
> And lost emong those rocks into him rold,
> Did lose his name: so deare his love he bought. (152–55)

Most simply, Colin points to a loss of self in love, just as Bregog's identity (his name) disappears in joining the Mulla. But Bregog's destruction
is curiously overdetermined: he "loses" himself by self-division, by going
underground, and by Old Mole's rocky revenge, as well as by mingling
his waters with the Mulla's. Several of these images recall not only death
but the neoplatonic process of emanation from a realm of ideal forms
into the time-bound, earthly cosmos, and the connection is germane to
the idea of the river-marriage.[21]

Rivers in Spenser's work often serve as metaphors for temporal
process, and his many river-marriages play with the patterns of flux and
stability, emanation and return, the many and the one, that characterize
this world. These two rivers quietly do Love's work in Time's cosmos
despite the forces arrayed against them. Time appears again in an otherwise unnecessary detail in the story, the mention of the ruins of "that
aunciente Cittie / Which *Kilnemullah* cleped is of old" (112–13). The
ruins may demonstrate that worldly power ultimately passes, while Love
endures: Colin insists with surprising force that Bregog's love continues
and will continue "so long / As water doth within his bancks appeare"
(94–95). It is no accident, as several critics have pointed out (Gaffney,
13–14; Oram 1990, 361–62), that the sequence of incidents also
recalls Ralegh's illicit marriage and its discovery by the queen. Here
again the forces of love oppose those of power, and love triumphs at the
cost of a great "name."[22]

After Colin's heightened celebration of Rosalind the last lines of the
eclogue return to pastoral humility in a quiet but profoundly moving way.

> So having ended, he from ground did rise,
> And after him uprose eke all the rest:
> All loth to part, but that the glooming skies
> Warnd them to draw their bleating flocks to rest. (952–55)

As in many eclogue closings, we return to the workings of the natural world, to the passage of the day and the weather. The action of "rising" recalls the aspiration of Colin's hymn, but it modulates here into an act of pastoral care. The "glooming skies" suggest night or bad weather and carry a faint threat: they suggest all the obstacles good shepherds must face. But above all the lines affirm Colin's loving community: he has come home.

With this resumption of the narrative voice the eclogue closes, neatly distancing the reader from its participants. Spenser's position, however, remains more problematic. He was Colin's creator, not Colin, and having voiced his critique of the court, he remained nonetheless bound to it—for his pension, for an audience, for support in an Ireland considerably less welcoming than Colin's. It is fitting that he chose to bind *Colin Clout* with *Astrophel,* an elegy-book dedicated to Sidney's widow, wife of the earl of Essex, the rising star of Elizabeth's court. Spenser's contribution to the book raises again the problem of the poet's involvement in the world of war and politics and suggests a complementary—and perhaps an opposing—stance.

### *Astrophel* and *The Dolefull Lay of Clorinda*

Sir Philip Sidney, to whom Spenser had dedicated *The Shepheardes Calender* in 1579, died seven years later in the Netherlands, fighting with English forces against the Spanish before the city of Zutphen. There he received a bullet wound in the thigh that turned gangrenous, causing his death 26 days later. In death he became a Protestant hero, celebrated with an extraordinary funeral and volumes of elegies. It is no surprise that Spenser and his fellow contributors to the *Astrophel* collection—Lodowick Bryskett, Matthew Roydon, Sir Walter Ralegh, Sir Edward Dyer, and perhaps Sidney's sister Mary, the Countess of Pembroke—added theirs to the number. The collection's late publication in 1595 is puzzling. By that time several of the book's seven elegies had already been published in *The Phoenix Nest* (1593), and Bryskett's "The Mourning *Muse* of *Thestylis*" had been entered on the Stationers' Register in 1587. *Astrophel* was certainly not written until after *The Ruines of Time* (1590), for in the preface to that poem Spenser apologizes for not having written Sidney's elegy.

*Astrophel* is a cool, rather distanced work and has been faulted for its lack of passionate feeling.[23] But Spenser may never have known Sidney well, and the poem's late date ensured that it would not express immediate grief. In its own way it is as daringly experimental as *Daphnaïda,* although different in kind. Both poems move the lyric form of the elegy toward narrative: in *Daphnaïda* the elegy receives a narrative frame, while in *Astrophel* lyric is almost entirely displaced by an allegorical account of Sidney's death. Spenser may have wished to give the book's later elegies a fictional framework (each succeeding poem begins with a stanza introducing a new lamenting shepherd). But the poem does more: in the context of Sidney's death it reexamines Colin's embrace of the pastoral life dramatized in the preceding poem, showing its limitations.

Spenser's decision to make his narrative a pastoral complicates it. The obvious reason for his choice is that, after Spenser, Sidney was England's most famous pastoral writer: several of the other poems in the collection are pastorals, and Bryskett's poem uses the pastoral name Sidney gave himself, "Philisides" (*Phi*llip *Sid*ney). But the choice creates a strain in decorum: Sidney's military death is an epic matter, and pastoral shepherds are not warriors. The other pastorals in the collection avoid the strain by imagining Sidney as a knight lamented by shepherds, or by imagining him as a shepherd and avoiding reference to the nature of his death. By contrast, Spenser chooses to highlight the conflict of modes by making Sidney a shepherd while referring allegorically to his death in battle. He further compounds the generic complexity (urged perhaps by the nature of Sidney's wound) by assimilating his story to the myth of Venus and Adonis, as he found it in Ovid's *Metamorphoses* and in an elegy by Ronsard.[24] Despite Venus's attempts to keep him with her, Adonis leaves to hunt the boar, which wounds him mortally in the thigh; Astrophel is similarly engaged in slaying wild beasts when wounded. The effect of these layers of reference—to Sidney's poetry, to his famous death, to the Adonis myth, to the ethos of pastoral poetry—is no small degree of cognitive dissonance. It is hard to see clearly what Spenser is doing.

Yet the poem's meaning develops out of its central collision of values—essentially the values of epic and pastoral—when the shepherd-narrator blames Astrophel for his own death. He has no sympathy for Astrophel's venture onto "forreine soyle" (92) in pursuit of savage prey, commenting, "What needeth perill to be sought abroad, / Since round about us, it doth make abroad?" (89–90). He stresses Astrophel's unwariness and describes him as attacking his prey "Full greedily" (104): the Spenserian adverb is at best an ambivalent one, and here suggests bloodthirstiness. This critical view of Astrophel's venture appears most fully in the picture of him slaughtering beasts:

> His care was all how he them all might kill,
> That none might scape (so partiall unto none)
> Ill mynd so much to mynd anothers ill,
> As to become unmyndfull of his owne.
> But pardon that unto the cruell skies,
> That from himselfe to them withdrew his eies. (109–14)

The narrator blames Astrophel for paying so much attention to the slaughter that he forgets his own safety. But the description suggests a shepherd (or hunter) gone berserk: the shepherd's "care" for his sheep is here given over to slaughter. Taking this criticism seriously, several recent essays have argued that Spenser here suggests that Sidney's military exploits were a mistake: that war is never justifiable.[25] But Spenser's other work makes no suggestion that he holds this humanist position, or that he sees war, however terrible, as avoidable. Both the prose of *A View of the Present State of Ireland* and the poetry of book 5 of *The Faerie Queene* treat war as an evil but, given the world's dangers, a necessary one. In book 6 of *The Faerie Queene* those not prepared to fight are likely to be humiliated, enslaved, or destroyed.

It seems more likely that Spenser is again playing with a pastoral figure whose limited view of things distorts his judgment. In an important article, Michael O'Connell points to the limitations of Astrophel's shepherd-narrator, who does not realize the Christian consolation that might attend Astrophel's death.[26] In the stanza quoted above he blames the "cruel skies" for distracting Astrophel from his own safety, and his accusation recalls those of Alcyon in *Daphnaïda* and the narrator of *Muiopotmos*. If events are not determined by cruel gods, they are a matter of luck; the narrator plays repeatedly with the word *happy* in the sense of "lucky," emphasizing that Astrophel is unlucky—a shepherd "not so happie as the rest" (12). His view of events omits the possibility of Christian salvation: all that remains of Astrophel at death is the flower into which he and Stella are transformed.

The view that the narrator does not fully understand the story gains additional support from his treatment of Astrophel as hunter. Traditional pastoral shepherds do not hunt: they use no violence except to protect their sheep against invading wolves. Pastoral masques and poems set the huntsman against the peaceful shepherd. Sidney's own masque *The Lady of May* sets the shepherd Epsilus against the hunter Therion, as does Spenser's fellow pastoralist Michael Drayton in *The*

*Muses Elizium* (1630), who has a shepherd, a fisherman, and a woodsman compete for the attentions of a maid, each praising his own way of life.[27] Astrophel's interest in the hunt, and with it the violence normally excluded from the shepherd's life, thus becomes for the narrator a topic for criticism. Yet Astrophel's associations with Adonis suggest an alternative set of values, ones by which hunting is a necessary part of full adulthood. Spenser used the Adonis myth several times in *The Faerie Queene,* but the treatment of the myth in the tapestry of Malecasta (III.i.34–38) illuminates most clearly Astrophel's choices. Venus hides her lover from his peers and from the world's dangers, embodied in the boar that will eventually kill him. But so protected, he remains a passive "Boy," kept by her ministrations "from bright heavens vew" (III.i.35.7): to avoid hunting is to deny time's imperatives. Spenser's evocation of the Adonis myth thus suggests that the narrator of *Astrophel* cannot understand a figure whose actions spring from a different set of values.

Sidney saw the battle in which he was fighting as a patriotic and religious necessity: he was defending the Protestant cause in the Netherlands against the Spanish king, a defense for which he had argued fervently and with limited success at court for all of his brief adult life. In his view, the determination of events in the world was ultimately governed by God's providence, and there was (from the point of view of the divine foreseer) no luck or fortune. Sidney's values are, so to speak, those of Christian epic, which valorizes the works of the warfaring saint; these values exist outside the bounds of conventional pastoral. In this reading, the narrator's misjudgment of his actions in *Astrophel* parallels the misjudgment of anyone in the actual world who would counsel withdrawal from military engagement with Spain.

*Astrophel* is followed and completed by *The Dolefull Lay of Clorinda,* whose authorship remains unclear. The narrator ascribes it to Astrophel's sister, whose biographical counterpart is Sidney's sister Mary, Countess of Pembroke. Mary, a brilliant translator of the Psalms, could certainly have written an elegy like the *Lay.* The case for Spenser's authorship is based entirely on internal evidence (see *VE,* 7:501–7). Like *Astrophel,* the *Lay* is written in sixains, and its diction and imagery also carry over from the earlier poem. The language sounds like Spenser's, and many phrases duplicate others in his works. Yet the ascription asks to be taken at face value. Margaret Hannay makes the fullest case for Mary's authorship in arguing that the poem is one of her comparatively immature works around which Spenser, writing later, built *Astrophel* and established the linkage.[28] While we are never likely to know for certain who wrote the poem, it is clear that the two elegies form a connected effort as the other *Astrophel* elegies do not.

For as O'Connell first pointed out, the Christian perspective that *Astrophel* lacks appears in its companion elegy. *The Dolefull Lay* is, unlike *Astrophel,* a Christian elegy and conforms to the conventional pattern exemplified in "November," where the shepherd-speaker moves through grief to a new vision of the dead shepherd among the blessed. Like many speakers in pastoral elegy, Clorinda begins in isolation: she sees no one to whom she can complain because she can see no audience whom her poem will benefit. The heavens are the "workers of my unremedied wo" (8) (her view here recalls that of the *Astrophel* narrator), while mortals are simply helpless, unable to act against fate. Accordingly, she decides to speak to herself alone, but as she continues she reaches out to the community to grieve in common: "Breake now your gyrlonds, O ye shepheards lasses, / Sith the faire flowre, which them adornd, is gon" (37–38).

The turn of the poem comes as Clorinda distinguishes between Astrophel's body and his soul. The first is "Scarse like the shadow of that which he was" (59), and she realizes that the other, an "immortal spirit" (61), cannot come within death's power. She can now picture Astrophel in Paradise, its pastoral imagery a metaphor for his lasting happiness. The opposition of the dead and living changes its value: the dead shepherd lives in "everlasting bliss," while "we here wretches waile his private lack, / And with vaine vowes do often call him back" (85, 89–90). Here Clorinda fully identifies herself with her fellow mortals; she is one of the many who live on earth for a while, but not forever. Her final farewell brings up one of the poem's key terms and changes its meaning: "But live thou there still happie, happie spirit, / And give us leave thee here thus to lament" (91–92). "Happie" here does not simply mean fortunate, but fully satisfied, happy as mortal beings can never be, and as the narrator of *Astrophel* can never imagine him. Her action thus suggests a coming to terms with her grief, a giving up of the dead shepherd, and a more just awareness of the world's limitations.

Except for *Colin Clout,* these midcareer pastorals do not belong among Spenser's greatest poems, but they suggest an unusual formal inventiveness as he adapted his pastoral for political and psychological themes. Chief among these are the conflict between the impulse to engage the world and the impulse to withdraw from it. If *Colin Clout* ends by repudiating the court, *Astrophel* insists on the heroism involved in continued military commitment. As the Shepherd of the Ocean,

Ralegh dramatizes the moral and political dangers of the court, and Colin embodies a refusal to cast himself adrift on its uncertain waters. But Astrophel's story evens the balance, implying that the shepherd who wants to keep his hands entirely clean may neglect the Lord's work. This dialectic will resume in the second installment of *The Faerie Queene*.

# Chapter Six

# 1595: *Amoretti and Epithalamion*

*Amoretti and Epithalamion* was entered on the Stationers' Register on 19 November 1594; Ponsonby's dedicatory epistle suggests that Spenser had sent it from Ireland in September. It commemorates the poet's wooing of Elizabeth Boyle and their marriage, probably on 11 June, the preceding summer solstice (Judson, 166). The book's three parts bring together ancient and modern genres in a characteristic Spenserian synthesis. The 89 sonnets of the *Amoretti* form a cycle of the kind Petrarch had made famous, dramatizing the progress of a love affair through a series of lyric instants. Those sonnets are succeeded by four anacreontic poems familiar from the compilation of short Greek poems known as The Greek Anthology and its imitations in Renaissance Latin and the vernaculars. The *Epithalamion,* or marriage-poem, that ends the volume is a classical genre revived in the Renaissance, but Spenser wrote the poem in the long, intricate stanzas of the Italian canzone. As usual, what he borrowed, he changed. He gave his sonnets a unique rhyme scheme, avoiding the antithetical structure of the Petrarchan form, and he varied the usually fixed length of his canzone stanzas from 17 to 19 lines.

The changes in verse form are the external signs of deeper alterations, which appear in the generic mixing. Despite a separate title page for the marriage-poem, the octavo volume was made to appear a single, unified work with a separate page for each sonnet of the *Amoretti* and each stanza of the *Epithalamion*. Yet this unity, like the harmonies that the book insists on, works with materials not easily reconciled. The book joins genres that embody three traditions of love poetry, and with them three different visions of love. Even omitting the anacreontic verses, sonnet sequences and epithalamia contrast markedly. The former consists of a lover's intensely subjective, fragmentary, and at times self-contradictory utterances, while the latter creates a ceremonious, even ritualistic, image of a public rite. Yet Spenser changes the meaning of both kinds by uniting them in the service of a Protestant ideal of sexuality sanctified in marriage. The egocentric intensity of the sonnet sequence modulates toward a mode of playful conversation with a loved other, and the public ritual of the marriage-poem is made personal. Spenser knits both forms into a plot of Christian wooing and wedding at once intimate and cosmic.

This achievement of large resonance makes neither the *Amoretti* nor the *Epithalamion* an unproblematic celebration of love. One of Spenser's great virtues as a writer is a comic honesty that enables him to admit the uncertainties, puzzles, and unresolved ambiguities of experience. This honesty appears abundantly in these poems, directly in the *Amoretti* and implicitly in the *Epithalamion,* and accounts for some of their most moving effects. On the one hand, the book embodies a loving criticism of self-dramatizing "Petrarchan" attitudes toward love. But on the other hand, Spenser's own hopeful attempt to link divine love with human, *agape* with *eros,* undergoes an uneasy, skeptical testing. If Spenser creates the first Western lyric sequence focused not on the lover's desire but on a portrait of relationship, he does so fully aware of the uncertainty surrounding all attempts at relationship in a mutable world.

## The *Amoretti*

**Petrarch and Petrarchism**    Spenser's *Amoretti* is arguably his most radical reworking of any literary convention, yet the poems in the sequence—often muted, prosy, subtly comic—hardly announce their originality. The strangeness of the sequence appears only against the background of the tradition in which he was working. This tradition is marked with the name of one man, Petrarch, whose brilliant, egocentric talent united the conventions of earlier love lyric and gave them a distinctive stamp, although his influence was diffused and changed by the often very different poets who came after him.

Francesco Petrarca, humanist and poet, was born in Arezzo on 20 July 1304 and died in Arqua, in the Euganean Hills, in 1374. The most famous humanist of his generation, he edited the text of Livy, wrote letters and dialogues, collected antiquities, served on diplomatic missions, and wrote poetry in Latin and Italian in recognition of which he was crowned laureate in Rome in 1341. He wrote a Latin epic, *Africa,* and a series of allegorical *Triumphs,* which left their mark on *The Faerie Queene.* His major lyric collection, the *Rime Sparse,* is a sequence of 366 poems largely concerned with the lady he calls Laura, whom, in a manuscript note, he says he first saw and adored on 6 April 1327. He continued to love and to write about her after her death on the same day twenty-one years later.[1] Repeatedly revised and added to, and given final shape only at the end of his life, the sequence dramatizes the speaker's powerful ambivalence toward his own desire.

The materials of Petrarch's sequence come from medieval tradition, both in the variety of verse forms (while largely composed of sonnets, many of the collection's most brilliant poems are longer lyrics, including sestinas and the canzones) and in the conventions of the relationship. The idealization of the lady's virtue and beauty, her coldness, the speaker's role as her quasi-feudal vassal, his pain and pleas for mercy all derive from Provençal lyric and the thirteenth-century Italian poets of the *dolce stile nuovo,* as do the familiar praises of the lady's eyes, her smile, her white skin and golden hair. Petrarch fuses these in a sequence predicated on intense ambivalence. His love for Laura remains frustrated: whereas Provençal poetry includes lyrics testifying to sexual consummation, Petrarch's feeling for Laura remains intense but unreturned. And whereas in Dante's *Vita Nuova* a similarly unconsummated worship is described as the first step toward the love of God, Petrarch's sequence often presents his obsession with Laura as a kind of idolatry, the worship of an earthly good in God's place.

The form of the *Rime Sparse,* or "Scattered Rhymes" (its Latin title, *Rerum Vulgarium Fragmenta,* reemphasizes the fragmentary nature of each poem), further develops this ambivalence. Whereas Dante's *Vita Nuova* interposes prose passages between poems to make a coherent narrative, Petrarch's sequence lacks such narrative coherence: omitting the narrative links, he sets the poems in an unbroken series to focus on the speaker's changing consciousness. The sequence so constituted creates two contrary impressions. It suggests in the short term a constant change as the speaker's attitudes shift and even contradict one another from sonnet to sonnet. But they do so without final resolution, and so the larger sequence embodies a psychological paralysis: the speaker remains trapped in his passion, neither approaching Laura more closely nor managing to turn his back on her. Petrarch bequeaths this combination of variation and stalemate to subsequent sonnet sequences. His self-division appears as well in a striking stylistic trait of Petrarchan poetry, the oxymoron, or verbal paradox, like "pleasant pain" or "loving hate," a figure ready-made for the expression of emotional ambivalence.

The sequence thus takes much of its power from the speaker's tortured sense of the incompatibility between earthly love—and ultimately all earthly goods—and the salvation of his soul. The opposition appears in two contrary themes in the *Rime*—a deep awareness of and attraction to natural beauty, registered in repeated descriptions of particular places and seasons, and an almost obsessive concern with death. Long before Laura dies, the speaker feels old, aware of a need to reform himself while remaining unable to do so. While occasionally—especially after her death—Petrarch casts Laura in the role of Dante's Beatrice, encouraging him to go beyond her to her Creator, she is more often a distraction, a separate object of worship, and hence a cause of his "scattering." He repeatedly puns on her name to develop this idea. As the *laurel,* or wreath, used to crown poets, her name is associated with the earthly fame that Petrarch gives his lady but that he also gains for himself by his writing: his glorification of her is potentially vain self-glorification. As a breeze (in Italian, *l'aura*), her name is associated with inspiration and pleasure but also with empty vanity. The final poem of the sequence, a canzone, is a prayer for help addressed not to Laura but to the Virgin Mary: in the end the poet is still a scattered creature praying for salvation but not assured of it.

The sequence focuses its intense scrutiny on the speaker's mind, not the lady's. We know that Laura is beautiful, that her hair is golden, that her eyes are expressive and at times chilly or angry, but we know little else about her. Like dozens of sonnet sequences that follow it, the *Rime* develops the thoughts of a man under the pressures of desire, not those of the woman he woos. Laura is always *removed:* she is praised, remembered, occasionally addressed, but the addresses are rhetorical, accusations of cruelty to which no reply is expected. The vagueness of her characterization led some of Petrarch's contemporaries, against his protestations, to question whether Laura really existed. While it is likely that she did, the egocentric focus of the sequence prevents us from knowing more than her effect on the poet's sensibility.

While Petrarch's talent marked the sonnet sequence for two centuries after his death, there were important differences between him and later poets, and indeed, the commentaries that accumulated around his poetry changed importantly how the *Rime* itself was understood.[2] The *blazon,* or portrait of the lady's body, which figures in many subsequent sequences, has no place in the *Rime,* where sexual desire tends to be implied or suggested by metaphor. Nor does the neoplatonic love theory, which energizes many fifteenth- and sixteenth-century sonnet sequences, play an important part in Petrarch's. Some of Petrarch's imitators, like Pierre Ronsard, wrote sonnet sequences different from and more sensual than his.

In England, as in other places, the history of Petrarchan imitation is simultaneously an affirmation of likeness and difference.[3] Wyatt's Tudor

Petrarchan imitations rework Petrarch's concern with transience to focus on the instability of worldly loyalties. Sidney's *Astrophil and Stella* (1590) modulates Petrarch's ambivalence into a staged battle between the forces of idealizing love and sexual desire. The sequence differs from Petrarch's in many ways—Astrophil is more impudent and more sexually demanding than Petrarch's speaker—but his wooing ultimately follows the same pattern of stalemate. While Astrophil addresses Stella with increasing urgency and even kisses her while she is sleeping, she eventually rebuffs him, and the sequence trails off in frustration.

**The Lady as Partner**  Like many sequences, the *Amoretti* opens with a sonnet suggesting the poet's view of his work and distinguishing it from that of others. Petrarch's *Rime* opens with a retrospective address to the reader, describing the poems as the effect of youthful error: they are, he says, a raving of which he is now ashamed. Sidney's first sonnet raises the problem of how best to persuade the lady to love him. Spenser's opening, by contrast with both of these, develops the idea of the sonnet as an intermediary between himself and his beloved, a means of communication and pleasure.

> Happy ye leaves when as those lilly hands,
> > which hold my life in their dead doing might
> > shall handle you and hold in loves soft bands,
> > lyke captives trembling at the victors sight.
> And happy lines, on which with starry light,
> > those lamping eyes will deigne sometimes to look
> > and read the sorrowes of my dying spright,
> > written with teares in harts close bleeding book.
> And happy rymes bath'd in the sacred brooke
> > of *Helicon* whence she derived is,
> > when ye behold that Angels blessed looke,
> > my soules long lacked foode, my heavens blis.
> Leaves, lines, and rymes, seeke her to please alone,
> > whom if ye please, I care for other none.[4]

This marvelously serene envoy to the book is concerned primarily with the picture of its reception. As Louis Martz has pointed out in a classic essay, there is no uncertainty about whether or not the lady will "deigne

. . . to look" at the poems: it is assumed that they will enjoy that happiness.[5] The sonnets, the opening insists, are meant for the lady, and while their publication and the frequent invocation of other readers suggests that she is not their only audience, she remains their primary one.

The certainty of the opening sonnet comes from its being written to a lady who will become a bride. Whereas the traditional Petrarchan scenario involves a stalemate, the lady distant and the lover frustrated, the *Amoretti* follows a courtship that ends with Spenser's marriage to Elizabeth Boyle in 1594; the goal of marriage is mentioned as early as sonnet 6. It is thus, almost uniquely among English Renaissance sonnet sequences, a success story. This fundamental shift in the direction of the sequence entails others. The traditional sonnet lover suffers intensely and dramatically: we see him hopelessly self-divided, burning and freezing at once. Spenser's sonnets rarely portray such intensity of suffering: at their unhappiest they sound merely exasperated or depressed. As a lover who is at least forty years old, perhaps older, and contemplating a second marriage, Spenser can adopt neither Astrophil's theatrics nor his goals. He envisions not merely bedding his lady but knitting "the knot, that ever shall remaine" (6.14). While there is no fundamental change in the character of the *Amoretti*'s two lovers—there is no evidence, for instance, that the speaker who praises the lady's pride in the fifth sonnet must learn to value her as he ought—the relationship between the two develops. The lady especially is moved to yield to the lover's persuasions and accept him, while the lover now confronts the new challenges of acceptance and marriage soon to come. The underlying mood of the *Amoretti* is hope of a fruition that will be blessed. As the opening sonnet insists, it is a happy sequence.

This radical shift in the plot of the sonnet sequence makes possible the humor so central to the *Amoretti*. As in much of his poetry, Spenser's meaning develops through an ongoing generic critique, using earlier versions of the same kind to encapsulate oversimplified or failed attitudes toward the subjects he treats. In the first two-thirds of the *Amoretti* he shows the deficiencies of Petrarchan tradition, but he does so, with some gusto, by playing the Petrarchan lover. He holds up traditional clichés for scrutiny, their inadequacy suggested by their very inappropriateness to the relationship he portrays. In this opening sonnet, for instance, the reference to the "sorrowes of my dying spright / Written with teares in harts close bleeding book" (7–8) is singularly out of keeping with the poem's stress on secure happiness. Literary lovers often protest that they are dying of love, and at times they keep their love a secret—hence the "close," or *hidden,* bleeding of the heart's book. But this sonnet begins a literal book in which the heart is anything but silent: the phrase is a fossilized Petrarchan convention. This play with traditional love language pervades the first two-thirds of the *Amoretti,* but it is especially marked in sonnets 10, 11, 12, 14, 16, 18, 23, 24, 30, 32, 41, 43, 44, 49, 54, 57, and the sonnets where the lady is compared, tongue in cheek, to a bloodthirsty beast—20, 31, 47, 53, and 56.

Unlike the ladies of other Petrarchan sequences, the lady of the *Amoretti* has a recognizable character. There is, of course, a limit on the degree to which a sequence written by one lover can see into the mind of the other, but the *Amoretti* moves unusually far for a lyric form toward an awareness of the lady as an independent soul. She is more distinct than the lady of other sequences: several times we hear her voice (18, 29, 75), and often we hear about her actions as she laughs at her lover or refuses to be impressed by him. She is self-possessed, sure of her worth, hesitant to commit herself, and capable of laughter. (Sonnet 16 gives life to one of the oldest of clichés when one of Cupid's arrows is broken by "a twincle of her eye"[11].) Several sonnets (28, 29, 75, perhaps 58 and 59) record the lovers' playful sparring. As Martz has noted, the lady is the primary audience for the part that the poet is playing: her discerning eye is expected to see through false theatrics (161–62).

Both the poet's comic overacting and the lady's good sense appear in sonnet 54, in which the metaphor of life as a theater operates to stress the lover's staginess. When he is happy in his love, he "masque[s] in myrth like to a Comedy," and when he is sad, "I waile and *make* my woes a Tragedy" (6–8, italics mine). The lady, however, refuses to take these dramatics seriously:

> Yet she beholding me with constant eye,
>> delights not in my merth nor rues my smart:
>> but when I laugh she mocks, and when I cry
>> she laughes, and hardens evermore her hart.
> What then can move her? If nor merth nor mone,
>> She is no woman, but a sencelesse stone. (9–14)

In the final couplet the speaker returns to acting the part of the frustrated lover, resorting to cliché as he accuses his lady of stony-heartedness. But this mock hand-wringing is undercut by the reference to the lady's "constant eye": it is her balance, her refusal to be moved by mere rhetoric, that makes her the poet's fit audience. Her constant eye enables Spenser to write a sequence that is partly a game, played for the intelligent amusement of two adults. To a degree unknown in English sonnet writing, the lady is a partner in separating true and false sentiment.

**Self-Pleasing Pride and Mutual Goodwill**     Above all, the lady is "proud," as the poet calls her, aware of her own worth. This pride involves what medieval writers would have called "Daunger," a stand-offishness accompanied by an unwillingness to give up her freedom; the lover's most exasperated sonnets focus on this withholding of self. Yet the speaker is ambivalent about his lady's pride: when he first mentions it in sonnet 5, he sees it as a sign of her integrity.

> For in those lofty lookes is close implide,
>> scorn of base things, and sdeigne of foule dishonor:
>> thretning rash eies which gaze on her so wide,
>> that loosely they ne dare to looke upon her.
> Such pride is praise, such portlinesse is honor,
>> that boldned innocence beares in her eies:
>> and her faire countenance like a goodly banner,
>> spreads in defiaunce of all enemies.
> Was never in this world ought worthy tride
>> without some spark of such self-pleasing pride. (5.5–14)

Here pride is not the sin of Lucifera's house, but the foundation for ambitious beneficence, a pleasure in the self necessary if one is to accomplish "ought worthy." The language of the sonnet has a touch of the heroic as it suggests that the lady's concern with "honor" (like Britomart's) is more than passive. Her "boldned innocence" suggests fearlessness derived from a clear conscience, but boldness is also a knightly quality.[6] The effect is complexly reiterated in the next lines, for the lady's "faire countenance like a goodly banner" has a long history in Petrarchan poetry. It appears in one of the most famous of Petrarch's sonnets, Rime 140, which Wyatt translated:

> The longe love, that in my thought doeth harbar
> And in myn hert doeth kepe his residence,

> Into my face preseth with bolde pretence,
>
> And therein campeth, spreding his baner.[7]

In Petrarch's poem and Wyatt's imitation, the banner is Love's as the lover lets his desire show in his face, an expression that causes the lady's displeasure. Spenser reverses the metaphor: the banner is the lady's, and she carries her attack to the enemy.

Yet at other times the speaker's irritation with this independence explicitly surfaces. No matter how much one may wish another's freedom, the actual consequences of such freedom are often hard to bear, especially if they involve the other's willingness to overlook one's generosity. In much of the sequence—up to sonnet 67, when the lady pledges her faith—the speaker vacillates about her pride, at times condemning it as vanity, at others praising its integrity, and at still others mocking his own impulse to complain. The vacillation appears most strikingly in the paired sonnets 58 and 59, where the speaker first scolds the lady for her self-assurance and then in an about-face praises it as a sign of constancy.[8]

Constancy is a central virtue in the work of a poet so concerned with earthly instability, and the lady's constancy is essential to her character. If in sonnet 54 her "constant eye" opposes the lover's exaggerated changes of mood, the same opposition occurs elsewhere. Petrarch's sequence presents his love for Laura as radically destabilizing, driving him from one stance to the next and leaving him unable to gain the stability afforded by the love of God. Spenser's sequence quietly assimilates his lady's constancy to this divine steadfastness. She is in sonnet 59 a "steddy ship" that in fair weather and foul "doth strongly part / the raging waves and keepes her course aright" (5–6). Elsewhere she becomes a guide: in sonnet 34 her anger leaves the speaker feeling like a ship wandering "in darknesse and dismay" (7) without a view of her starry light:

> Yet hope I well, that when this storme is past
>
> my *Helice* the lodestar of my lyfe
>
> will shine again, and looke on me at last,
>
> with lovely light to cleare my cloudy grief. (9–12)

*Helice* refers to the constellation of Ursa Major, which would enable the lover-mariner to steer his ship. But the name also recalls punningly the first sonnet's reference to "the sacred brooke / Of *Helicon* whence she

derived is" (9 –10). *Helicon* is the spring of the Muses, and this opening
sonnet stretches the allusion to locate a central creative source giving
form to the lady's beauty as well as to her lover's poems. Sonnet 34
makes the lady herself "my *Helice,*" a guiding Muse. Love for her illuminates, inspires, and causes the speaker to transcend himself.[9]

The lovers' disagreements focus on terms like "band," "bond," and
"tie"—links that at once affirm the relationship and limit personal liberty.[10] The middle and later books of *The Faerie Queene* repeatedly explore
love's dangerous ability to deteriorate into bondage, and the speaker of
the *Amoretti* is not free from uneasiness as he tries to find a vocabulary in
which marriage need not compromise freedom. This concern gives
unusual resonance to the conventional comparison in sonnet 37 of the
lady's tresses with a "golden snare," and its flip ending—"Fondnesse it
were for any being free, / to covet fetters, though they golden bee"
(13–14)—touches on a real worry. By sonnet 65, after the lady has
shown signs of relenting, the speaker tries to persuade her that the
bonds of matrimony are happy ones.

> The doubt which ye misdeeme, fayre love, is vaine,
>> That fondly feare to loose your liberty;
>> when loosing one, two liberties ye gayne,
>> and make him bond that bondage earst dyd fly.
> Sweet be the bands, the which true love doth tye,
>> without constraynt or dread of any ill:
>> the gentle birde feeles no captivity
>> within her cage, but singes and feeds her fill. (1–8)

Spenser is playing here with the idea of liberty not only as freedom in
general but as a particular civic *space* exempt by royal license from external control.[11] The lady and her lover are like cities and will, so to speak,
merge their liberties so that their joint space will be larger. The speaker
tries to redefine the bond: it will not be an external constraint but an
enclosure created by mutual desire against the world's encroachments.

> There pride dare not approch, nor discord spill
>> the league twixt them, that loyal love hath bound:
>> but simple truth and mutuall good will
>> seekes with sweet peace to salve each others wound.

> There fayth doth fearlesse dwell in brasen towre,
>
> and spotlesse pleasure builds her sacred bowre. (9–14)

In the protective space created by "loyal love," faith rules and pleasure can be "spotlesse." Yet the eloquence of the plea disguises a certain uneasiness. Indeed, the "pride" that dares not approach is not an external force at all but the lady's stubborn independence, and the bird comparison seems clumsy: the bird may like its prison, but it is nonetheless a prisoner. In the Elizabethan period marriage was, after all, a contract giving the husband legal powers over his wife, and so it is difficult fully to make the argument for marriage as freedom. Spenser attempts to do so by imagining marriage as an enclosure created by mutual goodwill, but it is precisely in his attention to this ambivalence, and his dramatization of the overcoming of the hesitation, that his sequence stands out from others. The attention to the potential for married liberty makes his sequence a door on a world radically different from that envisioned in other sonnet cycles.

The most brilliant treatment of voluntary ties occurs in sonnet 67, where the lady accepts her lover. Like the best of Spenser's poems, this work makes profound use of its predecessors even while departing from them. Indeed, part of Spenser's meaning depends on our knowing the previous works (Greene 1982, 29–53). The central image of Spenser's sonnet—the lady as a doe pursued by her hunter-lover—comes from Petrarch's sonnet 190, in which he follows a white doe symbolizing Laura from early morning until noon, which suggests the middle of his life. Then the doe vanishes: the poem looks toward Laura's death. The Petrarchan sonnet is animated by a sense of natural beauty and a feeling of reverent delight. The vision of the early sixteenth-century imitation of it by Sir Thomas Wyatt, however, differs radically. His hind (a red deer) is not followed in admiration but hunted: love is predation on the man's part and teasing elusiveness on the woman's. It turns out that the weary speaker is simply one of many hunters—one, indeed, who "cometh furthest behind." In the end he finds the chase vain, and the hind (or woman) fickle and unchaste.

Spenser's poem differs profoundly from both works. It begins by recalling Wyatt's imitation in the picture of the discouraged huntsman:

> Lyke as a huntsman after weary chace,
>
> Seeing the game from him escapt away:

> sits downe to rest him in some shady place,
>> with panting hounds beguiled of their pray,
> So after long pursuit and vaine assay,
>> when I all weary had the chace forsooke,
>> the gentle deare returnd the selfe-same way,
>> thinking to quench her thirst at the next brooke. (67.1–8)

The sonnet's opening recalls Wyatt's poem with its emphasis on the huntsman's weariness and his "vain assay." But surprisingly, the "gentle deare" (the punning is simple to the point of being mildly funny) returns. She does so in response to beneficent natural appetite: she needs to quench her thirst.

The rest of the poem departs from both Wyatt and Petrarch:

> There she beholding me with mylder looke,
>> sought not to fly, but fearelesse still did bide:
>> till I in hand her yet halfe trembling tooke,
>> and with her owne goodwill hir fyrmely tyde. (9–12)

The lover ceases to be a hunter. Instead, the deer comes to him of her own accord, and when he ties her, he does so with "her owne good-will"—the image of an external bond is reconceived as no more than voluntary agreement. The lady's "bond" is thus the sign of her liberty. The placement of "trembling" reemphasizes the mutuality of the lovers: it is not clear whether the deer or the speaker (as the reference to the doe's being "fearless" would suggest) trembles—or both. The sonnet ends on a note of wondering happiness.

> Strange thing me seemd to see a beast so wyld,
>> so goodly wonne with her owne will beguyld. (13–14)

Wyatt's bitter cynicism has vanished, and the mood approaches the admiration of Petrarch's original. But the ending differs from his as well. Petrarch's speaker sees from a collar around the doe's neck that Caesar has made it free: however blessed, the speaker will remain at a distance. Here, by contrast, the lady will become the speaker's bride, "goodly wonne with her owne will beguyld." The stress on "goodly" opposes this kind of winning to other, more sinister kinds; as often happens in sonnets, the emotional distance traveled appears in the repetition of a crucial word in a changed context. Whereas the lover's hounds have been "beguiled of their pray," the lady is now "beguyld" with her own will: far from being caught by guile, she has chosen to yield herself of her own free desire.

**Sexual Love and Christian Charity**   In sonnet 67 the lady's "will" or wish is also the word for sexual desire: if Petrarch's and Sidney's sequences oppose human love to divine, Spenser's insists on their connection. We have already seen in sonnet 65 an attempt to imagine marriage as an enclosure in which "spotlesse pleasure builds her sacred bowre"; the insistence on the spotlessness of pleasure points to a redeemed sexuality. In stressing the goodness of sexuality within marriage, Spenser touches on a familiar aspect of Protestant thought, but he goes beyond most Protestants in insisting that human, sexual love is not only a good but distantly akin to the love of God. The poem following the deer sonnet, set on Easter morning, explicitly establishes the comparison:

> Most glorious Lord of lyfe that on this day
> > Didst make thy triumph over death and sin:
> > and having harrowd hell didst bring away
> > captivity thence captive us to win,
> This joyous day, deare Lord, with joy begin,
> > and grant that we for whom thou diddest dye
> > being with thy deare blood clene washt from sin,
> > may live for ever in felicity.
> And that thy love we weighing worthily,
> > may likewise love thee for the same againe:
> > and for thy sake that all lyke deare didst buy,
> > with love may one another entertayne. (68.1–12)

Spenser begins the sonnet as if preaching. The "we" of the first 12 lines might be that of a priest praying for the whole Christian community, and the poem as a whole incorporates phrases from the Sarum Missal.[12] The sonnet's large temporal scope, encompassing the Crucifixion, the harrowing of hell, the present Easter, and the "felicity" of the afterlife, further suggests the solemnity of a public occasion. After the extended apostrophe of the first four lines, the next eight form a series of prayers—for joy in the day, for eventual salvation, for the spirit to respond to God's love in kind. The sonnet-sermon's theme is God's love as it appears in his sacrifice and in man's capacity to mirror that love in his own. Repeated words reemphasize the mirroring—"love," "deare," and the rhyming "we" and "thee." The eleventh and twelfth lines move easily from the love of God to the love of one's neighbor: all form parts of a web of binding charity.

Then in the couplet Spenser suddenly moves from the public to the intimate, just as he shifts from high style to the simplicity of low: "So let us love, deare love, lyke as we ought, / love is the lesson which the Lord us taught" (13–14). The final link in the web of charity is erotic love sanctified by marriage. The breathtaking shift suggests that there is no absolute division between love that involves the body and the love of God: the latter is simply a purer form of the "lesson" to be learned by all the faithful. Human love participates in the divine, as its distant reflection.

This association appears elsewhere. Prescott has pointed to a religious dimension in the seemingly secular allegory of the deer sonnet: in Psalm 42 the singer groans for God "when lyke in chase the hunted Hynde the water brookes doth glad desire"; the deer here and elsewhere was often allegorized by the Church Fathers as Christ (1985, 47–52). Just as the deer returns to the speaker of her own will, so God's grace is a gift. The religious dimension does not supersede the secular love story but, in characteristic Spenserian fashion, enriches it: the sacred echoes insist that the relation of the two lovers is infused with divine charity. No other English sonnet sequence suggests such a deep connection between the Christian and the erotic, and it is not surprising that both the *Amoretti* and the *Epithalamion* frequently echo the Song of Songs, whose sensuality was sanctified by its interpretation as the dialogue between Christ and the church.

A quiet structural device in the sequence, Spenser's appropriation of the church calendar, further links the earthly and the divine. Alexander Dunlop has pointed out that the *Amoretti* is divided into three parts: an initial twenty-one sonnets, a central group of forty-seven, and a final group of twenty-one.[13] The middle group begins with the sonnet 22 on Ash Wednesday, "this holy season, fit to fast and pray," and the following forty-seven sonnets cover the days of Lent, ending with sonnet 68 on Easter Day. The stress on the church calendar assimilates the trials of Spenser's wooing to the Lenten period and joins his joy in his lady with the Christian joy in the salvation Christ has won for sinners. The Lenten reading of the sequence has been challenged, and it is not the only way of reading the time period covered by the sonnets. But it is characteristic of Spenser to make the correlation, and such a reading illuminates his larger attempt to sanctify earthly love.

The Lenten calendar is a particular instance of the book's unusual treatment of time. In most sonnet sequences time appears as the destroyer of the beloved's beauty, against which the poet marshals his art. Petrarch's sequence is centrally concerned with time the devourer. References to the beauty and vitality of returning spring highlight the speaker's aging and his lack of progress; recurrent sonnets on the death of friends stress the brevity of all earthly life. By contrast, time in the *Amoretti* has a shape. The sequence presents a process of wooing that leads to marriage, which will result in the children wished for in the *Epithalamion.* While acknowledging time's destructive power, the sequence emphasizes its creative capacity as well—its ability to make on earth what will last hereafter. Spenser's reference to knitting the knot "that ever shall remaine" (6.14) should be taken literally: love in this world will survive in some form in the next.

Time makes a particularly prominent appearance in the sonnets succeeding the lady's acceptance, when the wooing moves toward fulfillment in marriage. Whereas the Easter sonnet looks back to the Resurrection and forward to eternity, sonnet 70 acknowledges the present spring as a time of decisive revelation:

> Fresh spring the herald of loves mighty king,
>> In whose cote armour richly are displayd
>> all sorts of flowers the which on earth do spring
>> in goodly colours gloriously arrayd.
> Goe to my love, where she is carelesse layd,
>> yet in her winters bowre not well awake:
>> tell her the joyous time wil not be staid
>> unlesse she doe him by the forelock take. (1–8)

It is hard to capture the full resonance of this wonderfully graceful sonnet. Most plainly it is an invitation poem, a *carpe diem* lyric inviting the lady to join the rites of spring. The playful vision of her "in her winters bowre not well awake" makes her into a slugabed like Herrick's classically modeled Corinna. But the poem (like the fifth stanza of the *Epithalamion*) also echoes the Song of Songs, and as in the deer sonnet, the scriptural echoes invest the human wooing with divine associations. "Awaken" is a common scriptural call to new spiritual awareness, leaving the old life for a new. (The Geneva Bible glosses a reference to sleep in the Song of Songs as being "troubled with the cares of worldly things."[14]) "Love's mighty king" gestures through Cupid toward God, and the invitation to "wayt on love amongst his lovely crew" extends to the faithful. Spring's advent shadows a vision of time redeemed in divine love, and salvation and human love make part of the same whole.

**Burdens of Mortality**    This vision of human love joining seamlessly with the divine is not, however, left unexamined. One can consider the problem in terms of the sonnet in which Spenser describes his first kiss:

> Comming to kisse her lyps, (such grace I found)
>     Me seemd I smelt a gardin of sweet flowres:
>     that dainty odours from them threw around
>     for damzels fit to decke their lovers bowres.
> Her lips did smell lyke unto Gillyflowers,
>     her ruddy cheekes lyke unto Roses red:
>     her snowy browes lyke budded Bellamoures,
>     her lovely eyes lyke Pincks but newly spred. . . .
> Such fragrant flowres doe give most odorous smell,
>     but her sweet odour did them all excell. (64.1–8, 13–14)

In comparing the lady to a garden, the poem at once evokes and controls the powerful sensuality of the Song of Songs (4:12). Flower comparisons are usually visual: cheeks like roses are a standard cliché. Spenser's focus on smell (like that of the biblical poem) gives the flowers a sensuousness that the standard iconography lacks. Yet this sensuality is carefully limited by the degree to which the comparisons are not literal: we are not meant to wonder, for instance, why her brows smelled one way and her cheeks another. Spenser surrounds the lady with a lovely flower catalog suggesting youth, growth, and beauty. The poem recalls the Renaissance paintings in which a human image is created from fruits or flowers. Spenser further controls the sensuality of the poem with the reference to grace in the opening line. The idea of grace, hovering as it does between the idea of the lady's mercy in granting the kiss and a divine mercy accorded to the sinning mortal, coupled with the wondering praise of the whole, limits the transgressive violence that turns the lady into a garden for the delight of her lover and stresses the delights of one of the lower senses.

And yet the sonnet is oddly disquieting, as if the reference to the lady's grace did not fully contain its sensuality. The harmony between spiritual and fleshly joys is not a stable but a momentary condition, an ideal for which the speaker argues but cannot always achieve. In sonnet 72 he notes that often when his spirit spreads its "bolder winges" toward heaven it is recalled by "thoght of earthly things / And clogd with burden of mortality" (1, 3–4). The spirit-bird descends from the heaven that is its destiny to dwell with the lady, where it "doth bath in blisse and mantleth most at ease" (9). The poem's opening is troubled, but by the final couplet it regains a wondering serenity: "Hart need not wish none other hapinesse, / But here on earth to have such hevens blisse" (13–14). Taken absolutely, the line is either intensely critical of the heart or heretical, but what Spenser is doing is making honest acknowledgment that the pleasures of earth—and especially those of love—can challenge the higher realm of the divine.

As the sonnets move toward fulfillment, the lover's sensual feeling becomes more, not less, evident, and his thoughts dwell increasingly on his lady's body, as in sonnet 86:

> Fayre bosome fraught with vertues richest tresure,
>> The neast of love, the lodging of delight:
>> the bowre of blisse, the paradice of pleasure,
>> the sacred harbour of that hevenly spright.
> How was I ravisht with your lovely sight,
>> and my frayle thoughts too rashly led astray?
>> Whiles diving deepe through amorous insight,
>> on the sweet spoyle of beautie they did pray.
> And twixt her paps like early fruit in May,
>> whose harvest seemd to hasten now apace:
>> they loosely did theyr wanton winges display,
>> and there to rest themselves did boldly place.
> Sweet thoughts I envy your so happy rest,
>> which oft I wisht, yet never was so blest. (76.1–14)

The model for this kind of sonnet is European: the poem itself imitates the second sonnet of Tasso's *Rime,* and many sonnets in French, for instance, celebrate a lady's breasts.[15] But the focus of Spenser's version is not in fact the lady's bosom but the lover's imagination of it. The imagination—always the least controlled and the most liable to passion of the inner senses—here is seen to stray, and the speaker's address to the bosom witnesses throughout a conflict between spirit and matter. When the bosom is "fraught with vertues richest tresure" and becomes "the sacred harbour of that heavenly spright," it is clearly seen in idealizing, neoplatonic terms: the beauty of the body is a sign for those who would see the beauty of the soul and should lead the beholder to that higher level. But between these neoplatonizing lines are phrases—"the neast of love," "the paradice of pleasure," and perhaps most striking, "the bowre of blisse"—that are markedly sensual in their weight.

The rest of the sonnet reemphasizes this sense of transgression as it imagines the thoughts "pray[ing]" on their "sweet spoyle of beautie." The speaker's personification of his own thoughts, so that it is they, not he, that place themselves in the lady's bosom, dramatizes an attempt to avoid responsibility and suggests an ambivalence: to touch that bosom is to be "blest," but it is also a violation. The sonnet is markedly Spenserian in making a problem out of the sexual drive while not abandoning the claim that flesh and spirit are or ought to be compatible. The poem draws on many poems by Catullus and subsequent poets about pets nesting in the bosoms of ladies, but those poems are for the most part simple in their desire: the lover is envious of the bird and would like to be where it is. Here the literal bird is replaced by the thought, and the poet dramatizes his uneasiness about the degree to which his eroticized imagination may be transgressing.

The nagging presence of desire appears throughout the later sonnets as the speaker scolds himself for libidinous impulses and indulges thoughts of conquering and "spoiling" that are inconsistent with his stress on mutual goodwill. The conflict between the two visions of love appears in the pervasive imagery of food. In Sidney's sequence *Astrophil and Stella,* Astrophil insists, after 13 lines of praise for Stella's disembodied virtue, on the priority of lust: "Ah, but desire still cries, give me some food" (Sylvester, 457). The opening sonnet of the *Amoretti* revises Sidney's metaphor when the speaker calls his lady "my soules long lacked foode, my heavens blis" (1.12). She is *soul*'s food: Spenser spiritualizes the referent, making the satisfaction it represents spiritual, not sexual. The food metaphor recurs often in the *Amoretti,* standing normally for spiritual and emotional comfort. The second sonnet, for instance, addresses his love of the lady, advising it to break forth from the heart in which it has lodged, "both to ease my smart / And also to sustayne thy selfe with food" (7–8). Sonnet 35, repeated as the 83rd, develops a conceit of the speaker as a Narcissus who, having looked on his lady, no longer finds anything to satisfy him in the world and yet cannot gaze enough on her.

Yet in the later sonnets the food imagery becomes decidedly material. Sonnet 76 imagines the lady's breasts "like early fruit in May / Whose harvast seemd to hasten now apace" (9–10), and the dream of the seventy-seventh reduces her to a "goodly table . . . All spred with juncats," among which are "twoo golden apples" (2–3, 5). This comic reduction of the lady to an edible woman suggests the difficulty of sanctifying desire. Sonnet 88, written in the lady's absence, develops the neoplatonic notion that her purified image in the memory satisfies the lover, who can "thereon feed [his] love-affamisht hart," but concludes that such nourishment is insufficient: "But with such brightnesse whylest I fill my mind / I starve my body and mine eyes doe blynd" (13–14).

The final section of the *Amoretti* is its most unsettled. The speaker appears by turns angry with himself and (in sonnet 86) with others who have slandered him. The biographical circumstances of these sonnets are obscure, but the speaker's success and the imminence of his marriage seem to tax his patience as nothing earlier has. The three final sonnets all develop his sense of loss when he is absent from his lady. The first recalls one of the late sonnets of *Astrophil and Stella:* he sees time itself (in the form of day and night) as weary and unsatisfying. The second gives the lie to the neoplatonic commonplace that the lady's remembered image can sustain him. The last presents him as once more aimlessly wandering in his lady's absence. Like most sonnet sequences, the *Amoretti* trails off unresolved.

## The Anacreontics

This lack of resolution is complicated by the Anacreontics, which Spenser placed after the sonnet sequence and which link it with the *Epithalamion.* These playful poems have a history going back to the Greek Anthology: they feature a mischievous, childlike Cupid who causes pain to lovers and whose actions often suggest erotic double entendres. (Spenser had already tried his hand at the form in "March.") Despite their brevity and playfulness, they are a form of allegory and as such a means of generalization: Cupid is love, and in describing Cupid's acts, the poet suggests how love works.

Cupid works, it would seem, primarily on the body. Unlike the tradition of the sonnet sequence, which insists on the primacy of sentiment, and the tradition of the epithalamion, which insists on the public, social dimension of marriage, anacreontic verse is primarily concerned with bodily love. Its erotic psychology deals primarily with physical pleasure and physical frustration. The description of Cupid hunting with Diana's dart in the second of the poems, for instance, suggests that chastity can be a means of increasing sexual attractiveness. The final poem develops an image of wounding and salving that has obvious sexual application. The poems would seem to embody a comparatively impersonal set of generalizations about love, a coolly comic vision of sexuality that contrasts with the Christian emphasis of both the *Amoretti* and the *Epithalamion.*

Yet it has been argued, largely convincingly, that the visions of Venus and Cupid have also a hidden, metaphorical dimension that places them in the Christian context.[16] Venus as an image of heavenly bliss and Cupid as her son, wounded and comforted, suggests the possibility of divine healing for the lover, a Christian as well as an erotic healing. It is altogether characteristic of Spenser to work on several levels at once and to suggest one view of love while hiding a second inside it. The practice, unmistakable in sonnet 67, may appear even here.

## The *Epithalamion*

Unlike the *Amoretti,* whose originality becomes clear only slowly, the *Epithalamion* strikes one at once as a major work. Its vitality, its mastery of rhetoric and verse form, its variety of mood, its moments of great intensity, its sheer size—a lyric of 433 lines connecting the events of a day in an Irish town with the workings of the "high heavens"—make it one of the most inclusively brilliant poems of a great poet. It has rightly been praised for realistic vividness and good humor in describing a middle-class wedding. But it is much more. A meditation on time, its serious, witty numerological patterning reflects the occasion it celebrates.[17] Its repeated gestures of invocation, wishing, command, and prayer suggest affinities with Renaissance ideas of poetic magic.[18] And its echoing of biblical and liturgical passages quietly relates this human marriage to the marriage between Christ and his church, and the soul's ultimate end in God.[19]

While the *Epithalamion* brings the *Amoretti*'s wooing to a joyful close and returns to many of its concerns, it does so in a different mode. More than the sonnet sequence, the *Epithalamion* is a visionary poem in the sense that it dramatizes its speaker's imagining of the divine forces that guide the world and give it meaning. In Spenser's poetry the marriage of man and woman is a *discordia concors,* a uniting of opposites; here his vision of the marriage celebration also reveals the harmonious union of heaven and earth. The poem is not, however, a statement of doctrine but an act of imaginative inquiry, and as in the *Amoretti,* the speaker's attempt to envision an encompassing harmony must contend with less exalted desires and fears. While the work's wonderful bel canto rhetoric manages to make the resulting strain graceful, that strain remains stubbornly present beneath the poem's melodious surface.

**Epithalamic Conventions**   While epithalamia varied greatly in form and content, they were by and large public poems celebrating the great occasion of a noble or a royal wedding.[20] The roots of the Renaissance form are Greek: we have fragments of epithalamia by Sappho, and wedding songs occur in Greek drama. The primary classical model for Renaissance writers, however, was Catullus, who wrote three Latin epithalamia, each with classical and Renaissance progeny. His long account of the wedding of Peleus and Thetis (in Catullus 64) looked toward the tradition of the epic or mythological epithalamium, a tradition that late classical authors like Statius and Claudian developed, using classical gods to praise the marriages of Roman emperors and nobility. Catullus 62, a much shorter poem, presents a contest between choruses of youths and maidens about the relative value of marriage and virginity (the boys argue for marriage, the girls—doomed to fail—for virginity).

The poem that set the pattern for Spenser's epithalamion, however, was Catullus 61, the *Epithalamion for Manlius Torquatus and Junius Aurunculeia.* This lyric epithalamion is structured by the marriage rites, the poem follows the bride's appearance, her entrance into her new house, her meeting with the groom, and their bedding together. It ends hoping for the birth of a son and wishing the couple joy in their married love.

While the poet praises the beauty and virtue of the couple, the marriage is not primarily a matter of individual happiness: it is a joining of two noble houses. The married couple now assumes adult roles: the bride must leave her parents' house, while the groom, notes the poet with playful mockery, must give up his favorite slave boy. The poet credits the pair with desire for one another, but their coupling is, so to speak, generic: they feel what any healthy, handsome young man and woman are expected to feel. The similes comparing the bride to a hyacinth, a daisy, or a poppy reemphasize the stress on this marriage as an impersonal, biological process. The societal orientation of the wedding is reemphasized by the presence of the community—the boys who hold Hymen's torches, the virgins accompanying the bride, the "honest matrons, well wedded to ancient husbands,"[21] who put her to bed.

In Catullus's lyric epithalamion, as in others, the poet-speaker plays a central role. He invokes Hymen, and he not only describes the unfolding ceremony but manages it: he tells the boys to raise Hymen's torches, commands the bride to cross the threshold, orders the matrons to put her to bed, and then summons the bridegroom. He prescribes the duties of man and wife to each other, makes bawdy jokes at the groom's expense, and at the end of the poem blesses the couple, wishing that they may beget a son. In all this he acts as society's voice, articulating its needs and announcing its values.

Renaissance writers revived the epithalamic form in both Latin and the vernaculars. Ronsard, Du Bellay, and others of the Pléiade wrote lyric epithalamia, and Spenser might have known two epithalamia in English by Sir Philip Sidney and Bartholomew Yonge. But with a few important exceptions, it is hard to find definite echoes of other epithalamia in Spenser's poem. Rather, the many epithalamia in Latin, Italian, and French had established a storehouse of *topoi* from which Spenser, like other Renaissance poets, would have drawn: these *topoi* included an invocation of the evening star, a praise of the bride, a description of revelry, and a blessing on the married couple. Nothing, however, could have predicted the radical changes that Spenser made in the form as he used it to create a work at once cosmic and personal.

**Epithalamic Pastoral**   Even for Spenser, the *Epithalamion* is an extraordinarily inclusive poem. Like the betrothal ending Redcrosse's quest in the first book of *The Faerie Queene,* it imagines an earthly ceremony whose music is echoed by the harmonies of the spheres. On the one hand, the marriage the poet envisions is a local, middle-class celebration in an Irish town surrounded by the Irish countryside. Spenser makes a point of involving this countryside: the first three stanzas of the poem proper invoke resident deities of place and even indulge in playful boasting about the excellence of the fish in the River Mulla (59). On the other hand, these local, humble celebrants join with stars and angels.

The pastoral coloration of much of the poem emphasizes a joining of the humble and the exalted in celebration. The *Epithalamion* insists on the cosmic dimensions of the celebration from the start:

> Early before the worlds light giving lampe
> His golden beame upon the hils doth spred,
> Having disperst the nights unchearefull dampe. (19–21)

The lines effortlessly create an effect of immense space as they move from the sun to the hills to the vanishing night. They remind one, as Richard Neuse has suggested, of God's "Let there be light," associating the marriage with the divine generosity in the creation of the world (167–68).

One metaphor for the universal participation of all things in the marriage—a metaphor whose literal truth Renaissance science insisted on—was musical. The Pythagorean-Platonic model of the universe was constructed according to mathematical ratios: each of the eight spheres vibrated as it turned, giving off a single note, which joined in a divine harmony. This harmony was echoed by literal music on earth and by the more metaphorical harmonies of a just state, an orderly family, and a temperate soul.[22] In the eighth verse the speaker mentions a variety of Irish instruments—"the pipe, the tabor, and the trembling Croud / That well agree withouten breach or jar" (131–32), and their concord is both musical and cosmic. The instruments agree with one another musically, but they also agree with other sounds, and with other musics. The boys later in the stanza cry aloud "As if it were one voyce. / Hymen Io Hymen, Hymen they do shout, / That even to the heavens theyr shouting shrill / Doth reach, and all the firmament doth fill" (139–42): their harmonious unanimity joins earth with heaven. The minstrels and boys echo the birds Spenser has already described in the fifth stanza:

> Hark how the cheerefull birds do chaunt theyr laies
> And carroll of loves praise.
> The merry Larke hir mattins sings aloft,
> The thrush replyes, the Mavis descant playes,
> The Ouzell shrills, the Ruddock warbles soft,
> So goodly all agree with sweet consent,
> To this dayes merriment. (78–84)

The playful fiction of the birds as a choir looks back to medieval love
poetry, but in this context it develops the pervasive musical metaphor.
Like the musicians, the birds "all agree with sweet consent," and the
punning on "sweet consent" ("pleasant harmony" and "gentle assent")
reemphasizes the concordance of wills on the part of all living creatures.
It is no accident that the refrain focuses on the woods' echo of his own,
human, song.

The modern-day Irish boys running up and down the street crying
"Hymen, Io Hymen," like the children in Catullus, suggest a different
inclusiveness, a combining of ancient and modern, Irish and Roman,
Christian and classical tradition. The pantheon of Greco-Roman gods—
the Muses, Jove, Juno, Cynthia, the "glad Genius" of generation—appears,
while other mythological figures are referred to in similes: Orpheus,
Aurora, Tithonus, Maia, Alcmena. At the same time the poem echoes passages from the Bible—from Isaiah, the Song of Songs, the Psalms, Revelation. The bride is described in terms recalling the bride of the Song of
Songs, but she is also compared to "Maia, when as Jove her tooke, / In
Tempe, lying on the flowry gras, / Twixt sleepe and wake, after she weary
was, / With bathing in the Acidalian brooke" (307–10). It was common
practice for Renaissance writers to refer to God the Father as "Jove"; the
late classical allegorizing of pagan mythology found Christian meanings in
the most unpromising classical myths. The Italian neoplatonists merely
developed this tradition when they argued that all religions look ultimately to the same divine truths. Spenser's syncretism here forms part of
this insistence on a harmony between classical and Christian.

The poem's cosmic aspect further appears in the invisible wit of its
numerology, its use of number to underscore the passage of time and,
with that, both the beauty of earthly life and its transience. In 1960, A.
Kent Hieatt drew attention to the poem's elaborate play with number;
while not all the conclusions of his seminal study have been accepted, its
essentials are irrefutable. The poem that follows the course of the wedding day has twenty-four stanzas, corresponding to the twenty-four
hours in a day; night is announced in the seventeenth stanza, just as there
would be sixteen hours and fifteen minutes of daylight on 11 June in
southern Ireland (Hieatt 1960, 8–15).[23] The poem has 365 long lines
corresponding to the days of the year, and sixty-eight short lines intended
to equal (Hieatt argued) the sum of the seasons, months, and weeks.

We know of no one who noticed the poem's numerology until
Hieatt's work, nearly three and a half centuries after it was composed,
and it is nearly impossible for a reader to pay simultaneous attention to

the meaning of the poem's words and the line numbers in which they occur. But such a simultaneous awareness is not necessary for an appreciation of the part that this patterning plays in the poem. It ties the structure of the poem to the order of time, imitating the numerical patterning that, for a platonist, is the world's skeleton. The poem thus imitates the order it celebrates, becoming in a special sense "for short time an endlesse moniment" (433).

Neuse has argued further that this numerological play suggests the speaker's attempt to gain a kind of magical control over the events of the wedding day. The stress in the lyric epithalamion on verbal gestures of invocation, command, and prayer has long been noticed, but in the context of Spenser's lyric these gestures take on special importance. In much of the poem the speaker invokes divine beings, from the nymphs of the forest to the powers of the "high heavens," asking them to let "this one day be myne" (125)—to make this wedding day conform to his wishes. Neuse argues that in associating himself with Orpheus in the opening stanza the speaker announces his status as an Orphic poet whose songs are also charms, able to effect changes in the actual world. In identifying the structure of his poem with that of time itself, the poet tries to make the world conform to his wishes.

**"My Selfe Alone"**   Yet Spenser's poem is not merely cosmic. It differs from previous examples of the genre primarily in treating the poet's own wedding, not that of a patron. The innovation is original and radical (it was not imitated by later Renaissance poets) because it reimagines the public form of the epithalamion from within. Where the speaker of the traditional epithalamion is a public figure, the speaker of this poem minimizes the role. The exuberant, officious voice of the traditional stage manager now blends with that of the groom whose approaching marriage makes him feel personal hope and fear. Spenser gives the public form some of the subjective intensity of a sonnet sequence; its range of feeling is vastly greater than that of previous marriage-poems. When the speaker asks the Hours and the Graces to "Helpe to addorne my beautifullest bride" (105), he seems filled with an overflowing joy, playing for the sheer pleasure of it with the polysyllabic superlative. Elsewhere he modulates into folksy humor, awe, anxiety, longing, serenity, and solemn prayer. As he imagines the events of the day from the inside, their meaning changes.

The song's invocation announces its personal nature. The public poetry of eulogy and lament that the speaker recalls at the opening contrasts with the intimacy of his new subject, "mine owne loves prayses" (14), and the social world of the traditional epithalamion shrinks further when he announces "So I unto my selfe alone will sing" (17). The imagined audience for most epithalamia is the social world they invoke—the bride and groom, their family, their friends, their dependents. The poem appears to speak *to* as well as *for* a community. By contrast, this epithalamion gives the speaker no audience but the surrounding trees: "The woods shall to me answer and my Eccho ring" (18). The refrain recalls the familiar picture of the solitary (often lovelorn) pastoral shepherd serenading the woods, and it stresses the speaker's isolation.[24] This emphasis problematizes the convention by which the speakers of lyric epithalamia follow the wedding in the present tense, organizing it and addressing its participants. If the speaker is alone in his singing, the poem that follows is held up as an imagined construction—not what happens, but what the speaker in his solitude hopes will happen.

As Neuse has pointed out, this isolation recalls the speaker's solitude in the final sonnets of the *Amoretti;* the metaphorical darkness mentioned in sonnet 88 reappears in the second stanza as the literal darkness before dawn (167–68). The lyric thus develops a fiction within a fiction: the speaker appears apart from the wedding in the first and last stanzas, and in the stanzas between we hear him feign for himself the events he anticipates.[25] The poem is thus an unfolding monologue, the speaker's attempt to imagine his future marriage—and especially his bride—in a moment of present isolation. The *Epithalamion* is one of many Renaissance preparation-poems in which the speaker readies himself for an event by enacting it imaginatively. Such poems often prepare for death—for instance, "The Passionate man's Pilgrimage," ascribed to Sir Walter Ralegh, or Donne's "A Hymne to God my God in my Sickness." In them the speaker "tune[s] the instrument" of his soul by imagining what will come afterward. In the *Epithalamion* the speaker prepares himself not for death but for marriage.

This preparation brings with it an awareness of vulnerability. The poem opens with a graceful 14-line period whose very orderliness in invoking the Muse and placing this work among earlier works suggests deliberate joy. Yet with the resolution of the period, the style and tone abruptly change:

> Ne let the same of any be envide,
> So Orpheus did for his owne bride,
> So I unto my selfe alone will sing. (15–17)

The lines become simple in their syntax, end-stopped, tense: the poet warns off envy as if his joy immediately put him in danger. The possibility of hostility or mishap occurs here for the first time and reappears later in the poem. (The speaker specifically mentions envy when he invokes Cynthia in stanza 21.) The speaker's sense of vulnerability seems to increase as his anticipated happiness increases, prompting similar defensive gestures. The comparison with Orpheus further complicates the meaning of Spenser's act, for the Orpheus myth recalls at once the poet's strength and his vulnerability. As the archetypal poet-magician, Orpheus was able to change the world with his song. But the reference to Orpheus's praise for his bride (or perhaps lament for her death[26]) calls up the memory of her loss and the poet's inability finally to release her from the underworld. It brings back the forces the poet has just asked the Muses to set aside—"death, or love, or fortunes wreck" (8).

**Mutability**  This sense of the world's potential hostility plays against the poem's vision of unanimous celebration and produces a strain of melancholy to which many critics have pointed. The melancholy is often associated with time. If the speaker hopes that this day will "for al the paynes and sorrowes past, / Pay . . . usury of long delight" (32–33), he nonetheless feels the mutability inherent in these celebrations: time that creates also destroys. When he invokes the Hours "Which doe the seasons of the yeare allot, / And al that ever in this world is fayre / Do make and still repayre" (100–102), he stresses their creative force, but "repayre" necessarily evokes the idea of decay.

The tension appears vividly in the tonal shifts of the poet's address to the sun in the seventh stanza. He begins by ordering the young men and women of the town to prepare themselves as escorts:

> Set all your things in seemely good aray
> Fit for so joyfull day,
> The joyfulst day that ever sunne did see.
> Faire Sun, shew forth thy favourable ray,
> And let thy lifull heat not fervent be
> For feare of burning her sunshyny face,
> Her beauty to disgrace. (114–20)

The repeated stress on the day's joyfulness seems a little willed here, as if the speaker felt it necessary to override an unspoken anxiety. (The slightly forced quality of the tone appears if one compares the lines with the entirely exuberant repetition of "my beloved love" in the second stanza.) The poet asks at once for good weather and favorable astrological influence, but his next request, "And let thy lifull heat not fervent be," abruptly performs another gesture of averting. While he is not seriously afraid that his bride will be sunburned, the sun he addresses is more than another planet. Because it marks the day's progression, it stands for time itself; elsewhere in Spenser's poetry its heat is associated with the difficulties of life in this world.[27] Like the time it measures, the sun's energies are at once "lifull," life-giving, and destructive.

So far the tone has been lighthearted, but now the speaker shifts into a heightened style and intensity of address:

> O fayrest Phœbus, father of the Muse,
>
> If ever I did honour thee aright,
>
> Or sing the thing, that mote thy mind delight,
>
> Doe not thy servants simple boone refuse,
>
> But let this day let this one day be myne,
>
> Let all the rest be thine.
>
> Then I thy soverayne prayses loud wil sing. (121–27)

The extended invocation, the suspended syntax, the seriousness of "If *ever* I did honour thee aright," the repetition of "this one day," all create a new intensity in the speaker's manner as he moves from the life-giving sun to the sun god who assists at poetic creation. As Apollo's servant he asks for the special gift of "this one day" that he can make his own and concedes, "Let all the rest be thine." This may mean, "Let me sing *my* song this day and *your* songs forever after," but the urgency of the request suggests that more is at stake. The speaker also invokes Apollo in his role of sun god, time's guardian, and his concession points to life's uncertainty after this charmed day.

This awareness of the world's precariousness exerts a pressure on the speaker's imagining of the wedding. At times—as in the central stanzas in church—he holds it at bay. But during the subsequent festivities his sense of mutability returns. After calling the young men of the town to ring the bells in celebration, he continues: "This day is holy; doe ye write it downe, / That ye for ever it remember may" (263–64). The very act of commemoration involves seeing the wedding as already *past,* a moment easily forgotten. As if the idea of mutability had surfaced in the speaker's mind, he refers to the sun that is now on the wane.

> This day the sunne is in his chiefest hight,
> With Barnaby the bright,
> From whence declining daily by degrees,
> He somewhat loseth of his heat and light,
> When once the Crab behind his back he sees. (265–69)

After the summer solstice, the length of the day and the height of the noon sun will diminish. The passage suggests an inevitable transience.

**The Bride**   Spenser's decision to make the form reflexive, dramatizing the speaker's imagination of his future wedding, also tends to remove the lady as a distinct consciousness. The *Amoretti* is unique among sonnet sequences for the way the lady stands forth as a person with her own views, her pride, her laughter, and her sense of self, but in the *Epithalamion* she shrinks from a presence to an image. Whereas Spenser addresses the lady often in the *Amoretti,* he speaks to her only three times in the marriage-poem. Each address is a moment of surprising intimacy: the first occurs when he playfully urges her to rise from bed. But these are exceptions. Ordinarily, while we learn much about how he imagines his bride, the dramatized "stubborn damsel" of the *Amoretti* disappears.

She disappears for a second reason, one connected with the epithalamic genre and perhaps with marriage itself. In consenting to marriage, the Bride has undertaken a formal and elaborately decorous role. From the moment she rises from her bed to be clothed in symbolic garments and to move through the prescribed ritual, she becomes an icon of "comely womanhood" (192)—a figure whose perfection transcends mere individuality. Spenser's elaborate rhetoric, most notable in the triple portrait of stanzas 9–11, responds to this change, making her into an ideal figure, an icon for joyful admiration. It treats her as a *discordia concors,* a harmonious uniting of opposites. The ninth stanza begins with a strikingly resonant image:

> Loe where she comes along with portly pace,
> Lyke Phœbe from her chamber of the East,
> Arysing forth to run her mighty race,
> Clad all in white, that seemes a virgin best. (148–51)

The Bride appears like a goddess in an epiphany, and Spenser's language recalls Psalm 19:5, in which the sun "commeth forthe as a bridegrome

out of his chambre, and rejoyceth like a mightie man to runne his race."
This feminizing of the biblical text (incidentally changing a sun god for
a moon goddess) surrounds the lady with an aura of sanctity while distinguishing her from God himself. (A similar effect occurs in the twelfth
stanza, where the cry "Open the temple gates unto my love" recalls Isaiah 26.2.) The Bride's hair is an emblem of chaste sexuality, unbound
according to Roman tradition but interwoven with pearls and flowers to
suggest her purity. While she is "lyke some mayden Queene" (158), the
speaker also stresses her modesty and her downcast eyes, "So farre from
being proud" (164). The pride here is primarily haughtiness, but context
also gives it a sexual dimension that is suggested in order to be denied.
This stress on downcast modesty is marked toward the end of the stanza
and contrasts with the picture of a laughing Elizabeth in the *Amoretti*.
The individual woman is submerged in the role of bride.

The tenth stanza moves inward, from the Bride's attire to her body. It
is a *blazon*—a physical description of the lady (popular in France), usually from the head downward. While the overt sexuality of the *topos* suggests one aspect of the speaker's response, he attempts to control that
erotic potential by modifying the convention. His initial address to
"merchants daughters" (167) recalls the address to the "daughters of
Jerusalem" in the Song of Songs 1:5. The echo at once connects the
Bride with the bride of the Song of Songs and reminds the audience of
the comic middle-class atmosphere of the wedding, an effect at once
humorous and exalted. The comparison that follows combines in typically Spenserian fashion the courtly and the homely:

> Her cheekes lyke apples which the sun hath rudded,
> Her lips lyke cherryes charming men to byte,
> Her brest like to a bowle of creame uncrudded
> Her paps lyke lyllies budded. (173–76)

The common comparison of the lady's parts to apples, cherries, cream,
and lilies here gains force with the rustic diction of "rudded" and the stress
on the edible evident in the first three lines. The lines recall the picture of
the lady as a table of "juncets" in the *Amoretti* (77). The potential danger
of this sexual intensity is avoided by the sudden retreat of the next lines:

> Her snowie necke lyke to a marble towre,
> And all her body like a pallace fayre,

> Ascending uppe with many a stately stayre,
> To honors seat and chastities sweet bowre. (177–80)

The metaphors of edibles give way to metaphors of architecture on the model of the Song of Songs 7:5—cool, stately, chastely indefinite. By an elaborate sleight of phrase the direction of the blazon is reversed: instead of downward we move upward to the "chastities sweet bowre," whose physical location remains unspecified. The stanza suggests the tension between the impulse to praise the lady's sexuality and the impulse to cover it.

The stress on chaste modesty recurs as the next stanza moves beyond the visible to what "no eyes can see" (185)—the lady's inner self, which must ultimately be known by faith. Where in the seventh stanza she is crowned with a garland, "lyke some mayden Queene" (158), here it is her virtue that reigns over her baser instincts "as Queene in royall throne" (194). Yet there is a difficulty in this idealization: it appears as rhetorical overkill when the speaker insists that no thought "of thing uncomely ever may / Thereto approch to tempt her mind to ill" (198–99). Here as later (cf. 234–37) the speaker insists on his bride's chastity with an intensity that suggests another gesture of warding-off. There is no doubt that these three stanzas are examples of triumphant rhetoric, but they also suggest the strains inherent in such impersonal praise. For the stress on mutuality that the sonnet sequence investigates is limited in a poem that focuses on the mind's eye, without the check of the lady's remembered actions.

The marriage service that forms the center of the poem also tends to abstract the lady from herself. In these stanzas the large spaces of the poem's opening and closing narrow to the church itself, and the pagan imagery, so profuse elsewhere, is excluded. (Even the woods now answer Christian anthems or angelic alleluias.) The Bride becomes a "Saynt" surrounded by virgins and angels, passive and obedient before "th' almighties vew" (211). The speaker orders the virgins to "Bring her up to th'high altar that she may / The sacred ceremonies there partake" (215–16), and in the following passage she becomes the object of the cherubs' peeping eyes while her own eyes remain on the ground, "governed with a goodly modesty, / That suffers not one looke to glaunce awry" (235–36). She is passive: her qualities are personified as acting in and for her. By contrast, the world around her, the "roring Organs" (217), the choristers with their joyful anthems, the holy priest, and the peeping angels are active. It is here that the lady most clearly becomes an image from whom virgins can learn obedience (212). She is the still, virtuous center of the scene, having renounced her individuality to partake in the sacred rite. Yet, as he addresses her directly for a second time, the Bridegroom imagines a moment that recalls the lady of the *Amoretti:* "Why blush ye love to give to me your hand, / The pledge of all our band?" (238–39). The hesitance recalls the lady who playfully mocked her languishing suitor.

**Night**     The poem's second center is not the church but the bedroom. But this is a different center, a private space opposed to the potentially malevolent world outside. Significantly, the refrain changes ("The woods no more shal answer"), warding off external intrusion. During these stanzas, uniquely in Spenser's poetry, the speaker reimagines night as a time of protected intimacy. The stanzas are at once joyful and anxious, sensuous and hesitant. The long-awaited bedding is also the moment of maximum anxiety in which conflict may break out between husband and wife. It is the section in which Spenser gives more than a stanza to averting potential danger.

The treatment of the Bride changes too. When the speaker orders the virgins to unclothe her and lay her like another flower among lilies and violets in bed, his orders yield to an imagined vision:

> Behold how goodly my faire love does ly
> In proud humility,
> Like unto Maia, when as Jove her tooke,
> In Tempe, lying on the flowry gras,
> Twixt sleepe and wake, after she weary was
> With bathing in the Acidalian brooke. (305–10)

The lines bring together pride, affection, awe, and perhaps a certain self-satisfaction. The resonance of "goodly" stresses the beneficence of the lady's beauty, as the oxymoron "proud humility" does the combination of pride and modesty that have characterized her from the start of the sonnet sequence. "Proud" here, however, has an unmistakable sexual resonance, and the movement off into mythical parallel deepens the sense of awe. Maia is the goddess of earth, and as such the speaker's making love to his bride invites a sense of divine powers at work—earth and sky. The mythological comparison is also, however, a means of moving the actual worry and danger of the relationship into a realm of fantasy. The Bridegroom imagines himself as Jove.

The process begun with the dismissal of the Bride's attendants continues with the welcoming of night as a protectress. At this moment the pronouns shift: the Bride is no longer "she" but one of "we" or "us," and the speaker imagines them united against external danger. It is in this stanza that the magical, Orphic concern of Spenser's song is most apparent: it is an attempt to avert imagined evil from the marriage-bed. The appeal to night to spread her wing "over my love and me, / That no man may us see" (319–20) is a warding-off of the evil eye, an avoidance of envy; the whole of the nineteenth stanza lists evils the lover would avert. These evils begin with fears at the center of the marriage: "Let no lamenting cryes, nor dolefull teares, / Be heard all night within nor yet without: / Ne let false whispers breeding hidden feares, / Break gentle sleepe with misconceived dout" (134–37). These fears, which also haunt Amoret in Busyrane's masque, include the dangers of malicious gossip that the characters face in book 6 of *The Faerie Queene.* They are most dangerous because they attack the marriage from the inside; as he continues, the speaker tries to minimize their force by making them increasingly external and fanciful. "The Pouke," witches, hobgoblins (the first and last creatures from folktale) yield to unpleasant animal sounds: the screech owl, the stork, the raven, and finally, as the list tumbles into absurdity—the fears of the opening having been met with humor—"th'unpleasant Quyre of Frogs" (349).

By the moment of consummation, we have moved under the guardianship of "stil Silence" so that "That sacred peace may in assurance rayne, / And tymely sleep, when it is tyme to sleepe, / May poure his limbs forth on your pleasant playne" (354–56). The consummation is thus introduced by a stress on sacred peace, assurance, and timeliness: for the moment, the world has been made secure for the forces of eros. The imagination of lovemaking presents an obvious problem of tact in a poem to be offered to the Bride; it also highlights the conflict between Spenser's insistence on the goodness of sexuality and his sense of its irrational power. He deals with both by displacing some of the lovemaking onto the "hundred little winged loves" (357)—figures at home in an anacreontic poem—who "filch away sweet snatches of delight, / Conceald through covert night" (362–63). These are the erotic, secular equivalents of the peeping angels in the marriage service, and they are meant, I think, to suggest something innocent about this private act. But the poet eventually goes beyond them:

> Ye sonnes of Venus, play your sports at will,
> For greedy pleasure, careless of your toyes,
> Thinks more upon her paradise of joyes,
> Then what ye do, albe it good or ill. (364–67)

Here the Bridegroom becomes "greedy pleasure," and his bride paradise.[28] "Greedy" is rarely a positive adjective in Spenser's lexicon, and the lines suggest, for a moment, the amoral imperatives of pleasure.

**Endings**   Between the lovemaking stanza and the next the speaker's tone changes quietly but absolutely. The change is signaled by his wondering question:

> Who is the same, which at my window peepes?
> Or whose is that faire face, that shines so bright,
> Is it not Cinthia, she that never sleepes,
> But walkes about high heaven al the night? (372–75)

This magical moment derives much of its force from the fact that the speaker's attempt to organize the day now ends: the lines suggest instead a quietude and a relaxed openness unique in the poem. The low style, the humor of "peepes," and the comforting picture of Cynthia as a watchful guardian reemphasize a sense of happy, postcoital calm. In the traditional epithalamion the poet now abandons his role as stage manager to offer good wishes; here the prayers become movingly personal. There is an echo of the previous anxiety in the possibility of Cynthia's envy (376), but the speaker concerns himself mostly with her function in presiding over childbirth. His petitions differ from earlier ones: where before he has asked the gods to "let this one day be myne" (125), he now looks to the future. He asks Cynthia and Genius, the god of generation, for the gift of fruitfulness, and Juno, goddess of wedlock, for a final permanence: "Eternally bind thou this lovely band" (396). The book's final treatment of a *band* looks beyond this life to the next.

These final stanzas move imperceptibly from the easy, low style of the first wondering questions about Cynthia to the grand style of the final petition, most of it a single, magnificent periodic sentence:

> And ye high heavens, the temple of the gods,
> In which a thousand torches flaming bright

Doe burne, that to us wretched earthly clods
In dreadful darknesse lend desired light;
And all ye powers which in the same remayne,
More than we men can fayne,
Poure out your blessing on us plentiously,
And happy influence upon us raine,
That we may raise a large posterity,
Which from the earth, which they may long possesse,
With lasting happinesse,
Up to your haughty pallaces may mount,
And for the guerdon of theyr glorious merit
May heavenly tabernacles there inherit,
Of blessed Saints for to increase the count. (409–23)

The stanza views earth from the perspective of eternity. Human beings are merely "wretched earthly clods / In dreadful darknesse," an image that recalls *The Faerie Queene*'s "wide deepe" (I.ii.1.5) in which mortals must wander, looking to the North Star for guidance. The prayer looks beyond the many pagan gods to an implicitly Christian deity who is "More than we men can fayne" and asks for a posterity who will become God's saints, using this world to gain the next.

So let us rest, sweet love, in hope of this,
And cease till then our tymely joyes to sing,
The woods no more us answer, nor our eccho ring. (424–26)

In the fashion familiar from some of the sonnet couplets, the final lines quietly revert to low style. This third and final address to the lady differs from the others in its sense of intimacy, of shared "tymely joyes." The adjective *timely* has occurred repeatedly in the final stanzas of the poem: "timely sleep" is invoked in stanza 20, "timely seed" in stanza 21, "timely fruit" in stanza 22. "Timely fruit" adumbrates the pun that "timely joyes" intensifies—these are not only joys fit for or appropriate to this time but joys *in time,* joys of this world as opposed to those of the next.

The canzone form usually ends with a *tournata,* or envoy, addressed to the song itself, sending it into the world. Similarly, in Spenser's notoriously difficult final stanza, the speaker shifts his stance:

> Song made in lieu of many ornaments,
> With which my love should duly have bene dect,
> Which cutting off through hasty accidents,
> Ye would not stay your dew time to expect,
> But promist both to recompens,
> Be unto her a goodly ornament,
> And for short time an endlesse moniment. (427–33)

For all the uncertainty of its middle lines, the skeleton of this sentence is the speaker's clear request to his "Song" to be for his love "for short time an endlesse moniment." As in the opening stanza, the speaker stands once more outside the imagined drama of his poem. This return from the heightened, magical world of the wedding to the everyday of the singing moment—from what Berger would call the "second world" of the imagination to the primary world of everyday life—is common in Spenser's poetry.[29] It occurs when Immerito speaks at the end of *The Shepheardes Calender,* and within that poem, in Colin's return to himself at the end of "November"; it is responsible for the periodic punctuation of *The Faerie Queene* with proems regarding his own time. But here the movement is accomplished with triumphant finesse, for the poem that has been so far a means of solitary dreaming is now shared as a gift. The *Amoretti* adopts this stance from the start: in his first sonnet the poet sends the sequence to his bride. Here, by contrast, making the poem a gift is a final act of disengagement from the imagined fiction, offering it as a "goodly ornament" in the place of others that have been lost.

We are unlikely to learn more about these other ornaments or about the "hasty accidents" that have cut them off. But the reference to "accidents"—transient, imperfect, mutable—reemphasizes the uncertainties of the world to which the speaker returns. The gift of his poem is his response to this mutability, for it is both a proof of his love for his lady and an attempt to make the "short time" of the wedding an "endlesse moniment." The poem's honesty insists, of course, on the complementary reading of "for short time": all of time is only "short time" in God's eyes, and so the poem's immortality is limited. But this facing of mutability with an offering of love is a gesture as affirmative as any in Spenser's poetry.

## Chapter Seven
# 1596: *The Faerie Queene*

*The Faerie Queene* that Spenser published on returning to England in 1596 contained a slightly revised version of books 1–3 (the major alteration was a new ending to book 3), along with three new books, 4–6. The second installment continues the poem; it also quietly shifts its emphasis. Obvious narrative and thematic continuities appear in the ongoing stories of Britomart and Artegal, Marinell and Florimel, Timeas and Belphoebe. More grandly, the second half completes the first in treating the social virtues related to the private virtues of the earlier books. James Nohrnberg, for instance, argues that " 'friendship' is the 'chastity' of the social body, or the capacity in it for a pure love; justice is its 'goodly frame of temperance,' or its ideal constitution; and courtesy is its 'holiness,' meaning its capacity for hallowing, for reverence, for acts of faith in others, and for the reception of grace" (779). Many parallels between books support such a vision of the whole.

Yet the second installment also departs from Spenser's original epic plan insofar as it appears in the letter to Ralegh. There he envisions twelve books of private virtues embodied in Arthur, followed possibly by "the other part of polliticke vertues in his person, after that hee came to be king" (16). Yet Friendship, Justice, and Courtesy are not private virtues, dealing as they do with the social and political world. Spenser seems to have curtailed the plan announced in the letter. On such an account, the parallels between books come from his continuous improvisation as he marks analogies between outwardly different orders of reality.

Paradoxically, this concern with the public virtues comes at the same time that the poem loosens its epic moorings. If Virgil dominates the opening books, especially 1 and 2, the Virgilian presence, as John Watkins has most recently pointed out, lessens in the second installment.[1] Even when in book 5 the epic deals directly with matters that Virgil wrote about—the bitter needs of empire, the problematic attempt to ensure peace by violence—the poem departs from Virgil's model. Certain specifically epic *topoi* appear less often. No extended genealogies occur, and the only prophecy comes during Britomart's ambiguous dream at the Temple of Isis. Instead of Virgil, Spenser looks

to Chaucer, whom he invokes in book 4 as the "well of English unde-
fyled," and to medieval romances. In book 6 Spenser recalls the marvelous narratives of Greek romance, but the purposeful epic progress of
the earlier books slackens.

It is not certain why this shift should have occurred, but the project
as Spenser conceived it in the 1580s may no longer have satisfied him.
While the poem only rarely loses its humor and serenity, its second half
is more problematic than the first, less hopeful, less sure of its audience.
A biographical explanation is possible. The poem's first audience, Queen
Elizabeth, had appeared in the eyes of the New English, Spenser among
them, as irresolute and unwilling to follow good advice. His stay at
court may have given his view of himself as its teacher a check: in *Colin
Clout* Colin claims that "all the rest do most-what fare amis, / And yet
their owne misfaring will not see" (757–58). But if an epic poet is not a
teacher, what is his function? What is the relation between the ideals he
envisions and the imperfect actuality he faces?

The material of the later books inevitably raises these questions. The
study of the mind in relation to God or to the body is largely timeless:
internal battles need not refer outward to historical particulars. When
Spenser does invoke history, as he does in book 1, he does not proceed
further than the earlier sixteenth century—a distance that makes it
easy to accommodate history to providential myth. But an honest
attempt to treat the contemporary world exposes a gap between ideal
and actual.[2] Spenser attempts courageously to deal with contemporary
politics in the final half of book 5 but produces the most self-divided
section of the epic as the narrative alternately spotlights and hides its
unease.

This new uncertainty appears in two developments: an increased
attention to the epic's poet-narrator, and a corresponding attention to
the gap between the ideal truths he communicates and the actuality
they are meant to affect. The changed nature of the narrator becomes
apparent in the proem to book 4. Whereas in the proem to book 1 the
speaker is a generic figure, a Virgilian poet turning from pastoral to
epic, here, by contrast, the speaker appears as a particular man under
attack from the authorities.

The rugged forhead that with grave foresight
    Welds kingdomes causes, & affaires of state,
    My looser rimes (I wote) doth sharply wite,

For praising love, as I have done of late,

And magnifying lovers deare debate;

By which fraile youth is oft to follie led,

Through false allurement of that pleasing baite,

That better were in vertues discipled,

Then with vaine poemes weeds to have their fancies fed. (IV.proem.1)[3]

The "rugged forhead" belongs to Lord Burleigh, whose disapproval of Spenser's work must have also included *Mother Hubberds Tale,* called in after its publication in 1591. The proem thus dramatizes the situation of the historical Spenser vulnerable to the criticism of Elizabeth's most powerful counselor. It signals what Judith Anderson has called "the growth of a personal voice" in the epic, as in all the later poems (125). It emphasizes the poet's exposed situation as he defends his work against charges of immorality.

He responds with a defiant appeal to higher authority. After defending love as the root of honor and virtue, he dismisses Burleigh: "To such therefore I do not sing at all, / But to that sacred Saint my sovereigne Queene" (IV.proem 4.1–2). The poet enlists Elizabeth as a protector in whom Love demonstrates its virtues, but his sense of the queen as audience is shaky. The final stanza asks Cupid to chase "imperious fear" from Elizabeth and remove "awfull Majestie":

In sted thereof with drops of melting love,

Deawd with ambrosiall kisses, by thee gotten

From thy sweete smyling mother from above,

Sprinckle her heart, and haughtie courage soften,

That she may harke to love, and read this lesson often. (IV.proem.5.5–9)

This proem differs from the others in not directly addressing the queen. In the proem to the first book the poet apostrophizes Elizabeth as a Muse; in the second he speaks to her playfully about the reality of his fiction; in the third he asks her to see herself in his imagined mirrors. But here the bond is less sure. Elizabeth's qualities—"imperious fear," "awfull Majestie," "haughtie courage"—hardly inspire faith that she will obey her poet-teacher in hearkening to Love. The proem to the fourth book may have been added late: while there is no external evidence, it seems close in feeling to the final stanzas of book 6. But elsewhere in the

poem's second half Spenser makes us aware of a narrator who is himself
exposed to slander and unsure of support.

This poet increasingly foregrounds the fictional nature of his work,
setting its ideal truths against the actual world they are meant to influence. Throughout *The Faerie Queene* Spenser will stand back from his
poem to comment on it, often with comic or ironic intention (see, for
instance, I.vi.5 and III.viii.27). But the poem now insists on its status as
a fiction.[4] Some episodes end with unwarranted neatness, opposing the
shapeliness of fiction to the ragged uncertainties of the actual. Spenser
develops the first major episode of book 4 in this problematic way.
When Cambell, Canacee, Triamond, and Cambina appear in canto 2,
they seem a textbook embodiment of that book's concern with Concord—with the harmonious bonds tying individuals and societies
together. They form a group of four, the number associated with Concord, united by the three essential bonds that connect individuals—
bonds of kinship, of love, and of friendship (IV.ix.1–2). Their names—
Agape ("divine love") and her three sons Priamond ("first world"),
Diamond ("second world"), and Triamond ("third world")—insist on an
allegorical significance that critics have developed in detail.[5] Triamond
gaining his brothers' souls images the bond of friendship: true friends,
like true lovers, share a single soul. In its allegorical outline their story
moves from discord to concord, hostility to friendship: Cambina's arrival
with her tamed lions and her caduceus is an emblem of peace arising
from strife.

Yet such an account of the episode avoids its narrative texture, which
Spenser goes out of his way to make awkward. When, for instance,
Agape begs the Fates to lengthen the lives of her children, they tell her
sternly that "what the Fates do once decree, / Not all the gods can
chaunge, nor *Jove* him self can free" (IV.ii.51.8–9). Yet two stanzas later
they grant her request to add the life of each son, as he dies, to those of
the remaining sons. The abruptness of this about-face must be purposeful: Spenser could have avoided the Fates' initial refusal, but instead he
makes them contradict themselves. Similar awkwardness invests
Agape's solution. To say that the Fates spin out human lives and eventually cut them off is to make a metaphor, but Spenser literalizes it by
allowing the lives to be treated as individual threads that can be added
to one another like bits of string too short to be saved.

Allegory is, of course, often silly if taken literally, but this account
foregrounds the silliness, a treatment continued in Spenser's account of
the battle. Allegorical battles can be genuinely frightening, like the fight

in book 2 between Arthur and Maleager. Yet Spenser makes this battle absurd: I think particularly of Cambell's picking Priamond's broken blade out of his own head and hurling it like a knife to slit his opponent's "wesand pipe" (IV.iii.12); Diamond's standing headless because his second life has not yet vacated his body (IV.iii.20–21); or the mutual deaths of Cambell and Triamond followed by their mutual resurrection (IV.iii.34–35).[6] The tendency for the episode's narrative texture to undercut its seriousness is compounded by the deus-ex-machina appearance of Cambina, who reconciles the parties by magic when her counsel will not work. Concord seems to depend on enchanted potions and magic wands.

This story thus creates an allegorical image of an ideal—Concord—while foregrounding the ideal, bookish quality of the account, a bookishness reinforced by its attribution to the "antique stories" of Chaucer (IV.ii.32). The final stanza wraps things up in with comedic absoluteness:

> Where making joyous feast theire daies they spent
>> In perfect love, devoide of hatefull strife,
>> Allide with bands of mutuall couplement;
>> For *Triamond* had *Canacee* to wife,
>> With whom he ledd a long and happie life;
>> And *Cambel* tooke *Cambina* to his fere,
>> The which as life were each to other liefe.
>> So all alike did love, and loved were,
> That since their days such lovers were not found elswhere. (IV.iii.52)

The neat, balanced pairings of this stanza emphasize the exclusion of disorder or "hateful strife"—strife that will appear necessary to love later in the Temple of Venus. The reference to an idealized past stresses these lovers' unlikeness to any modern lovers—and to lovers outside literature. The episode presents an ideal in a way that foregrounds its remove from actual life; it contrasts with later episodes that show just how hard Concord is to attain.[7]

As Cervantes would demonstrate, writing a second part to a long work often generates a retrospective tendency, a rethinking of one's earlier ideas. The second half of *The Faerie Queene* presents a "Faerie Revisited"—a return to themes and situations that Spenser had already treated but came to see differently. This occurs most clearly in moments of self-quotation or self-parody, as when in book 6 Colin leaves his Eng-

lish and Irish pastoral landscapes to camp out on Mount Acidale. The
episodes ask us to set these later books against the earlier ones and to
consider how both relate to actual experience. While Spenser's art
always returns to the same images, expanding their meaning in new
ways, these later books stress a new sense of the gap between the poet's
ideal images and the resistant world he faces.

## Book 4: Bonds of Love and Hate

In many ways books 3 and 4 function as a single unit. Book 4 lacks an
independent quest, and Cambell and Triamond, its titular heroes, figure
only sporadically in the plot, most of which follows characters and
explores material from the earlier book. Yet book 4 presents this material
from a new perspective, for Friendship is a more public virtue than
Chastity. While Friendship can include erotic love between men and
women (Edmund Tilney named his 1567 dialogue on marriage *The
Flower of Friendship*), it also includes ties between members of the same
sex. Both heterosexual lovers and famous friends like Hercules and
Hylas, David and Jonathan, inhabit the Temple of Venus, the male
friends associated with a higher and more virtuous love than the others
(IV.x.26). Spenser's Friendship encompasses the harmonious order
appearing in the relations of the planets, the placement of the elements,
and the safety of commonwealths, as well as the bonds uniting groups
and joining individuals. The Latinate term for this order is *concord* (like
Temperance, ultimately a musical term [Spitzer, 17ff.][8]) which, as
Spenser says, guarantees the stability of the universe, binding the elements themselves in "inviolable bands" (IV.x.35.4). The Pythagorean
number associated with Concord is four, and the fourth book plays with
groups of four, like the titular heroes and their ladies, or Amyas, Placidas,
Aemylia, and Poena (Fowler 1964, 24–33; Hieatt 1975, 75–94).

Spenser's Concord is dynamic rather than static. He dramatizes its
nature in the Temple of Venus when Concord appears between Love and
Hate. These "brothers"—attraction and repulsion, the impulse to
embrace and the impulse to do battle—are fundamental forces governing the world:

> Nathlesse that Dame so well them tempred both,
>     That she them forced hand to joyne in hand,
>     Albe that *Hatred* was thereto full loth,

> And turn'd his face away, as he did stand,
>
> Unwilling to behold that lovely band. (IV.x.33.1–5)

Concord does not simply negate Hate but holds it in fruitful unity with its opposite (Williams, 79–80). Spenser here avoids equating Concord with Love, emphasizing instead that Concord binds contraries together, an idea at once psychological and cosmological. In the creation myths of *Colin Clout* (835–54) and *Fowre Hymnes,*[9] Love (there indistinguishable from Concord) "tempers" warring elements by creating intermediate terms to bind one to another. In its psychological dimension the emblem suggests that Love and Hate, attraction and hostility, are necessary to the relations of Britomart and Artegal, as they are to many other loves in book 4. This uniting of opposites is the precondition of the divine bounty imaged in Venus—hence Concord acts as the gatekeeper of her Temple.

Concord's opposite in the book, Ate (in Greek, "strife"), is not mere "hate" or opposition but an urge to destroy the bonds that Concord creates. The figure appears as early as Homer's *Iliad,* but she owes more to the irrational destructiveness of Virgil's fury Allecto in the seventh book of the *Aeneid.* Like Concord, she operates in both public and private spheres. Her dwelling houses her trophies, fragments of ruined civilizations, "Altars defyl'd, and holy things defast . . . Nations captived, and huge armies slaine" (IV.i.21.5, 8). Like many evils in the second half of *The Faerie Queene,* she operates through language, especially slander. The unwieldiness of her form may stress her disharmony, or it may suggest that her anarchic violence will ultimately defeat itself: her tongue and mind are double, her feet different sizes, each moving in different directions. She attacks everyone at random, and her successes in the book do not last long. Yet her infernal energy never relents.

Her influence appears in the counter-tetrads of the book, groups of four held together by weak or inadequate bonds. Spenser sets against the tetrad of Cambell, Canacee, Triamond, and Cambina that of Paridell, Blandamour, Duessa, and Ate herself. The rivalries of Paridell and Scudamour (disguised at times as comradeship), their sexual greed, and their repeated recourse to battle emphasize the weakness of their ties. The narrative traces the shift in their relations from comradeship to bloody hatred and back; bonds based only on mutual advantage remain unstable (IV.ii.29). An equally schematic instability appears at the end of canto 9 when Arthur and Britomart encounter Paridell, Blandamour, Druon, and Claribell in an all-male tetrad of anti-lovers. The four all

hate women in one way or another but differ as their antagonism
appears as rejection or seduction, changeableness or rigid absoluteness.
They engage in dreamlike combat, changing their allegiances moment
by moment.

Ate's influence dominates the first half of book 4, which chronicles a
succession of nasty battles. These create in aggregate an impression of
mindless, largely male aggression that is strengthened by repeated,
heavy-handed epic similes. When Paridell attacks Scudamour, Spenser
compares them to waves that

> Forcibly driven with contrarie tydes
> Do meete together, each abacke rebowndes
> With roaring rage; and dashing on all sides,
> That filleth all the sea with fome, divydes
> The doubtfull current into divers wayes. (IV.i.42.2–6)

The chaotic image suggests that the knights are moved by irrational
forces driving them to a continual, meaningless conflict.

In theory the code of chivalry, with its stress on service to one's king,
one's lady, and one's God, provides a means of controlling this aggression and giving it purpose. Book 4 experiments with chivalry in the
tournament of cantos 4 and 5, considering its capacity for creating or
strengthening bonds. Tournaments often figure in romances, as do the
particular motifs of this one—the magical prize, the exchange of armor,
the disguised knight. They usually provide occasions for the hero to distinguish himself, showing his fitness for the knighthood he claims. Yet
Spenser treats this tournament and its rules with genial irony. While
stressing the brutality of the battles, he robs them of their seriousness,
partly by limiting the damage done: no deaths occur in these lists,
despite references to bloody wounds and fatal weapons. When Triamond, wounded so sorely that he cannot return to the lists, hears that
Cambell has been taken by the opposing side, he at once dons Cambell's
armor and returns without difficulty to the fight. Like cartoon characters, these knights seem indestructible and therefore trivial.

The tournament further dramatizes how the forms of chivalry limit
love between men and women. The binding of friendship requires freedom, as Spenser insists in the *Amoretti,* but treating the lady as a fount of
transcendent beauty on the one hand and a prize on the other makes
such freedom difficult. In theory the lady's will is all-powerful, but in

fact she is the knight's possession: neither role allows for free exchange. In the procession before the tournament Satyrane carries Florimel's girdle like a sacred object:

> Bearing that precious relicke in an arke
> Of gold, that bad eyes might it not prophane:
> Which drawing softly forth out of the darke,
> He open shewd, that all men it mote marke. (IV.iv.15.2–5)

Satyrane shows Florimel's girdle to the assembly as a priest might hold up the Host to a congregation. Yet the girdle remains very much an object, meant not for worship but for possession, a *prize* to go to the winner. Like the girdle, the ladies are also potential possessions, and indeed the tournament's prizes include both belt and Florimel herself— or, since Florimel is absent, the False Florimel, whom everyone takes for the true one. The farcical moment in the fifth canto when the girdle exposes the unchastity of most ladies present only heightens the sense of a conflict between the ideal of womanly chastity and the actual ladies it does not fit. It also catches the reader in an uncomfortable bind. How are we to respond to this Ariostan revelation? Are we to join the overtly vicious Squire of Dames in cynical laughter? Are we to engage in moral condemnation? Neither stance seems adequate.

Braggadocio's role in these cantos highlights the moral confusions of chivalry. He exemplifies knighthood as empty pretense and, as such, arouses in his companions both censure and smugness. When he excuses himself from battling for the False Florimel, "they all gan smile, / As scorning his unmanly cowardize" (IV.iv.11.1–2), and the lady in question berates him for his unknightly behavior. Yet when he continues to ride with them, cheerfully impervious to shame, the group does not expel him. Instead, they make "That masked Mock-knight . . . their sport and play" (IV.iv.13.1–4), the butt of their jokes. He is necessary to the others because, while his imposture degrades the ideal of knighthood, it also supports their sense of superiority. Blandamour, who has obtained the False Florimel by attacking an unprepared Ferraugh, is no pillar of chivalry, but Braggadocio makes him look good. This complacency, along with ungratified lust, fuels the general outrage at the tournament's end when the False Florimel chooses Braggadocio as her protector. Although Satyrane has insisted on her freedom of choice (IV.iv.25.9), and although she chooses rightly, selecting the knight whose worth most closely approximates her own, the others fall into a rage, and their threats (IV.v.27) show no concern for the lady's will.

Like Cambell and Triamond, Britomart and Artegal move from battle to friendship, but their narrative explores more fully the problematic psychology of love and hate. Aggression in both hero and heroine is figured repeatedly in the armor both wear—armor that is the outward sign of knighthood. In book 3 Britomart's armor suggests her complement of male and female, thorn and rose. She arms herself for self-protection (III.iii.53) and overcomes the various male aggressors she meets without difficulty. Her self-protectiveness extends to an instinctive hiding of her quest,[10] and in the fourth book the disguise hinders friendship. In the book's first episode Britomart continues to pretend she is a man to Amoret (who sees her as a potential rapist [IV.i.5−6]), "to hide her fained sex the better, / And maske her wounded mind" (IV.i.7.3−4). The impulse behind the macho facade is an instinctive fear of abandoning a protective mask. Only when she gains unquestioned dominance, having knocked yet another knight off his horse, can she announce herself as both knight and lady, reasserting the balance of her nature. The victory enables her to relax with Amoret in a bed that can now be a place of "safe assurance" and mutual disclosure as they talk all night about their loves (IV.i.15−16). The generosity apparent when she rescues Amoret and gains entrance for the defeated knight enables her to escape her armor in the solace of mutual communion.

Artegal's armor differs. He first appears in Merlin's mirror wearing "*Achilles arms*" (III.ii.25.6), which associate him with the supreme warrior of the *Iliad,* but when he appears in book 4, he is attired like a walking wood and bears on his shield the motto "*salvagesse sans finesse*" (wildness without refinement). He thus recalls Satyrane, who leaves the wood for civilization, but differs from him in advertising his savagery. The elaborate getup is in fact, like its counterparts in actual Elizabethan tournaments, highly artful, and it announces an aggressive male pride that scorns what is civilized—and indeed what is feminine (see IV.vi.28.8−9). Where Britomart's armor balances her femininity, Artegal's insists on a willed one-sidedness: in Spenser's terms, he embodies Hate untempered by Love. Yet his rejection, like Marinell's, suggests a vulnerability he will not admit. Achilles, whose arms he bears, was also known in the Renaissance for his concupiscence.[11] While he is not sexually licentious, Artegal, like Redcrosse and many of

Spenser's other heroes, is moved by passions that grow more powerful for being denied.

His difference from Britomart's other opponents appears when they battle a second time, largely on foot. Until now her chastity has kept her above other knights and a spear's length away from them. But her love for Artegal leaves her vulnerable, and when he kills her mount, she must oppose him on equal terms. The battle dramatizes the antagonism as well as the attraction in sexual feeling: the fight quite literally uncovers both antagonists as they cut away one another's armor (IV.vi.15, 19). This violent disarming culminates when Artegal shears off Britomart's visor, revealing her as a woman.

> With that her angels face, unseene afore,
>
> Like to the ruddie morne appeard in sight,
>
> Deawed with silver drops, through sweating sore,
>
> But somewhat redder, than beseem'd aright,
>
> Through toylesome heate and labour of her weary fight. (IV.vi.19.5–9)

Britomart's angelic, sweating face typifies the comic mixing of idealization and physical realism in Spenser's art. Overcome at the sight, Artegal instinctively drops his sword and "of his wonder made religion" (IV.vi.22.3), kneeling to her as a goddess. As Lauren Silberman shrewdly points out, the reaction is wrongheaded: Artegal makes love into something else (110). While Britomart may recall both Venus and Diana, she remains merely human, and the need to recognize shared humanity is central to Spenser's idea of love.

Glauce prevails on the others to raise their visors and show themselves "such as indeed they were" (IV.vi.25.9) and gives the following reconciliation a larger meaning when she advises Artegal not henceforth to be "rebellious unto love, / That is the crowne of knighthood, and the band / Of noble minds derived from above, / Which being knit with vertue, never will remove" (IV.vi.31.6–9). Having revolted against Cupid, a potential within his own psyche, Artegal must now acknowledge him and accordingly his bond with Britomart. Yet the lovers remain uneasily bound: Artegal's wooing is a hunt (IV.vi.33, 40–41), and having gained his suit, he leaves her to complete his quest. Britomart forces herself to comply: if love depends on freedom, she must allow her lover his. She makes do by seeking Amoret: "For vertues onely sake, which doth beget / True love and faithfull friendship she by her did set" (IV.vi.46.8–9). Virtue's duties replace Love's solace.

The resolution of the battle between Britomart and Artegal looks toward others in the second half of the book. After much suffering, Amoret presumably meets Scudamour,[12] who recounts how he first won her; Belphoebe pardons Timeas; Aemylia gets her Amyas, and Poena her Placidas; and Florimel finds Marinell. Yet like Britomart's reconciliation with her lover, these happy endings are often less happy, or less final, than they seem. The bonds of love seem at times as problematic as Ate's battles. These cantos explore the difference between true and false bonds—between the loving bonds that develop from freedom and those created by coercion, ambition, or fear.

The interwoven plots of cantos 7–9 set the Timeas-Belphoebe-Amoret episode against that of Aemylia-Amyas-Placidas-Poena. The allegorical figure of Lust, who captures both Amoret and Aemylia, links them. Both plots explore desire's ability to affect bonds of friendship. The plots have clear correspondences: Lust captures Aemylia when she goes to meet Amyas, and Corflambo captures Amyas at the same time. The allegory suggests that their passions overcome and "imprison" both lovers, as, for instance, Orgoglio does Redcrosse. Amoret, too, is captured by Lust when she walks unwarily through the wood "for pleasure, or for need" (IV.vii.4.2). But unlike book 1, the narrative treats this yielding to passion without overt moral judgment: it concerns itself with lust's social effects.

The two episodes also contrast with one another, for while the Amyas-Placidas plot proceeds with unperturbed conventionality, the Timeas plot uses its conventions to comment on the politics of the Elizabethan court. The wild man, the distressed heroine, the angry lady, and the hero turning hermit are common romance motives. But the allegory ties these conventional motives to an actual court scandal. In the third book Spenser associates Timeas and Belphoebe with Ralegh and the queen, and the fourth book explores the same relationship. Between the two installments came Ralegh's disastrous secret marriage to Elizabeth Throckmorton, its discovery by the queen, and his subsequent disgrace. The difficulty of the episode comes largely from the obliquity with which Spenser treats this explosive material, insisting on the connection and ensuring deniability. Caution is necessary, for Spenser insists quietly that the queen/Belphoebe's furious reaction is a mistake (Oram 1990, esp. 354–59).

The allegory of Lust's battle with Timeas gives a sympathetic version of Ralegh's involvement with Elizabeth Throckmorton: his attempt to overcome his desire results, confusingly, in his yielding to it. Lust uses Amoret as a shield and takes a delight in her hurts that suggests their sexual dimension (IV.vii.26–27): examining the unconscious Amoret, Timeas finds she has one wound "of his owne rash hand" (IV.vii.35.9). Returned from killing Lust, Belphoebe finds Timeas bending over Amoret, decides that he has been unfaithful, and rejects him, as the queen banished Ralegh from court. The allegory suggests quietly how the private bonds of love can ruin careers, undoing the public ties between subject and prince, at least when those ties depend on a fantasy of courtship. The happy ending Spenser gives to the incident—Belphoebe once more accepts Timeas, an ending unlike Elizabeth's continued coldness toward Ralegh—implicitly suggests to the queen how she ought to act. But even this ending, as Timeas dwells with Belphoebe "all mindlesse of his owne deare Lord [Arthur]" (IV.viii.18.4), suggests that he is wasting his time.

By contrast, the Amyas-Placidas plot develops a serenely happy ending. The episode dramatizes the claims of friendship over love, a point made at the opening of the ninth canto. What is most striking about this episode is its easy denial of difficulty, as the ideal friends stand in for one another and the lusty Aemylia and the willful Poena find happiness in their marriage to the two friends. The tetrad thus created recalls that of Cambell and Triamond: it is another instance of an idealized romance avoiding the problems of class and character that dominate the treatment of Timeas.

Canto 8 joins both plots with a remarkable passage in which Arthur, Amoret, and Aemylia stay in the house of Sclaunder. Both episodes hinge on the proper understanding of appearances, and misapprehension and vicious gossip pose a threat in both, as they must have in the Ralegh-Throckmorton story. Sclaunder insists that Arthur is sleeping with the women he protects, and the narrator addresses the audience in a surprising speech:

Here well I weene, when as these rimes be red
  With misregard, that some rash witted wight,
  Whose looser thought will lightly be misled,
  These gentle Ladies will misdeeme too light,
  For thus conversing with this noble Knight;
  Sith now of dayes such temperance is rare
  And hard to finde, that heat of youthfull spright
  For ought will from his greedie pleasure spare,
More hard for hungry steed t'abstaine from pleasant lare. (IV.viii.29)

The speaker's vision of his corrupt age moves him to accuse his readers, some of whom will not believe in Arthur's virtue. The suspicion cannot be taken literally: no one reading the episode would accept, against the author's silence and romance convention, that Arthur would indulge in hanky-panky with his ladies. But the comment dramatizes the narrator's increasing isolation from the very group his epic intends to teach. If slander ruins language—then and now—how is the poet himself to be free from misreading?[13]

The differences between books 3 and 4 appear in their treatment of Scudamour. In book 3 he is an impatient lover, burning with desire to cross Busyrane's moat and relapsing into tantrums when he cannot. His inability to rise above passion—mirrored in the fire that scorches him—prevents him from joining Britomart to rescue Amoret. In book 4 the narrative frames his story differently: he is a knight who, despite (or perhaps because of) his knightly prowess, fails at friendship. Jealousy in book 3, as imaged in Malbecco, is a sickness of love; by contrast, Scudamour's jealousy in book 4 is a version of discord, created by Ate's slanders in a social situation (IV.i.46–53). Knowing little of Amoret, Scudamour takes Ate's words as truth. When Amoret tries on Florimel's girdle (IV.v.19), Scudamour seems not to notice her: perhaps an Amoret capable of buckling Florimel's belt, a symbol of chastity, around her waist does not match the image Ate has planted in his mind.

In both books Scudamour demonstrates an adolescent self-centeredness; he is unable to see beyond his longing and his grief. The grief appears vividly in his stay with Care. *Care* is an ambiguous word in Spenser's lexicon, appearing in *The Shepheardes Calender* as both the shepherd's beneficent attention to his sheep and Colin's solipsistic sorrow. Scudamour's Care, an infernal version of Colin's, resembles Despaire, a cave-dwelling, melancholy, starved, hollow-eyed blacksmith who "to small purpose yron wedges made." The wedges, glossed by the narrator as "unquiet thoughts" (IV.v.35.8–9), suggest the invasiveness of Scudamour's obsessions. This is another house of Ate dominated by restless fantasy (Care's six servants, as William Nelson pointed out, parody the Pythagorean idea of musical harmony [1963, 250]). While Scudamour's sleeplessness results most immediately from slander, its roots appear in his account in canto 10 of how he claimed Amoret in the Temple of Venus.

Love is a divine mystery in *The Faerie Queene,* and Spenser keeps it mysterious by presenting the Temple of Venus through the eyes of a narrator who does not understand it, an unexpectedly novelistic device.[14]

Just as Scudamour remains uncertain about the material of Venus's altar
(IV.x.39) and sees Venus only through a veil (IV.x.41), so his whole
account places a screen between the reader and this ambiguous paradise.
Scudamour's consciousness does not, as it might in a realistic novel,
entirely control the narration: he offers information he cannot have
when he describes Concord, Love, and Hate. But his views are conditioned either by his limited, rigid chivalric code or by a sour cynicism
rarely adequate to his needs. His opinions usually consist of proverbial
clichés. Describing Delay, he comments that she tries "time to steale,
the threasure of mans day, / Whose smallest minute lost, no riches render may" (IV.x.14.8 –9). In forcing Amoret to leave with him, he shakes
off his "shamefast fear / Which Ladies love I heard had never wonne"
(IV.x.53.6 –7). The "I heard" is revealing: he takes his wisdom second-
hand.

Although Scudamour describes Concord joining Hate and Love, he
does not use what he sees to make sense of events. For him life is either
Hate or Love: the two do not mix. He begins his account of the Temple
entirely in the mode of aggressive, military action. When he has
knocked his quota of knights off their horses, he claims the shield and
advances to the gate before the bridge, presided over by Doubt and
Delay. These allegorical figures mark an initial complication. The
episode has begun as a romance adventure in which a young knight performs a feat of arms, winning a shield and (by implication) a lady, but it
now becomes a courtship allegory with characters—Doubt, Delay,
Daunger—who recall the allegorical wooing in *The Romance of the Rose.*
Yet unlike the narrator of *The Romance of the Rose,* Scudamour does not
see these figures as representatives of the lady but as military opponents.
Whereas Daunger traditionally embodies the lady's stand-offishness,
Scudamour sees him in literal military terms, an identification that
recalls the Ovidian view of love as military conquest (*Amores,* I.9.1:
"Militat omnis amans, et habet sua castra Cupido" [Every lover is a soldier, and Cupid has his war camp]). It also suggests the assumptions
about women that such a view involves: if they are really the enemy,
then it is no accident that he sees in Daunger's deformed hindparts an
ambush of "hatred, murther, treason and despight" (IV.x.20.6).

After the bridge Scudamour moves from a fantasy of combat to a fantasy of unalloyed pleasure. He has "past all perill" (IV.x.21.1), and the
garden of Venus seems like a paradise in which "thousand payers of lover
walkt, / Praysing their god, and yeelding him great thanks, / Ne ever
ought but of their true loves talkt, / Ne ever for rebuke or blame of any

balkt" (IV.x.25.6–9). This is Love without Hate, hence without the
complicating and humanizing conditions that make it earthly love.
There is an irony in the picture of specialized lovers who speak of love
only, leaving no room for the give-and-take of actual exchange. Scudamour insists repeatedly on the unalloyed pleasure of the place and
envies the lovers who "being free from feare and gealousye,"

> Might frankely there their loves desire possesse;
> Whilest I through paines and perlous jeopardie,
> Was forst to seeke my lifes deare patronesse:
> Much dearer be the things, which come through hard distresse.
>
> (IV.x.28.6–9)

The final line tries to discount an envy of lovers who have everything
made—who have none of the problems that come with everyday life.

Yet this vision of pleasure omits the garden's pain. Within the Temple
of Venus are a "Great sorts of lovers piteously complayning" (IV.x.43.2),
and one lover sings a hymn to Venus because he is "Tormented sore"
(IV.x.43.8). The statue of Venus is itself mysterious, veiled, bisexual; it
recalls the medieval figure of Nature and the classical figure of Lucretius's
Venus while transcending both.[15] The hymn, which imitates the invocation of Lucretius's *On the Nature of Things,* envisions the goddess as a
source of generation who causes the earth to bloom, the animals to mate,
and the world to renew itself. Its scope transcends Scudamour's limited
knightly perspective: it makes his efforts part of an impersonal drive to
populate the world. Despite her association with pleasure, Venus concerns herself less with individual happiness than with the creation of life.

On finding Amoret, Scudamour is torn with doubt, "For sacrilege me
seem'd the Church to rob, / And folly seem'd to leave the thing
undonne" (IV.x.53.3–4). Sacrilege wins out, and Scudamour removes
his "glorious spoyle of beautie" (IV.x.58.3) from the Temple, despite her
pleading. He is encouraged when he sees the statue of the goddess "with
amiable grace / To laugh at me and favour my pretence" (IV.x.56.3–4).
The meaning of Venus's laugh remains obscure: it recalls the familiar
male wisdom that women really want to go to bed even when they
protest, but it may also suggest that Venus is willing to sacrifice Amoret
or any other individual woman for her larger plans.

This is wooing as a military operation—quite literally "shield love"
(Scud-amour)—whose defects have already appeared in book 3 when

Britomart comes across Amoret paralyzed by her fear of her lover. When Britomart reads Busyrane's riddling advice, "Be Bold, Be Bold, Be Not Too Bold," she needs to consider the dangers of her own impetuousness, but the words gain in meaning when applied to Scudamour, who has misunderstood the nature of his quest for love (Hieatt 1975, 102–13). Lovers may need Doubt and Delay, for instance, if they wish to understand one another. If Scudamour is to find in Amoret a wife as well as a prize, he has to approach her differently, and the poem presents no evidence that he realizes this necessity. His progress suggests the stages of a wooing: after initial Doubt and Delay one treats directly with Daunger and comes eventually to knowledge of the linked opposites of Love and Hate. But he misreads the signposts. As a result, two figures that bar his way as he enters Venus's realm—Doubt and Daunger— resurface in Busyrane's masque, having never been adequately dealt with. At the opening of the canto Scudamour refers to Amoret as "this peerelesse beauties spoile" (IV.x.3.3), implying their physical reuniting, but the meeting remains undramatized. True recognition is forestalled.

The originality of Spenser's imagination appears in his treatment of the most familiar epic *topos,* the catalog, which he makes into a celebration of marriage, of England, of concord, of the temporal world itself. In epics the catalog appears largely in lists of warring armies and ships. It develops the magnitude of the epic action and incorporates a sense of the *local* represented by particular warriors. Spenser never creates the traditional lists of opposing armies: accounts of collective military action never seem to have appealed to his imagination. He signals the epic nature of his task by a formal invocation to Clio, the Muse of history (IV.xi.10), but the following enumeration is a catalog of rivers. With a characteristic Spenserian shift, the epic leaves the human dimension for the larger structures of the world.

The marriage of rivers has, of course, a local, patriotic dimension. The catalog celebrates England and Ireland by praising their rivers, with loving attention to their courses, the cities that border on them, their swiftness, their fish, their history and local legends. The political ramifications of the description surface when Themes himself appears, bearing on his head the city of London, or Troynovant "like to a Coronet" (IV.xi.27.6): the reminder that London is "New Troy" touches on the imperial myth of England as the inheritor of the legacy of Troy and Rome.[16] This canto may revise the *Epithalamion Themesis* that, E.K. mentions, the young Spenser had written—a poem that probably celebrated the earl of Leicester, through whose lands the Thames and Medway make their way. Fowler has suggested that the naval area of the Medway embodied England's might and that the whole episode celebrates the marriage between Elizabeth and her people (172–75). The only time the narrator addresses his audience directly, he encourages it to colonize the Amazon's "land of gold" (IV.x.22.5), creating an English empire to rival that of Spain.

For Spenser to have done so much would be no more than Drayton attempted in the next generation in his mammoth *Poly-Olbion* (1622), an epic-size celebration of British rivers and the British countryside. But Spenser goes beyond Drayton's concern with the local and the patriotic; the river-marriage clearly touched on something important to his imagination (Roche 1963, 167–84).[17] We have already met it in the marriage of Bregog and Mulla in *Colin Clout;* Spenser will return to it again in the *Mutabilitie Cantos.* The river-marriage is itself a familiar minor form in Renaissance Italian and neo-Latin literature,[18] but it gains special importance in Spenser's work because it serves as a metaphor for the world of becoming. Unlike most epic writers, Spenser usually dispenses with the epic machinery of divine and infernal beings planning the lives of the mortals below. (The closest he comes to such a council is the ad-hoc meeting between Duessa and Night in book 1—tactics at best, not strategy.) Instead, he represents through emblematic description—the Castle of Alma, the Garden of Adonis, the Temple of Venus, the Marriage of Rivers, the Dance of the Graces in Acidale—how and why the world works.

The association of the river with time appears at least as early as Heraclitus's remark that one can never put one's foot in the same river twice. Crossing the bridge to Venus's isle, Scudamour hears "underneath, the river rolling still / With murmure soft, that seem'd to serve the workmans will" (IV.x.15.8–9). The resonant line revives this association ("rolling still" punningly presents a paradox of motion and continuity) and reminds one that the stasis of the Temple is surrounded by the world of process. The river-marriage develops the concern with time and change on a grand scale but pairs it with a sense of ultimate order and unity, embodied in the marriage. This canto celebrates not only England and Elizabeth but the whole world of becoming, the world of time, in the house of Proteus, god of change.

Change appears most obviously in Spenser's attention to history—not only the local histories and legends of British rivers but the histories of the world. Neptune's sons include "famous founders . . . / Of puissant Nations, which the world possest" (IV.xi.15.1–2), including the giant

Albion himself. As the archetypal *imperium,* Troy holds a central place. We hear about it just after the introduction of Ocean and Tethys, for their son, Nereus, has the gift of prophecy and foretold Troy's fall (IV.xi.19). A stanza later Spenser mentions "Divine Scamander, purpled yet with blood / Of Greekes and Troians, which therein did die" (IV.xi.20.7−8). The celebration of rivers, which reminds one of the New Troy that is England, recalls as well the fall of Old Troy and the fragility as well as the creation of new civilizations.

For a platonist the world is a perpetual dialogue between the One and the Many: the One, potential beyond time, spills over in its fullness, shaping matter in an approximation of its forms, while matter gradually loses the imposed shape, reverting to formlessness. Many platonists concern themselves primarily with the human need to return to the radiant, timeless perfection of the One, away from what Milton calls the "smoke and stir of this dim spot" (*Comus.* l.5).[19] Yet for one platonic tradition the world is not merely a pale reproduction of the forms but good in its fruitful multiplicity.[20] This canto celebrates that multiplicity, and Spenser emphasizes here, as in the Garden of Adonis, the idea of fruitfulness. Looking back at the canto, the narrator comments:

> O what an endlesse worke have I in hand,
>> To count the seas abundant progeny,
>> Whose fruitfull seede farre passeth those in land,
>> And also those which wonne in th'azure sky? (IV.xii.1.1−4)

But there are other forms of fruitfulness: of fish (33, 35, 43), of cities, of myths, even of scholars (26, 34). The very idea of marriage—of two becoming one—embodies in condensed form the idea of the movement between the one and the many, and toward the end of the description of the Irish rivers Spenser falsifies geography to picture three rivers that rise in the same place, part, and join once more before losing themselves in the larger sea: "All which long sundred, doe at last accord / To join in one, ere to the sea they come, / So flowing all from one, all one at last become" (IV.xi.43.7−9).[21]

While the river-marriage celebrates time and change, Marinell and Florimel have been kept artificially separate from the world of process. Both are imprisoned by immortals, Florimel by Proteus in "sad thraldomes chayne" (IV.xi.1.5), and Marinell by his mother, "like her thrall; / Who sore against his will did him retaine, / For fear of perill, which to him mote fall" (IV.xi.7.6–8). While Cymodoce tries to protect her son against Proteus's prophecy that a woman will kill him (III.iv.25.9), her fears originated in his mortal nature; she tries to protect him from the dangerous world itself in the womblike security of the sea. Florimel shares Marinell's mortality, which Spenser stresses by excluding both from the feast, at which Marinell cannot eat immortal food (IV.xii.4). Exiled from the gods' table, he wanders about Proteus's domain until he hears Florimel's lament.

In her lament Florimel asks that Marinell be imprisoned with her: "So had I rather to be thrall, than free; / Such thraldome or such free-dome let it surely be" (IV.xii.10.8–9). As in the *Amoretti,* Love's bands limit some freedoms while offering a possibility of new life. Moved initially with "soft remorse and pitty rare" (IV.xii.12.5), Marinell for the first time looks beyond himself. The comic sequel, in which he sickens with love, forcing his mother to help him, highlights the difference between her immortal protectiveness and his mortal needs. The narrator comments drily: "It's late in death of daunger to advize, / Or love forbid him, that is life denayd" (IV.xii.28.6–7). Cymodoce has the choice of allowing her son to die or to risk his life in his own way, by loving Florimel; he will die in either mortal or immortal bands. (There is a sexual pun buried in Proteus's prophecy that a woman will "dismay or kill" him.) The marriage of the Thames and the Medway thus becomes the occasion for recommitting Florimel and Marinell to the world of process—the world that the marriage itself celebrates.

## Book 5: Approximations of Justice

Whereas Friendship encompasses the bonds between individuals and the larger Concord of the universe, Justice focuses more narrowly on the political order. The two overlap. Aristotle points out that both virtues regulate communities (*NE,* 1159b25–1160a), and like Friendship, Justice has cosmic equivalents: the sun and moon run "in equall justice" (V.vii.iv.9), dividing day and night between them. Nonetheless, the Book of Justice distinguishes itself from the Book of Friendship by its concern with rule. Few of its incidents concern the righting of private wrongs; most deal with governorship. This is a book of princes, and Elizabeth appears in her public role as she attempts to secure public order and establish just relations between states.

Such order is not easy to ensure. The proem, a miniature complaint, attacks an age in which human nature has grown stony and the constellations, evidence of Concord's bonds in book 4 (x.35), stray from their proper paths. The proem dramatizes a nostalgic gloom increasingly present in the later books of the epic, and its final eulogy of the queen's justice seems incongruous after nine stanzas of accusatory lament. Later canto 8 will scrutinize the queen's justice as well as praise it. The fifth book stresses the difficulty of imposing an imperfect, temporary justice on this corrupt world, and the emphasis results in a peculiar harshness. The snappish quarrels of book 4 lead to frequent battles, but its only deaths are those of the half-realized brothers Priamond and Diamond, along with the allegorical figures of Lust and Corflambo. By contrast, book 5 is littered with corpses and disfigurements, from the headless lady of the first canto to the poet of the eighth, his tongue nailed to a post outside the queen's throne room. Giants play a significant role in book 5, and in the seventh canto Spenser relates them to the Titans, who revolted against the gods until driven back and slain. The urge to rebellion and lawless violence returns repeatedly, and its presence necessitates a constant wary repressiveness.

In turning to the resistant world in which Justice must operate, book 5 brings the historical allegory of book 1 up to date, considering the events of the preceding twenty years both nationally and internationally—in England, France, the Low Countries, and Ireland. The attention to recent history constitutes an act of faith as the poet attempts to connect the ideals of justice with the particulars of the actual. Yet the faith becomes increasingly strained. In its unmanageable particulars recent history does not square easily with the ideal providential patterns that one can find in more distant events. Sidney argues in his *Defence of Poetry* that history is a poor moral teacher largely because it deals with what *has* happened as opposed to what ought to happen. Accordingly, in the final cantos of book 5 Spenser often departs from the actual even while pretending to deal with it. At its greatest, the book acknowledges the ambivalences of history, the just ruler's difficulty in balancing conflicting claims. At its weakest it flattens into a polemical defense of common sixteenth-century positions—justifying the repression of Anabaptists, or women, or Ireland—that leaves modern readers feeling morally uneasy. "Spenser was the instrument," C. S. Lewis wrote, "of a detestable policy in Ireland, and in his fifth book the wickedness he had shared begins to corrupt his imagination."[22] Much of the book does support a violent repressiveness, as when Talus shoulders the Egalitarian Giant off his cliff onto the rocks below. Yet the poem remains alert in various ways to what such repressiveness costs, as it does in the pathetic simile describing the Giant's fall.[23] In book 5 more than in any other, the poet confronts the constrictions of the actual world and the awareness that moral action usually involves choosing the lesser of two evils.

Spenser places Artegal, his knight of Justice, in a line of culture-bearers that includes Bacchus and Hercules. Both figures were allegorized in the Renaissance as bringers of law and civilized knowledge, but both were also morally ambiguous, tainted by violent irrational excess.[24] Both Artegal and Hercules—with whom Spenser repeatedly compares Artegal—subdue tyrants and restore law. Yet Hercules' womanizing leads to his death, and his love for Omphale causes him to abandon his heroic identity, obeying her, wearing women's clothes, and engaging in the women's work of spinning. Artegal's weaknesses appear in the account of his rearing by Astrea, goddess of Justice, in "a cave from companie exilde" (V.1.6.7). This secret upbringing keeps Artegal clear of human corruption but limits his knowledge of human beings. He practices justice on the beasts of the wood (V.i.7–8), and while the detail may imply that all fallen human beings share a bestial savagery, it also suggests that Artegal lacks experience in more complex cases (Patterson 1993, 91). When he appears in book 4, he does so as the salvage knight, and men notice his justice less than his "overruling might" (V.i.8.4).

Astrea, whose ideal nature will not abide the corruptions of the iron age, abandons the world to Artegal, leaving her groom to assist him:

> His name was *Talus,* made of yron mould,
>
> Immoveable, resistlesse, without end.
>
> Who in his hand an yron flale did hould,
>
> With which he thresht out falshood, and did truth unfould. (V.i.12.6–9)

Where the companions of the other questing knights of *The Faerie Queene* are moral guides or (in Glauce's case) morally supportive companions, Talus is simply an extension of Artegal's power. He is an instrument: his "end" needs to be given him by his master. Iron himself, he embodies the violence necessary to impose law in the iron age: in Jane Aptekar's oft-quoted words, he is "a bloodhound and a police helicopter, an executioner and an army" (41–42); Lewis would add that on occasion he is a torturer ("Talus is the rack as well as the axe" [348]). He can get out of hand: at least once Artegal is forced to recall him from unnecessary slaughter (V.xi.65).

After the multiple plots of books 3 and 4, book 5 returns to the single narrative of earlier books, and like them, it is structured in part as a fall and recovery. After initial easy successes, Artegal is imprisoned by Radigund; rescued, he returns to his original quest with a new maturity.[25] But Artegal's virtue is not a private one, and his adventures also develop the nature of Justice. Spenser makes use of a familiar threefold distinction between Justice, which enforces laws; Equity, which modifies those laws in accord with particular circumstances; and Mercy, which forgives wrongs instead of punishing them. The book explores Justice proper (mentioned in the proem to canto 4) in cantos 1–4.20, Equity (mentioned in the proem to canto 7) in cantos 4.21–7, and Mercy (mentioned in the proem to 10) from canto 8 to the end.[26] As the book progresses it takes fuller account of the actual world, in which Artegal can only attempt an approximation of Justice.

The early episodes of the poem present schematic cases, instances of lawlessness, oppression, rebellion, and fraud; Artegal's wit and power sweep away opposition. The first is a textbook case. Sir Sanglier, who cuts off his lady's head, provides an instance of power unrestrained by civilized laws, power not only to take the Squire's lady away and kill his own but to make the Squire afraid to accuse him. Artegal solves the problem by imitating the most famous legal judgment of the Old Testament, that of Solomon. One moral is clearly that successful justice needs the aid of a certain guile.[27]

In canto 2, Artegal triumphs over contrasting threats to hierarchical order, from the nobility and the common people. Pollente and his golden-footed, silver-handed daughter are allegorical images of power and riches, extorting what they want from the weak and the poor. Like Sir Sanglier, Pollente embodies power without the constraint of law, although he acts not from lust but from greed. Power used for personal gain creates gold; accordingly, Spenser's allegory makes Munera, his daughter, the *result* of his acts. The independent might of the great nobility posed a problem for the Elizabethan regime and was a particularly vexing problem in Ireland, where the great Anglo-Norman landholders—the Old English—often opposed the New English attempting to assert the crown's rights. With necessary severity Artegal beheads Pollente and cuts off the daughter's hands and feet (purging the body of filthy lucre) and drowns her, appropriately, in the "durty mud" (V.ii.27.4).

By contrast, the egalitarian Giant represents a threat from below. Unlike Pollente, he does not appear greedy, although he is followed by a crowd who hope to make themselves rich (V.ii.33.4). He is an idealist—

he is almost certainly associated with the Munster Anabaptists, who practiced community of goods—and he bears the scales associated with Astrea as he attempts to deliver justice.[28] The basis of his claim perverts the golden-age argument prominent in the proem to book 5—a perversion anticipated by the Fox in *Mother Hubberds Tale*. He argues that the original equality of all things has been lost: just as the sea has encroached upon the land, so nations have "run awry" (V.ii.32.6); his reform will suppress tyrants and redistribute wealth, just as he will throw down the "mountaines hie, / And make them levell with the lowly plaine" (V.ii.38.1–2). The Giant's language here echoes God's biblical power (see Luke 3.5) because he has assumed God's role: his human justice replaces trust in providence with a fantasy of restored perfection in this world.[29] Accordingly, Artegal criticizes the Giant's implicit theology: his attack also echoes the Bible, emphasizing God's guidance and the Giant's ignorance.[30] He further challenges the Giant's literalism in attempting to balance right and wrong as if they were physical, measurable quantities. Right exists in the mind, and it balances extremes, sitting not in either pan of the scales but "in the middest of the beame alone" (V.ii.48.9). When the Giant will not be persuaded, eloquence gives way to violence: Talus casts him from his cliff to die on the rocks.

Artegal prevails again in the next episodes. Whereas the tournament of book 4 ends in disarray, the tournament of book 5 ends neatly, with malefactors getting their just deserts. Artegal exposes Braggadocio's transparent attempt to claim credit for the tournament victories and restores Guyon's horse, after which Talus ends the false knight's career by shaving his beard, defacing his shield, and scattering his arms. The false Florimel presents a greater threat. She seems temporarily to outshine the true Florimel, even in the eyes of her lover (V.iii.18–19), but when Artegal confronts her with the true lady, her nullity appears and she evaporates like a rainbow (V.iii.24). The episode of the two brothers resolves with equal neatness as it moves from the threat of fratricide to the security of law. In Artegal's words, "equall right in equall things doth stand" (V.iv.19.1): the same principles that enable the younger brother to claim the land from the elder brother's island also enable the latter to claim the sea-borne dowry. Providence ultimately governs the world's changes and here creates a quid pro quo for the brothers. This is the most perfect of Artegal's judgments.

The schematic quality of these incidents clarifies their principles, but it also foregrounds their fictional nature—their distance from the complexity of actual life. Many episodes also suggest a troubling rigidity to

Artegal's judgment, a tendency to act according to abstract formulae. In the first episode, for instance, he follows Solomon precisely, but Solomon's situation differed. He was judging between two women, each of whom claimed an infant, and discovered the truth in the absence of other testimony by his threat to divide the child. In the case of Sir Sanglier, however, a witness exists, the Squire's lady, whom Artegal does not bother to question.[31] Artegal goes literally by the book, following Solomon and ignoring the new circumstances. His lack of interest in the lady's testimony accords with the savage masculinity he has exhibited in book 4 and makes his justice seem mechanical. Similar literal-mindedness appears after he executes Pollente and his daughter. He seizes their "mucky pelfe" and "burning [it] all to ashes, powr'd it down the brooke" (V.ii.27.9). Attempting to destroy evil at its root, he attacks the gold as if it were the cause of wrong, not its instrument, forgetting that the source of evil lies ineradicably in the fallen human heart.[32] The acts suggest great naïveté or frustrated rage at a world in which other Pollentes and Muneras remain to prey on others.

A different blindness guides him at the tournament, where, by borrowing Braggadocio's armor, he makes possible the attempted fraud. In romances knights often disguise themselves in other knights' armor, as Cambell does in book 4, and by and large these disguisings have a purpose. In book 4, for example, Cambell wishes Triamond to take the credit for his acts. But Artegal assumes Braggadocio's armor without considering the effects of his acts: either he mechanically follows a romance script or he unrealistically expects Braggadocio to change character and give away his seeming glory. When the mock-knight claims credit, Artegal, furious at "that boasters pride and gracelesse guile," issues forth, "And unto all himselfe there open shewed" (V.iii.20.3, 5). While the unmasking is just, it is hardly impartial: Artegal concerns himself with his private glory.

The second half of canto 4 begins a new movement in the poem as Artegal comes across a more serious form of disorder—a whole society in revolt. Its emblem is the mob of women gathered around a knight, ready to give him a shameful death because he will not don women's clothes and do their work. Each aspect of the emblem—the mob of women, the inappropriate demand, the unknightly punishment—reinforces the picture of a social order gone wrong.

> Such is the crueltie of womenkynd,
>> When they have shaken off the shamefast band,

> With which wise Nature did them strongly bynd,
> T'obay the heasts of mans well ruling hand,
> That then all rule and reason they withstand,
> To purchase a licentious libertie.
> But vertuous women wisely understand,
> That they were borne to base humilitie,
> Unlesse the heavens them lift to lawfull soveraintie. (V.v.25)

While the final line excepts unusual female rulers like Elizabeth, whom God has placed on the throne, the stanza stresses that Nature normally "binds" women to obedience. In denying these natural bonds, Radigund and her followers lose their humanity, becoming Spenserian equivalents of Goneril and Regan.

It is not entirely clear why, in book 5, Spenser should take a harder line than he does in books 3 and 4 about the heroic potential of women.[33] Perhaps, despite his disclaimer, an uneasiness about Elizabeth's authority surfaces in the book about rule, or perhaps his concern with justice makes him more sensitive to the fragility of order. He certainly insists with unusual force on the traditional hierarchy. His treatment of Radigund makes her a woman revolting against her own nature. Her name recalls a saint who—perversely, in Protestant eyes— refused to consummate her marriage. She is the epic's third variation on the *Venus armata,* or armed lady, but she assumes a different stance in the world of gender relations. Britomart enters it to pursue a dynastic goal; Belphoebe avoids it; Radigund wishes to dominate it. In her attempt she mirrors the worst qualities of Spenser's men. If Scudamour tries to possess his lady in the Temple of Venus, Radigund reverses the relation, binding men with literal chains. The ideal of mutual trust and mutual goodwill advanced in the *Amoretti* is impossible for either. Her initial anger stems from her rejection by Bellodant the Bold, who will not "be wonne unto her will" (V.iv.30.6), and although "will" keeps its Elizabethan sense of "carnal desire," the line suggests more generally that the knight will not do what she wants. Driven by anger and pride, she insists on her will.

Accordingly, the ironies of the episode develop around references to bonds and bondage. Having thrown off Nature's bonds, Radigund enslaves Artegal but, humiliatingly, she falls in love with him, as she has with Bellodant. Privately she admits to Clarinda, her confidant, that she wishes for gentler bonds of love.

> Therefore I cast, how I may him unbind,
> And by his freedome get his free goodwill;
> Yet so, as bound to me he may continue still.
>
> Bound unto me, but not with such hard bands
>     Of strong compulsion, and streight violence,
>     As now in miserable state he stands;
>     But with sweet love and sure benevolence,
>     Voide of malitious mind, or foule offense. (V.v.32.7–33.5)

Radigund can imagine a relationship based on "free goodwill" but, unable to give up the security of domination, she remains imprisoned by her own will.

Artegal's imprisonment is another fall necessary for self-knowledge: like Redcrosse and Guyon, he thinks himself invulnerable, and he turns aside from his public quest for private gratification only to be left helpless. He has no business delaying his journey (see V.xi.41), and his motives are suspect.

> Now sure (said he) and by the faith that I
> To Maydenhead and noble knighthood owe,
> I will not rest, till I her might doe trie,
> And venge the shame, that she to Knights doth show. (V.iv.34.1–4)

He echoes Redcrosse's intemperate desire to encounter Despair (I.ix.32.1–2): the language of knightly aspiration suggests that Artegal sees the battle as another romance adventure in which he will represent "noble knighthood" and gloriously avenge its shame on its detractors. But he underestimates his opponent. Radigund is not an ordinary adversary: she is a woman, and like Redcrosse's encounter with Despair, combat with her does not fit within the normal parameters of chivalric battle. In the manner of romance knights, Artegal accepts the food his opponent sends to his tent, requites it with gifts, and agrees that if he loses he will "obey / [Her] law, and ever to [her] lore be bound" (V.iv.49.2–3). His confidence in his virtue, both moral and physical, keeps him from attending to the circumstances of his acts.

The battle recapitulates the fight between Artegal and Britomart in book 4, with significant differences. In both, the victorious Artegal uncovers the face of his female antagonist only to stand amazed by her beauty and yield. When he sees Radigund's face, "his cruell minded hart / Empierced was with pittifull regard, / That his sharpe sword he threw from him apart, / Cursing his hand that had that visage mard" (V.v.13.1–4). But whereas Artegal's only reason for opposing Britomart is revengeful pride, his opposition to Radigund is not a private matter, based as it is on the injustice of her acts. His "pittifull regard" is a version of false mercy: sentiment strengthened by sexual feeling, which leaves him forgetful of why he is fighting in the first place. His mercy results in Turpine's hanging (V.v.18), as well as his own imprisonment.

The result of this yielding is a radical injustice:

> So was he overcome, not overcome,
>> But to her yeelded of his owne accord;
>> Yet was he justly damned by the doome
>> Of his owne mouth, that spake so warelesse word,
>> To be her thrall, and service her afford. (V.v.17.1–5)

Because he has given his word, his knight's honor now works against him, and he finds himself "justly" condemned to allow Radigund's injustice. The lines recall ironically the "accord" between lovers like Britomart and Artegal, as does the stanza's ending: "No fayrer conquest, than that with goodwill is gayned" (V.v.17.9). The sexual element in the defeat highlights the loss of Artegal's public role. Unlike Hercules, who renounces his monster-killing duties for a life of pleasure (V.v.24), Artegal traps himself by inappropriately giving his word and allowing himself to act on his pity—both acts stemming from his vision of himself as a glorious knight, not an agent of justice.

What follows at least begins Artegal's necessary education. No longer able to trust to his physical prowess, he adopts a certain patience. When Clarinda tests him, he declares

> . . . that to a courage great
> It is no lesse beseeming well, to beare
> The storme of fortunes frowne, or heavens threat,
> Then in the sunshine of her countenance cleare
> Timely to joy. (V.v.38.1–5)

This speech is, admittedly, delivered warily to one of his captors, but it does stress a moral rather than a physical endurance. He develops a capacity to temporize, offering to sue for Radigund's "favour" (V.v.41.2). The narrator comments on his treatment of Clarinda: "So daily he faire semblant did her shew, / Yet never meant he in his noble mind, / To his owne absent love to be untrew" (V.v.56.1–3). His situation gives rise to an unheroic but necessary wiliness, an understanding of how to negotiate from a position of weakness.

Beyond the episode of the Egalitarian Giant, the initial cantos of the book have little historical particularity, but Radigund's golden hair would associate her with Mary, Queen of Scots, who was Elizabeth's most serious, long-term rival. Later, in the eighth canto, Spenser treats Mary's trial and death in static terms; here he suggests the violence implicit in the long sparring match between the cousin queens. When Britomart hears of Artegal's capture, Spenser treats her jealousy comically, but he also notes the "felnesse of her heart" (V.vi.18.6) as she sets out to kill the woman who stands between her and her divinely ordained line. In various forms the Mary-Elizabeth contest dominates the center of book 5, from the fourth through the eighth cantos. While the episode of Dolon's treachery may suggest Britomart's worry about sexual betrayal, it may also touch, as Rene Graziani has argued, on a Catholic plot to set off twenty pounds of gunpowder under Elizabeth's bed.[34]

Britomart's rescue is also a matter of equity. In Aristotelian terms, Justice concerns itself with enforcing general laws, whereas Equity modifies the general law to fit particular situations. In Elizabethan England equity was associated not with the common law but with the queen's Courts of Chancery. At the poem's literal level, Artegal is caught in the "law" of his given word and cannot free himself from his imprisonment: he needs Britomart to rescue him. His plight parallels England's plight—in need of Elizabeth's determined might to meet the danger that Mary poses. (As O'Connell points out, Mary's regal status made it hard to try her under common law; it was necessary to invoke the queen's power of equity [1977, 145–46].) The seventh canto thus opens by announcing it will treat "That part of Justice which is Equitie" (V.vii.3.4) and proceeds to do so, in Britomart's dream and in her subsequent mortal combat.

Britomart's vivid dream in the Temple of Isis provides the book with an ambivalent prophecy; the ambivalence appears when Spenser first describes the statues of the Egyptian deities. Associating Osyris and Isis with Justice and Equity (V.vii.2–3), he pictures Isis with one foot on the ground and the other on a crocodile whose tail twines familiarly about her middle, "So meaning," the narrator comments on Isis, "to suppresse both forged guile, / and open force" (V.vii.7.3–4). Although the crocodile embodies "forged guile," he also images Osyris, whose uncontrolled justice is in danger of becoming its opposite. A similar ambivalence invests the "mother earth" on whom Isis's abstemious priests sleep, but who gave birth to both the giants and the vines whose wines stir up "old rebellious thought" (V.vii.11.5). Earth (and human nature) is at once fruitful and rebellious, always in danger of self-destructive revolt.

The priest interprets Britomart's dream in terms of Merlin's prophecy, according to which the crocodile/Osyris (Artegal) will beget a child on the idol/Isis (Britomart) for the good of England. Isis's subduing of the crocodile recalls Britomart's overcoming of Artegal in the fourth book and his subsequent wooing. Yet this interpretation omits much of what gives the dream its potency, in particular the crocodile's sinister nature: associated with "forged guile" in the initial description of the statue, it threatens to eat Britomart/Isis after devouring the flames that threaten her Temple. The crocodile is both necessary and dangerous: like the lion beneath Mercilla's throne, it needs restraints.[35] Although the priest's reading cheers Britomart, her dream remains more troubling than he admits.

Britomart's battle with Radigund differs markedly from Artegal's. She refuses Radigund's conditions (V.vii.28) and attacks with a jealous intensity that causes both women to forget their tactics (V.vii.29.4). Comparing them to a tiger and a lioness (V.vii.30), Spenser distinguishes the royal beast from the mere predator while simultaneously equating their mutual violence. He suggests that the savagery of the battle is at once unnatural and necessary when he describes them hacking at one another's breasts (V.vii.29), or when he compares their blood on the ground to "fruitles seede, of which untimely death should grow" (V.vii.31.9). Both women, sources of life, concern themselves with death; having beaten Radigund, Britomart kills her without hesitation.

Although there is little internal allegory in this book, the conflict also has aspects of a psychomachia: Radigund's desire to make Artegal her slave enacts one of Britomart's repressed wishes. For Britomart to create a relationship with Artegal in which each can love the other freely, she must give up the claim of ownership, overcoming the Radigund impulse in herself. Accordingly, when she first sees Artegal, Spenser compares her to Penelope, whose constancy expresses itself in domesticity rather than warlike action (V.vii.39). The simile anticipates the position she now assigns herself as she restores the rule of men, repealing "the liberty of women . . . / Which they had long usurpt" (V.vii.42.5–6). This somewhat depressing—to modern readers—retreat from heroic activity forms part of a program of self-mastery that Spenser suggests is necessary for Artegal's future queen. The episode ends—insofar as it ends—with Britomart's new helplessness as she waits despondently for Artegal's success. We see no more of her.

The last section differs from earlier ones in making history, implicit in the Britomart/Radigund opposition, the primary reference of the allegory. Yet the messiness of this history frustrates resolution: sometimes Spenser departs from historical fact in insisting on closure, and sometimes, as in the final stanzas, he displays the degree to which, as Merlin says, the end is not. This does not mean that Spenser is wrong to attempt these cantos: they embody an act of faith, as he tries to square the ideal constructions of his fiction with the actuality he knew. But the many battles in this section are marked by weariness and frustration. In canto 8 Arthur cannot get at the Souldan in his high chariot and so must stay unheroically at a distance, deflecting his enemy's darts. Similarly, in canto 9, Malengin's speed and capacity for transformation leave him ungraspable until Talus's superhuman speed and determination enable Artegal and Arthur to capture him. In these cantos Talus executes tasks, like subduing French Catholics or catching Irish rebels, that actual English armies could not carry out. He seems increasingly a fantasy of power—the fantasy of one of the New English deeply distressed by the actual limits of the queen's armies, purse, and will.

In the battle with the Souldan, which shadows the English defense against the Spanish Armada, the allegory works successfully, largely because Spenser was building on established belief: English Protestants already saw the astonishingly complete English victory as God's work. The Souldan's attack from his "charret hye" (V.viii.28.4) suggests the large Spanish galleons, which were outmaneuvered by the smaller, quicker English ships, and Arthur's unveiled shield recalls the storm that drove the Spanish fleet onto the Scottish and Irish coasts. Spenser's treatment of the shield suggests a new stress on human capacity, which accords with the fifth book's focus on the external world. In book 1 Orgoglio's defeat is entirely God's work: the giant blinds himself by striking the cover from Arthur's shield. In book 5 man proposes before God disposes, and Arthur chooses to unveil the shield when nothing else will serve.[36]

Malengin's capture, on the other hand, seems the product of wishful thinking. His name means "evil wit," and he may embody the rebellious

Irish with his "long curld locks, that downe his shoulders shagged / And on his backe an uncouth vestiment / Made of straunge stuffe, but all to worne and ragged" (V.ix.10.6–8); his deceitful tongue (V.ix.5), however, links him with Catholic priests. Although, like Proteus, he changes form when captured, Arthur does not ask him for knowledge. He transforms himself, appropriately enough, into a serpent. Talus strikes him with his flail, "That all his bones, as small as sandy grayle / He broke, and did his bowels disentrayle" (V.ix.19.4–5). The scene presents a fantasy of crushing permanently the forces he embodies.

Spenser's ambivalence toward the queen he served appears most clearly in his portrait of her as Mercilla in canto 9. Its positive emphases recall the portrait of Alma in the corresponding canto of book 2: where that queen ruled over the good body, this one presides over the good realm. In Spenser's iconic portrait she appears an ideal ruler, a vigilant peacekeeper and justiciar (Aptekar, 13–23; Cain, 136–41). She sits with a sword at her feet, rusted from long peace but ready for use when necessary (V.ix.30). The potentially rebellious Lion underneath her feet is restrained with an iron chain and collar (V.ix.33), and she is attended upon by Justice, Law, Equity, and Peace. Her name links her with the God-like virtue of Mercy, and her role as God's intermediary is apparent when the narrative details the cloth of state spread above her "like as a cloud, as likest may be told . . . Whose skirts were bordred with bright sunny beams . . . Mongst which crept litle Angles through the glittering gleames" (V.ix.28.4, 6, 9).

She judges the treasonous Duessa, who here embodies Mary, Queen of Scots, beheaded in 1587. Even though the canto appeared nine years after her death, its subject remained sensitive, and the account brought an angry protest from Mary's son, James VI of Scotland. Elizabeth had kept Mary in confinement for nearly nineteen years, despite being urged by her Protestant subjects to execute her. Alive and the next successor to the English crown, Mary was a focus for Catholic plots against the queen's life, and Mary repeatedly encouraged such plotting. Elizabeth remained, however, deeply reluctant to shed royal blood, and when prevailed upon to sign Mary's death warrant, she blamed the execution on William Davison, Second Secretary of the Privy Council, imprisoning him for eighteen months.

While Spenser's account weighs contrasting arguments, he makes it clear that Duessa must die. On Duessa's side are Pity, Regard of Womanhood, Nobility of Birth, Grief, and "*Daunger* threatning hidden dread, / And high alliance unto forren powre" (V.ix.45.5–6). On the other side are Zeal, "Kingdoms care," Authority, Law of Nations, Religion, and Justice. With some irony Spenser makes Ate, glad to ruin anyone, side with the prosecution. Although these accusers show the necessity of Duessa's death, Mercilla, unwilling to pass judgment, drops a tear and exits. The portrait certainly presents Elizabeth with the face she wanted to see, stressing her mercy and leaving the fact of Mary's execution to indirect mention in the next canto. But it also contains an implicit critique: Mercilla's avoidance of judgment demonstrates the unwillingness to make up her mind that exasperated Elizabeth's counselors and subjects (Cain, 141–44). In the Artegal/Radigund battle Spenser shows that pity can be destructive, and Mercilla's pity seems similarly flawed. Although Arthur is briefly moved by Duessa's plight, Artegal stays firm in his condemnation.

One detail makes Mercilla's justice still more ambiguous. The two central stanzas of the canto describe how the entrance to Mercilla's chamber is occupied by a poet whose tongue was "for his trespasse vyle,"

> Nayld to a post, adjudged so by law:
> For that therewith he falsely did revyle,
> And foule blaspheme that Queene for forged guyle,
> Both with bold speaches, which he blazed had,
> And with lewd poems, which he did compyle. (V.ix.25.2–6)

While the passage may simply warn against misusing language, Spenser adds that the poet's name, "Bon Font" (Well of Goodness), was written in "cyphers strange, few could rightly read" (V.ix.26.3). The phrase seems ready-made for Spenserian allegory, and indeed, official anger at Spenser's *Mother Hubberds Tale* had caused the calling-in of the *Complaints* volume. The image suggests that the Law, which has crossed out "Bon" and substituted "Mal," so that "Bon Font" becomes "Mal Font" (Well of Evil), has misjudged the poet. The grotesque emblem speaks to the poet's physical vulnerability and the Law's authoritarian power. It darkens the subsequent image of Mercilla's justice (DeNeef, 131–32).

In reviewing recent English actions across the British and Irish Channels, Spenser divides the last cantos of book 5 between Arthur and Artegal. Arthur's freeing of Belge gives a positive, if nearly unrecognizable, version of the English military attempt to aid the States General in the 1580s. Belge's seventeen sons are the provinces of the Low Countries, of which the Spanish had recaptured twelve. Arthur may stand for Spenser's old patron, the earl of Leicester, whom the queen sent to aid the States General in 1585, and whose mission ended two years later in futile bickering between Leicester, Sir John Norris, and the States General. The city freed by Arthur is Antwerp, which the Spanish conquered and continued to hold during Spenser's lifetime.[37] Spenser reworks these depressing facts as a series of romance combats between Arthur and Geryoneo, or his Monster. Geryoneo is a new version of the three-bodied Spanish monster that Hercules conquered as one of his twelve labors; emblem books make Hercules an image of Concord, and so Geryoneo embodies a perversion of that ideal (Aptekar, 140–52). The woman-headed monster, which Spenser associates with the Inquisition, recalls both Error and the crocodile in the Temple of Isis: thus it, too, figures a perversion of Justice.

The next episode deals with a major embarrassment of Protestant policy: Henry of Navarre's conversion to Catholicism (1593) to pacify his Catholic subjects and secure his throne. Artegal denounces Sir Burbon's faintheartedness in surrendering his shield and, with it, his chivalric (and by implication, religious) identity. Yet, like the English, he continues to support Burbon's attempt to win the ungrateful Lady Flourdelis. Spenser's frustration may appear again in Talus's violent attack on the "rude rout" (V.xi.47.2) opposing Burbon's right to his lady: the iron man sweeps aside all opposition like a wish—quite unlike the English forces sent to Henry's aid.

Artegal's primary mission is to free Irena, whose name conflates the Irish word for "Ireland" with the Greek word for "peace." She has been held captive by Grantorto (Great Wrong), another version of Spain, the last of the giants of this book. Although one might expect that Spenser's situation in Ireland would lead to an exfoliation of historical and moral allegory, the opposite occurs. Artegal appears at the last minute, developing a familiar romance cliché, but there is no richness of historical or moral allegory to give the battle meaning. Perhaps Spenser's awareness of how far the Irish situation was from triumphant victory prevented him from using his skill in the episode. In any case, having started to reform the "ragged common-weale" (V.xii.26.4) with Talus's merciless help, Artegal is forced to break off his task and return "in heaviness" to the Faerie Court.

Up to this point the writing of the final cantos seems willed: Spenser is fulfilling a promise he has made to himself. But with the appearance of Envy and Detraction and the bite of the Blatant Beast there is an abrupt, savage rise in the quality of the verse. The passage may refer to the recall from Ireland in 1582 of Lord Grey, under attack from factions

at home, but it need not be so specific. For the New English the frequent changes of policy and attitude on the part of the crown were a
source of continual frustration: court slanders undo the work of Justice.
Artegal finds himself unable to fight the hags: all he can do is ignore
them: "Yet he past on, and seem'd of them to take no keepe"
(V.xii.42.9). The episode with Radigund prepares him for this stoic
endurance, but he can do no more with these enemies. He must leave
them to the knight associated with the court's unwritten laws and with
the gift of speech itself, the knight of Courtesy.

## Book 6: A Corruptible, Necessary Virtue

Courtesy is the slipperiest of the virtues of *The Faerie Queene*.[38] Like all
Spenser's virtues, its meaning is broad. Most narrowly it concerns courtly
manners, and the book often deals with questions of proper behavior:
does Aladine's lady disgrace herself by carrying her knight on his shield?
When is it acceptable to lie? (Calidore engages in necessary prevarication
in canto 3, and Pastorella does so in canto 11.) Under what conditions
should a seeming commoner like Tristram fight (and kill) a knight?
What is the "proper" way for a knight to woo a shepherdess? Critics have
traced many connections between book 6 and Castiglione's *The Book of
the Courtier,* the greatest of the Renaissance courtesy books.[39] But Spenser
(and indeed, Castiglione) sees more at stake. The concern with manners
develops into an examination of what we mean by civilized behavior—
and hence, by civilization. In the proem Spenser argues that while courtesy appears a humble virtue, it "brancheth forth in brave nobilitie, / And
spreds it selfe through all civilitie" (VI.proem.4.4–5). It makes "civility"—civilization itself—possible. Later Colin will speak similarly of the
Graces, bestowing "all gracious gifts" on men:

> Sweete semblaunt, friendly offices that bynde,
> And all the complements of curtesie:
> They teach us, how to each degree and kynde
> We should our selves demeane, to low, to hie;
> To friends, to foes, which skill men call Civility. (VI.x.23.1, 5–9)

Courtesy in its largest sense is the aggregate of essential rules that make
societies work, the ways in which individuals and classes of people
behave toward one another so that cohesive community is possible.

Yet in the proem's fourth stanza the narrator makes a familiar shift, blaming courtesy as practiced in the degraded present age, which "being matcht with plaine Antiquitie, / Ye will them all but fayned showes esteeme, / Which carry colours faire, that feeble eies misdeeme" (VI.proem.4.7–9). Modern courtesy is no more than external show, the false appearances of *Colin Clouts Come Home Againe*. The fifth stanza develops this attack in detail:

> But in the triall of true curtesie,
>> Its now so farre from that, which then it was,
>> That it indeed is nought but forgerie,
>> Fashion'd to please the eies of them, that pas,
>> Which see not perfect things but in a glas:
>> Yet is that glasse so gay, that it can blynd
>> The wisest sight, to thinke gold that is bras.
>> But vertues seat is deepe within the mynd,
> And not in outward shows, but inward thoughts defynd.
>
> (VI.proem.5)

If courtesy is merely fashioned for the eyes of those "that pas" (those who judge? those who do not last?), then it has little to do with truth. The image of the "glas" has—as it often does—a double reference: it points to the narcissistic courtier looking at himself in a mirror, a member of the House of Pride, but it also recalls the glass of this world through which Paul says we necessarily see "darkly" (1 Corinthians 13:12). Courtesy is a worldly quality, and the world distracts attention from virtue whose seat is "deepe within the mynd."

The opposition between the world and the mind raises the central problem of whether courtesy can even be a virtue. If it consists in external appearances, how can one distinguish true courtesy from its corrupt imitation? "Sweete *semblant*" is by definition a way of seeming, ambiguously related to truth. Blandina, Sir Turpine's mildly corrupt lady, has as sweet a semblant as Serena or Pastorella. Courtesy rarely appears in the Renaissance lists of virtues with Holiness, Temperance, and Justice.[40] Rather, it provides the subject of courtesy manuals, which concern themselves less with morality than with the skills necessary to succeed at court. Even Courtesy's association with courts, insisted on in the opening canto of the book, has problematic aspects: most writers held up courts as centers of corruption, as Spenser does in parts of *Colin Clout.* Is not Courtesy by its nature corrupting? Is civilization, with its courts and cities, an unmitigated good?

As in the final stanzas of the proem to book 5, the final praise of Elizabeth contrasts markedly with what precedes it. This idealized picture makes her the creative center of her court, a "pattern" or platonic form of courtesy itself, and the mirror metaphor reappears with new meaning: as God's intermediary the queen is illuminated by divine virtue and in turn passes its light on to her courtiers (VI.vi.proem.6). In the final stanza Spenser rings a new change on the idea of Elizabeth as a source of virtue: "Right so from you all goodly vertues well / Into the rest, which round about you ring" (VI.proem.7.6–7). Like the Graces Colin will invoke later, the queen participates in a benevolent cycle of giving and receiving: the poet takes his image of courtesy from her and returns it to her again in his poem. This is a very different court from that criticized only stanzas earlier, and as in *Colin Clout,* Spenser makes no attempt either to lessen the contradiction or to explain it. It leaves the proem split between an ideal vision of courtesy, with its praise of the queen, and a satiric attack on courtesy as currently practiced, alerting the reader to the divergence between them.

The theme of courtliness gone wrong appears in the Blatant Beast, which Spenser associates by its thousand tongues with the traditional figure of Fame, and by its poisonous iron teeth with the iron age of the present. The Beast's most important aspect, as critics have pointed out, is its relation to language: "Blatant" comes most likely from Latin *blatero,* to babble, and it is often associated with the courtly vice of slander. But the Beast can speak truly, as the poem implies he does when he exposes monastic abuses (VI.xii.24). It is less the Beast's capacity for lies than his purpose that distinguishes him. The Beast is an ally of Ate, using speech to destroy, and its tongues speak "reprochfully, not caring where nor when" (VI.xii.27.9). Book 6 concerns itself centrally with speech: the need to speak graciously, to settle quarrels, to give advice, to persuade, is constantly on exhibit, yet Calidore's quest explores the truth that the skill that makes civilized intercourse possible can also destroy it. One of the Beast's two genealogies (VI.i.8) echoes the creation of courtesy itself (cf. VI.proem.3), and its doglike nature suggests the fawning nastiness often attacked in satires of courtiers: it is thus a kind of anticourtesy. Calidore, who excels in "gracious speech," hunts a creature that embodies the misuse of his own gift.

The book's titular virtue determines the mode in which it is written. The personification allegory typical of earlier books of *The Faerie Queene* occurs rarely here; where it does it almost never portrays a battle *within* the mind. Spenser concerns himself with interactions between people or between individuals and groups; he usually develops the first by episodes that are typical rather than allegorical, and the second by per-sonifications like the Blatant Beast and Mirabella's giant Disdain. Disdain, although "sib to great Orgoglio" (VI.vii.41.8), differs from him in kind: he embodies *social* forces that punish individuals like Mirabella. He does not embody Mirabella's scorn of her lovers, although he stands for a social echo—a consequence—of that scorning. Similarly, the three villains, Defetto, Decetto, and Despetto, who attack Timeas in canto 5 do not represent aspects of Timeas's psyche, as the three Forsters of book 3 seem to do. They embody forces that a disgraced man—one bitten by the Blatant Beast—will find attacking him at court.

Although all the books of the second part of *The Faerie Queene* touch on the relation between the poet's fiction and the actual world, this book, more than any other, foregrounds its status as a fiction, a work that is *made up* (Berger 1988, 215–25). It does so from the opening stanza of the proem, in which the narrator begins not by announcing his subject but by stressing his pleasure in writing.

> The waies, through which my weary steps I guyde,
>> In this delightfull land of Faery,
>> Are so exceeding spacious and wyde,
>> And sprinckled with such sweet variety,
>> Of all that pleasant is to eare or eye,
>> That I nigh ravisht with rare thoughts delight,
>> My tedious travell doe forget thereby;
>> And when I gin to feele decay of might,
> It strength to me supplies, & chears my dulled spright. (VI.proem.1)

The narrator has earlier compared the writing of the poem to a journey, but this passage emphasizes not seagoing labor (cf. I.xii.1) but renewing pleasure. The opening contrasts, as critics have noted, with the grim plodding of the last parts of book 5. The act of writing now allows the narrator a sense of joyful freedom; it is a source of strength restoring him after the "decay of might" caused by fatigue or age. In E.K.'s terms, this is recreative poetry, not moral, and in the second and third stanzas it becomes clear that this healing develops out of the narrator's immersion in the ideal realm of his vision, far from the actuality of "wicked worlds disdaine" (VI.proem.3.4). If in this book courtesy is a virtue moving naturally toward the corrupt world, the poet's imagination moves away from it, toward an untouched ideal.

Having emphasized the act of making, Spenser structures the rest of the book to remind the reader of its fictive nature. Characters remain simple and the plot active: the frequent narrative repetitions point to an author pulling the strings (Berger 1988, 218–20). A couple dallying on the ground in canto 2 yields to another couple in the same situation in canto 3; Serena among the cannibals looks toward Pastorella among the brigands. The frequent interruptions of the plot and the increasing number of unresolved episodes further intensify the reader's awareness of the poem as a made thing. Among other questions, the poem asks about the nature and value of these fictions: Are they a retreat from the actual? Do they have a social purpose? What is the relation between the deep joy of the opening proem and the actual world that the poet must face?

As in book 3, the plot of book 6 drops its hero early only to pick him up again toward the end, dividing the book into three sections: an initial part (VI.i–iii.26) in which Calidore solves handily a series of problems; a middle part (VI.iii.27–viii) from which he is absent and in which the problems treated become increasingly intractable; and a final part (VI.ix–xii) in which Calidore reappears and, after an extended pastoral sojourn, completes his quest. Like book 3, it develops by theme and variation, drawing its ideas together in an emblematic center. But the "center" of book 6, Colin's vision of the Graces on Mount Acidale, occurs, unlike the Garden of Adonis, late in the poem. It remains more problematic than the Garden, for it suggests a gap between the vision the poet sees and the world to which he speaks.

In a manner now familiar, the opening section presents Calidore with three deceptively easy problems: Briana's enforcement of Crudor's perverse wishes; Tristram's slaying of an unnamed knight; and the first section of the Calepine-Serena episode. The first two incidents raise the issue of knights who misuse their status to gratify their appetites. As in the opening of book 5, the hero resolves each problem neatly. He overcomes first Briana's seneschal and later her lover, Crudor, causing a sudden alteration of character in both of them: Briana is "wonderously now chaung'd from that she was afore" (VI.i.46.9). In the second incident the young knight has already killed his discourteous foe; Calidore needs only to recognize Tristram's innate nobility, making him a squire and starting him on his way to the tragic end that he will eventually achieve—offstage—in romance legend. His subsequent white lie (VI.iii.18) further saves a lady's reputation.

The third episode suggests how much the moral world of book 6 differs from that of book 1. Calidore finds Serena and Calepine dallying "in covert shade," the knight having removed his armor "for that him selfe he thought from daunger free" (VI.iii.20.3, 6). The tableau recalls Redcrosse and Duessa before Orgoglio's arrival, but the likeness stops there. When Redcrosse removes the whole armor of God, he abandons his role as God's agent, and his dalliance with Duessa confirms his spiritual sickness. By contrast, the armor on this grassy ground is physical, not spiritual, and the lovers are morally blameless. Yet the world of book 6 remains radically unsafe, and the young knight has foolishly left himself vulnerable to physical and (allegorically) social danger. The very assumption that one is safe makes one easy prey to hidden predators, and as Serena wanders off "Without suspect of ill or daungers hidden dread" (VI.iii.23.9), the Blatant Beast attacks. The episode's allegory implies that dallying with one's lover can affect one's reputation and demonstrates how quickly one's enemies may pounce. Serena will sicken with the Beast's poisoned bite until she reforms her behavior in canto 7.

The interlaced adventures of the book's center continue its examination of discourtesy and social predation in relation to several other issues. One is whether courtesy can be learned. Is it a product of nature or of nurture? The book's analysis parallels Montaigne's meditation on cannibals and Shakespeare's *Tempest* (1623) in asking how far civility can be taught. The primary instance of nurture is the infant whom Sir Calepine finds in the paws of a bear and gives to Bruina to become Sir Bruin's heir. Calepine argues that the baby's character is a tabula rasa on which one can write what one wishes (VI.iv.35–36), and in this case his argument seems justified: the narrator comments that the baby will become a famous knight (VI.iv.38).

Against this instance Spenser sets the Wild Man, whose natural goodness shows itself despite his lack of training. The Wild Man presents an extreme version of the argument for nature: while his upbringing has left him "mis-shapt" (VI.v.1.5), he can still rescue Calepine, pity Serena, and, recognizing Arthur's virtue, follow him faithfully. Spenser attributes the Wild Man's goodness to his noble blood, which, given the right occasion, "breake[s] forth" (VI.v.1.9) in virtuous action. Nonetheless, Spenser treats him comically: his inability to speak—to master the essential civilized skill—keeps him from the dignity of full humanity. He treats Calepine's physical wounds, but significantly, he cannot cure the infected bite of the Blatant Beast. By contrast, Tristram is a woods-dweller whom Spenser treats seriously. Like the Wild Man, he shows his native nobility in his acts, but he has had sufficient court training to make him material for a knighthood.

The innate baseness of some people persists regardless of civilized training. The figure of Turpine (in Latin, *turpis,* "base") dramatizes the limits of civility. Like Sans Loy of book 1, he has the technological advantages of a knight without the spiritual discipline that should guide them, but unlike Sans Loy, he is driven by a humiliating fearfulness that issues in sadistic spite. The dilemma Turpine poses is that of what to do with a knight so base that he will not abide by chivalric rules. Symbolically stripped of his armor by Arthur as punishment for his unknightly behavior, he refuses to accept the shame Arthur has meted out and dons a new suit once Arthur has turned his back. Arthur's final enraged act—hanging Turpine by his heels from a tree—punishes him further, but it suggests as well Arthur's frustrated inability to deal with the figure. Where many similar villains simply lose their heads, Turpine remains alive, perhaps because, like Despair in book 1, he embodies an aspect of human nature that will continue as long as this world lasts.

Mirabella (*mira* ["wondrously"] plus *bella* ["beautiful"]) embodies a different, though related, problem of civility. Originally of base stock, she has abused her natural gifts (VI.vii.28), and her story recalls that of Columbell and the Squire of Dames, in which a courtly lady uses her beauty as a means of power. Mirabella has taken sadistic pleasure in scorning her lovers, and the story of her judgment by Cupid seems an allegory of how scorn long lavished on others is at last returned in kind. She has misused the traditions of love in playing the haughty mistress; now her repentance will do little to alleviate the public contempt she suffers. Most of her rescuers cannot defeat the giant Disdain: attempt-ing to free her, they are imprisoned and whipped along with her, suffer-ing the fate of anyone who dares to side with a person subject to public opprobrium. Arthur alone can overcome the giant, but he cannot kill him for fear of killing Mirabella. This puzzling detail may suggest that he embodies a public context that Mirabella needs in order to live: she cannot exist in solitude.

The societal dimension of Spenser's subject leads him at times to cre-ate a kind of poetic anthropology: this is the only book of *The Faerie*

*Queene* to play in some detail with groups—with the cannibals, the shepherds, the brigands. The cannibals obviously oppose the example of the Salvage Man, for in them wildness and baseness coincide. Predators on the civilized world, they live by plunder: here, as in the case of the brigands, the native Irish may have been in Spenser's mind.[41] The rough comedy of the episode stems from the one-sidedness of the cannibals' greed: they see the naked Serena primarily as food, but when they gaze on her, Spenser's account satirizes more than savages:

> Her yvorie necke, her alablaster brest,
>> Her paps, which like white silken pillowes were,
>> For love in soft delight thereon to rest;
>> Her tender sides, her bellie white and clere,
>> Which like an Altar did it selfe uprere,
>> To offer sacrifice divine thereon;
>> Her goodly thighes, whose glorie did appeare
>> Like a triumphall Arch, and thereupon
> The spoiles of Princes hang'd, which were in battel won. (VI.viii.42)

This stanza is a courtly *blazon,* describing the lady from top to toe, the form that Spenser uses without irony in the *Epithalamion.* Shorn of context, it might fit without alteration into an erotically charged romance episode. Here, however, it suggests with brilliant comedy the degree to which the *blazon* form makes women into objects, dividing them into edible portions. The cannibals concern themselves only secondarily with Serena as a sexual being; their major debate concerns whether she should make one meal or many (VI.viii.37). But the treatment of the *blazon* suggests the element of savagery in the highly sophisticated poets—and readers—who turn women's thighs into triumphal arches on which to hang their imagined spoils.[42]

Book 6 develops the dialect of civilization and savagery partly through images of clothing and nakedness.[43] Truth—and especially divine Truth—is traditionally naked, without the clothes that would hide its essence from the viewer. But in this world, by and large, clothing—and armor—remain necessary. The Graces may appear naked in Colin's vision, but Serena's actual nakedness causes helplessness and embarrassment. References to armor also raise the issue of civilized covering: in the second canto Aladine's lack of armor leaves him vulnerable.

Arms signal rank: Tristram gains the armor of the knight he has killed and with them his new status as squire, and Arthur punishes Turpine by disarming him. Yet at times characters dispense with arms: Calepine pursues the bear without his armor, which would slow him down, and the Wild Man is mysteriously invulnerable to weapons. The Hermit of canto 5 seems able to hang up his armor, after a life spent in good works. Like the Wild Man at the other end of the spectrum, he lives apart from "all this worlds incumbrance" (VI.v.37.9), devoting himself to his salvation. Like Contemplation in book 1, he has reached the age when he can rightfully give over his work, and his place, in the world. He can, however, still heal Timeas and Serena where the Wild Man failed. He knows the world: his advice, secular and practical, focuses on the circumspection necessary to preserve reputation in a world full of malicious eyes (VI.vi.7, 14). His civility appears in his language, for "he the art of words knew wondrous well" (VI.vi.6.3).

Calidore, of all the characters, is the one most conversant with costume, shifting easily between armor and shepherd's garb, and in Calidore, Spenser analyzes the complex mixture of strength and weakness in courtesy. Unlike Redcrosse, or even Artegal, he does not grow: he remains what he seems at the beginning of the book, a fully courteous knight. The opening cantos suggest his typical strengths: he is cautious, well-mannered, judicious, coolheaded, patient. He works to benefit others, righting the wrongs of the first canto and reconciling Briana to Crudor; he judges Tristram sensibly and takes pleasure in helping him toward knighthood. He seriously pursues the Blatant Beast. Yet the ambiguities of courtesy surface in his initial portrait (VI.1.2–3), which praises his natural "gentlenesse of sprite / And manners mylde" while suggesting that they are useful qualities for an aspiring courtier.

> Ne was there Knight, ne was there Lady found
>> In Faery court, but him did deare embrace,
>> For his faire usage and conditions sound,
>> The which in all mens liking gayned place,
>> And with the greatest purchast greatest grace. (VI.i.3.1–5)

These lines do several things at once. While they emphasize Calidore's deserved popularity, their mention of a *lady*'s embrace gives a sexual resonance to his "faire usage and conditions sound"; similarly, references to his having gained liking from all and grace from the greatest suggest a quiet manipulativeness. Yet, lest the treatment appear simply critical, the sentence continues:

> Which he could wisely use, and well apply,
> To please the best, and th'evill to embase.
> For he loathd leasing, and base flattery,
> And loved simple truth and stedfast honesty. (VI.i.3.6–9)

While the lines shift the description once again toward eulogy, not all its statements are true. Calidore may love simple truth, but he does not practice it: he tells a white lie to Priscilla's father, and in the later cantos of the poem he finds that simple truth—or simple anything—is not to his purpose. As a knight of Courtesy, Calidore appears better or worse according to the situation he finds himself in, like a gray figure set against a black or white ground.

Calidore's sojourn with the shepherd community clarifies both his strengths and his limitations.[44] The episode reworks a familiar motif in epic, the moment when the hero turns aside from his quest to sojourn temporarily with country folk. Versions of this motif occur when Una dwells with the Satyrs and Florimel with the Witch. Yet Spenser builds into his account of Calidore's stay the question of whether it is a serious "truancy" from his quest for the Blatant Beast. The narrator himself makes the charge at the opening of canto 10 ("Who now does follow the foule *Blattant Beast?*"), but in the second stanza he adopts Calidore's point of view, dismissing court life as superficial, a hunting "after shadowes vaine / Of courtly favour, fed with light report / Of every blaste, and sayling alwaies in the port" (VI.x.2.7–9). It is difficult simply to dismiss this criticism of the court as Calidore's rationalization, for the proem to book 6 has already insisted on it.

The shepherds who enable Calidore's pastoral retreat stand apart from Spenser's earlier shepherds in their conspicuous literariness. In *The Shepheardes Calender* and *Colin Clout* Spenser gives his figures English names, often comic ones—Hobbinol, Piers, Thenot. The names of Melebee and Corydon, by contrast, come from Virgil's first and second eclogues, while Pastorella derives her name from the genre. (Her name may indeed suggest an even more marked generic play; it recalls the *pastourelle,* a medieval narrative kind in which, typically, a knight riding along sees a peasant maiden and tries to seduce her. So Calidore sees Pastorella.[45]) Unlike Spenser's earlier shepherds, they seem to live an untroubled, simplified life: Melibee says that, although he has little, he also has little to disturb his contentment (VI.ix.20–22). He stands for a particular literary ideal, or idyll: a desire "for innocence and happiness, to be recovered not through conversion or regeneration, but merely through a retreat."[46] It is a dream of happiness gained by discarding the anxieties, as well as the comforts, of civilized life.[47]

The account of the shepherds suggests, however, that the simple life is never, for Calidore, really an option. Whereas they remain conventional literary swains, good-natured, childlike, literal-minded, Calidore is a knight playing shepherd. They offer him refreshment (imaged in the drink he receives "to quench his thirstie heat" [VI.ix.6.8]), ease and a chance to woo Pastorella, but he can never forget his courtly training. When the knight and the old shepherd engage in a dialogue on shepherd life, they speak largely at cross-purposes: Melibee speaks of the need to rise above one's fate by accepting it with stoic resignation, and Calidore interprets him to mean that one can determine one's own fate (VI.xi.30–31). Calidore belongs to a world of action, not a world of contemplation. He makes a meaningful social gaffe—his only *faux pas* in the book—when he tries to pay Melibee with gold, assuming that the currency of the outer world will work here. Melibee insists that this kind of exchange has no place in Arcadia (VI.ix.32–33).

Calidore's treatment of Pastorella gives evidence that he can never live the shepherd's life in more than form. He woos her with the cleverness of an aspiring courtier, and his methods involve the *sprezzatura* characteristic of court culture. He uses the boor Coridon to show up his own superiority (VI.ix.42, 44) and eventually to disguise the success of his affair with Pastorella (VI.x.37). *Mutatis mutandis,* he still uses court tactics in his pastoral surroundings, just as he will eventually attack the brigands wearing armor beneath his shepherd's cloak. Whatever the charm of the world he sojourns in, he can never be a member of that world in more than costume.

Calidore's tendency to remain locked in his own nature appears in the symbolic watershed of the final cantos, Colin's vision of the Graces on Mount Acidale. The Graces, who originated in the classical period, had come in the Renaissance to embody all the divinely civilizing gifts of culture: they are conduits of divine beauty, handmaidens of the Venus who is for neoplatonists the source of generative form. Colin's calling them down with his song at once demonstrates the poet's visionary art and dramatizes its fragility. The preparation for the vision of the Graces stresses the separateness of their realm from that of the shepherds—

even the idealized shepherds of pastoral. It is the center of a series of concentric circles—of wood, mountain, plateau, dancing maidens. As the perfect form the circle is the appropriate vehicle for this vision of divine perfection and embodies the ultimate source of the many circles that have appeared in the book—the circle of courtiers around the queen (VI.proem.6), of shepherds surrounding Pastorella (VI.ix.8), and (parodically) of cannibals surrounding Serena. The center of the circle is, ambiguously, both Colin's Rosalind and Venus herself: she is that center of beauty that Colin's loving art enables him to see.

This vision of divine order prompts a startling break in the poem's narrative frame as the narrator steps forward, addressing his shepherd-surrogate in the present tense:

> Pype jolly shepheard, pype thou now apace
> Unto thy love, that made thee low to lout;
> Thy love is present there with thee in place,
> Thy love is there advaunst to be another Grace. (VI.x.16.6–9)

Epic narrators address their characters as early as Homer, often at moments of heightened feeling.[48] Here, however, there is an unusual intimacy, since Colin as visionary poet already embodies an aspect of the narrator. The narrator abandons himself to an imaginative identification with the Colin he has created, a Colin who, like him, uses his music to bring into the world an image of the ideal order deep within the mind. For a moment the poem turns lyric: we watch not Colin but the narrator as he loses himself—just as Colin loses himself—in the loving vision he has created.

The narrative movement resumes abruptly in the next stanzas as imagination yields to ordinary sight and Calidore steps into Colin's circle. Calidore is suspicious of what he sees and decides to determine what it is—"Whether it were the traine of beauties Queene, / Or Nymphes, or Fairies, or enchaunted show / With which his eyes mote have deluded beene" (VI.x.17.5–7)—by entering Colin's domain. Calidore is hardly to be blamed. His intrusion onto fairy ground, dispelling its enchantments, is a familiar romance motif that Spenser uses to emphasize a difference of sensibilities. The poet envisions the ideal while the practical knight of Courtesy necessarily regards it with skeptical suspicion. It is a familiar pairing—Colin Clout and the Shepherd of the Ocean embody roughly the same opposed attitudes in *Colin Clouts Come Home Againe*—

and Spenser the poet-courtier necessarily encompassed both. Yet the episode suggests the incompatibility of the two temperaments. Calidore's entrance destroys the vision and drives Colin to break his pipe, the gesture with which he first appears in *The Shepheardes Calender.* The gesture now, however, takes on new meaning. There it suggests the narcissistic frustration of the poet unable to make his song into magic that will reshape the world according to his desire. Here it marks the frustration of the poet who cannot sustain a vision of the ideal under the pressure of the world as it is. Afterward the two emissaries of different worlds speak together reasonably and graciously, discussing meaning in the absence of the vision. But the graciousness and the discussion do not substitute for the loss.

The discussion does, however, prompt a breaking of the narrative frame. In the course of explaining his vision to Calidore, Colin launches into praise of his lady and then turns abruptly to Elizabeth: "Sunne of the world, great glory of the sky, / That all the earth doest lighten with thy rayes, / . . . / Pardon thy shepheard, mongst so many layes, / As he has sung of thee in all his dayes, / To make one minime of thy poore handmayd" (V.x.28.1–2, 4–6). If the stanza is meant as apology, it is strikingly ill advised. It seems unlikely that the queen, reading Colin's praise of Rosalind, would feel herself slighted: shepherds praise their pastoral loves all the time. What the address does is to replace Colin's voice with Spenser's and to display the division in the poet's allegiance. Is Spenser Calidore or Colin? Does he owe allegiance to Elizabeth Boyle or to his queen? Like *Colin Clouts Come Home Againe,* the passage dramatizes the tension between vocational selves.[49]

If Acidale shows Calidore's limitations, the brigands' raid and its aftermath show his necessity. When he implies to Melibee that the life of the shepherd is beyond the reach of Fortune's power (VI.ix.27–28, 31), he naively forgets that all earthly things are subject to disaster; shepherds are safe in this world only if there are knights ready to protect them. Spenser even allows the suggestion that the brigands can destroy the shepherd society *because* Calidore is absent: the doggerel quatrain prefacing canto 10 suggests (against the witness of the rest of the text) that the raid takes place while he watches the Graces—that is, while he is not there to intervene.

The brigands, vicious beyond even the cannibals whom they partly resemble, form Spenser's most emphatic vision of secular evil. Both cannibals and brigands live on the borders of civilized lands (the latter live in a cave on an island), practicing no cultivation themselves but taking what they will by attacking civilized folk. Yet where the cannibals are driven by physical appetite—albeit degraded appetite—the brigands are driven by an even less natural hunger for gold. (The monetary exchange Melibee refuses is the motive force of the brigands' society.) Whereas the cannibals' religion limits their lusts—their priest refuses to let them rape Serena before they consume her (VI.viii.43.9)—the brigands recognize no value but money, and when their leader insists on keeping Pastorella, they turn on him. They epitomize, in short, the menaces of a world without rules. It is likely that Spenser intended a connection between them and the native Irish, whom he saw similarly as lawless predators; by extension, the shepherds are luckless English settlers. In terms of the poem's concern with fiction, the brigands represent another instance of the "real world" breaking in on the ideal, a more emphatic intrusion than Calidore's innocent destruction of Colin's vision.

The story of Pastorella's survival and rescue develops the account of courtesy in several ways. She is forced to temporize in her relations with the chief of the brigands if she is to avoid rape: it is an elementary lesson in the necessity of seeming. The chief, with an inchoate chivalry, is willing to die to keep her, and the resulting nightmarish battle reduces the brigands to hungry dogs attacking one another (VI.xi.17). Calidore's rescue, however, depends on the smooth tongue with which he persuades Coridon to lead him to the brigands and insinuates himself into their company. At the same time the episode curiously deepens the nature of courtesy, drawing on myths of descent to the underworld in order to rescue the dead—Demeter and Persephone, Christ's harrowing of Hell.[50] Pastorella, sick and wounded among corpses, seems dead before she revives (VI.xi.50.8–9). At its deepest level Calidore's courtesy recalls the divine rescue that brings life out of death.

The book's ending takes the characteristic open-endedness of Spenserian romance to an extreme by creating a parodically closed and triumphant ending and then allowing it to unravel. Spenser makes the final four cantos of book 6 bookish beyond even the norm for this epic. The self-conscious pastoral of cantos 9 and 10 has already been mentioned, while the eleventh and twelfth cantos derive materials from a new source, the Greek romances of the second and third centuries A.D. These violent prose adventure stories, with their stress on chance and fortune, include motifs that Spenser employs—thieves who enslave the heroine, threaten her chastity, and fight among themselves; noble foundlings with identifying birthmarks—to call attention to the plot's conspicuous literariness. When Pastorella turns out to be a noble lady fit for Calidore to marry, the ending is both quite unlike life and quite conventional.

The Blatant Beast turns out to be surprisingly vulnerable. Spenser describes the battle between Calidore and the Beast in comic close-up: "He grind, hee bit, he scratcht, he venim threw" (VI.xii.31.8): the detail suggests that the Beast has ceased to be a *meaning* and been reduced to a romance *beast* that can be captured by a romance knight (Berger 1988, 220–21). Yet the social viciousness the Beast embodies cannot be permanently contained, and the Beast escapes; it reappears, in the form of the extreme Protestants of Henry VIII's time, attacking indiscriminately monastic abuses and religious images—images that form the basis of the poet's own art.[51]

With this shift the narrative becomes present and personal:

Ne may this homely verse, of many meanest,
Hope to escape his venemous despite,
More than my former writs, all were they clearest
From blamefull blot, and free from all that wite,
With which some wicked tongues did it backebite,
And bring into a mighty Peres displeasure,
That never so deserved to endite.
Therfore do you my rimes keep better measure,
And seeke to please, that now is counted wisemens threasure. (VI.xii.41)

Once again—and here decisively—the narrative frame breaks and epic yields to personal lament. Spenser has increasingly tended to punctuate *The Faerie Queene* with moments of personal revelation, but this grim anticlimax turns against the original purpose of the work. The Beast has attacked him and he counsels his rhymes—bitterly, possibly ironically— to keep "better measure" and "seeke to please." This is the debased pleasure that the court asks of poets in *Colin Clout* or *The Teares of the Muses:* the speaker turns away from the educational task that he set himself at the opening of the first book.

*The Faerie Queene* ends with the poet addressing neither the queen nor his audience but his rhymes and, by implication, himself. The figure of Burleigh—the "mighty Pere" against whom the poet appeals to the queen in the proem to book 4—now seems to carry the day. The search for an audience has also become increasingly problematic, and where the proem to book 6 stresses the sheer delight of the fictional world for the writer, there now seems nowhere else to appeal. Jarred out of the world of romance, the poet can only speak to himself, muttering bitterly that he needs to keep his head down.

## Chapter Eight
# 1596–1609: Last Poems

Spenser died, probably at the age of 47, three years after the 1596 edition of *The Faerie Queene* was published. His last major poems—*Prothalamion* (1596), *Fowre Hymnes* (1596), and the posthumously published *Mutabilitie Cantos* (1609)—differ greatly from one another, but like the second half of the epic, they all share a retrospective quality, looking back on the earlier poetry from the perspective of middle age. They deal in various ways with time, change, and the uses of the imagination. Each dramatizes an act of *feigning*—of making things up as the speaker tries to understand the world and his place in it. In each case the speaker works through a sequence of imaginings toward a more comprehensive, if not to a final, vision.

### Fowre Hymnes

*Fowre Hymnes* was published in 1596 with a reprint of *Daphnaïda*. In the dedication to the Countesses of Cumberland and Warwick, Spenser asserts that he wrote the first two in honor of earthly love and beauty in the "greener times of [his] youth," but finding "that the same too much pleased those of like age and disposition, which being too vehemently caried with that kind of affection, do rather sucke out poyson to their strong passion, than hony to their honest delight, I was moved by the one of you two most excellent Ladies, to call in the same" (*YESP,* 690).[1] Since too many copies of these hymns had got abroad for them to be recalled, he "resolved at least to amend, and by way of retractation to reforme them" with two hymns of heavenly love and beauty. The dedication thus gives the four poems a biographical shape: the first two are the work of youth, while the second pair embody the second thoughts— the revision—of wiser age.[2] It raises questions of biography (how accurate is this account of their genesis?) and of meaning (how are the first hymns opposed to the later ones?).

The biographical question does not admit of much certainty. It seems unlikely that Spenser would tell the countesses that one of them had asked him to recall earlier work unless there were some truth in the sce-

nario. Yet the disclaimer that one's love poetry belongs to the period of
one's youth is an Elizabethan convention,[3] and the compliment Spenser
pays to the countesses as being "rare ornaments of all true love and
beautie, both in the one and the other kinde" implies that he is willing to
allow earthly beauty some value and expects that they will as well. The
earlier hymns do not appear in the lists of Spenser's unpublished works
unless they are *The hell of lovers* or the *Purgatorie* mentioned by Ponsonby
in the preface to the *Complaints*. The *Fowre Hymnes*'s versification suggests
that both the "earlier" poems and the "later" ones are late work: if
Spenser wrote the first two as a young man, he revised them extensively
for inclusion in the final group.[4]

Whatever its historical accuracy, the dedication emphasizes the
work's concern with the speaker's growth. It presents a conversion—a
turning from one kind of love to another, or more precisely, from the
shadow of divine love to the reality. For all the neoplatonic argument in
the opening hymns, the poem is lyric, not philosophy, and dramatizes
the speaker's search for love—love whose definition changes during the
poem. The speaker's relation to the historical Spenser is complex, as
always when he makes biography into fiction. Like Colin in *Colin Clout,*
he embodies one aspect of the poet's more complex nature. Simply
equating him with the poet reduces the poem to untrustworthy biography; it implies that, since the final stanzas of the "Hymne to Heavenly
Beautie" declare all worldly goals worthless, Spenser was either hypocritical or confused when, in the simultaneously published *Prothalamion,*
his heart is set on worldly advancement. During this period and after he
was busy acquiring additional property in Cork (Judson, 174–75);
earthly riches surely had meaning for him. In his treatment of the narrator Spenser looks back at attitudes struck by an earlier self and submits
them to loving parody and criticism. But he shapes the narrator's character with the freedom that fiction confers.

As with *The Shepheardes Calender, Fowre Hymnes* creates its meaning
out of the relations of its parts; criticism has shown how intricate
Spenser made those relations.[5] The four have structural similarities: each
opens with an invocation, followed by an account of creation, and closes
looking toward grace. The members of each pair contrast with one
another: whereas the odd-numbered hymns tend, for instance, to be
narrative in method, the even-numbered hymns tend to emphasize
argument in its more restricted modern sense. But the central contrast
occurs between the largely secular, this-worldly emphasis of the first
pair and the explicitly Christian orientation of the second pair. The third

hymn begins by repudiating the earlier poems and offers itself as a substitute for their false doctrine. The narrator's repeated words and images—light, fire, wounds, food, disease, healing—shift in meaning as he understands his initial experience as part of a fuller truth (Bjorvand, 15–45; DeNeef, 78–88).

Renaissance writers inherited the hymn form, like so many others, from classical antiquity. Greek poets wrote hymns to classical gods, describing their attributes, and the "Homeric" hymns often included narrative sections.[6] In the Middle Ages Christian poets used the form to celebrate the One God, and with the Reformation vernacular hymns were sung in English churches (Spenser uses the most popular hymn stanza for "July"). The classical hymn praising pagan deities and heroes reappeared in the Renaissance alongside the Christian form. It was popular in neo-Latin poetry, and among vernacular poets Ronsard in particular wrote hymns to gods like Bacchus, abstractions like Death or Justice, and heroes like Hercules or Castor and Pollux. In his hands the hymn became a half-lyric, half-narrative form, which enabled the poet freely to develop ideas associated with his subject. George Chapman had anglicized this Continental form in 1594 with two hymns jointly titled *The Shadow of Night*. An uneasy relation between "pagan" and "Christian" subjects thus formed part of hymnic tradition. When Ronsard wrote "Hercule Chréstien" (Christian Hercules, 1555), which he included among his hymns, he asserted that Hercules could be seen as Christ, whose exploits were adumbrated by the pagan figure. But his attempt to fit Hercules into the context of revelation suggests how much it was necessary to *argue* that pagan and Christian were compatible.

In *Fowre Hymnes* Spenser makes use of this tension, dramatizing a movement from one kind of hymn to another, from earthly love (however exalted) to the divine love that makes other goals seem inadequate shadows. The poem thus traces the speaker's hesitant, uncertain journey toward divine truth. The first two hymns develop a neoplatonizing vision of the Good that is fulfilled only in the final vision of the heavenly hymns. The relation between the two sets resembles the familiar relation between type and fulfillment; to borrow Ralegh's description of pagan mythology, the first hymns present "crooked images" of the "true history" informing the later ones.[7] Yet the poem does not present a record of salvation achieved. It charts the narrator's path toward the divine love he describes but never fully attains: like the *Mutabilitie Cantos,* the poem ends looking toward a final end.

**"An Hymne in Honour of Love"**    In the proem to the first hymn
the speaker announces his condition.

> Love, that long since hast to thy mighty powre,
> Perforce subdude my poore captived hart,
> And raging now therein with restlesse stowre,
> Doest tyrannize in everie weaker part;
> Faine would I seeke to ease my bitter smart,
> By any service I might do to thee,
> Or ought that else might to thee pleasing bee. (1–7)

This plaintive lover owes much to Chaucer's mildly comic speakers,
overawed by a conquering deity. The clichéd self-pity of "my poore captived hart" and the lover's eagerness to propitiate Cupid recall the
Chaucerian persona, an association strengthened by the rhyme royal
stanza Chaucer often used for his serious poetry and by the mock-
pathetic references to the speaker's wits, which have been "enfeebled
late, / Through the sharpe sorrows, which thou hast me bred" (15–16).
The dutiful lover swears homage to a mastering Cupid and sings his
praises in the hope that the god will relent and aid him in winning his
lady.

The Cupid praised in these opening verses is not the neoplatonic figure who appears intermittently in the poem but the powerful, sadistic,
conqueror god celebrated in the first of Petrarch's *Trionfi*, "The Triumph
of Love." As a deity of "victorious conquests" (11) he ruthlessly creates
"wyde wounds" with his "cruell darts" (13–14). The echoes of Petrarch
are explicit: in the sixth stanza the speaker advises the young women he
addresses to "Prepare your selves, to march amongst his host" (40). The
line recalls "The Triumph of Love," in which Love appears like a Roman
general above a procession of enslaved lovers. But in Petrarch the triumph of Love leads to a succession of later triumphs—of Death, Fame,
Time, and ultimately Eternity—each victor in turn yielding to the next.
Here, by contrast, the triumph of Love seems at once random and
absolute: Cupid's "wondrous triumphs" (18) have no larger meaning
than the triumphs of the god of Love in the House of Busyrane.

Yet in the fourth stanza, and intermittently thereafter, the speaker
views Cupid differently, in neoplatonic terms. This deity sits like the
Cupid of *Colin Clout* in "*Venus* lap above" (24), begot both by Venus and
by "Plentie and . . . Penurie" (53). The reference to "Plenty and Penurie"

is neoplatonic, and Spenser signals the speaker's shift into the alternate tradition by employing similar paradoxes in the rest of the stanza.[8] This god of Love is a creator responsible for separating the confused elements of the universe and linking them in "Adamantine chaines" (89). He presides over all generation, causing beasts to mate and man to "enlarge his lasting progenie" (105), a phrase suggesting both physical offspring and works of the mind. He enables the lover to glimpse a beauty beyond the beauty of the flesh, making him "mount above the native might / Of heavie earth, up to the heavens hight" (188–89). The lines suggest the familiar neoplatonic view of love as a force born with an apprehension of physical beauty that nonetheless drives the lover beyond the "heavie earth" of the body as he ascends to a vision of Beauty itself.[9]

Although Spenser is sometimes a syncretic poet, blurring the differences between the traditions he joins, this poem insists on those differences. In this hymn the speaker tries unsuccessfully to reconcile his experience of painful earthly desire with a notion of love as an elevating force. The first he couches in Petrarchan terms, the second in neoplatonic. At times the contradiction issues in direct questioning, as when, after praising Cupid's achievements, he returns abruptly to his own unhappiness:

> How falles it then, that with thy furious fervour,
> Thou doest afflict as well the not deserver,
> As him that doeth thy lovely heasts despize,
> And on thy subjects most doest tyrannize? (158–61)

Through the first two hymns the speaker tries to adopt a neoplatonizing view of love, but he cannot: he is a Protestant Aristotelian, concerned with this world, and his imagination refuses the serene flight of a true platonist, inevitably returning to his worldly frustration. As he veers from one view of love to the other, his language changes. Having shifted from the Petrarchan Cupid to the creator-god, the speaker returns in stanza 18 to Petrarchan clichés—the "imperious boy" with "sharp empoisoned darts," the wretched lovers, and the lady's frozen breast. This plaintive explosion subsides as the speaker returns to the idea of love as a virtuous discipline, and by stanza 24 he explains his setbacks as a spiritual trial separating true love from easy lust. After a neoplatonizing account of the lover's vision of his lady, he reverts to earthly pains in discussing the lover's jealous torments. When he praises love again, he does so in a most un-neoplatonic fashion by envisioning sexual fulfillment in a "Paradize / Of all delight" (280–81).

The speaker is most obviously neoplatonic in this hymn when he describes how the lover's imagination works to refine his beloved's image.

> Such is the powre of that sweet passion,
> That it all sordid basenesse doth expell,
> And the refyned mynd doth newly fashion
> Unto a fairer forme, which now doth dwell
> In his high thought, that would it selfe excell;
> Which he beholding still with constant sight,
> Admires the mirrour of so heavenly light. (190–96)

Spenser's ambiguous pronouns suggest how the lover's imaginative vision of his beloved enables him to transcend himself. The first two lines describe love's purifying of the lover's mind, so that it is "refyned . . . Unto a fairer forme." But the following lines ("which . . . thought") suggest that it is the *beloved*'s mind that has been refined. The lines sketch out the neoplatonic commonplace that the lover recreates a purified image of the beloved in his imagination—an image closer to the absolute Beauty that has shaped the beloved in the first place. Yet the following phrase ("that . . . excell") seems to refer again to the lover's high thought: by refining the beloved's image, he himself rises above his ordinary nature. Both occur at once: by purifying his image of the beloved, the lover purifies himself.

Yet this idealizing may encourage the solipsistic worship of a fantasy: the lines remain unclear on whether the lover admires the beloved or himself. The speaker's doubts about this imagining surfaces in the next stanza:

> Whose image printing in his deepest wit,
> He thereon feeds his hungrie fantasy,
> Still full, yet never satisfyde with it,
> Like *Tantale,* that in store doth sterved ly:
> So doth he pine in most satiety,
> For nought may quench his infinite desyre,
> Once kindled through that first conceived fyre. (197–203)

The image of the beloved becomes the lover's food, whose imagination (his "hungrie fantasy") it nourishes; the nourishment is limited, however. The picture of Tantalus suggests not the satisfaction of love achieved but desperation: desire is infinite, and the food the imagination offers is insufficient.[10] This image may merely rework the neoplatonic commonplace that any particular lady is never enough for a desire satisfied only by Beauty itself, but it also recalls *Amoretti* 88, in which the lover, absent from his beloved, finds her image insufficient: "But with such brightnesse whylest I fill my mind, / I starve my body and mine eyes doe blynd" (13–14). Love's imperfection reappears five stanzas later, where the list of famous lovers—Leander, Aeneas, Achilles, Orpheus—consists of amatory disasters.

The imagination's potential deceptiveness appears in the repeated verb *to feign*. On the one hand, it denotes (from the Latin *fingere*) the act of fashioning or imagining. As a faculty for making things up its associations are dominantly negative: one fains (or feigns) what does not exist.[11] On the other hand, it denotes (from the Old English *faegen*) the act of rejoicing. In the earlier hymns the lover's *feigning* forms part of his loving. The beloved is "Fairer than fairest, in his fayning eye, / Whose sole aspect he counts felicitye" (216–17): the eye at once imagines the beloved and enjoys her. The lover, too, is a "Thrise happie man . . . / [who] faines himselfe, and doth his fortune blesse" (209–10). Here the lover's faining is rejoicing, but it may suggest as well a reconceiving of the self under love's influence. Yet what the lover feigns may be unreal. When he purchases "lyking" in the lady's eye, "What heavens of joy, then to himselfe he faynes" (240): he has exaggerated his lady's kindness. Soon after, tormented by jealousy, his imagination pictures "to his fayning fansie . . . / Sights never seene, and thousand shadowes vaine, / To breake his sleepe, and waste his ydle braine" (254–56). The imagination acts as a double-edged sword, able to idealize the beloved and equally able to picture her infidelity. For a thoroughgoing neoplatonist, what the actual lady does is unimportant, but the speaker is not so serenely free of earthly desire.

The speaker's confusion appears again at the end of the hymn when he describes the sensuous "Paradize / Of all delight" (280–81) the lover finally attains after the "paines of Purgatorie" (278). It is a place of "joyous happie rest,"

> Where they doe feede on Nectar heavenly wize,
> With *Hercules* and *Hebe,* and the rest

> Of *Venus* dearlings, through her bountie blest,
> And lie like Gods in yvorie beds arayd,
> With rose and lillies over them displayd.
>
> There with thy daughter *Pleasure* they doe play
> Their hurtlesse sports, without rebuke or blame,
> And in her snowy bosome boldly lay
> Their quiet heads, devoyd of guilty shame,
> After full joyance of their gentle game. (282–91)

This picture departs strikingly from the neoplatonic script in abandoning the infinite desire of the *eros* for happy rest and chastely sensual play.[12] The departure from neoplatonic convention comes as a mild shock after the neoplatonic language of earlier stanzas. Nor is the vision Christian. However appealing the picture of innocent, happy, and playful sexuality, its source is not an epithalamion resulting from a real courtship but the fantasy of a rejected lover.

The poem's final stanzas insist on this context when the speaker asks Love to help him "come at length unto the wished scope / Of my desire, or . . . my selfe assure, / That happie port for ever to recure" (296–98). Spenser repeats elsewhere that earth offers no assurance, so that this hope of earthly security seems delusory. The next stanza's offer of a "heavenly Hymne, such as the Angels sing" (302) reemphasizes the substitution of *eros* for *agape*. *Fowre Hymnes* was published with a reissue of *Daphnaïda,* and Alcyon, that poem's protagonist, seems to embody a darker version of this first hymn's wandering speaker. Both focus on the loves of this world and forget those of the next.

**"An Hymne in Honour of Beautie"**    By the second hymn the speaker has changed. His vacillation between Petrarchism and neoplatonism has vanished, and he has become the spokesman almost in spite of himself for a neoplatonic Cupid. He begins in midflight, caught in a rush of divine inspiration. "Ah whither, Love, wilt thou now carrie mee? / What wontlesse fury dost thou now inspire / Into my feeble breast, too full of thee?" (1–3). The claim to be inspired by a divine *furor* or madness appears often in neoplatonic writers, especially the poets of the French *Pléiade*.[13] The speaker steps forward as Venus's spokesman, trying with his praises to raise "The ravisht harts of gazefull men" (12) to admire her heavenly light. He assumes a divine authority: instead of addressing Cupid or Venus, many stanzas now lecture an imagined group of "faire Dames" (162).

Yet while the hymn treats philosophic material, it does so to dramatize the speaker's still-uneasy quest for love. His main purpose in praising Venus, he says in the fourth stanza, is not to ascend to a vision of Beauty but to gain his earthly lady. He asks Venus to beautify her "sacred hymne":

> That both to thee, to whom I meane it most,
> And eke to her, whose faire immortall beame,
> Hath darted fyre into my feeble ghost,
> That now it wasted is with woes extreame,
> It may so please that she at length will streame
> Some deaw of grace, into my withered hart,
> After long sorrow and consuming smart. (22–28)

While the speaker insists that he means his praise "most" to Venus, the stanza focuses largely on the lady who has wasted his feeble spirit. Even Venus's pleasure has as its end the gaining of some "deaw of grace" from the lady. The poem's purpose thus diverges from the ultimate goal of neoplatonic loving and suggests a limitation in the speaker's understanding of what he is doing, a shortsightedness that will result in the hymn's bathetic ending.

The speaker first develops the nature of Venus, or Beauty, which he argues must be more than a harmony of colors and shape, for two reasons: such harmony alone cannot move men as Beauty can, and whereas colors decay with time, Beauty's power is eternal (64–105). Instead, Beauty is the "goodly Paterne" (32), or form, by which Love created the world. Its vivifying influence shapes the "grosse matter of this earthly myne" (46) into the world we know.

> For through infusion of celestiall powre,
> The duller earth it quickneth with delight,
> And life-full spirits privily doth powre
> Through all the parts, that to the lookers sight
> They seeme to please. (50–54)

The language makes the form-giving principle of Beauty seem a divine energy pouring into inert matter to give it life. In individual human beings the form is the soul, which creates in the womb a house of matter for herself, adorning it with the heavenly riches of its origin. Since the soul shapes the body, a beautiful body is testimony to a beautiful soul (120–40).

This assertion raises the hymn's first serious difficulty, for the speaker must now explain why some beautiful souls do not have beautiful bodies and—worse—why some beautiful bodies lack beautiful souls. He accounts for the first by the continued tension between form and matter: at times "by chaunce, against the course of kynd, / Or through unaptnesse in the substance fownd" (143–44), the soul cannot prevail against the imperfection of matter. But he raises the second possibility only to avoid it. For a neoplatonist, the soul is ultimately good, although often distracted and blinded by the body's appetites and fears. The idea of a bad soul raises the disturbing specter of Christian sinfulness. The speaker avoids this idea, treating instead the soul's vulnerability to external attack or seduction; he concludes that the soul itself remains beautiful—"things immortall no corruption take" (161)—and the ensuing sin is that of the seducer, not the seduced (155–56).[14]

The speaker further appeals to a Christian truism—that all things of this world can be corrupted if wrongly used ("Nothing so good, but that through guilty shame / May be corrupt, and wrested unto will" [158–59]). But he does not consider how the "will" comes to be corrupt in the first place. For a thoroughgoing neoplatonist, the problem is simple: the soul's contact with matter corrupts and blinds it. To reverse the blindness one rejects the body and ascends inward and upward to the mind. But this neoplatonist has already shown unwillingness to leave the body behind, and he does not mention this alternative. For a Christian, on the other hand, matter is neutral and the will's corruption derives from Adam: it is not matter but pride that blinds us and prevents us from acknowledging our inherited evil and dependence on God. An uneasy awareness of these unpleasing alternatives makes the speaker rather awkwardly elide the problem, turning instead to lecture "faire Dames" (162). Avoiding consideration of human sinfulness—a consideration that would undercut the argument that the incorrupt soul imprints itself in the beautiful body—he stresses the need for chastity and wisdom in choosing one's lover.

Such a lover possesses a similar soul and has been born under the influence of the same star. But in treating the similarities the speaker raises a second problematic issue—the lover's creation of the beloved's image. As in the earlier hymn, the topic elicits considerable ambiguity: true lovers draw "out of the object of their eyes"

> A more refyned forme, which they present
> Unto their mind, voide of all blemishment;
> Which it reducing to her first perfection,
> Beholdeth free from fleshes frayle infection. (213–17)

The problem with this scenario of the mind's stripping away the lady's corruptible matter to envison her original perfection is its tendency toward an unreal grandiosity. The language describing the lover's "conform[ing]" the lady's image to the light within has overtones of narcissism:

> Thereof he fashions in his higher skill,
> An heavenly beautie to his fancies will,
> And it embracing in his mind entyre,
> The mirrour of his owne thought doth admyre. (221–24)

"His fancies will" is an ambiguous phrase: *will* is a corruptible faculty, even if one omits the sexual associations of the word. The account of the lover's idealizing permits two readings. It describes the traditional neoplatonic ascent to a truer, less material view of the beloved, stressing the innate sympathy between like souls. But it also suggests a narcissistic idolatry as the speaker makes an idol of the beloved and disregards the actual lady he faces. The speaker betrays an underlying fear that this feigning may again be delusion.[15]

The following stanzas further suggest that uneasiness. The playful account of what lovers' sharper-sighted eyes can see—the "Armies of loves" (240) and the "thousand Graces"—are clichés of actual courtship. Again the halfhearted neoplatonist goes only halfway. For neoplatonic *eros* to work, the lover must ascend beyond the individual and beyond the flesh, but this lover is unwilling to do so; he remains at the level of the particular and the material.

This stalemate accents the hymn's curious ending. The last two stanzas return not to the triumph of Beauty but to the lover's condition as he addresses his lady.

> When your faire eyes these fearefull lines shal read,
> Deigne to let fall one drop of dew reliefe,
> That may recure my harts long pyning griefe,

And shew what wondrous powre your beauty hath,
That can restore a damned wight from death. (283–87)

The exaggeration and the clichéd language of the final line look back to
the first hymn. The speaker's vision of a transcendent love seems incompatible with the "damned" condition he claims for himself. The lover's
exaggerated rhetoric has a bathetic effect, pointing to his continued
unease.

**"An Hymne of Heavenly Love"**    Spenser links the second pair of
hymns to the first with an intricate series of parallels and contrasts.[16]
The wounded, self-sacrificing Christ in the third hymn opposes the
wounding, ruthless archer-Cupid in the first; Sapience in the fourth
hymn corrects Venus in the second. The earlier hymns concern *eros,* the
love driving the self toward Beauty; the later hymns concern *agape,* the
selfless love that God extends to his creatures and that they can only
attempt to imitate. Whereas the proems of the first hymns were self-
concerned and self-serving, the speaker here attempts to turn away from
his own condition except as it prevents him from worshiping God. The
contrast recalls the familiar Christian pattern of type and fulfillment—
of the flawed Old Testament event that is perfected in Christ's life. Fully
understood, the neoplatonic Venus foreshadows the characteristics of
Sapience. Spenser's retractation involves a reworking of the poem's
images so that the initial vision of love appears as a figure of Christian
truth, inadequately understood.

   In the opening stanza of the third hymn the speaker admits that he
needs the aid of Love's wings to help him rise above this "base world" to
a divine vision, and the second stanza explicitly repudiates the earlier
hymns. Regardless of what Spenser may have felt, his speaker unequivocally rejects the "mad fit" (9) of secular love: "But all those follies now I
do reprove, / And turned have the tenor of my string, / The heavenly
prayses of true love to sing" (12–14). These hymns thus announce
themselves from the start as a turning point or conversion. Later the
speaker tells himself that "All other loves, with which the world doth
blind / Weake fancies, and stirre up affections base, / Thou must
renounce, and utterly displace" (262–64). Sensual love blinds the imaginations ("weake fancies") of its devotees; one must renounce it to see
clearly.

   Accordingly, these hymns concern themselves with the redeployment
of the imagination. If in the first hymns the imagination elevates the

lover as he reforms the image of the beloved in accordance with ideal Beauty, it here reshapes him by humbling him with an account of God's love. In "An Hymne of Heavenly Love" God creates man in his own image: "For love doth love the thing belov'd to see, / That like it selfe in lovely shape may bee" (118–19). The lines echo earlier hymns in which the lover creates the beloved in *his* own image, as a mirror to himself; it is only God's love, *agape,* not *eros,* that remains free from the egocentricity implicit in the earlier feigning. Verbs of seeing now recur frequently in contexts that suggest a new understanding of vision. In these later hymns the speaker's difficulty comes in imagining his subjects, whereas the initial hymns merely stress the difficulty of putting conceptions into words. The later hymns exhort the mind to transcend the limiting imaginations of this world: "Lift up to [God] thy heavie clouded eyne, / That thou his soveraine bountie mayst behold" (222–23). The art of the hymn tries with God's aid to strip away the clouds of the fallen imagination.

Like the first of the secular hymns, "An Hymne of Heavenly Love" is largely narrative in form. Both start with the world's creation, although the picture has now changed: the neoplatonic vision of Cupid and Venus yields to a picture of God the Father generating out of his overflowing goodness the rest of the Trinity, the angels, and mankind. By recalling the earlier hymns, the later ones rewrite their pagan truths as Christian belief. In the sixteenth stanza, for instance, the speaker describes God creating man "According to an heavenly patterne wrought, / Which he had fashiond in his wise foresight" (108–9): the account of creation here places the divine "patterne" in the mind of God. The speaker now sets the atemporal platonic cosmology of the earlier hymns into the traditional Christian history of creation and fall. And the Fall—that aspect of human existence that the earlier hymns necessarily avoid—here occupies center stage as the reason for man's sinfulness and the condition of God's greatest generosity. Accordingly, the hymn's central stanzas deal with Christ's incarnation: "In flesh at first the guilt committed was, / Therefore in flesh it must be satisfyde" (141–42).[17] In this moment the divine comes into fullest contact with the human, and the speaker, potentially at least, overcomes the blindness that has limited the loves of the earlier hymns. The divine enters the human spirit, not by man's action in reshaping the lady, but in God's humiliation of himself by becoming flesh.

The hymn as a whole forms a meditation on God's overflowing bounty and goodness, proceeding chronologically with an account of

Christian history from creation to Christ's death on the cross.[18] The purpose of such meditations, a defined, semiliterary form in the sixteenth
century, was to inspire a movement of pious feeling through vivid imagining of spiritual truth, opening the soul to God's presence. This poem
is personal in a new way in *Fowre Hymnes*. Imagining the Crucifixion, the
speaker addresses himself:

> With sence whereof whilest so thy softened spirit
> Is inly toucht, and humbled with meeke zeale,
> Through meditation of his endlesse merit,
> Lift up thy mind to th'author of thy weale,
> And to his soveraine mercie doe appeale;
> Learne him to love, that loved thee so deare,
> And in thy brest his blessed image beare. (253–59)

The speaker now tries to submit his imagination to this new discipline
of learning to love. He addresses neither Cupid, Venus, nor the reader
but himself, in a dramatized attempt at self-awakening:

> And looke at last how of most wretched wights,
> He taken was, betrayd, and false accused,
> How with most scornefull taunts, and fell despights
> He was revyld, disgrast, and foule abused,
> How scourgd, how crownd, how buffeted, how brused. (239–43)

Yet this rhetoric of self-address and self-humiliation is hortatory
rather than visionary. It is less a meditation than a command to meditate, a scolding of the recalcitrant self. After imagining the crucified
Christ, he continues: "Then let thy flinty hart that feeles no paine, /
Empierced be with pittifull remorse" (246–47). The attack on the stony
heart suggests that the speaker is not sufficiently moved by the picture
of Christ's suffering, however much he might like to be. The final stanzas of the poem imagine what the speaker *would* feel were he to come to
an awareness of God's love.

> Then shalt thou feele thy spirit so possest,
> And ravisht with devouring great desire

> Of his deare selfe, that shal thy feeble brest
> Inflame with love, and set thee all on fire. (267–70)

The difference between this prescription and a fully successful meditation is the absence of a moment of colloquy in which the speaker loses
himself in addressing God. The speaker desires such a moment but fails
to achieve it. The final stanzas anticipate the time when the soul commits itself fully to God: "Thenceforth all worlds desire will in thee dye, /
And all earthes glorie on which men do gaze, / Seeme durt and drosse in
thy pure sighted eye" (274–76). But the speaker has not achieved this
visionary state. The restlessness of the earlier hymns recurs in muted
form: the speaker still looks to the future, his quest unfinished.

**"An Hymne of Heavenly Beautie"**   Like the second hymn, the
fourth begins in a rush of inspiration:

> Rapt with the rage of mine own ravisht thought,
> Through contemplation of those goodly sights,
> And glorious images in heaven wrought,
> Whose wondrous beauty breathing sweet delights,
> Do kindle love in high conceipted sprights:
> I faine to tell the things that I behold,
> But feele my wits to faile, and tongue to fold. (1–7)

The speaker is again "ravisht," possessed by the divine spirit he has looked
toward earlier, and allowed a measure of the vision that he has sought.
Perhaps the discipline of the previous poem has worked. As he beholds the
sights of heaven, his capacity to speak about what he sees fails him: "I
faine to tell the things that I behold" uses "faine" in its meaning of "joy,"
but the sense of "make up" is present as well, for any telling of these
divine truths in human language must fall short of the reality.

Yet the speaker's purpose in this feigning has changed, and with it his
role: in the second stanza he prays for illumination "that I may show /
Some litle beames to mortall eyes below" (11–12). As in "An Hymne in
Honour of Beautie," the speaker becomes an inspired teacher. Whereas
in "An Hymne of Heavenly Love" he addresses himself, he now prepares
to address the reader, showing him how to see. Like the speaker of the
first two hymns, the reader has fed on "vaine delight," and the speaker
must provide new food.

His central task in this context is to make the reader *see,* enabling him
to know God with his inner eye. Verbs of seeing and beholding, which
suggest the problem announced in the first stanza, occur unusually
often in this hymn. If the speaker's tongue fails when confronted with
the Beauty beyond earthly language, how can one bring a sense of the
divine to the human? The speaker's initial—and very traditional—
response is to display God through his works:

> Beginning then below, with th'easie vew
> Of this base world, subject to fleshly eye,
> From thence to mount aloft by order dew,
> To contemplation of th'immortall sky. (22–25)

These four lines encapsulate the progression of the poem's first half,
from the easy to the difficult, the visible to the invisible, the fleshly to
the spiritual. The upward progression emphasizes the order of the cosmos: each level of creation is more "cleare" ("bright") than the last one,
and so, by analogy, the realm beyond the end of the universe, beyond
the "fleshly eye," is brighter still.

The speaker makes room in this hierarchy of the invisible for the
heaven "where those *Idees* on hie / Enraunged be, which *Plato* so
admyred, / And pure *Intelligences* from God inspyred" (82–84). The pattern of Beauty in the second hymn—an idea of its own—recurs in a
Christian context. The ideas are as much a part of the structure of the
cosmos as the spheres or the nine orders of angels that surround God.
This incorporation of the platonic ideas in a Christian scheme looks back
to Augustine (Bieman, 115–32), but in this context it takes the idea of
Beauty in the earlier hymn and makes it good by showing that it is not
so much wrong as partial, in need of a Christian context for full comprehension.

Yet the speaker's opening rapture gradually falters. Spenser typically
treats the desire for God, not its fulfillment, and by the sixteenth stanza
the speaker turns from his audience to address himself: "Cease then my
tongue, and lend unto my mynd / Leave to bethinke how great that
beautie is, / Whose utmost parts so beautifull I fynd" (106–8). Whereas
in the opening verse the tongue fails, it is now the mind that needs to
refresh itself with an awareness of not only the external glory of God's
kingdom but its spiritual qualities. The following stanzas dwell on the
limitations of human beings, who, unable to look on the physical sun,
are the more incapable of perceiving God's majesty (120–26).

This increased stress on human limitation causes a shift in the means by which the speaker tries to mirror the divine. The hymn's second half imagines God less through his works than through revelation. The speaker avoids the attempt to show divine things directly, and he turns in discussing heaven to traditional metaphorical language derived largely from the Bible: "His throne is built upon Eternity. . . . His scepter is the rod of Righteousnesse. . . . His seate is Truth, to which the faithfull trust" (152, 155, 159).[19] The speaker will not try to describe God or even to develop a new metaphor for him; he uses biblical language accommodated to the human capacity for knowledge.

This language appears most clearly in the description of Sapience (Wisdom), which is heavily indebted to the Book of Proverbs. One common tradition associates this half-Hebraic, half-Greek figure with Christ, and hence with the creation of the world that the first half of the hymn has praised.[20] Through her God's works are accomplished on earth: "Both heaven and earth obey unto her will, / And all the creatures which they both containe: / For of her fulnesse which the world doth fill, / They all partake" (197–200). The lines recall the Venus in the second hymn whose "life-full spirits privily doth powre / Through all the [world's] parts" (52–53). The comparison with Venus is explicit in the thirty-first stanza, where the speaker denies that the goddess herself could not "once come neare this beauty soverayne" (217). The *sovereign* Beauty is at once governing and healing: it is the supreme glory of which Venus is only a shadow. Had Anacreon, who praised Venus, "Seene but a glims of this, which I pretend, / How wondrously would he her face commend, / Above that Idole of his fayning thought" (220–22). Anacreon's Venus is feigned, while Sapience represents truth beyond fiction.

Yet in considering the artists who have rendered the divine, the speaker returns to his own situation, and the assured exposition of the earlier parts of the poem ceases. He dwells on his own inadequacy: "How then dare I, the novice of his Art, / Presume to picture so divine a wight?" (225–26). He retreats from the role of a divine visionary: angels see Sapience face to face, but "Enough is me t'admyre so heavenly thing" (236). In mortal life moments of vision, like the one with which the poem started, do not last long.

The recurring metaphor of food suggests how far the speaker has come and how far he has yet to go. Whereas in "An Hymne in Honour of Love" the lover is compared to Tantalus "feed[ing] his hungrie fantasy, / Still full, yet never satisfyde with it" (198–99), the lovers of God in this final hymn are content:

So full their eyes are of that glorious sight,
And senses fraught with such satietie,
That in nought else on earth they can delight,
But in th'aspect of that felicitie,
Which they have written in their inward ey;
On which they feed, and in their fastened mynd
All happie joy and full contentment fynd. (281–87)

This account of final satisfaction, however, describes not the speaker but
the lover of God who has gained his desire. The stanza echoes the end of
"An Hymne in Honour of Love," in which the speaker thinks of the
happy lovers who "feede on Nectar heavenly wize" (282) and wishes himself among them. Again the speaker envisions what he would like but
has not so far achieved. The final section of the poem (stanzas 35–41)
once more turns away from his own experience to contemplate that of
the "thrise happie" (239) man who can envision Sapience. But this final
vision will come only after death, and so the final stanzas turn back to
the self-address of the third hymn.

Ah then my hungry soule, which long hast fed
On idle fancies of thy foolish thought,
And with false beauties flattring bait misled,
Hast after vaine deceiptfull shadowes sought. . . .
Ah ceasse to gaze on matter of thy grief.

And looke at last up to that soveraine light,
From whose pure beams al perfect beauty springs,
That kindleth love in every godly spright,
Even the love of God which loathing brings
Of this vile world, and these gay seeming things;
With whose sweete pleasures being so possest,
Thy straying thoughts henceforth for ever rest. (288–91, 294–301)

The speaker ends by exhorting himself, not the reader. The final vision,
here as in the *Mutabilitie Cantos,* is still to be enjoyed, and like that
poem, this one ends looking toward a rest that signifies an end to straying. The visionary remains a pilgrim on the road.

## Prothalamion

One of Spenser's few occasional poems, *Prothalamion* celebrates the betrothal of Elizabeth and Katherine Somerset, two daughters of Edward Somerset, the fourth earl of Worcester. We do not know the exact date of the betrothal, which probably occurred between mid-August and late September, but the double marriage was celebrated on 8 November 1596. The two brides were married to Henry Guildford and William Petre, both followers of the earl of Essex, who figures crucially in *Prothalamion's* final stanzas. The poem very likely builds, in ways we cannot now see, on the implications of the occasion itself, which involved a uniting of families under the auspices of the queen's last favorite. It is thus very different from *Fowre Hymnes,* but like that poem, it depicts the unfolding drama of the speaker's active thought.[21]

Poetry was sometimes associated with the celebration of Renaissance betrothals,[22] but Spenser seems to have made up the poem's title and to have fashioned it out of other kinds—epithalamium, dream-vision, pastoral masque. Like an epithalamion, this poem pictures the bride's progress toward her future husband (a double procession here) and creates a strong sense of celebratory ritual. The sixth stanza's song of blessing recalls the epithalamic speaker's formal good wishes at the poem's close, and as in many epithalamia, including Spenser's own, the natural world unites with the human to celebrate the marriage. Yet the poem differs greatly from the epithalamic norm, and these changes make an essential part of its meaning. It describes an event in the remembered past, not the unfolding present, and alters the principals so that the brides by metathesis become birds—swans. The poem's speaker, far from being the central occasion's stage manager, appears at the start isolated from the community he observes. Each of these alterations has meaning.

The poem also recalls the visionary emblems of *The Ruines of Time* and the *Visions* in the *Complaints.* The second stanza begins, "There in a Meadow, by the Rivers side, / A Flock of *Nymphes* I chaunced to espy," and the third starts, "With that I saw two Swannes of goodly hewe": either might begin a stanza of *The Visions of Petrarch.* (The verse form, an elaborate Italian canzone stanza divided into three by rhyme scheme and short lines, also recalls Petrarch's visionary poetry.) Yet if Spenser returns to an earlier mode, he does so in his new manner. In the second stanza, "I chanced to espy" stresses the uneasy wandering of the speaker: he differs markedly from the impersonal visionary of the *Ruines,* who records divine hieroglyphics and responds with proverbial truth. *Prothalamion*'s speaker presents another version of Spenser, a disappointed courtier whose early patron, Leicester, is dead, and who hopes in time to sing Essex's deeds. The poem's subject is partly this Spenser's transcendence, through his public vocation, of an initial melancholy isolation.

**Birds, Brides, Flowers, and Rivers**   Like much of Spenser's poetry, *Prothalamion* meditates on process. Its title, *Prothalamion* (*pro* [before] plus *thalamos* [bedchamber]), distinguishes it from an epithalamion (*epi* [upon]) in stressing the movement *toward* marriage. An Elizabethan betrothal was the legally binding commitment to marry, the start of the bride's passage from girl to matron with responsibilities for a household. Many poems recognize that the passage could be daunting. Catullus's epithalamia (for instance, 61:80–81; 62:20–24, 39–47) emphasize the opposition between maidenhood and marriage, stressing the bride's unwillingness to give up her girlhood and her family for the new house of her husband.

   Like Catullus, the speaker imagines the brides' unwillingness—in this case by picturing them in their maiden state as immaculate swans. The poem's final stanza describes them immediately before their betrothal as "two faire Brides, their Loves delight" (176), but earlier they are not brides but birds associated with a purity unstained and untrammeled by the everyday.

> Two fairer Birds I yet did never see:
> The snow which doth the top of *Pindus* strew,
> Did never whiter shew,
> Nor *Jove* himselfe when he a Swan would be
> For love of *Leda,* whiter did appeare:
> Yet *Leda* was they say as white as he,
> Yet not so white as these, nor nothing neare;
> So purely white they were,
> That even the gentle streame, the which them bare,
> Seem'd foule to them, and bad his billowes spare
> To wet their silken feathers, least they might
> Soyle their fayre plumes with water not so fayre,
> And marre their beauties bright,

> That shone as heavens light,
>
> Against their Brydale day, which was not long. (39–53)

Yet the insistence on a hyperbolic purity creates an awareness of its opposite. The additional comparisons—snow, Jove, Leda—bring with them the memory of Jove's seduction of Leda, which resulted in the birth of Helen of Troy and hence a world of blood and mire and ruined empires far removed from "heavens light." Compensating, the speaker insists that Leda and Jove were "nothing neare" the swans, "So purely white they were" (Berger 1965, 512–13). But his authorial protectiveness suggests that this fantasy of absolute purity is vulnerable. The concern is mirrored in the protectiveness of the river, which, punningly, seems "foule to them" and avoids wetting their feathers lest he mar their beauty.

Such perfection cannot last. When the speaker says that the swans' beauty "shone as heavens light / Against their Brydale day, which was not long," "Against" may mean "in preparation for," but it may also mean "in opposition to." The unearthly purity of the birds will not survive marriage but will change into something less perfect and more human (Berger 1965, 514). The birds are brides-to-be, and the speaker plays with their human nature in a crucial genealogical pun. When the nymphs stand amazed at the swans, having never seen "a sight so fayre, / Of Fowles so lovely" (60–61), the narrator comments:

> For sure they did not seeme
>
> To be begot of any earthly Seede,
>
> But rather Angels or of Angels breede:
>
> Yet were they bred of *Somers-heat* they say,
>
> In sweetest Season, when each Flower and weede
>
> The earth did fresh aray,
>
> So fresh they seem'd as day. (64–70)

Although the birds seem to be angels, they are in fact the progeny of "Somers-heat"—of Somerset and of the generative heats of the season.[23] The pun emphasizes that for all their bird-idealization, these birds are women, daughters of an earl and members of a family. Yet it redeems the animal in the human: "In sweetest Season" stresses life's fresh renewal; even the sexual associations of "in season" emphasize a "sweet" and proper generativity. This familiar paradox—that women (and men) are both angels and animals—reappears in the punning of "Fowles" (60–61): these are fair fowls, but the word carries its earthly baggage.

The opposition between untouched purity and human love reappears as an opposition between motion and stasis. The birds appear almost motionless as they are borne on the river's stream: they come "softly swimming" (37) and "floating on the Crystal Flood" (57). When the nymphs look at them, "they stood amazed still, / Their wondring eyes to fill" (58–59). The image recalls the wondering stasis attendant on the epiphany of a changeless classical goddess. Yet the swans are swimming "downe along the Lee" toward the Thames and, ultimately, the human world of London: they journey away from the purity of heaven and toward the impurities of love.[24] Their road is the river, Spenser's most familiar image of process. The opposition of swan and river has already appeared when the river fears that he may "Soyle their fayre plumes with water not so fayre / And marre their beauties bright," as in the end he will. Spenser's brilliant refrain focuses on time: "Against their Brydale day, which was not long: / Sweete *Themmes* runne softly, till I end my Song." The bridal day is not far off, but it, too, will not last long: the joyful rite will yield to a new world of social duties. The Orphic appeal to the river whose name recalls "times," like the apostrophe to the sun in the *Epithalamion,* asks for a world made temporarily sweeter and softer by the poet's song—and quieter, for if the song is to be heard, nature must cooperate. With the song's ending, its protective charm will lapse.

Spenser develops the shift from stasis to movement through the poem's third major image, the flowers that appear in several stanzas. These have several meanings,[25] but the most important is their traditional association with virginity. Spenser describes them as the "honour of the field" (74), and the nymphs who gather them are agents of process, "Daughters of the Flood," whose hair is unbound as if they were themselves brides (23). "And each one had a little wicker basket, / Made of fine twigs entrayled curiously, / In which they gathered flowers to fill their flasket" (24–26). As in the Garden of Adonis, Spenser stresses the fruitfulness—the abundance—time makes possible. The slightly awkward repetition (after *basket*) in "To fill their *flasket*" enables him to stress the act of *filling*. Against the wish for untouched purity is the hope of plenty, imaged here in the "store of vermeil Roses" (33). The uniting of abundance and transience appears when the nymphs strew flowers on the water:

> Then forth they all out of their baskets drew,
> Great store of Flowers, the honour of the field,
> That to the sense did fragrant odours yield,
> All which upon those goodly Birds they threw,
> And all the Waves did strew,
> That like old *Peneus* Waters they did seeme,
> When downe along by pleasant *Tempes* shore
> Scattred with Flowres, through *Thessaly* they streeme,
> That they appeare through Lillies plenteous store,
> Like a Brydes Chamber flore. (73–82)

The traditional association of the lilies with purity tempers the sensuous abundance of "Lillies plenteous store," and the final line joins richness, sensuousness, and mutability with shocking power. "Like a Brydes Chamber flore" superimposes on the fluid transience of the river the intimate enclosure of the bridal chamber in which consummation will take place.

The second part of the stanza also moves toward the moment of humanization in which birds will become brides.

> Two of those *Nymphes,* meane while, two Garlands bound,
> Of freshest Flowres which in that Mead they found,
> The which presenting all in trim Array,
> Their snowie Foreheads therewithall they crownd,
> Whil'st one did sing this Lay,
> Prepar'd against that Day. (83–88)

For a moment the allegory falters as the nymphs crown the "snowie Foreheads" of the swans. Swans do not have crownable foreheads, and the image seems silly unless one recalls (as one does automatically) that brides, not birds, receive garlands. The fiction of the brides as swans turns momentarily transparent, anticipating the final stanza's resolution of the swans back into the women. The song that follows, sung by one of the nymphs, is striking precisely for its ordinariness—its common eulogistic diction and familiar epithalamic good wishes. Although the nymph addresses the brides as "birds," they are "the worlds faire ornament / And heavens glorie" (91–92): both this-worldly and otherworldly. The song celebrates the "happy hower" (92) that leads them to their lovers. The good wishes—for joy, content, peace, plenty, and fruitful issue—are the standard wishes of the community on such occasions: they sum up what a human bride can hope for. With the reference to Venus's ability to "remove / All loves dislike, and friendships faultie guile / Forever to assoile" (98–100), the singer refers directly to the dangers of the world the brides are about to enter. She cannot know that Venus *will* smile on the brides: all the community can do is to offer its best wishes.

**Poet and Patron**    In stanzas 1, 8, and 9, Spenser frames this meditation on the brides' commitment of themselves to a world of process, the primary subject of stanzas 2–7, with a second, related story involving the speaker's relation to the larger world. It dramatizes the speaker's own commitment—or recommitment—to the stream of time and to his vocation as poet.[26] His sympathy with the brides' imagined wish to stay unmarried stems from his own analogous impulse to retreat from a world in which time has not run softly, and the poem charts his gradual return. It opens with an elaborate suspended sentence that sets his discontent against the temperate beauty of the countryside:

> Calme was the day, and through the trembling ayre,
> Sweete breathing *Zephyrus* did softly play
> A gentle spirit, that lightly did delay
> Hot *Titans* beames, which then did glyster fayre:
> When I whom sullein care,
> Through discontent of my long fruitlesse stay
> In Princes Court, and expectation vayne
> Of idle hopes, which still doe fly away,
> Like empty shaddowes, did aflict my brayne,
> Walkt forth to ease my payne
> Along the shoare of silver streaming *Themmes,*
> Whose rutty Bancke, the which his River hemmes,
> Was paynted all with variable flowers,
> And all the meades adornd with daintie gemmes. (1–14)

This treatment of the speaker's frustration with his fruitless stay at court restates the repeated Spenserian concern with useless, destructive "care" or grief. It looks back as far as *The Shepheardes Calender,* although Colin's cares—or Scudamour's, or Alcyon's—are amorous, not political. These cares have continued up to the present, for the speaker's hopes *"still* doe fly away, / Like empty shaddowes" (italics mine). As in the past he leaves the social world of the city for the relief of the country, so in the present he re-presents that countryside in an idealizing language of pastoral fantasy with its mythologized natural forces (*Zephyrus* and *Titan*), its "silver streaming *Themmes,"* and its painted flowers (Berger 1965, 510–12).

The speaker thus stands, at the opening of the poem, in both the past and the present, gloomily opposed to the city-world he has left. He is ready to see in the brides (whose thoughts he can never share) a reluctance to leave a state of virginal purity for the toils of marriage and to protect them in the idealizing rhetoric of his song. It is not he who wishes the brides joy in the sixth stanza, as would the speaker of an epithalamion, but one of the nymphs, a representative of the larger community from which he feels himself excluded. Yet as the poem develops, his sympathetic identification with the brides in their eventual joy leads him beyond the limiting self-concern with which he began. The nymph's words are, after all, his words at one remove, and in the seventh stanza he envisions an echoing landscape attempting (like him) to lend its "best service" (124) to the swans, a joyful unanimity that leads to a radically changed tone when he returns in the eighth verse to the city:

> At length they all to mery *London* came,
> To mery London, my most kyndly Nurse,
> That to me gave this Lifes first native sourse:
> Though from another place I take my name,
> An house of auncient fame.
> There when they came, whereas those bricky towres,
> The which on *Themmes* brode aged backe doe ryde,
> Where now the studious Lawyers have their bowers,
> There whylome wont the Templer Knights to byde,
> Till they decayd through pride. (127–36)

London now appears merry because the speaker's immersion in the joys of the brides has enabled him to see his own situation afresh. He mentions his name—and hence his connection with the greater world—with pride and sees the city itself as his "most kyndly Nurse" because she has brought him up in a tradition of civility, a tradition that has resulted in the writing of this poem. The city, symbolically riding on the "brode aged backe" of the river, embodies process, not personal but historical.[27] The medieval order of the Templars has given way to the "studious Lawyers," arms to laws, and the vision of process recalls the poet to his own changes:

> Next whereunto there standes a stately place,
> Where oft I gayned giftes and goodly grace
> Of that great Lord, which therein wont to dwell,
> Whose want too well, now feeles my freendles case:
> But Ah here fits not well
> Olde woes but joyes to tell
> Against the bridale daye which is not long:
>     Sweete *Themmes* runne softly till I end my Song. (137–44)

As the poet recalls Leicester's lost patronage and his present situation, he is tempted to self-pity, but he explicitly rejects that temptation in the name of poetic decorum. This decision has vocational implications: as he looks outward toward the "joys" it is his present task to tell, he returns to a renewed sense of his role as poet.

It is as a public poet that, in the ninth stanza, he addresses the earl of Essex, "a noble Peer, / Great *Englands* glory and the Worlds wide wonder" (145–46). His praise is certainly extravagant, and it has the practical end of attracting a new patron. But the recording of merited praise is also what a heroic poet does, and the praise of Essex's "dreadfull name" (147) extends to England in its battle against Spain. The suddenly heightened style of this stanza marks the poet's reassumption of his role as England's epic bard as he speaks directly to the earl:

> Faire branch of Honor, flower of Chevalrie,
> That fillest *England* with thy triumphes fame,
> Joy have thou of thy noble victorie,
> And endlesse happinesse of thine owne name
> That promiseth the same:
> That through thy prowesse and victorious armes,
> Thy country may be freed from forraine harmes:
> And great *Elisaes* glorious name may ring

Through al the world, fil'd with thy wide Alarmes,
Which some brave muse may sing
To ages following,
Upon the Brydale day, which is not long:
    Sweete *Themmes* runne softly till I end my Song. (150–62)

The passage transforms the language of the poem's earlier praises in this new, heroic context so that it becomes *England*'s betrothal song. The poet wishing Essex joy of his victory recalls the nymph who wishes the brides joy of their marriage: the speaker can now take his proper place—the place of an epithalamic writer—offering his good wishes at the poem's end. The "endlesse happinesse" of the earl's name parallels the earlier wish for "endlesse Peace" in marriage (101); filling baskets with flowers reappears as filling the world with the earl's fame and that of his queen. In this national context the "Brydale day" of the refrain cannot be the marriage of the two daughters, but the queen's accession day on 17 November, which was often celebrated as the marriage of the queen to her people.[28] The stanza attempts to bind together the earl's fame, Elizabeth's, and that of the poet himself, the "brave muse" who will sing of them "to ages following."

The final stanza brings the various strands of the poem together. The poet presents an idealized vision of the city with its "high Towers" from which Essex issues "Like Radiant *Hesper* when his golden hayre / In th'*Ocean* billowes he hath Bathed fayre, / Descended to the Rivers open vewing, / With a great traine ensuing" (164–67). The earl's seeming descent to the river is coordinated with the movement of the star upward, arising out of the Ocean's billows, so that he moves simultaneously downward toward the world and upward toward the heavens: immersion in process leads to glory beyond it. The image of Essex as Hesper, the evening star, reworks the familiar Spenserian image of the single guiding star that enables human beings to find their way in darkness (see, for instance, *Faerie Queene*, I.i.7, I.ii.1; *Amoretti*, 34; and *Epithalamion*, 286–93). But Hesper, as Spenser's readers would know, is the evening star and the guide for lovers invoked frequently toward the end of epithalamia: he becomes a guardian spirit watching over this marriage and over all England.

The two grooms appear in the earl's train like Castor and Pollux, and the mythological comparison recalls the dangerous reference to Leda in stanza 3: if Leda bore Helen of Troy, she also bore these heroes, later transformed into stars (*YESP,* 763, notes to lines 42–44). They descend to meet their brides at "the Rivers side" (175), the place of process itself. The final lines stress the harnessing of time:

> Which at th'appointed tyde,
> Each one did make his Bryde,
> Against their Brydale day, which is not long:
>      Sweete *Themmes* runne softly, till I end my Song. (177–80)

"Tyde" is time as well as the movement of water: here the ceremony appoints the tide, making it fruitful. The women become brides in preparation for the actual wedding, giving formal consent to their new lives. The final line is curiously inconclusive, since the speaker asks the river to continue to run even as the song ends. Perhaps this is a final gesture toward another song the poet hopes to write?

This poem, as Patrick Cheney has emphasized, looks in a very different direction from the end of the final book of *The Faerie Queene, Fowre Hymnes,* or the *Mutabilitie Cantos* with their fatigue and desire for a final sabbath. It advertises Spenser's patriotism, his epic ambitions, and his continued willingness to serve his queen and her favorite. It also shows his unending search for a patron. It is a poem about the attempt to rise above private woes and to become once more a public poet. Spenser had many faces, and this one turns resolutely toward the world and the river's open view.

## The *Mutabilitie Cantos*

We know little about the composition of the *Mutabilitie Cantos.* In 1609 Matthew Lownes republished books 1–6 of *The Faerie Queene* and added a poem entitled: "TWO CANTOS / OF / *MUTABILITIE:* / Which, both for Forme and Matter, appeare / to be parcell of some following Booke of the / *FAERIE QUEENE* / UNDER THE LEGEND / OF / *Constancie.* / Never before imprinted." We do not know how Lownes acquired the poem, nor when Spenser wrote it, although it is probably a late work.[29] It remains unknown who named the piece *Constancy* or divided it into cantos 6, 7, and two stanzas of 8, although it is difficult to imagine anyone but Spenser doing the latter. (The division with its two-stanza tail looks like a characteristically meaningful Spenserian joke.) While resembling the rest of *The Faerie Queene* in its stanza form, the poem is self-contained and, unlike the other books, lacks a human hero: with its inset pastoral myth it resembles a short Ovidian narrative like *Muiopotmos*.

In any event, the cantos embody a coda to Spenser's epic and his career. They look back at earlier work, notably the *Complaints* and *The Shepheardes Calender*, from a new viewpoint. They present an inventory of Spenserian themes and motives, including a complaint about mutability and the loss of the golden age; the revolt of a Titan; a parodic epic conflict between classical deities; an (Irish) pastoral interlude; a rewritten Ovidian myth; a comic fall; a river-marriage; a trial judged by a mysterious bisexual Nature; an allegorical procession of the seasons; and an expression of longing for final rest in God. Like many Spenserian poems, they mix the personal and the philosophical, the local and the universal, the playful and the serious.

They embody Spenser's most comprehensive consideration of process, the abiding concern of his poetry since the translations of the *Theatre for Worldlings*. Because mutability, or change, is associated with the fallen world, the cantos present in their quiet, undramatic way a theodicy, or defense of God's goodness in the face of the world's evil. The Fall appears explicitly in the opening stanzas and recurs in comic form in the inset myth of Faunus and Diana; the poem attempts to put it in its proper place. In this effort the cantos draw on much of Western culture (the variorum edition of the poem lists more than 100 relevant titles in its index of sources and analogues) and look particularly to the tradition of epic in which theodicy is a traditional concern, to Ovid and to Chaucer.

Like *Fowre Hymnes,* this poem dramatizes the education of the narrator's imagination as he tries to understand a truth beyond human comprehension.[30] The narrator intrudes directly four times: these punctuations of the poem—his opening complaint (vi.1–5), his shift into pastoral digression (vi.37), his seventh-canto invocation (vii.1–2), and his final solitary meditation on Nature's decision (viii.1–2)—signal its generic and philosophic changes. He moves from an Ovidian, anthropomorphic view of the forces behind events to a Christian vision that unfolds God's goodness while leaving his nature a mystery. Like the narrator of many pastoral elegies, he begins in "pagan" darkness and moves toward an awareness of Christian truth. These shifts allow no simple, final view of the problem of evil as they present it in increasingly inclusive, if never conclusive, form.

The narrator begins with a personification:

> What man that sees the ever-whirling wheele
>     Of *Change,* the which all mortall things doth sway,
>     But that therby doth find, & plainly feele,
>     How MUTABILITY in them doth play
>     Her cruell sports, to many mens decay? (vi.1.1–5)

The opening line announces a theme—Change—and by the fifth line
Change has become a female divinity who, like the goddess Fortuna,
sadistically raises men up only to cast them down again. The narrator's
genealogy of Mutability soon becomes a complaint about the world's
corruption for which she is blamed.

> For, she the face of earthly things so changed,
>     That all which Nature had establisht first
>     In good estate, and in meet order ranged,
>     She did pervert, and all their statutes burst:
>     And all the worlds faire frame (which none yet durst
>     Of Gods or men to alter or misguide)
>     She alter'd quite, and made them all accurst
>     That God had blest; and did at first provide
> In that still happy state for ever to abide. (vi.5)

The lines dramatize an essential confusion in the narrator's thinking, for
as Berger has pointed out, in envisioning Mutability as a Titaness he
loses track of what she refers to (1988, 252). Mutability is the name of a
process, a word for the changes that have resulted from Adam's fall. But
this stanza makes Mutability not only the effect of the Fall but its cause.
Human beings, according to this view of events, are mere passive sufferers and lose their responsibility for the world's original evil (Zitner, *MC*,
18–20). Mutability, the destroyer of God's order, appears as a force
comparable to God himself, able to undo his work. The parodic narrative that follows plays with this tendency to conceive of Mutability as if
it were an independent force, and it makes her a Titan struggling for
territory with the Olympian gods. The narrator thus begins by envisioning a cosmos in which divine forces appear as anthropomorphic deities.
    The great literary storehouse of such thinking is Ovid's *Metamor-
phoses,* which develops an account of a world without stability or justice.
The gods of Ovid's poem are powerful, greedy, capricious, petty, and

often foolish: they look like projected images of human rulers. In the poem's final book Ovid sums up this picture of the world by having Pythagoras, half-visionary, half-crank, argue that nothing is stable except change itself. The *Metamorphoses* thus speak, as Michael Holahan has argued, directly to the issues of Spenser's poem, creating a picture of a world without purpose or justice.[31] The *Cantos* suggest the limits of such a vision.

The narrator's original, simplified picture of Mutability as the source of all evil begins to dissolve in the opening narrative. While she may appear to be another Eve in her attempt to rise beyond her proper sphere, Jove's view of her as a "fraile woman" (vi.25.7) or as the "off-scum of that cursed fry," the Titans (vi.30.1), is markedly one-sided. On reaching his palace she appears "of stature tall as any there / Of all the Gods, and beautifull of face / As any of the Goddesses in place" (vi.28.3–5). Change is not always ugly. She pities the fate of fallen men (vi.11.5), for she embodies all attitudes toward change, including an awareness of its cost. Sheldon Zitner remarks that Mutability and the Olympian gods engage in a family squabble (*MC,* 16), and Spenser's treatment makes her their equal or their superior.

It does so in part by treating the Olympian gods with parodic Ovidian humor. While Renaissance writers, including Spenser, often treated the Olympians in terms of moral or scientific allegory,[32] his treatment here deprives them of allegorical dignity. Mutability and Cynthia squabble over her ivory throne like two fishwives (vi.11–13), and the resulting eclipse causes the other gods to run in disorder to Jove's palace (vi.15). Later, when she asserts her claim, they stand "all astonied, like a sort of Steeres" (vi.28.6). In having Jove send Mercury down to arrest her, Spenser repeats the familiar epic *topos,* dramatizing the imposition of divine will on the world (Greene 1963, 7, 214–17), but in this case the result is anticlimactic. When Mercury arrives and asserts his authority, Mutability frowns and announces that she plans to take over Jove's kingdom as well as Cynthia's. Stalemated, Mercury returns to Jove, his mission unaccomplished. The parodic treatment of the gods extends to Jove himself, who, despite the portentous rhetoric describing his "black eye-brow" (vi.22.2), does very little. When Mutability enters his palace, the gods rise in disorder, but Jove, "all fearelesse, forc't them to aby; / And in his soveraine throne, gan straight dispose / Himselfe more full of grace and Majestie, / That mote encheare his friends, & foes mote terrifie" (vi.24.6–9). With all the foolishness of an earthly ruler, Jove tries to look his best.

Spenser further stresses Jove's weakness by giving Mutability an excellent case. Medieval and Renaissance accounts divided the universe into three spheres: the terrestrial, below the moon and seemingly dominated by random change; the celestial, encompassing the physical universe above the moon, where change was recurrent and circular; and the supercelestial, the realm of God beyond alteration. Mutability rules the terrestrial sphere at the start of the poem, as she does at the end. The question is whether she will dominate the celestial realm as well. Despite Jove's contemptuous rhetoric, Spenser gives Mutability stronger genealogical credentials than the Olympians, for as the daughter of the Titans, she descends from Saturn's elder brother. In fact Jove bases his claim less on legal descent than on superior strength, having overthrown Saturn, his father, as well as the Titans. When he claims the heavens "by Conquest of our soveraine might, / And by eternall doome of Fates decree" (vi.33.5–6), he gives the game away. To claim the heavens by conquest is to admit the right of challengers: if Mutability can in turn conquer the gods, the universe is rightly hers. Jove's second line of defense, "doome of Fates decree," does claim legitimacy by right but does so by positing a power beyond that of the gods—the power of fate. This defense allows Mutability's appeal to the god of Nature. As a subordinate power Jove is partial to his own cause (vi.35.1); he must unwillingly order "*Dan Phoebus* Scribe her Appellation seale" (vi.35.9). The legal appeal ends the war in heaven and prepares for Nature's judgment.

Yet first the narrator intrudes, marking a change in modes. He begins by returning to earth: the trial, he says, will occur "upon the highest hights"

> Of *Arlo-hill* (Who knowes not *Arlo-hill?*)
> That is the highest head (in all mens sights)
> Of my old father *Mole,* whom Shepheards quill
> Renowmed hath with hymnes fit for a rurall skill. (vi.36.5–9)

The passage accomplishes a dizzying return to the familiar—to the local landscape Spenser celebrates in *Colin Clouts Come Home Againe.* "Who knowes not *Arlo-hill?*" is partly foolery, suggesting that this Irish place has been made famous by Spenser's verse, but it also sets Arlo-hill in a line of visionary mountains from Sinai to Acidale. While the narrator points to the indecorum involved in this shift from epic to pastoral (vi.37.1), the shift to the local and the humble enables Spenser to suggest in small the patterns that govern the universe. The pastoral fable bears effortlessly the burden of epic.

This myth presents another assault on the moon goddess by an irreverent intruder,[33] but it lacks the portentous epic machinery of the canto's opening. Its unpretentious comedy treats the Fall differently and more subtly. Instead of attempting to spell out divine mysteries, it points toward them, suggesting their meaning in playful myth without insisting on literal likeness. Its token Irish "fall" occurs when Faunus persuades Molenna to place him where he may see Diana naked, bribing her with cherries and "Queene-apples" as well as an offer to unite her with the River Fanchin. The myth's comic surface suggests that the Fall originates in a mortal creature's desire to know more of Godhead than he should. Faunus's peeping at Cynthia's "somewhat" and breaking into silly laughter suggests the foolish inability of any mortal to comprehend divine mysteries. In all likelihood there is also self-reference here, for Faunus peering at Cynthia also images the poet in his attempt to understand truths beyond his comprehension.

The episode limits the dimensions of the Fall, partly by departing from its primary source in the *Metamorphoses* (Ringler, 292–97). The story of Actaeon constitutes one of the most brutal moments in Ovid's poem. Unlike Faunus, Actaeon comes across the bathing Diana by accident while hunting; the furious goddess turns him into a deer so that his own hounds, not recognizing their master, tear him to pieces. The story displays without comment a world in which divine powers are unjust and pitiless and bad luck can strike at any time. The allegorizing of the story in the Middle Ages and the Renaissance tended to avoid the harshness of Ovid's treatment and to moralize the gods: it included the moral that "we ought not to be inquisitive in spying and prying into those matters, which be above our reache."[34] Such a moral fits Spenser's story much better than Ovid's, in which Actaeon has no intention of seeing Diana. But Spenser's version gentles the terrible Ovidian version, for despite her fury, Diana acts within limits. Although some of the nymphs would geld Faunus, they yield to the greater imperative that Faunus be able to continue his species (vi.50.3–4). Diana scares Faunus thoroughly by hunting him in a deerskin but does no more: there is a limit to divine wrath.

Further, the results of the Fall are mixed. In anger Cynthia leaves the Ireland in which she has taken pleasure, cursing it to abound in wolves and thieves (vi.55). Her abandonment recalls Astrea's departure after the golden age; in Christian terms, it figures the loss of man's direct contact with God after leaving the Garden of Eden. But the Fall also results in a marriage. Molenna receives Faunus's payment and mingles with the Fanchin: "So now her waves passe through a pleasant Plaine, / Till with the *Fanchin* she her selfe doe wed, / And (both combin'd) themselves in one faire river spred" (vi.53.7–9). Spenser emphasizes marriage when he first describes Molenna, whose rising occurs by a grove of oaks "That as a girlond seemes to deck the locks / Of som faire Bride" (vi.41.3–4). As in the Bregog myth of *Colin Clout,* this river-marriage involves both loss and gain, suggesting that the Fall issues in both disaster and fruitfulness. All things come at a price.

Whereas canto 6 begins, like Ovid's *Metamorphoses,* by stating its subject, canto 7 begins anew with an invocation. The description of the Muse sets the subject in a new context:

> . . . who but thou alone,
> That art yborne of heaven and heavenly Sire,
> Can tell things doen in heaven so long ygone;
> So farre past memory of man, that may be knowne. (vii.2.6–9)

All the Muses are daughters of Jove or (as Spenser often has it) of Apollo (see *The Teares of the Muses,* 1–2). The narrator's stress on this particular Muse's heavenly origins and her unique ability to tell of things done "in heaven so long ygone" suggests that he is not referring to Clio or Calliope. She is the spirit presiding over "An Hymne of Heavenly Love" and "An Hymne of Heavenly Beautie," whom Renaissance readers would probably equate with a Christianized Urania, Muse of astronomy, or with divine Wisdom herself.[35] The truths of this Muse transcend human grasp, "so farre past memory of man, that may be knowne." The anthropomorphic comedy of the sixth canto leads in the seventh to the unfolding of divine mysteries.

Accordingly, the poem's genre changes again. The posturing Olympian gods fade to voices in a trial or debate, and they appear later allegorized as the planets. The mysterious Nature who judges differs from them in kind. Like the Venus of book 5, she is terrible and beautiful, a veiled, androgynous figure presiding over earthly generation. The narrator refers the reader for fuller descriptions to Chaucer's *Parliament of Foules* and Alan de Lisle's *De Planctu Natura* (Nature's Complaint): the references, like the invocation of the Muse, dramatize primarily the speaker's own lack of certain knowledge (Zitner, *MC*, 48–50; Curtius, 106–27). In Chaucer and Alan, Nature is God's second-in-command, carrying out the work of creation through generation, according to the divine blueprint of providence. But Spenser goes further, associating Nature with the God of Nature to whom Mutability has appealed. She is "Great *Nature*, ever young yet full of eld, / Still mooving, yet unmouved from her sted; / Unseene of any, yet of all beheld" (vii.13.2–4)—the familiar paradoxes describe a deity whose nature is beyond time and human comprehension. Spenser compares her to the vision of the trans-figured Christ on Mount Thabor (vii.7); veiled, she is unknowable except as "an image in a glass" (vii.6.9), which recalls Paul's God seen "through a glass darkly" (1 Corinthians 13:12). The poem now re-presents the quarrel of Titan and Olympian as a problem in a Christian cosmos.

Mutability's case divides into three parts: her argument about the sublunary world; a procession making her claim to both the sublunary world and the celestial world above the moon; and her argument about the celestial world. She echoes Ovid's Pythagoras (*Metamorphoses,* XV.237–51) in showing that the world's four elements and their crea-tures change repeatedly "in restlesse wise" (vii.18.9), following it with the allegorical procession that dominates the canto. Here, as often in Spenser, a procession dramatizes an idea with resonant ambiguity: the picture of months and seasons develops Mutability's view of the world and simultaneously confutes it. For the temporal procession presents at once an image of change and order.

The inclusion of several cycles—the seasons followed by the months, for instance—displays the ordered continuity of time. Here, as in the Garden of Adonis, the cycles display the world's fruitfulness.[36] The 12 months participate in agricultural tasks: March sows seeds; May pro-duces flowers; June plows; September harvests; October makes wine. Even January and February, the dead months of the year, are absorbed in pruning as well as in cutting wood to warm themselves. Exceptions are April and May, whose sexuality appears in flowers, and December who is not concerned with agriculture so much as a fruitfulness of the spirit, feasting because "His Saviours birth his mind so much did glad" (vii.41.4). The procession shifts the implications of God's judgment that Adam would labor in the sweat of his face: like November, who has been "a fatting hogs of late, / That yet his browes with sweat, did reek and steem" (vii.40.3–4), the months perspire with gusto.

This procession glances backward to the beginning of Spenser's career, the vision of inevitable process in *The Shepheardes Calender.* Yet while that pastoral progression stresses care and waste, this one empha-sizes creation and fruitfulness. In "October" Piers advises Cuddie to write divine poetry, making flight to heaven, and the *Mutabilitie Cantos* fulfill Cuddie's program, but they do so not by abandoning the world but by celebrating it. Of the final poems Spenser published, *Fowre Hymnes* looks entirely toward heaven, and *Prothalamion* toward earthly glory. The *Mutabilitie Cantos* look in both directions, acknowledging the restless insufficiency of this world while nonetheless exalting the good-ness of what God has created.

In response to Mutability's attack, Jove allows her claim to the earth but insists on the traditional division between the sublunary and celes-tial regions. Since we use the sun and moon to calculate the time, they must themselves be above it: "who is it . . . / That *Time* himselfe doth move and still compell / To keepe his course?" (vii.48.4–6). Mutability responds by citing the scandal of change in the heavens that contempo-rary astronomers attested to, change that Spenser has already men-tioned in the proem to book 5. Mercury and Mars move out of their Ptolemaic courses; Venus cannot be seen in daytime; and the sun suffers eclipses (vii.50–52). The celestial realm shares the disorder of the earth.

Nature fixes her eyes on the ground—the world's substance—before looking up cheerfully to give her judgment.

> I well consider all that ye have sayd,
>> And find that all things stedfastnes doe hate
>> And changed be: yet being rightly wayd
>> They are not changed from their first estate;
>> But by their change their being doe dilate:
>> And turning to themselves at length againe,
>> Doe worke their owne perfection so by fate:
>> Then over them Change doth not rule and raigne;
> But they raigne over change, and doe their states maintaine. (vii.58)

The crucial term here is "their first estate": things do not change from their essential nature. Rather, their existence in the world unfolds their potential in temporal sequence, seed becoming shoot, growing into plant, plant blooming, giving fruit, dying and returning again to earth. The potential being in the plant "dilate[s]" by developing itself in time's appointed stages. The plant's essence, its "first estate," thus determines the changes that ensue.

By extension, all change, however dismaying from ground level, forms part of a plan that guides the cosmos. Nature concludes with a Christian warning.

> Cease therefore daughter further to aspire,
>> And thee content thus to be rul'd by me:
>> For thy decay thou seekst by thy desire;
>> But time shall come that all shall changed bee,
>> And from thenceforth, none no more change shall see. (vii.59.1–5)

All things will change at the end of the world, and thereafter earthly change—mutability as we know it—will cease. Nature does not deny Mutability her rule of earthly things. She remains in charge of the earth, and—since Nature never speaks to the astronomical question—perhaps even in charge of the celestial realm. The judgment does not contradict Mutability's arguments so much as put them in a new context, insisting that an unseen order lies behind apparent randomness. For her not to aspire "further" may mean "no further than earth" or "not beyond the world of appearances," or it may refer to the temporal limit implicit in the time when change will cease. It may include all of these. The stanza ends with the neatness of a joke:

> So was the *Titaness* put downe and whist,
>> And *Jove* confirm'd in his imperiall see.
>> Then was that whole assembly quite dismist,
> And *Natur's* selfe did vanish, whither no man wist. (vii.59.6–9)

The sudden vanishing of Dame Nature attests to the brevity of clear vision: for a moment she has given judgment, her veil removed. But with that she vanishes, and we return to the confusions of our world.

It is this renewed confusion that the two stanzas of the final canto dramatize. Epic moves typically between heaven and earth, between the long vision of the world's destiny and the daily blindness of muddy battle. Nature's judgment belongs to the realm of the long vision; the last section of the poem returns us to the narrator, whose experience of daily disorder is not so easily satisfied. We move from the dialogue of canto 7 to the solitary monologue—a meditative lyric—of canto 8.

When I bethinke me on that speech whyleare,
    Of *Mutability,* and well it way:
    Me seemes, that though she all unworthy were
    Of Heav'ns Rule; yet very sooth to say,
    In all things else she beares the greatest sway.
    Which makes me loath this state of life so tickle,
    And love of things so vaine to cast away;
    Whose flowring pride, so fading and so fickle,
Short *Time* shall soon cut down with his consuming sickle. (viii.1)

It turns out that Nature's reassurance in fact creates an increased awareness of the world's impermanence. The speaker remains divided, loving
earthly things and wishing simultaneously to rid himself of that love,
centered as it is on what Time will consume.

    In this ambivalence he turns from Nature's judgment to her promise:

Then gin I thinke on that which Nature sayd,
    Of that same time when no more *Change* shall be,
    But stedfast rest of all things firmely stayd
    Upon the pillours of Eternity,
    That is contrayr to *Mutabilitie:*
    For, all that moveth, doth in *Change* delight:
    But thence-forth all shall rest eternally
    With Him that is the God of Sabbaoth hight:
O that great Sabbaoth God, graunt me that Sabaoths sight. (viii.2)

The dissatisfaction with this world yields to a desire for the next, the
desire for final rest that appears in the first book of *The Faerie Queene* and
even in Spenser's translations in the *Theatre for Worldlings.* The final line
spells "Sabboath" in two ways and may, as critics have suggested, pun on
two possible meanings for the word—as "armies" and as "rest" (Bieman,
238–40; Berger 1988, 269–73). The narrator asks the God of rest for
final peace. But he also looks forward to the time when he will see the
God of Hosts; on such a reading, the prayer is not for an immediate end
but for ultimate salvation. In both cases the poem ends, like "An Hymne
of Heavenly Love," hoping for a final vision. With quiet originality
Spenser concludes this "imperfect" or incomplete canto in prayer, because
this life is necessarily unfinished, and its completion lies in God's hand.

## Chapter Nine
# Refashioning Spenser

The afterlife of Spenser's writing is the story of its refashioning. Good writers take from their predecessors what they can best use for themselves, and Spenser offered various possibilities to different readers. Whether this remaking of the earlier poet is a matter of Oedipal "misreading" or of self-affirmation in finding a father to imitate, Spenser was treated as he had treated others.[1] He was made new. He became a model for poets to absorb and reshape in ways that emphasized their difference from him, as he had displayed his difference from Chaucer, Ariosto, and Virgil. This refashioning of Spenser was the more complete as subsequent generations lost contact with the conventions upon which his poetry depended for meaning, making it easier to take the part for the whole.

Spenser left obvious legacies to his immediate followers. Crucially important, as Richard Helgerson (1983, 21–100) and others have shown, was his status as the first English poet to give his career a Virgilian shape—to present himself as a "laureate" poet writing a national poem to compete with those of the Continent. His success encouraged a belief in the capacities of English poetry and indeed the English language; early comments on his work often have a nationalistic flavor.[2] *The Faerie Queene* furnished the primary model for the long poem in English for the next half-century, just as *The Shepheardes Calender,* his most popular poem during his lifetime, became a model for the eclogue-book. Stylistically he offered to subsequent writers a poetic language unlike common speech—sonorous, deliberate, slightly archaic. And he bequeathed the stanza he had created for his epic.

Spenser's immediate seventeenth-century followers—among others, Michael Drayton, William Browne, the young George Wither, Giles and Phineas Fletcher, and Henry More—spoke of him with reverence and, as Joan Grundy points out, followed him in seeing the poet's calling as an exalted one.[3] Most of them wrote pastoral, at least on occasion, and they all wrote long poems. Browne wrote *Brittania's Pastorals* (1613–16), an unfinished, ceaselessly proliferating narrative; Drayton, the immense *Poly-Olbion* (1612, 1622), a geographical and historical account of England, also unfinished; Giles Fletcher, *Christ's Victorie and Triumph in Heaven and Earth* (1610); his brother Phineas, *The Purple Island* (1633), a psychomachea modeled on the Castle of Alma, and *The Locusts, or, Apollyonists* (1627), a short epic on the Gunpowder Plot; and More, the philosophical poem *The Praexistency of the Soul* (1647) in Spenserian stanzas. Yet despite their enthusiasm for Spenser and the verbal echoes of his poetry, their engagement with his work seems superficial—either mechanical in its imitation, like *The Purple Island,* or so different as to have little underlying resemblance, as with Wither and More.

The two poets of this group who internalized Spenser most fully, Michael Drayton and Giles Fletcher, changed him radically, and in different ways. Drayton saw and emulated a Spenser who had written England's great patriotic poem. While Drayton wrote in many different modes (beside his pastorals and *Poly-Olbion* he wrote odes, imaginary epistles, satires, biblical narratives, a sonnet sequence, and a historical epic on the wars between Edward II and his barons), his poetry returns to the celebration of England. Yet Drayton's mature work differs significantly from Spenser's, avoiding allegorical romance in favor of the literal truths of geography and history. The apparent mythmaking of *Poly-Olbion,* with its river-nymphs and spirits of place, exists to provide narrators for the mass of information about rivers, mountains, forests, mines, battles, and local legends that he includes in his poem. Unlike Spenser's sturdy nymphs and satyrs, these creatures are mostly bodiless voices. Drayton's work looks toward the later seventeenth century in dividing into fact and fancy, the truth of the actual (*Poly-Olbion* and *The Barrons Wars* [1603]) and the pure play of imagination (*Nimphidia* [1627] and *The Muses Elizium* [1630]). Spenserian faith in the imagination's access to truth about the world's divine patterning has weakened; in its place is a cautious, Baconian attention to fact.

Fletcher seems at first closer to Spenser, in both his use of allegory and his concern with divine truths. *Christ's Victorie and Triumph,* which treats Christ's incarnation, temptation, crucifixion, and resurrection, is the best post-Spenserian allegory until Milton. Fletcher's closeness to Spenser appears as well in his use of the divine numerology that undergirds so many Spenserian texts.[4] Yet despite its reworking of the Bower of Bliss, the Cave of Despair, and the Cave of Mammon in its account of Christ's temptation, *Christ's Victorie* moves in a very different direction from *The Faerie Queene.* Like Drayton's work, Fletcher's poem abandons the world of romance fiction-making, in this case for the truth of the

Bible; its underlying kinship is with Spenser's "Hymne of Heavenly Love" and "Hymne of Heavenly Beautie." The poem's narrator looks away from moral life on earth to a timeless realm beyond human knowledge; his witty, paradoxical rhetoric points toward that realm while admitting its incapacity to picture it in human terms.[5] Fletcher's poem has none of Spenser's shrewd, stubborn, humorous balance: Fletcher's Spenser is an enthusiast.

The greatest Spenserian, in Kathleen Williams's phrase, is Milton, who gives the impression of knowing the earlier poet better than anyone before or since.[6] Spenser is everywhere in Milton's work: Comus is a male Acrasia; Satan sits on his throne in Pandemonium like Lucifera in the House of Pride; Sin is shaped like Error; and in *Paradise Regained* Christ undergoes a testing that recalls Guyon's in the Bower of Bliss. Even Samson, in Milton's least Spenserian poem, must confront temptation and despair.[7] Spenser's presence in Milton's work comes partly from a temperamental affinity resulting in comparable themes—temptation, despair, concord, nature's enormous abundance, the dangerous good of sexuality. The increasingly free-standing narrator of the later books of *The Faerie Queene* furnishes a model for the epic narrator of *Paradise Lost* (1674), himself a character in the poem.

Milton's Spenser is a profoundly moral psychologist—"a better teacher than *Scotus* or *Acquinas*," as Milton calls him in *Areopagitica*[8]— able to dramatize the testing of Guyon in the House of Mammon. A much greater poet than Drayton and Fletcher, Milton absorbed more of Spenser, yet reshaped what he found in accord with his own genius. While Milton's original plan for an epic looked to Arthurian romance for its subject, his earliest English poem shows him already aware of his own direction. The stanza of the *Nativity Ode* (1629) recalls the Spenserian stanza in its final alexandrine, but it treats a religious subject.[9] With the exception of the third of the *Fowre Hymnes*, Spenser avoided recounting biblical narrative directly: his use of the Bible is allusive and structural. Milton usually does the contrary: unlike Spenser (and like Giles Fletcher), Milton focuses on a biblical subject, treating pagan mythology in passing as, in Ralegh's phrase, "crooked images of some one true history" (*History*, 2:176).

Milton's most Spenserian poem is *Comus* (1637), which conflates a surprising number of Spenserian contexts. Comus recalls Acrasia in the Bower of Bliss, but when he tempts the lady he also reenacts the struggle in the third book of *The Faerie Queene* between Busyrane and Amoret. In each scene a male enchanter tries to impose a perverse understanding of love on a female victim; it is necessary not only to overcome him but to reverse his influence (cf. *Faerie Queene*, III.xii.34–36, and *Comus*, 813–18). In both episodes a benevolent female figure frees the victim, symbolically teaching her how to love rightly. In Milton's masque the figure is Sabrina, who appears in the history Arthur reads in the Castle of Alma (*Faerie Queene*, II.x.19). Sabrina is invoked by a song (866–83) that echoes the roll call of deities in the river-marriage; what she bestows on the lady, in psychological terms, is the concord Spenser's river-marriage celebrates, a state of joyful motion imaged in the dance with which the masque ends.[10]

Yet the very form of *Comus* suggests again a crucial difference between Milton and Spenser. The masque is not description but conversation: where Spenser characteristically unfolds the mind by depicting place, Milton tends increasingly to do so, like Shakespeare, in dialogue.[11] By comparison with *The Faerie Queene, Paradise Lost* is a dialogue-heavy epic, concerned with dramatizing states of mind through speech. The internalization of epic—its concern less with deeds than with the states of mind that make them possible—occurs in Milton through soliloquy and dialogue. *Paradise Lost* begins with its most Spenserian milieu, a hell that mirrors its despairing inhabitants, but it is already a talky hell: speeches make up more than two-fifths of the first two books. (In book 9 the percentage rises to nearly three-fifths.) The Spenserianism of the opening books comes to a climax in the brilliant *homage* of Sin and Death, an allegory developing out of Spenser's analysis of narcissism and despair in the House of Pride. But after the second book of the epic Milton turns away from allegory to represent his characters' development primarily through what they say and do. By book 10 Milton depicts Adam's encounter with despair entirely through soliloquy.

Milton's turn away from allegory was already overdue in the 1660s. For the afterlife of Spenser's work cannot be separated from the fortunes of the allegorical mode so central to both *The Faerie Queene* and *The Shepheardes Calender*. Allegory as a way of *reading* texts, central to the thought processes of the Middle Ages and the Renaissance, fell into disfavor in the seventeenth century,[12] and the habit of writing allegory subsequently atrophied. In the advertisement to his *Temple of Fame* (1715) Pope looks back on allegory as "a sort of writing" "discontinu'd of late."[13] Allegory was never entirely replaced by other modes: there were many Spenserian imitations in the seventeenth century, including a continuation of *The Faerie Queene* by Ralph Knevet (1633). *Pilgrim's Progress*, the most famous allegory in English, appeared in 1678, but the differences between Bunyan's narrative and Spenser's are instructive. The allegory of *Pilgrim's Progress* is simple. By and large there is a one-to-one relationship of figure to referent, and characters exhibit the qualities of their names—Christian, Pliable, Talkative, Faith. Powerful in its bare-bones clarity, the allegory lacks Spenser's easy movement between various dimensions of meaning. (Characters in the eighteenth-century genre of the novel would further develop away from allegorical type to particular example.[14]) Similarly, when Pope comments on *The Shepheardes Calender* in his *Discourse on Pastoral Poetry* (1704), he notices only one out of the many dimensions of the poem—the relation between the life of an individual and the movement of the seasons. The richness of allegorical reference in Spenser's eclogue-book vanishes.

Just this richness of meaning struck neoclassical critics as incoherent or suspiciously obscurantist. Despite their disagreements, Joseph Addison, Joseph Spence, and Thomas Warton all found *The Faerie Queene* insufficiently unified, and its characters insufficiently like actual people. Spence argued that if you choose to represent an idea as a "human personage, it should not be represented with any thing inconsistent with the human form or nature": Talus, as an *iron* man, presents an inconsistency.[15] Talus's nature as an embodied metaphor is not allowed. Similarly, even while defending Spenser's work as a product of its age, Warton faulted it for mixing "divine truth, and profane invention" (Mueller, 64), and when he praised *The Faerie Queene,* it was for the passages, like the masque of Cupid, that seem closest to the static tableaus of eighteenth-century personification-allegory (61). (One eighteenth-century meaning for "allegory" was indeed "personification.") Spenser's capacity to bring together various kinds of meaning in a single character or event now seemed confusing or, at worst, blasphemous.

Yet Spenser never suffered eclipse. He remained a great English poet, however faulty by neoclassical standards: his *Works,* published in 1611, 1617, and 1679, were reedited by John Hughes in 1715, and in 1758 two editions of *The Faerie Queene* appeared within a year.[16] Recent work suggests that he was often read informally in eighteenth-century public schools, and Richard Frushell lists 250 Spenserian imitations between 1660 and 1800.[17] While he was no longer claimed as a Virgilian poet, some critics (beginning with his editor, John Hughes, in 1715) attempted to develop an alternative set of literary principles in which allegory would have its own place and its own rules. In his *Letters on Chivalry and Romance* (1762) Bishop Hurd developed a new conception of literary unity, arguing that Spenser should not be judged by classical but by "Gothic" standards: if his epic lacks the unity of a single action, it possesses the unity of a common design, picturing the 12 virtues necessary to a single illustrious character.

Poets continued to read and use him. Dryden looked to *Mother Hubberds Tale* and *Colin Clouts Come Home Again,* and Pope brilliantly reworked Spenser's allegory in *The Rape of the Lock* (1712). In that mock-epic the sylphs unfold the radiant superficiality of Belinda's mind—just as the figures met by the heroes in the early books of *The Faerie Queene* suggest their mental states—but in the social context of eighteenth-century drawing rooms. Faerie comes to Windsor and is transformed. In the *Rape* Pope's Cave of Spleen is indebted to Spenser's various caves (including the Cave of Morpheus), and even more so to Spenser's anatomy of frustration and despair.[18] By contrast, James Thomson's *The Castle of Indolence* (1748) displays its Spenserian credentials more openly: it is written in Spenserian stanzas, echoes Spenser's language, and foreshadows a view of Spenser that would be important in the Romantic period. The poem's opening canto presents an enchanter, Indolence, who captures the unwary and imprisons them in a life of inaction. Indolence is a brilliantly persuasive rhetorician, an eighteenth-century mixture of Archimago, Acrasia, and Despaire, who suggests that worldly activity is futile: better to dream in his enchanted castle. *The Castle* associates Spenserian poetry with a pleasurable yielding to an escapist—and ultimately a despairing—imagination. While in the second canto a Knight of Industry, like Guyon in Acrasia's Bower, overcomes the enchanter and destroys his castle, his exhortation to labor is an eighteenth-century challenge to the perceived ethos of Spenser's romance-epic.

During the Romantic period Spenser once more became a major influence, especially with the second generation of Romantics. One sign of this revival is the Spenserian stanza's reappearance in major poems—Wordsworth's *Guilt and Sorrow* (1798), Shelley's *Revolt of Islam* (1817) and "Adonais" (1821), Byron's *Childe Harold's Pilgrimage* (1812), and Keats's *The Eve of Saint Agnes* (1820), among others. Spenser's ability to render psychological states through description, his mythmaking, and his creation of a dreamlike, visionary world all attracted Romantic poets, but in very different ways. Two Romantic versions of Spenser may suggest the range. Shelley looked to the neoplatonism of Spenser's work and reconceived it with a philosophical intensity and purity quite unlike the original. *Adonais,* which begins as a pastoral elegy in Spenserian stanzas, ends with a despairing turn toward the platonic One in the absolute of death—a movement utterly unlike Spenser's abiding concern with this world's ills. Keats, on the other hand, turned to the poet of Acrasia's Bower. Spenser is for him the great poet of the senses, and in *The Eve of Saint Agnes* he uses Spenserian stanzas to create a world whose meaning lies in its celebration of imagined sensuous intensity.

It was in this period that Spenser became for many what Charles Lamb called the "poet's poet," a figure whose poetic brilliance lay in his capacity to create a removed fantasy world.[19] This view of Spenser focuses on the sensuousness of his imagery, the delicacy of his description, the inventiveness of his narrative, to envision a poet whose art, instead of engaging the actual, offers an alternative to it. It is a picture already present, implicitly at least, in Thomson's *Castle of Indolence*. The tendency to see Spenser as an Elizabethan escapist is compatible with Coleridge's distinction in *The Statesman's Manual* (1816) between allegory and symbol. If allegory is "but a translation of abstract notions into a picture-language,"[20] it creates simple, mechanical, one-to-one equivalences, without much imaginative force. The allegory of *The Faerie Queene*—the aspect of Spenser's poetry that makes it an exploration of human moral behavior—was increasingly discounted as external to the poem's real effects: Hazlitt commented that if Spenser's readers "don't meddle with the allegory, the allegory won't meddle with them" (Mueller, 75–76). It is no accident that, at the start of the Victorian period, Tennyson would introduce "The Lotos-Eaters" (1832) with a series of Spenserian stanzas.

This gradual (and always incomplete) trivialization of Spenser's poetry derived in part from large cultural changes that separated aesthetic from moral categories.[21] These changes were not welcome to many poets: Shelley's insistence that poets are the unacknowledged legislators of the race has more in common with Spenser's view of the poet as the court's teacher than it does with the idea of the poet as a craftsman of intricate beauty. The first great modern reading of Spenser's work was John Ruskin's brilliant, condensed account of the allegory of book 1, an account facilitated by his familiarity with medieval iconography and habits of thought.[22]

Subsequent critics have worked to regain the kinds of knowledge—historical, philosophical, generic, iconographic—necessary to see more clearly what Spenser thought he was doing. Central to this awareness is Spenser's insistence that Beauty and Virtue are ultimately One, and that the poet's allegory mediates between realms of being, suggesting the uneasy fruitfulness of this world as it participates—incompletely and temporarily—in the ideal.

# Notes and References

*Chapter One*

1. William Nelson, *The Poetry of Edmund Spenser* (New York: Columbia University Press, 1963), 10; hereafter cited in text.

2. "October," 79. All quotations of Spenser's shorter poems follow William Oram et al., *The Yale Edition of the Shorter Poems of Edmund Spenser* (New Haven: Yale University Press, 1989).

3. *The Works of Ben Jonson*, 11 vols., ed. C. H. Hereford, Percy Simpson, and Evelyn Simpson (Oxford: Clarendon, 1925–52), 1:137; hereafter cited in text. The comment comes from Drummond's conversations with Jonson.

4. *Mulcaster's Elementarie*, ed. E. T. Campagnac (Oxford: Clarendon, 1925), 274, 269.

5. This dialogue, concerned with the fear of death, was attributed to an "Edw. [*sic*] Spenser." For arguments about attribution see *The Axiochus of Plato*, translated by Edmund Spenser, ed. Frederick Morgan Padelford (Baltimore: Johns Hopkins University Press, 1934), and the commentary in *VP* 487–96; see also Harold I. Weatherby, "AXIOCHUS and the Bower of Bliss: Some Fresh Light on Sources and Authorship," *Spenser Studies* 6 (1985): 95–113.

6. *The Works of Thomas Nashe*, vol. 1, ed. Ronald B. McKerrow (Oxford: Blackwell, 1958), 302.

7. *Spenser's Prose Works*, ed. Rudolf Gottfried (Baltimore: Johns Hopkins University Press, 1949), hereafter cited in text as *VP*. This work is volume 9 of *The Works of Edmund Spenser: A Variorum Edition*, ed. Edwin Greenlaw, Charles Grosvenor Osgood, Frederick Morgan Padelford and Ray Heffner (Baltimore: Johns Hopkins University Press, 1932–49), cited in notes as *VE*.

8. Sir Phillip Sidney, *An Apology for Poetry*, ed. Geoffrey Shepherd (Manchester: Manchester University Press, 1965), 133.

9. See W. H. Wepley, "Edmund Spenser: Being an Account of Some Recent Researches into his Life and Lineage . . . ," *Notes and Queries* 162 (January–June, 1932): 182–83, hereafter cited in text; Douglas Hamer, "Some Spenser Problems," *Notes and Queries* 180 (January–June 1941): 183–84; 206–9; Mark Eccles, "Elizabethan Edmund Spensers," *Modern Language Quarterly* 5 (1944): 413–27.

10. See S. K. Heninger, "The Typographical Layout of Spenser's *Shepheardes Calender* and Sansovino's Sannazaro," in *The Word and the Visual Imagination*, ed. Karl Joseph Höltgen, Peter M. Daly, and Wolfgang Lottes (Erlangen, Germany: Universitätsbibliothek, 1988), 33–71.

11.   Richard Helgerson, *Self-Crowned Laureates: Spenser, Jonson, Milton, and the Literary System* (Berkeley: University of California Press, 1983), 29; hereafter cited in text.

12.   Lodowick Bryskett, *Literary Works,* ed. J. H. P. Pafford (Amersham, England: Gregg International Publishers, 1972), 6.

13.   On Spenser's knowledge of and interest in Ireland, see Sheila Cavanaugh, " 'Such Was Irena's Countenance': Ireland in Spenser's Prose and Poetry," *Texas Studies in Literature and Language* 28 (1986): 24–50.

14.   *The Life and Correspondence of Lodowick Bryskett,* ed. Henry R. Plomer and Tom Peete Cross (Chicago: University of Chicago Press, 1927), 33.

15.   See, for instance, Nicholas Canny, *The Elizabethan Conquest of Ireland: A Pattern Established 1565–1576* (New York: Barnes and Noble, 1976), 125–36.

16.   Quoted in Alexander Judson, *The Life of Edmund Spenser* (Baltimore: Johns Hopkins University Press, 1945), 134, 135, 163; hereafter cited in text.

17.   On the composition of the *View* see *VP,* 503–05; and Jean Brink, "Constructing the *View of the Present State of Ireland,*" *Spenser Studies* 11 (1990): 203–28.

18.   Quoted in Brink, "Constructing the View," 207.

19.   The bibliography on the *View* is growing rapidly in complexity and quality. See Willy Maley, "Spenser and Ireland: A Select Bibliography," *Spenser Studies* 9 (1988): 227–42, for work through the mid-1980s. See also the article *"A Vewe of the Present State of Ireland"* by David B. Quinn in *The Spenser Encyclopedia* (Toronto: University of Toronto Press, 1990), 713–15, hereafter cited in the text.

20.   C. S. Lewis, *The Allegory of Love* (Oxford: Oxford University Press, 1936), 348.

21.   Nicholas Canny, "Spenser and the Development of an Anglo-Irish Identity," *Yearbook of English Studies* 13 (1983): 1–19.

22.   Many of the fine essays in Patricia Coughlin, ed., *Spenser and Ireland: An Interdisciplinary Perspective* (Cork: Cork University Press, 1989), hereafter cited in the text, stress these contradictions.

23.   Ciaran Brady, "Spenser's Irish Crisis: Humanism and Experience in the 1590's," *Past and Present* 111 (May, 1986): 17–49, hereafter cited in the text. Canny and Brady argued the issue further in "Debate: Spenser's Irish Crisis," in *Past and Present* 120 (August, 1988): 201–15. See also Brady's "The Road to the *View*: On the Decline of Reform Thought in 7 ⸗⸗ ⸗r Ireland," in *Spenser and Ireland,* 25–45.

24.   Annabelle Patterson, *Reading Between the Lines* (Madison: University of Wisconsin Press, 1993), 80–115, hereafter cited in the text; see also Patricia Coughlin, "Ireland and Incivility in Spenser," in *Spenser and Ireland,* 46–74.

25.   Lines 29–35. See also Wepley, "Edmund Spenser," 182–83.

26.   Harold Stein, *Studies in Spenser's Complaints* (New York: Oxford University Press, 1934), 2–34, makes the fullest argument for Spenser's putting

the volume together; he is followed by Ronald Bond (*YESP*, 217–22). More recently, Jean R. Brink has questioned whether Spenser had any part at all in collecting and printing this volume; see "Who Fashioned Edmund Spenser? The Textual History of the *Complaints*," *Studies in Philology* 88 (1991): 153–68; hereafter cited in text.

27.   Richard Rambuss, *Spenser's Secret Career* (Cambridge, England: Cambridge University Press, 1993), 86–87.

28.   See A. L. Rowse, *Sir Walter Ralegh: His Family and Private Life* (New York: Harper, 1962), 158–69, for details.

29.   Spenser's gradual renunciation of the dream of acting the courtier-poet is a primary concern in John Bernard, *Ceremonies of Innocence* (Cambridge, England: Cambridge University Press, 1989), esp. 107–10, 126–34, 153–62, 163–85.

30.   *Acts of the Privy Council* (1598–99), 204–5, quoted in Judson, *Life of Spenser*, 200.

31.   On the nature and attribution of this work see *VP*, 533–37; and Ciaran Brady, "A Briefe Note of Ireland," in *The Spenser Encyclopedia*, 111–12.

32.   William Camden, *Annales, or The History of the most Renowned and Victorious Princesse Elizabeth, late Queen of England . . . written in Latin and translated into English, by R. N{orton} . . .* [London, 1635], reprinted in *Edmund Spenser's Poetry*, 3d ed., ed. Hugh MacLean and Anne Lake Prescott (New York: Norton, 1993), 661; hereafter cited in text.

*Chapter Two*

1.   All quotations in this chapter from *The Shepheardes Calender* are taken from Oram et al., *Yale Edition of the Shorter Poems*.

2.   For an account of the importance of the *Calender* in the context of English literary history, see Paul Alpers, "Pastoral and the Domain of Lyric in Spenser's *Shepheardes Calender*," *Representations* 12 (1985): 83–100.

3.   Marot also wrote a poem—imitated in Spenser's "December"—in which he plays a shepherd, "Colin," addressing his king, although "Colin Clout" is calculated to recall Skelton's satire.

4.   Typical representatives of each position are: S. K. Heninger, "The Implications of Form for *The Shepheardes Calender*," *Studies in the Renaissance* 9 (1962): 309–21, and his recent entry on "*The Shepheards Calender*" for *The Spenser Encyclopedia*, 645–51; Helgerson, *Self-Crowned Laureates*, 55–82; John King, *Spenser's Poetry and the Reformation Tradition* (Princeton: Princeton University Press, 1990), 14–46, hereafter cited in text; and Harry Berger, Jr., *Revisionary Play: Studies in the Spenserian Dynamics* (Berkeley: University of California Press, 1988), 277–452, hereafter cited in text. Most critics, of course, combine various approaches.

5.   On this aspect of the *Calender* treated from a Bakhtinian perspective, see Roland Greene, "*The Shepheardes Calender*, Dialogue and Periphrasis," *Spenser Studies* 8 (1987): 1–33.

6.  On the first eclogue, see Michael C. J. Putnam, *Virgil's Pastoral Art* (Princeton, N.J.: Princeton University Press, 1970), 20–81; Eleanor Windsor Leach, *Vergil's Eclogues: Landscapes of Experience* (Ithaca, N.Y.: Cornell University Press, 1974), 113–42; Paul Alpers, *The Singer of the Eclogues* (Berkeley: University of California Press, 1979), 65–95. Annabel Patterson, *Pastoral and Ideology* (Berkeley: University of California Press, 1987), hereafter cited in text, discusses the deeply political implications of European pastoral poetry from Virgil on.

7.  On the view of the shepherd as representative, see William Empson, *Some Versions of Pastoral* (Norfolk, Conn.: New Directions, 1960), 11–20; and Paul Alpers, "What Is Pastoral?" *Critical Inquiry* 8 (1982): 437–60.

8.  George Puttenham, *The Arte of English Poesie,* ed. Gladys Doidge Willcock and Alice Walker (1936; rpt., Darby, Pa.: Darby Books, 1969), 38; hereafter cited in text.

9.  Virgil, *Eclogue* X.75: "Surgamus: solet esse gravis cantantibus umbra"; translation in Alpers, 1979, 63.

10.  Patrick Cullen, *Spenser, Marvell, and Renaissance Pastoral* (Cambridge, Mass.: Harvard University Press, 1970), 1–26; hereafter cited in text. Cullen's reading of *The Shepheardes Calender* has had a strong and continuing influence, because the Arcadian/Mantuanesque opposition he establishes so clearly illuminates the conflicts within the poems. My reading is deeply indebted to his book.

11.  This point is made by Lee Piepho in "The Organization of Mantuan's *Adulescentia* and Spenser's *Shepheardes Calender:* A Comparison," *Acta Contentus Neo-Latini Bononiensis: Proceedings of the Fourth International Congress of Neo-Latin Studies, Bologna,* ed. R. J. Schoek (Binghamton, N.Y.: Center for Medieval and Early Renaissance Studies, 1980), 576–82.

12.  Reference to weather as shorthand for the Fall is a poetic commonplace; it appears, for instance, in the opening of the *Second Shepherds Play,* which sets Christ's birth against the cold that the Shepherds lament at the onset of the drama.

13.  Louis Montrose, " 'The Perfecte Patterne of a Poete': The Poetics of Courtship in *The Shepheardes Calender,*" *Texas Studies in Literature and Language* 21 (1979): 44; hereafter cited in text.

14.  For a somewhat different reading of the cup, see David Miller, "Authorship, Anonymity and *The Shepheardes Calender,*" *Modern Language Quarterly* 40 (1979): 228–29.

15.  See Lynn Staley Johnson, The Shepheardes Calender: *An Introduction* (University Park: Pennsylvania State University Press, 1990), 6–7, 37–44, hereafter cited in text, for the most extended account of the three kinds, and the argument that the three divisions reflect the traditional triad of practical (moral), contemplative (plaintive), and divine (recreative) wisdom.

16.  See ibid., 115–17, for a fuller discussion of the meanings of "complaint." See also John Desmond Peter, *Complaint and Satire in Early English Literature* (Oxford: Clarendon Press, 1956), 1–13, 60–103.

17. Harry Berger Jr., *The Allegorical Temper: Vision and Reality in Book 2 of Spenser's* Faerie Queene (New Haven, Conn.: Yale University Press, 1957), 120–60; hereafter cited in text.

18. The association of rough language with satire is commonplace in Renaissance criticism and practice. Renaissance Protestants saw Langland's poem as a proto-Protestant work; for a critic like George Puttenham, he is of interest primarily for his attack on the church and his language: "He that wrote the Satyr of Piers Ploughman, seemed to have bene a malcontent of that time, and therefore bent himselfe wholy to taxe the disorders of that age, and specially the pride of the Romane Clergy, of whose fall he seemeth to be a very true Prophet, his verse is but loose meetre, and his termes hard and obscure, so as in them is litle pleasure to be taken" (*Arte*, 62). The identification is discussed most fully in King, *Spenser's Poetry,* 319–37. See also his *Spenser's Poetry and the Reformation Tradition* (Princeton, N.J.: Princeton University Press, 1990), 20–31.

19. See Anthea Hume, *Edmund Spenser: Protestant Poet* (Cambridge, England: Cambridge University Press, 1984), 21–26, hereafter cited in text, who argues that Wolves are Roman Catholic priests and Foxes are Roman-leaning clergy of the Church of England.

20. See also William Nelson, *The Poetry of Edmund Spenser* (New York: Columbia University Press, 1963), 46; hereafter cited in text. For the argument that the moral eclogues are *not* balanced but meant to bear a strong Protestant message, see Hume, *Spenser,* 13–40, and David Norbrook, *Poetry and Politics in the English Renaissance* (London: Routledge and Kegan Paul, 1984), 64, hereafter cited in text.

21. Harry Berger Jr., "Mode and Diction in the *Shepheardes Calender,*" *Modern Philology* 67 (1969): 147–49.

22. In "Spenser's 'E.K.' as Edmund Kent (Kenned/of Kent): Kyth (Couth), Kissed, and Kunning-Conning," *English Literary Renaissance* 20 (1990): 374–407. Louise Schleiner reviews various speculations about E.K.'s identity and offers a persuasive argument for Spenser's authorship of E.K's commentary, possibly with the help of Gabriel Harvey.

23. For readings of the *Calender* that argue for a homoerotic relation between Colin and Hobbinol, see Jonathan Goldberg, "Colin to Hobbinol: Spenser's Familiar Letters," *South Atlantic Quarterly* 88 (1989): 107–26; and Bruce R. Smith, *Homosexual Desire in Shakespeare's England* (Chicago: University of Chicago Press, 1991), 94–97.

24. William Ringler proved in "Spenser, Shakespeare, Honor, and Worship," *Renaissance News* 14 (1961): 159–61, that the *Calender* was originally addressed to the earl of Leicester, who is formally addressed "His Honor"; the proper title for a gentleman like Sidney was "His Worship." When, presumably at the last moment, Spenser decided to dedicate the book to Sidney, he never changed the introductory title.

25. "Of Friendship," in Frances Bacon, *Essays, Advancement of Learning, New Atlantis, and Other Pieces,* ed. Richard Foster Jones (New York: Odyssey Press, 1937), 82.

26. Richard Helgerson, *The Elizabethan Prodigals* (Berkeley: University of California Press, 1976), 1–16; hereafter cited in text.

27. See, for instance, Paul E. McLane, *Spenser's* Shepheardes Calender: *A Study in Elizabethan Allegory* (Notre Dame, Ind.: University of Notre Dame Press, 1961), 61–76.

28. See Leo Spitzer, *Essays on English and American Literature* (Princeton, N.J.: Princeton University Press, 1969), 180–92.

29. Norbrook, *Poetry and Politics,* 84–89, has a more cautious formulation.

30. The motto to "Aprill" signals such a vision: it is Aeneas's initial exclamation when he sees Venus disguised as a nymph in book 1 of the *Aeneid* and exclaims, "O dea certe" ("Most surely a goddess").

31. The fullest account of the structure of Colin's song appears in Thomas Cain, "The Strategy of Praise in Spenser's *Aprill,*" *Studies in English Literature* 8 (1968): 45–58.

32. Preface to *The Battle of the Books* in Jonathan Swift, *Gulliver's Travels, A Tale of a Tub, The Battle of the Books, etc.* (London: Oxford University Press, 1956), 540.

33. In dramatizing this rustic literal-mindedness, Spenser is playing with a long-standing pastoral tradition. Boccaccio's Sylvius in his pastoral elegy "Olympia" cannot recognize the metaphorical nature of his dead daughter's description of heaven, and in the eighth eclogue Mantuan makes his rustics as literal-minded and as limited as possible.

34. I am indebted to Anne Lake Prescott for this point.

35. One critical tradition identifies Dido and Elisa, in part because Dido's name in the *Aeneid* is Elissa. The reading has political implications: Dido's "death" is a metaphor for Elizabeth's marriage to the Duc D'Alençon and the subsequent wasting away of her kingdom. The greatest hindrance to this reading is the poem's stress on Dido's apotheosis: there is no room in the D'Alençon scenario for a happy Dido among the saints. Yet the obvious echoes of "Aprill" in "November" make the association difficult to dismiss entirely. For various versions of this argument, see McLane, *Spenser's* Shepheardes Calender, 47–60; Johnson, *An Introduction,* 128–30; Donald Cheney, "The Circular Argument of *The Shepheardes Calender,*" in *Unfolded Tales,* ed. George M. Logan and Gordon Teskey (Ithaca, N.Y.: Cornell University Press, 1989), 152–61.

36. On Marot's poem, see Anne Lake Prescott, "Musical Strains: Marot's Double Role" in *Contending Kingdoms* (Detroit: Wayne State University Press, 1991), 56–60; and in its relation to Spenser's poem, Patterson, *Pastoral and Ideology,* 107–32.

37. See John King, *English Reformation Literature: The Tudor Origins of the Protestant Tradition* (Princeton: Princeton University Press, 1982), 319–39.

*Chapter Three*

1. Virgil, *The Aeneid,* rev. ed., trans. W. Jackson Knight (London: Penguin, 1958), 27; hereafter cited in text as *Aeneid.* Although the lines appear

in some of the manuscripts, they are now generally considered to be by a later hand.

2.  *Orlando Furioso,* canto I, stanza i, ll. 1–2, trans. Barbara Reynolds (Harmondsworth, England: Penguin, 1975), I.117.

3.  Critics have often pointed to the relation between the Spenserian stanza and the eight-line stanza of Chaucer's "Monk's Tale," which matches the first eight lines of the Spenserian stanza exactly. But the verse form of "The Monk's Tale" has no final couplet, and its effect is altogether different. What Spenser does is retain the final couplet of the more popular narrative stanzas but integrate the rhyme into the body of the poem and—in an extraordinarily original move—make the final line an alexandrine, entirely avoiding the neatness of a simple couplet opposition. The final long line answers not only to the first line of a couplet but to the whole stanza.

4.  Anne Lake Prescott has argued cogently that the basis of book 1 is the allegory of a knight's pilgrimage, a figure going back to Saint Bernard. See "Spenser's Chivalric Restoration: From Bateman's *Travayled Pylgrime* to the Redcrosse Knight," *Studies in Philology* 86 (1989): 166–97.

5.  *Classical* romances, of which Spenser makes considerable use toward the end of book 6, are a distinct subgenre, important in book 6 of *The Faerie Queene;* they will be considered in relation to that book. For an excellent overview of the genre see the article "Romance" in *The Spenser Encyclopedia,* 609–18, by Patricia Parker.

6.  Thomas P. Roche, ed., *The Faerie Queene* (London: Penguin Books, 1978), 15; all quotations from *The Faerie Queene* are taken from this edition.

7.  Thomas M. Greene, *The Descent from Heaven: A Study in Epic Continuity* (New Haven, Conn.: Yale University Press, 1963), 406; hereafter cited in text. See Greene's earlier discussion (12–19) of the characteristic epic concern with earthly heroism and the divine will. My account of the epic is deeply indebted to Greene's book.

8.  *Coleridge's Essays and Lectures on Shakespeare and Some Other Old Poets and Dramatists,* ed. Ernest Rhys (London: J. M. Dent, 1907), 233. Coleridge goes on: "It is in the domains neither of history or geography; it is truly in the land of Faerie, that is, of mental space."

9.  Kenelm Digby, *A Discourse Concerning Edmund Spencer,* reprinted in R. M. Cummings, ed. *Spenser: The Critical Heritage* (New York: Barnes and Noble, 1971), 150; hereafter cited in text. Cf. A. C. Hamilton, *The Structure of Allegory in* The Faerie Queene (Oxford: Clarendon Press, 1961), 43: "Once we allow that in reading Spenser's poem we should focus upon the image, rather than upon some idea behind the image, our understanding gathers around our response to the poem's literal level because it arises from it."

10.  Merritt Hughes, ed. *John Milton: Complete Poems and Major Prose* (New York: Odyssey Press, 1957), 728–29.

11.  See, for instance, A. Bartlett Giamatti, *Play of the Double Senses* (Englewood Cliffs, N.J.: Prentice-Hall, 1975), 67–77; and James Nohrnberg,

*The Analogy of* The Faerie Queene (Princeton, N.J.: Princeton University Press, 1976), hereafter cited in text.

12.  Walter Davis, "Arthur, Partial Exegesis, and the Reader," *Texas Studies in Literature and Language* 18 (1977): 553–76.

13.  John Erskine Hankins, *Source and Meaning in Spenser's Allegory* (Oxford: Clarendon Press, 1971), 99–119, hereafter cited in text; Nohrnberg, *Analogy,* 102–282.

14.  That Spenser is allegorizing the fortunes of the English church is probable, but the precise details remain unclear. Humphrey Tonkin is the most recent to identify Arthur with Henry VIII, in *The Faerie Queene* (London: Unwin Hymen, 1989), 85; hereafter cited in text.

15.  Cf. Tristram White, an early seventeenth–century reader of Spenser, who commented in 1614: "The Poet in his *Faerie Queene,* playing upon the Etymologie of this Name, doth also allude to *Tilth,* though after a very wittie manner, thus 'Thence she thee brought into this lond' [*Faerie Queene,* I.x.60]." *The Martyrdom of Saint George of Cappadocia: Titular Patron of England,* reprinted in Cummings, *Critical Heritage,* 131.

16.  For this commonplace see, for instance, the opening prayer of Augustine's *Confessions,* trans. R. S. Pine-Coffin (London: Penguin Books, 1961), 21: "you have made us for yourself and our hearts find no peace until they rest in you."

17.  See John W. Shroeder, "Spenser's Erotic Drama: The Orgoglio Episode," *English Literary History* 29 (1962): 140–59; hereafter cited in text. As usual, Spenser links Orgoglio with several areas of meaning; in "The Orgoglio Episode in *The Faerie Queene,*" *ELH* 26 (1959): 171–87, S. K. Heninger Jr. associates him convincingly with the earthquakes heralding the Last Judgment and with Phillip II of Spain.

18.  Cf. Henry More in *An Explanation of the Grand Mystery of Godliness* (1660): "Methinks *Spenser's* description of *Una's* Entertainment by Satyrs in the Desart, does lively set out the condition of Christianity since the time that the Church of a Garden becam a *Wilderness.* They danc'd and frisk'd and play'd about her, abounding with externall homages and observances; but she could not inculcate any thing of that *Divine law of life* that she was to impart to them." Quoted in Cummings, *Critical Heritage,* 176.

19.  Spenser's deferred endings are a critical commonplace; for a discussion of them in the generic context of romance, see Patrica Parker, *Inescapable Romance: Studies in the Poetics of a Mode* (Princeton, N.J.: Princeton University Press, 1979), 54–113.

20.  The original division between book 1 as concerned with the realm of grace and book 2 as concerned with nature was argued in a seminal essay by A. S. P. Woodhouse, "Nature and Grace in *The Faerie Queene,*" *English Literary History* 16 (1949): 194–228. Subsequent criticism has considerably modified Woodhouse's thesis, but it remains the starting point for understanding the second book. In the analysis that follows I have been particularly influenced by

Berger, *Allegorical Temper;* Maurice Evans, *Spenser's Anatomy of Heroism* (Cambridge, England: Cambridge University Press, 1970), hereafter cited in text; and two luminous essays by Hugh MacLachlan, "The 'Carelesse Heavens': A Study of Revenge and Atonement in *The Faerie Queene*," *Spenser Studies* 1 (1980): 135–63; and "The Death of Guyon and the Elizabethan *Book of Homilies*," *Spenser Studies* 4 (1983): 93–114, both hereafter cited in text.

 21. Hence Spenser's comment apropos of Cymocles' vacillation between concupiscent and irascible passions: "A harder lesson, to learne Continence / In joyous pleasure, then in grievous paine" (II.vi.1.1–2). The tripartite division of the soul between a debased set of appetites (the concupiscent), an impulse to noble anger (the irascible), and reason goes back to Plato's *Republic* (4.430E–44E). For background, see Robert Reid, "Spenserian Psychology and the Structure of Allegory in Books 1 and 2 of *The Faerie Queene*," *Modern Philology* 79: 359–75.

 22. On Pyrocles and Cymocles, see Georgia Ronan Crampton, *The Condition of Creatures* (New Haven, Conn.: Yale University Press, 1974), 144–55.

 23. So Hudibras and Sans Loy in canto 2; Furor in canto 4; Pyrocles in canto 5; Cymocles in canto 6; and Pyrocles' refusal to take Archimago's good advice in canto 8.

 24. Aristotle, *Nichomachean Ethics,* 119b, trans. W. D. Ross, in *Introduction to Aristotle,* ed. Richard McKeon (New York: Random House/Modern Library, 1947), 373; hereafter cited in text as *NE.*

 25. Rosemund Tuve, *Allegorical Imagery* (Princeton, N.J.: Princeton University Press, 1966), ch. 2, esp. 65–66, 77–78; hereafter cited in text.

 26. George Sandys, *Ovide's Metamorphoses,* ed. Karl H. Hulley and Stanley T. Vandersall (Lincoln: University of Nebraska Press, 1970), 654.

 27. See MacLachlan, "Death of Guyon," 106–7, for a discussion of the Palmer as right reason.

 28. For a discussion of the Medina episode arguing that Spenser is exposing the inadequacy of temperance conceived of as a mean see Lauren Silberman, "The Faerie Queene, Book II and the Limitations of Temperance," *Modern Language Studies* 17 (1987) 9–22.

 29. For a fuller account of how Spenser transforms Ariosto's story in the Phedon incident, see Paul Alpers, *The Poetry of the Faerie Queene* (Princeton, N.J.: Princeton University Press, 1967) 54–69; hereafter cited in text.

 30. The clearest disagreement occurs between Berger, *Allegorical Temper,* 1–38, and Alpers, *Poetry,* 235–75. For Berger, Guyon is a psychologically motivated character who yields to the sin of *curiositas* in deciding to explore Mammon's world; for Alpers, Guyon's actions are not to be understood psychologically: he is an ideal figure whose journey through Mammon's realm is Spenser's means of treating the misuse of riches. Subsequent criticism has tended to develop from these basic positions. For a fine overview of the canto, see the article on "Mammon" by Anne Lake Prescott in *The Spenser Encyclopedia,* 451–52.

31. See Alpers, *Poetry,* 275; and A. Kent Hieatt, *Chaucer, Spenser, Milton* (Montreal: McGill-Queens University Press, 1975), 196; hereafter cited in text.

32. See Hugh MacLachlan's article on "Philotime" in *The Spenser Encyclopedia,* 542.

33. I am indebted to Harold Skulsky for this point.

34. See Merritt Y. Hughes, "Spenser's Acrasia and the Circe of the Renaissance," *Journal of the History of Ideas* 4 (1943): 381–99.

35. The letter to Ralegh makes Britomart's quest the undoing of Amoret's enchantment, but the narrative never mentions Amoret's situation until the eleventh canto, and it stresses throughout Britomart's quest for Artegal.

36. See especially Alpers, *Poetry,* 160–99; and John Watkins, *The Specter of Dido* (New Haven, Conn.: Yale University Press, 1995), 144–60.

37. On this motif, see Leigh DeNeef, "Spenser's *Amor Fuggitivo* and the Transfixed Heart," *English Literary History* 46 (1979): 1–20; hereafter cited in text.

38. Although the stories Britomart cites all appear in the *Metamorphoses,* Spenser's verbal borrowings in this episode come largely from the pseudo-Virgilian *Ciris,* the story of Scylla, who betrays her father Nisus and his city to King Minos, with whom she is infatuated. The *Ciris* is close in outlook to the *Metamorphoses* (the story appears in book 8 of Ovid's poem): its gods are unjust, and Scylla's ungovernable desire destroys all other ties, eventually causing her city's destruction and her own metamorphosis into a sea-hawk (*ciris*).

39. This ending in uncertainty is modeled on the *Aeneid* (VI.860–86), in which Anchises' catalog of Aeneas's descendants ends in lament for the death of Augustus's heir Marcellus and the consequent unsettling of the Roman succession.

40. See Georgia Ronan Crampton, "Spenser's Lyric Theodicy: The Complaints of *The Faerie Queene* III.iv," *English Literary History* 205–21; Hugh MacLean, " 'Restless Anguish and Unquiet Paine': Spenser and the Complaint, 1579–1590," in *The Practical Vision: Essays in English Literature in Honor of Flora Roy,* ed. Jane Cambell and James Doyle (Waterloo, Canada: Wilfred Laurier University Press, 1978), 29–47.

41. Kathleen Williams, *Spenser's World of Glass: A Reading of* The Faerie Queene (Berkeley: University of California Press, 1966), 101; hereafter cited in text.

42. See Michael O'Connell, *Mirror and Veil: The Historical Dimension of Spenser's* Faerie Queene (Chapel Hill: University of North Carolina Press, 1977), 107–14, hereafter cited in text; and William Oram, "Spenser's Raleghs," *Studies in Philology* 87 (1990): 341–62; hereafter cited in text.

43. For background to the Garden of Adonis, see Robert Ellrodt, *Neoplatonism in the Poetry of Edmund Spenser* (Geneva, Switzerland: Librairie E. Droz, 1960), 70–90, 102–3; Nelson, *Poetry of Spenser,* 206–23; Hankins, *Source and Meaning,* 234–85; and Nohrnberg, *Analogy,* 519–68.

44.  Plotinus, *Enneads* III.3.

45.  See Isabel MacCaffrey, *Spenser's Allegory: The Anatomy of Imagination* (Princeton, N.J.: Princeton University Press, 1976), 258–67; hereafter cited in text.

46.  Maureen Quilligan discusses the emphatic femaleness of the Garden in *Milton's Spenser: The Politics of Reading* (Ithaca, N.Y.: Cornell University Press, 1983), 190–97; hereafter cited in the text.

47.  In a striking observation, Evans, *Spenser's Anatomy*, 179–72, identifies the Hyena with time; Hugh MacLean and Anne Lake Prescott associate it with slander in *Spenser's Poetry*, 35 (note to III.vii.22.5).

48.  On this episode, see Thomas Roche, *The Kindly Flame: A Study of the Third and Fourth Books of* The Faerie Queene (Princeton, N.J.: Princeton University Press, 1964), 72–88, hereafter cited in text; Berger, *Revisionary Play*, 172–94; and MacCaffrey, *Spenser's Allegory*, 104–15.

49.  The classic statement of this thesis occurs in Thomas Roche Jr., "The Challenge to Chastity: Britomart at the House of Busyrane," *Publications of the Modern Language Association* 76: 340–44. On the other hand, Berger, *Revisionary Play*, 178–84, argues that the House presents the fantasy of a male imagination attempting to impose its view of love on Amoret. See also Lauren Silberman, *Transforming Desire: Erotic Knowledge in Books 3 and 4 of* The Faerie Queene (Berkeley: University of California Press, 1995), 61–67, for whom Busyrane becomes a repressive Petrarchan poet, attempting to punish Amoret's willing love for Scudamour.

50.  For the punning here, see Jonathan Goldberg, *Endlesse Worke* (Baltimore: Johns Hopkins University Press, 1981), 78–79; hereafter cited in text.

51.  See Donald Cheney, "Spenser's Hermaphrodite and the 1590 *Faerie Queene*," *Publications of the Modern Language Association* 87: 192–200.

*Chapter Four*

1.  *YESP*, 223; all quotations from the *Complaints* are taken from this edition.

2.  See Harold Stein, *Studies in Spenser's* Complaints (New York: Oxford University Press, 1934), 3–24; hereafter cited in text.

3.  On the complaint form, see John Peter, *Complaint and Satire in Early English Literature* (Oxford: Clarendon Press, 1956), 1–39, 60–103; and Hugh MacLean, "Complaints," in *The Spenser Encyclopedia,* 177–81.

4.  *The Riverside Chaucer,* ed. Larry D. Benson et al. (Boston: Houghton Mifflin, 1987), lines 1–7; all Chaucer quotations are taken from this edition.

5.  Jan van Dorsten, "*Complaints: Visions,*" in *The Spenser Encyclopedia,* 188.

6.  Kent Van den Berg, " 'The Counterfeit in Personation': *Prosopopoia, or Mother Hubberds Tale,*" in *The Author in His Work,* ed. Louis Martz and Aubrey Williams (New Haven, Conn.: Yale University Press, 1978), 85–102; hereafter cited in text.

7.  See, for instance, the first book of Joachim Du Bellay, *La Défence et illustration de la langue françoise,* ed. Henri Chamard (Paris: Librairie Marcel Didier, 1966).

8.  See Richard Rambuss, *Spenser's Secret Career* (Cambridge, England: Cambridge University Press, 1993), 84.

9.  See, however, Prescott's argument, in *French Poets and the English Renaissance* (New Haven, Conn.: Yale University Press, 1978), 46–48, hereafter cited in text, that Spenser follows Augustine in seeing seven as the number of this world and eight as the number of rest.

10.  W. L. Renwick, ed., *Complaints* (London: The Scholartis Press, 1928), 189; hereafter cited in text.

11.  See Gerald Snare, "The Muses on Poetry: Spenser's *The Teares of the Muses,*" *Tulane Studies in English* 17 (1968): 31–52, for an indispensable account of the tradition behind the poem. For a larger discussion of the Muses in European literature, see Ernst Robert Curtius, *European Literature and the Latin Middle Ages,* trans. Willard R. Trask (New York: Pantheon, 1953), 228–46; hereafter cited in text.

12.  For the idea of measure, see Frances Yates, *The French Academies of the Sixteenth Century* (1947; Nendeln, Liechtenstein: Kraus Reprint, 1968), 36–76. The underlying musical metaphor is the subject of Leo Spitzer, *Classical and Christian Ideas of World Harmony,* ed. Anna Granville Hatcher (Baltimore: Johns Hopkins University Press, 1963).

13.  For a discussion of the Latin poem, see Glen Most, "The 'Virgilian' Culex," in *Homo Viator: Classical Essays for John Bramble,* ed. Michael Whitby, Philip Hardie, and Mary Whitby (Bristol, England: Bristol Classical Press, 1987), 199–209. Spenser's translations have been discussed in Oliver Farrar Emerson, "Spenser's *Virgils Gnat,*" *Journal of English and Germanic Philology* 17 (1918): 94–118; and Henry G. Lotspeich, "Spenser's *Virgils Gnat* and Its Latin Origina," *English Literary History* 2 (1935): 235–41.

14.  For the modern reader—or indeed, for any reader after the eighteenth century—it is easy to forget that the pentameter couplet was only one of many narrative forms available to an Elizabethan writer, and not the dominant one. The Italian example (followed with variation by Spenser in *The Faerie Queene*) was for narration in stanzas; Stephen Hawes used stanzas; the writers of *A Mirror for Magistrates* used rhyme royal; and Surrey translated *The Aeneid* into blank verse. The primary exemplar of decasyllabic couplets was Chaucer. Gasgoigne in *Certain Notes of Instruction* associates couplets, or "ryding rime," with Chaucer, commenting that "it serveth most aptly to wryte a merie tale" (quoted in Gregory Smith, *Elizabethan Critical Essays,* vol. 1 [Oxford: Oxford University Press, 1904], 56).

15.  *The Arte of English Poesie,* ed. Gladys Doidge Willcock and Alice Walker (Cambridge, England: Cambridge University Press, 1936), 238. My account of *Prosopopoia* is indebted to Van den Berg, " 'The Counterfeit.' "

16.   See Thomas Greene, "The Flexibility of the Self in Renaissance Literature," in *The Disciplines of Criticism,* ed. Peter Demetz, Thomas Greene, and Lowry Nelson Jr. (New Haven, Conn.: Yale University Press, 1968), 241–64; and Stephen Greenblatt, *Renaissance Self-Fashioning from More to Shakespeare* (Chicago: University of Chicago Press, 1980), esp. 1–9 and 223–54.

17.   Ernst Cassierer, Paul Oskar Kristeller, and John Herman Randall Jr., eds., *The Renaissance Philosophy of Man* (Chicago: University of Chicago Press, 1948), 224–29.

18.   My reading in what follows is strongly influenced by Van den Berg's. But see Kenneth John Atchity, in "Spenser's *Mother Hubberds Tale*: Three Themes of Order," *Philological Quarterly* 52 (1973): 161–72, which argues that the narrator is merely a "translucent" (169) mask for Spenser's own views.

19.   The reference in the opening to Astrea leaving earth is a common analogy for the loss of Eden in Christian terms.

20.   See Thomas Greene, "*Il Cortegiano* and the Choice of a Game," in *The Vulnerable Text* (New York: Columbia University Press, 1986), 46–60.

21.   This paragraph is indebted to Van den Berg, " 'The Counterfeit,' " 97–99.

22.   Alfred W. Satterthwaite, *Spenser, Ronsard, and Du Bellay: A Renaissance Comparison* (Princeton, N.J.: Princeton University Press, 1960), 93.

23.   Kent A. Hieatt, "The Genesis of Shakespeare's *Sonnets*: Spenser's *Ruines of Rome: by Bellay,*" *Publications of the Modern Language Association* 98 (1983): 800–14.

24.   Don Cameron Allen, *Image and Meaning: Metaphoric Traditions in Renaissance Poetry* (Baltimore: Johns Hopkins University Press, 1960), 20–41.

25.   On these poems, see William Keach, *Elizabethan Erotic Narratives* (New Brunswick, N.J.: Rutgers University Press, 1976); Clark Hulse, *Metamorphic Verse* (Princeton, N.J.: Princeton University Press, 1981); and Leonard Barkin, *The Gods Made Flesh* (New Haven, Conn.: Yale University Press, 1986), 171–242.

26.   Judith Dundas puts it nicely: "Only in fun are allusions made to the 'wavering wit' and 'unstaid desire' of the gay Clarion. It is as though the usual moralizing expressions were here being treated as lightly as the heroic genres. We must pretend to shake our heads at the butterfly's behavior, but let us not be deceived by the mock morality any more than by the mock epic." *Muiopotmos*: A World of Art," in *Yearbook of English Studies* 5 (1975): 33.

27.   Ronald Bond, "*Invidia* and the Allegory of Spenser's *Muiopotmos,*" *English Studies in Canada* 2 (1976): 144–55.

28.   For the Calvinist reading of *Muiopotmos,* see Andrew Weiner, "Spenser's *Muiopotmos* and the Fates of Butterflies and Men," *Journal of English and Germanic Philology* 84 (1985): 203–20.

29.   See S. K. Heninger Jr., *Sidney and Spenser: The Poet as Maker* (University Park: University of Pennsylvania Press, 1988), 363–67, for a brilliant

account of this indeterminacy at a generic level. "From its titles and opening stanzas, 'Muiopotmos' activates certain expectations through its generic signals, but these signals are systematically jammed" (377).

*Chapter Five*

1. For a detailed account of Spenser's borrowings, see *VE*, 7:430–36; and Duncan Harris and Nancy L. Steffen, "The Other Side of the Garden: An Interpretive Comparison of Chaucer's *Book of the Duchess* and Spenser's *Daphnaïda*," *Journal of Medieval and Renaissance Studies* 8 (1978): 17–36, hereafter cited in text.

2. In Ovid's version of the Alcione myth the queen changes into a Halcyon; Chaucer characteristically avoids the supernatural ending and has her die.

3. *Daphnaïda*, 14. All quotations from Spenser's shorter poems follow *YESP*.

4. A. Bartlett Giamatti, *Exile and Change in Renaissance Literature* (New Haven, Conn.: Yale University Press, 1983), 33–75.

5. On the relation of seven to judgment and penance in the poem, see Maren-Sofie Röstvig, *The Hidden Sense* (Oslo, Norway: Universitetsforlaget, 1963), 82–87.

6. See Prescott, *French Poets,* 47; Alastair Fowler, in *Spenser and the Numbers of Time* (London: Routledge and Kegan Paul, 1964), 58–59, hereafter cited in text, cites Augustine, *Epistle,* LV.ix.19.

7. William A. Oram, "*Daphnaïda* and Spenser's Later Poetry," *Spenser Studies* 2 (1981): 141–58.

8. *Colin Clout*'s dedication to Sir Walter Ralegh is dated 27 December 1591.

9. Nature's mourning is commonplace in pastoral elegy; its rejoicing is less common. A famous example occurs in the second half of Virgil's fifth eclogue, when Daphnis is transformed into a god.

10. Richard Mallette, "Spenser's Portrait of the Artist in *The Shepheardes Calender* and *Colin Clouts Come Home Againe,*" *Studies in English Literature* 19 (1979): 19–41, esp. 39–41.

11. Cf. Psalm 119:103; and Proverbs 16:24.

12. The identities of some of these poets have been confirmed; others can only be guessed at. The best set of identifications appears in Carmel Gaffney, "Colin Clouts Come Home Againe" (Ph.D. dissertation, University of Edinburgh, 1982), 32–87; hereafter cited in text.

13. The material in the following paragraphs is condensed from two articles by William A. Oram: "Elizabethan Fact and Spenserian Fiction," *Spenser Studies* 4: 33–47; and "Spenser's Raleghs," *Studies in Philology* (1990), 341–62.

14. For the dating, see Agnes Latham, ed., *The Poems of Sir Walter Ralegh* (Cambridge, Mass.: Harvard University Press, 1962), xxxvi–xlv.

15.  See, for instance, Horace, *Odes,* I.3; and Virgil, *Eclogue,* IV.31–32.

16.  See, for instance, *Richard III,* I.4.9–33.

17.  A curiously exact parallel passage occurs in Donne's *Satire III,* 15–26.

18.  See John Bernard, *Ceremonies of Innocence: Pastoralism in the Poetry of Edmund Spenser* (Cambridge, England: Cambridge University Press, 1989), 122–34.

19.  Robert Ellrodt, *Neoplatonism in the Poetry of Edmund Spenser* (Geneva, Switzerland: Librairie E. Droz, 1960), 92–93, hereafter cited in text, argues that the first part of the hymn (771–834) is not neoplatonic, while the second part (835–94) is. Yet Spenser is rarely "pure" in his writing: the later lines blend the neoplatonic language with a tradition of paraphrasing Genesis.

20.  David Birchmore, "The Image of the Centre in *Colin Clouts Come Home Againe,*" *Review of English Studies* New Series 28 (1977): 393–406. The account below differs slightly from Birchmore's.

21.  Cf. Wyman H. Herendeen, *From Landscape to Literature: The River and the Myth of Geography* (Pittsburgh: Duquesne University Press, 1986), 234–37.

22.  Ellrodt, *Neoplatonism,* 219–23, argues convincingly that the myth was probably added or revised before publication in 1595.

23.  See, for instance, the comments in *VE,* 7:483–84, 486–87.

24.  Pierre Ronsard, "Adonis," in *Oeuvres Complètes,* 2 vols., ed. Gustave Cohen (Paris: Bibliothèque de la Pléiade, 1950), 2:25–33.

25.  See, for instance, Theodore Steinberg, "Spenser, Sidney, and the Myth of Astrophel," in *Spenser Studies* 11 (1990): 187–201.

26.  Michael O'Connell, "*Astrophel:* Spenser's Double Elegy," *Studies in English Literature* 11 (1971): 27–35; hereafter cited in text.

27.  *The Muzes Elizium,* Sixt Nimphall, in *The Works of Michael Drayton,* vol. 3, ed. J. William Hebel (Oxford: Blackwell, 1931), 293–300.

28.  Margaret Hannay, *Philip's Phoenix* (New York: Oxford University Press, 1990), 63–67.

*Chapter Six*

1.  For a brief account of Petrarch's life and Laura's status, see the introduction to *Petrarch's Lyric Poems,* trans. and ed. Robert M. Durling (Cambridge, Mass.: Harvard University Press, 1976).

2.  See William J. Kennedy, *Authorizing Petrarch* (Ithaca, N.Y.: Cornell University Press, 1994).

3.  Discussions of imitation appear in Thomas Greene, *The Light in Troy* (New Haven, Conn.: Yale University Press, 1982), hereafter cited in text; and Way Reed Dasenbrock, *Imitating the Italians* (Baltimore: Johns Hopkins University Press, 1991), 15–51. My indebtedness to both books is great, and my view of what Spenser does with Petrarch is close to Dasenbrock's in many particulars.

4.   Sonnet 1, 1–14. Quotations from *Amoretti and Epithalamion* follow *YESP*.

5.   Louis M. Martz, "The *Amoretti:* Most Goodly Temperature," in *Form and Convention in the Poetry of Edmund Spenser,* ed. William Nelson (New York: Columbia University Press, 1961), 147–48; hereafter cited in text.

6.   One of the most relevant associations is, of course, the directive Britomart finds in the House of Busyrane to "be bold," but "not too bold": boldness here clearly has a sexual component, involved as it is in self-assertion.

7.   Wyatt quotation from Richard S. Sylvester, ed., *English Sixteenth-Century Verse* (1974; New York: Norton, 1984), lines 1–4; hereafter cited in text.

8.   Sonnet 58 is problematic in being preceded by the phrase "*By her that is most assured to her selfe.*" This would suggest that some or all of the sonnet is the lady's words, yet the couplet "Why then doe ye proud fayre, misdeeme so farre, / That to your selfe ye most assured arre" is obviously the voice of the lover: "proud faire" is used of a lady, not a gentleman. It has been argued that "By" means "To," but so far no one has discovered any linguistic evidence for such a reading. A possible solution would be to attribute the first 12 lines of sonnet 58 to the lady—its burden is consistent with her speech in sonnet 75 (ll.5–8)—while assuming that the couplet represents the speaker's turning the tables on her: if she does not believe in self-assurance, why does she practice it? The following sonnet would still represent the speaker's change of mind.

9.   This vision of love as driving the lover to transcend himself is a commonplace of neoplatonizing language and appears in *The Faerie Queene* (see, for instance, III.iii.1–2); it appears as well in the most overtly neoplatonic of the *Amoretti,* the eighth, written before Spenser knew Elizabeth Boyle but incorporated by him into the sequence. See L. Cummings, "Spenser's *Amoretti VIII:* New Manuscript Versions," *Studies in English Literature* 4 (1964): 125–35.

10.   In this paragraph I am indebted to Myron Turner, "The Imagery of Spenser's *Amoretti,*" *Neophilologus* 72 (1988): 284- 99.

11.   *Oxford English Dictionary,* definition 7.

12.   See Anne Lake Prescott, "The Thirsty Deer and the Lord of Life: Some Contexts for *Amoretti* 67–70," *Spenser Studies* 6 (1985): 33–76; hereafter cited in text. This witty, learned, densely argued article should be read in its entirety.

13.   See Alexander Dunlop, "The Unity of Spenser's *Amoretti,*" in *Silent Poetry,* ed. Alastair Fowler (London: Routledge & Kegan Paul, 1970), 153–69. Prescott, "Thirsty Deer," 58–60, further develops Dunlop's discussion by accounting for the 89 sonnets in the sequence ("the total number of days for which communion collects and readings were assigned in the reformed prayer-book"), and the ties between the sequence and the *Book of Common Prayer* have been demonstrated in detail in William Johnson, *Spenser's Amoretti: Analogies of Love* (Lewisburg, Penn.: Bucknell University Press, 1990). Dunlop's thesis has been criticized by a number of writers, most cogently by Carol Kaske in

"Spenser's *Amoretti and Epithalamion* of 1595: Structure, Genre, and Numerology," *English Literary Renaissance* 8 (1978): 271–95; hereafter cited in text.

14.   *The Geneva Bible: A Facsimile of the 1560 Edition,* intro. Lloyd E. Berry (Madison: University of Wisconsin Press, 1969), 281v.

15.   See *VE: The Minor Poems,* 2:488.

16.   See Robert S. Miola, "Spenser's Anacreontics: A Mythological Metaphor," *Studies in Philology* 77 (1980): 50–66; for a contrary version of the Anacreontics, see Kaske, "Spenser's *Amoretti.*"

17.   A. Kent Hieatt, *Short Times Endlesse Monument* (New York: Columbia University Press, 1960), passim; hereafter cited in text.

18.   Richard Neuse, "The Triumph over Hasty Accidents: A Note on the Symbolic Mode of the *Epithalamion,*" *Modern Language Review* 61 (1966): 163–74; hereafter cited in text.

19.   See Douglas Anderson, "Unto My Selfe Alone: Spenser's Plenary Epithalamion," in *Spenser Studies* 5 (1984): 154–55; hereafter cited in text.

20.   My account of epithalamia owes a great deal to Thomas Greene, "Spenser and the Epithalamic Tradition," *Comparative Literature* 9 (1957): 215–28; hereafter cited in text.

21.   *Catallus, Tibullus and Pervigiliam Veneris,* Loeb Library Edition, trans. F. W. Cornish (1913; rpt., Cambridge, Mass.: Harvard University Press, 1962), 61:ll.182–83; hereafter cited in text.

22.   See Leo Spitzer, *Classical and Christian Ideas of World Harmony,* ed. Anna Granville Hatcher (Baltimore: Johns Hopkins University Press, 1963), hereafter cited in text; and S. K. Heninger, *Touches of Sweet Harmony: Pythagorean Cosmology and Renaissance Poetics* (San Marino, Calif.: Huntington Library, 1974), 256–84.

23.   See also J. C. Eade, "The Pattern in the Astronomy of Spenser's *Epithalamion,*" *Review of English Studies* 23 (1972): 173–78.

24.   The *locus classicus* of the shepherd singing to the woods occurs in the opening lines of Virgil's first eclogue. The essays by Greene ("The Epithalamic Tradition"), Neuse ("Triumph over Hasty Accidents"), and Anderson ("Unto My Selfe Alone") all treat from different perspectives the isolation of the speaker of Spenser's poem.

25.   As Enid Welsford points out: "The presupposition of the whole poem, *including* the first and last stanzas, is that the poet is describing the wedding as being recalled or, more probably, foreseen, in his own imagination; the presupposition of the marriage hymn proper, *excluding* the first and last stanzas, is that it is a kind of silent song, chanted mentally by him during the actual celebration and consummation of his marriage." *Spenser:* Fowre Hymnes and Epithalamion: *A Study of Edmund Spenser's Doctrine of Love* (New York: Barnes and Noble, 1967), 71, hereafter cited in text.

Welsford does not relate these two presuppositions—or fictions, as I would prefer to call them—but it seems logical enough that in stanzas 2–23 we have a fiction within a fiction—the poet-speaker *before* his wedding imagines himself going through it *later*. This way of reading the poem seems to me at times implied in Neuse's essay.

26.  Welsford notes that Spenser's vision of Orpheus singing "to himself alone may have been suggested by Virgil's moving account of his lamentation after Eurydice's death" in *Georgics,* IV.464–66; ibid., 174.

27.  See, for instance, *The Faerie Queene,* I.ii.29; and *Prothalamion,* ll.1–4.

28.  One might read the passage differently. "Greedy pleasure" might subsume both Bride and Bridegroom, and the "paradise of joyes" be mutual. Perhaps in this case precision is purposely avoided.

29.  Harry Berger Jr., *Second World and Green World* (Berkeley: University of California Press, 1988), 3–40.

*Chapter Seven*

1.  John Watkins, *The Spectre of Dido* (New Haven, Conn.: Yale University Press, 1995), 175–78.

2.  This problem has been central to much writing on the second part of *The Faerie Queene*. In particular, see Judith Anderson, *The Growth of a Personal Voice:* Piers Plowman *and* The Faerie Queene (New Haven, Conn.: Yale University Press, 1976), hereafter cited in text; and Thomas Cain, *Praise in* The Faerie Queene (Lincoln: University of Nebraska Press, 1978); hereafter cited in text.

3.  Quotations from *The Faerie Queene* follow the edition of Thomas Roche (London: Penguin Books, 1978).

4.  A small index of this new emphasis appears in the increased self-reference at the ends of cantos. At the close of book 1, canto 6, the poet announces that he will defer the battle between Satyrane and Sans Loy until later, and at the end of canto 12 he compares the end of the book to a seaman's temporary haven. No such self-reference occurs at the canto ends of book 2, and only three occur in book 3. But in book 4 eight cantos end by referring to the progress of the poem, in book 5 five do so, and in book 6 seven.

5.  See Roche, *Kindly Flame,* 15–31; and David W. Birchmore, "Triamond, Agape, and the Fates: Neoplatonic Cosmology in Spenser's Legend of Friendship," *Spenser Studies* 5 (1985): 45–64; and Patrick Cheney, "Spenser's Completion of *The Squire's Tale*: Love, Magic and Heroic Action in the Legend of Cambell and Triamond," *Journal of Medieval and Renaissance Studies* 15 (1985): 135–55.

6.  Lauren Silberman comments: "The series of violent but impermanent deaths inflicted on Pri-Di-Triamond makes the episode begin to resemble a Monty Python parody rather than a traditional joust." *Transforming Desire: Erotic Knowledge in Books III and IV of* The Faerie Queene (Berkeley: University of California Press, 1995), 162; hereafter cited in text.

7.  See Mark Heberle, "The Limitations of Friendship," *Spenser Studies* 8 (1987): 101–18.

8.  For background on the Pythagorean thinking underlying Spenser's concord, see S. K. Heninger, *Touches of Sweet Harmony* (San Marino, Calif.: Huntington Library, 1974).

9. See the "Hymne in Honour of Love," 71–91.

10. See, for instance, her unwillingness to admit her real feeling for Artegal to Redcrosse, whom she has befriended earlier (III.ii.5–16).

11. See T. K. Dunseath, *Spenser's Allegory of Justice in Book 5 of* The Faerie Queene (Princeton, N.J.: Princeton University Press, 1968), 59; hereafter cited in text.

12. Scudamour's failure to notice Amoret, sighing for her loss at precisely the moment when he should finally be rejoicing in her presence (IV.ix.38), is a notorious crux in the poem. I follow Hamilton (*Faerie Queene*, st. 38n) in assuming that Arthur presents her between stanzas 39 and 40; Scudamour seems to refer to her in IV.xi.3. But the omission is very puzzling. See Goldberg, *Endlesse Worke*, 63, for the argument that Scudamour does not recognize Amoret because he is narcissistically absorbed in the telling of his tale.

13. See Leigh DeNeef, *Spenser and the Motives of Metaphor* (Durham, N.C.: Duke University Press, 1982), 121–22; hereafter cited in text. The whole of his book develops Spenser's concern with misreading.

14. On Spenser's play with storytelling, see James Nohrnberg's article on *"The Faerie Queene,* Book IV," in *Spenser Encyclopedia,* 274–276; and Goldberg, *Endlesse Worke,* 31–82.

15. In "The 'Covert Vele': Chaucer, Spenser, and Venus," *English Literary History* 24 (1994): 639–59, Judith Anderson argues convincingly that Spenser conflates the figures of Venus and Nature in Chaucer's *Parliament of Fowles,* producing a "morally mixed" figure between Acrasia, on the one hand, and Nature in the *Mutabilitie Cantos,* on the other. For discussions of Nature, see also the *VE,* 4:228–37; and Curtius, *European Literature in the Latin Middle Ages,* 106–27.

16. For background on England as the inheritor of the mantle of empire, see Frances A. Yates, *Astraea* (London: Routledge & Kegan Paul, 1975), 34–59; hereafter cited in text.

17. Wayne H. Herendeen, *From Landscape to Literature* (Pittsburgh: Duquesne University Press, 1986), gives a rich account of the Renaissance river-marriage and discusses Spenser's river-marriages in particular (225–54).

18. See Rudolf Gottfried, "Spenser and the Italian Myth of Locality," *Studies in Philology* 34 (1937): 107–25.

19. *John Milton: Complete Poems and Major Prose,* ed. Merritt Y. Hughes (New York: The Odyssey Press, 1957), 90.

20. On this tradition, see Elizabeth Bieman, *Plato Baptized* (Toronto: University of Toronto Press, 1988), esp. 1–54; hereafter cited in text. Gordon Braden, in "Riverrun: An Epic Catalogue in *The Faerie Queene,*" *English Literary Renaissance* 5 (1975): 25–48, stresses Spenser's celebration of multiplicity, and Silberman (130–39) treats the episode as it views world and text as "both unfoldings of a larger, infolded, and never-fully knowable whole" (130).

21. For an extended account of the marriage of the Thames and the Medway as an image of concord, see Roche, *Kindly Flame,* 167–84.

22.  C. S. Lewis, *The Allegory of Love* (Oxford: Oxford University Press, 1936), 349; hereafter cited in text.

23.  On the simile, with an argument emphasizing the episode's ambivalence, see Annabel Patterson, *Reading between the Lines* (Madison: University of Wisconsin Press, 1993), 86–99; hereafter cited in text.

24.  See Jane Aptekar, *Icons of Justice: Iconography and Thematic Imagery in Book 5 of* The Faerie Queene (New York: Columbia University Press, 1967), 163–71; hereafter cited in text. Eugene Waith, *The Herculean Hero in Marlowe, Chapman, Shakespeare and Dryden* (New York: Columbia University Press, 1962), more fully discusses Hercules in the dramatic tradition.

25.  Dunseath, *Spenser's Allegory*, 86–140, makes the fullest argument for Artegal's fall, recovery, and growth as an agent of Justice.

26.  James E. Phillips, "Renaissance Concepts of Justice and the Structure of *The Faerie Queene*, Book V," *Huntington Library Quarterly* 33 (1970): 103–20, reprinted in *Essential Articles for the Study of Edmund Spenser*, ed. A. C. Hamilton (Hamden, Conn.: Archon Books, 1972), 471–87; hereafter cited in text as *EA*.

27.  See Aptekar, *Icons of Justice*, 108–24, on the importance of guile in the just man.

28.  See *VE*, 5:336–41; on the giants more generally, see Aptekar, *Icons of Justice*, 27–38. While the episode may refer to the Munster Anabaptists, who took over the city in 1534, the fear of revolt from below goes beyond any particular incident. See O'Connell, *Mirror and Veil*, 136–39.

29.  This episode leans heavily on the Bible; see the citations in A. C. Hamilton, *The Faerie Queene* (London: Longman, 1977), 541–42.

30.  See, for instance, 2 Esdras 4, Job 28, and Daniel 4:32.

31.  "We may wonder if it would not be simpler (not to say more legal) if [Artegal] just took the testimony of the lady who witnessed the crime instead of offering to cut her in two." Michael O'Connell, "*The Faerie Queene*, Book V," in *The Spenser Encyclopedia*, 281.

32.  See the First Letter of Paul to Timothy 6:10 for this criticism. In " 'Nor Man It Is': The Knight of Justice in Book V of Spenser's *Faerie Queene*," *Publications of the Modern Language Association* 85 (1970): 70; Judith Anderson speaks of a "perfunctory, robotistic, and inhuman element in Artegal's justice."

33.  On views of women rulers, see James E. Phillips Jr., "The Woman Ruler in *The Faerie Queene*," *Huntington Library Quarterly* 5 (1941): 211–34; and "The Background of Spenser's Attitude toward Women Rulers," ibid., 5–32. In "Rule Virginia: Protestant Theories of Female Regiment in *The Faerie Queene*, *English Literary Renaissance* 15 (1985): 247–76, Pamela Benson argues that Spenser's treatment of women rulers in book 5 is consistent with his position earlier in the poem.

34.  Rene Graziani, "Elizabeth at Isis Church," *Publications of the Modern Language Association* 79 (1964): 376–89.

35. For versions of the legal dimension to the allegory, see O'Connell, *Mirror and Veil,* 144–47; and Tonkin, *Faerie Queene,* 159–64.

36. A. C. Hamilton makes this point in his edition of *The Faerie Queene* (London: Longman, 1977), 586 (note to V.viii.37.6–9).

37. James Bednarz, in "Geryoneo," *The Spenser Encyclopedia,* 331, argues that the episode may in fact refer to the Veluwe fort near Zutphen, which the earl was instrumental in capturing late in 1586, but Spenser magnifies the capture so that it looks like that of Antwerp.

38. My thinking about book 6 has been shaped by two classic essays: Harry Berger Jr., "A Secret Discipline," reprinted in Berger, *Revisionary Play,* 215–42; and Richard Neuse, "Book VI as Conclusion to *The Faerie Queene,*" *English Literary History* 35 (1968): 329–53, reprinted in *EA,* 366–88, hereafter cited as Neuse, *EA.* I have also benefited greatly from Humphrey Tonkin, *Spenser's Courteous Pastoral* (Oxford: Clarendon Press, 1972); hereafter cited in text.

39. On Spenser and the tradition of courtesy books, see Daniel Javitch, *Poetry and Courtlines in Renaissance England* (Princeton, N.J.: Princeton University Press, 1978), esp. 18–49, 107–62; and Tonkin, *Spenser's Courteous Pastoral,* 163–72.

40. Hankins, *Source and Meaning,* 11–13, argues that courtesy is a knightly virtue and associates it with affability and urbanity, but his examples are medieval rather than Renaissance.

41. See Robert Stillman, "Spenserian Autonomy and the Trial of New Historicism: Book Six of *The Faerie Queene,*" *English Literary Renaissance* 22 (1992): 299–314.

42. See Donald Cheney, *Spenser's Image of Nature: Wild Man and Shepherd in* The Faerie Queene (New Haven, Conn.: Yale University Press, 1966), 106; and Theresa Krier, *Gazing on Secret Sights* (Ithaca, N.Y.: Cornell University Press, 1990), 114–15, 148–49.

43. The material in this paragraph was first suggested to me by Thomas Greene.

44. Critics have divided on the question of whether Calidore's stay with the shepherds is a "truancy" or a chance to learn truths necessary for his quest. For representative opinions, see Cheney, *Spenser's Image,* 214–27; Tonkin, *Spenser's Courteous Pastoral,* 111–31; and Paul Alpers, "Spenser's Late Pastorals," *English Literary History* 56 (1989): 797–817, hereafter cited in text.

45. Lauren Silberman pointed this out to me.

46. Renato Poggioli, *The Oaten Flute: Essays on Pastoral Poetry and the Pastoral Ideal* (Cambridge, Mass.: Harvard University Press, 1975), 1.

47. The degree to which Melebee's words are to be taken as genuinely authoritative has been the subject of considerable debate. See Berger, *Revisionary Play,* 233; Alpers, "Spenser's Late Pastorals," 797–817; and Judith H. Anderson "Prudence and Her Silence: Spenser's Use of Chaucer's *Melebee,*" *English Literary History* 62 (1995): 29–46.

48.  See, for instance, Homer, *Odyssey*, 14.55, 15.325; and Virgil, *Aeneid*, IX.446–49.

49.  On this conflict, see Donald Cheney, "Spenser's Fortieth Birthday and Related Fictions," *Spenser Studies* 4 (1983): 3–31, esp. 1–9; and Alpers, "Spenser's Late Pastorals," 810–15.

50.  See, for instance, Williams, *Spenser's World of Glass*, 221–22.

51.  In *Spenserian Poetics* (Ithaca, N.Y.: Cornell University Press, 1985), Kenneth Gross comments: "The pretense is reformation, but the practice is deformation" (232).


*Chapter Eight*

1.  All quotations from *Fowre Hymnes* and *Prothalamion* are taken from *YESP*.

2.  See Mary I. Oates, *"Fowre Hymnes:* Spenser's Retractations of Paradise," *Spenser Studies* 4 (1983): 143–69, for a valuable discussion of the meaning of "retractation." Oates's view that the poems dramatize the speaker's progress seems to me true to the *Hymnes,* although I think the psychoanalytic terms in which she charts that progress are not adapted to the particular problems on which the *Hymnes* focus.

3.  See Helgerson, *Elizabethan Prodigals,* 1–15, on this convention.

4.  See Ellrodt, *Neoplatonism,* 13–24, 219–23, for the most convincing arguments in dating the hymns.

5.  See Einar Bjorvand, "Spenser's Defense of Poetry: Some Structural Aspects of the *Fowre Hymnes,"* in *Fair Formes,* ed. Maren-Sofie Rostvig (Totowa, N.J.: Rowman and Littlefield, 1975), 13–53, hereafter cited in text; and Welsford, *Spenser's Doctrine of Love.*

6.  See Phillip B. Rollinson, "A Generic View of Spenser's *Fowre Hymnes,"* *Studies in Philology* 68 (1971): 292–304.

7.  Sir Walter Ralegh, *The History of the World,* in *Works,* 8 vols., ed. William Oldys and Thomas Birch (Oxford: 1829), 2:176.

8.  The double parentage brings together several traditions: see Welsford, *Spenser's Doctrine of Love,* 145–47. The paradoxical age of love is discussed in *De Amore,* Marsilio Ficino's commentary on Plato's *Symposium* (V.10); see *Marsilio Ficino's Commentary on Plato's Symposium,* ed. and trans. Sears Reynolds Jayne (Columbia: University of Missouri Press, 1944), 178.

9.  For a literary version of this ascent, see Bembo's speech at the end of the fourth book of Castiglione's *The Book of the Courtier,* ed. and trans. Charles S. Singleton (Garden City, N.Y.: Doubleday/Anchor, 1959), 336–60.

10.  See Anne Lake Prescott, "Tantalus" in *The Spenser Encyclopedia,* 676–77.

11.  See William Rossky, "Imagination in the English Renaissance," *Studies in the Renaissance* 5, (1958) 49–73; and Murry W. Bundy, *The Theory of*

*Imagination in Classical and Medieval Thought* (Urbana: University of Illinois Press, 1927).

12.  See, for instance, Welsford, *Spenser's Doctrine of Love,* 40–41.

13.  On the *furores,* see Frances Yates, *The French Academies of the Sixteenth Century* (1947; Nendeln, Liechtenstein: Kraus Reprint, 1968), 80–94.

14.  See Augustine, *City of God,* I.16, on the soul's purity despite rape. The problem is simply that the speaker's discussion of external violence done to the unwilling ignores the more difficult problem of the truly vicious soul in a beautiful body.

15.  A characteristic equivocation occurs in lines 230–31, where the lover counts the created image "fairer, than it is indeede, / And yet indeed her fairenesse doth exceede." The lines are almost impossible to pin down—and that is their point.

16.  The parallels and contrasts are most fully developed in Bjorvand, "Spenser's Defense."

17.  Bjorvand, "Spenser's Defense," 25, argues that stanza 5, the central stanza of the whole poem, treats Christ as the second person of the Trinity, in his divine aspect, while stanza 21, the central stanza of the hymn, treats Christ in his human aspect.

18.  See Leigh DeNeef, "Spenserian Meditation: The 'Hymn of Heavenly Beautie,' " *American Benedictine Review* 25 (1974): 317–34. The classic work on meditation as it appears in English Renaissance poetry is Louis L. Martz, *The Poetry of Meditation* (New Haven, Conn.: Yale University Press, 1955).

19.  See *YESP,* 743–47, for the scriptural references.

20.  Paul associates Christ with Wisdom in 1 Corinthians 1:24; see also Augustine *De Trinitate,* 7.3. See Ellrodt, *Neoplatonism,* 164–70. For fuller references, see *YESP,* 745–47.

21.  In this assumption as in much else, I follow the reading of Harry Berger Jr., "Spenser's *Prothalamion:* An Interpretation," *Essays in Criticism* 15 (1965): 363–80, reprinted in *EA,* 509–23; hereafter cited in text.

22.  See Dan S. Norton, "The Tradition of Prothalamia," in *English Studies in Honor of James Southall Wilson,* ed. Fredson Bowers (Charlottesville: University Press of Virginia, 1951), 223–41.

23.  See Daniel H. Woodward, "Some Themes in Spenser's *Prothalamion,*" *English Literary History* 29 (1962): 34–46.

24.  When the swans turn into the Thames to swim *up*river to Essex House, Spenser skips immediately to "mery London": the movement of the swans is thus emphatically *with* the current of the river—downward, as if away from heaven.

25.  Alistair Fowler, *Conceitful Thought* (Edinburgh, Scotland: Edinburgh University Press, 1975), 61–73.

26.  See Patrick Cheney, *Spenser's Famous Flight* (Toronto: University of Toronto Press, 1993), 240–45.

27.  Lawrence Manley, "Spenser and the City: The Minor Poems," *Modern Language Quarterly* 43 (1982): 224–25.

28.  Yates, *Astrea,* 29–111; and Roy Strong, *The Cult of Elizabeth* (London: Thames & Hudson, 1977).

29.  See Edmund Spenser, *The Mutabilitie Cantos,* ed. Sheldon P. Zitner (London: Thomas Nelson and Sons, 1968), hereafter cited in text as *MC,* 2–4; and Russell J. Meyer, " 'Fixt in Heavens Hight': Spenser, Astronomy, and the Date of the *Cantos of Mutabilitie,*" *Spenser Studies* 4 (1983): 115–31.

30.  In its treatment of the narrator, this essay is indebted to Harry Berger Jr.'s discussion of the poem in "The Mutabilitie Cantos: Archaism and Evolution in Retrospect," in *Revisionary Play;* and to Zitner, *MC,* 26–28.

31.  Michael Holahan, "*Iam opus exegi:* Ovid's Changes and Spenser's Brief Epic of Mutabilitie," *English Literary Renaissance* 6 (1976): 244–70; hereafter cited in text.

32.  On this allegorization see Jean Seznec, *The Survival of the Pagan Gods,* trans. Barbara F. Sessions (New York: Pantheon, 1953).

33.  See William Ringler, "The Faunus Episode," *Modern Philology* 63 (1965): 12–19, reprinted in *EA,* 289–98; hereafter cited in the text.

34.  Abraham Fraunce, *The Countesse of Pembrokes Yvychurch* (London, 1592), reprinted in *The Renaissance and the Gods,* vol. 13, ed. Stephen Orgel (New York: Garland, 1976), 43.

35.  See "An Hymne of Heavenly Love," st. 7, and "An Hymne of Heavenly Beautie," st. 2–3. See also Du Bartas, "L'Uranie"; and Milton, *Paradise Lost,* VII.1–12.

36.  See Sherman Hawkins, "Mutabilitie and the Cycle of the Months," in *Form and Convention in the Poetry of Edmund Spenser,* ed. William Nelson (New York: Columbia University Press, 1961), 76–102.

*Chapter Nine*

1.  On the act of interpreting as Oedipal, see Harold Bloom, *A Map of Misreading* (New York: Oxford University Press, 1975), 9–80; 125–43; and as an act of connection with the past, see Greene, *Light in Troy,* 28–53.

2.  See Richard Foster Jones, *The Triumph of the English Language* (London: Oxford University Press, 1953), 178–79; and R. M. Cummings, ed., *Spenser: The Critical Heritage* (New York: Barnes and Noble, 1971), 110, 127, 128, 137, and passim.

3.  Joan Grundy, *The Spenserian Poets* (London: Edward Arnold, 1969), 42–71; hereafter cited in text.

4.  See James Bobrick, "The Numerological Structure of Giles Fletcher's *Christ's Victorie and Triumph,*" *Texas Studies in Literature and Language* 21 (1979): 522–52.

5.  On this tendency to gesture toward the divine, see Jerome S. Dees, "The Narrator of *Christ's Victorie and Triumph:* What Giles Fletcher Learned from Spenser," *English Literary Renaissance* 6: 453–65.

6.  Kathleen Williams, "Milton, Greatest Spenserian," in *Milton and the Line of Vision*, ed. Joseph Anthony Wittreich (Madison: University of Wisconsin Press, 1975), 25–55.

7.  On the connections between *Samson Agonistes* and *The Faerie Queene*, see Patrick Cullen, *Infernal Triad* (Princeton, N.J.: Princeton University Press, 1974), 182–250.

8.  Hughes, ed., *Complete Poems and Major Prose*, 728–29.

9.  See Kenneth Gross, " 'Each Heav'nly Close': Mythologies and Metrics in Spenser and the Early Poetry of Milton," *Proceedings of the Modern Language Association* 98 (1983): 21–36.

10.  I have argued this reading of *Comus* more fully in "The Invocation of Sabrina," *Studies in English Literature* 24 (1984): 121–39. See also Quilligan, 1983, 209–12.

11.  See Angus Fletcher, *The Transcendental Masque* (Ithaca, N.Y.: Cornell University Press, 1971), 40–60, on Shakespeare and the masque.

12.  See Don Cameron Allen, *Mysteriously Meant* (Baltimore: Johns Hopkins University Press, 1970), 279–311.

13.  *The Poems of Alexander Pope*, vol. 2, Twickenham Edition, ed. Geoffrey Tillotson (London: Methuen & Co., 1940), 252.

14.  See, for instance, Leopold Damrosch, *God's Plot and Man's Stories* (Chicago: University of Chicago Press, 1985).

15.  Joseph Spence, "The Defects of Our Modern Poets, in Their Allegories," in *Spenser's Critics*, ed. William R. Mueller (Syracuse, N.Y.: Syracuse University Press, 1959), 32–37, 35; hereafter cited in text as Mueller.

16.  Ralph Church published *The Faerie Queene of Edmund Spenser* in 4 volumes (London, 1758); John Upton followed with *The Faerie Queene of Edmund Spenser* in 2 volumes (London, 1758–59).

17.  See Richard Frushell, "Spenser and the Eighteenth-Century Schools," *Spenser Studies* 7 (1986): 175–98; and Frushell's superb article in the *Spenser Encyclopedia*, "Imitations and Adaptations 1660–1800" (396–403). Frushell lists whole works that imitate Spenser; a list that included poems in which the Spenserian imitation forms only a part would be considerably longer.

18.  See Douglas Lane Patey, "Love Deny'd: Pope and the Allegory of Despair," *Eighteenth-Century Studies* 20 (1986): 34–55.

19.  See, for instance, William Hazlitt, "On Chaucer and Spenser" (Mueller, 73): "He paints nature not as we find it, but as we expected to find it; and fulfills the delightful promise of your youth. He waves his wand of enchantment—and at once embodies airy beings, and throws a delicious veil over all actual objects."

20.  *The Collected Works of Samuel Taylor Coleridge*, 18 vols., ed. Kathleen Coburn et al. (Princeton, N.J.: Princeton University Press, 1969– ), 6:30; hereafter cited in text as Coleridge, *Works*.

21.  On this development, see Douglas Lane Patey, "The Eighteenth Century Invents the Canon," *Modern Language Studies* 18 (1988): 17–37; and

" 'Aesthetics' and the Rise of the Lyric in the Eighteenth Century," *Studies in English Literature* 33 (1993): 587–608.

    22.   The account appears in an appendix to Ruskin, *The Stones of Venice,* vol. 3, reprinted in *VE,* book 1, 422–24.

# Selected Bibliography

## PRIMARY WORKS

Greenlaw, Edwin, et al., eds. *The Works of Edmund Spenser: A Variorum Edition.* Baltimore: Johns Hopkins University Press, 1932–49. The standard edition of Spenser's *Works,* now dated but valuable for its identification of references, source material, and criticism up to the 1940s.

### The Faerie Queene

Hamilton, A. C., ed. *The Faerie Queene.* London: Longman, 1977. A heavily annotated edition, very useful for students.

Roche, Thomas, ed. *The Faerie Queene.* Harmondsworth: Penguin, 1978. A more sparingly annotated edition, with short, packed introductions to several books.

### The Shorter Poems

Oram, William, et al., eds. *The Yale Edition of the Shorter Poems of Edmund Spenser.* New Haven, Conn.: Yale University Press, 1989. Complete and annotated, with substantial introductions to the individual poems.

Renwick, W. L., ed. *The Shepheardes Calender, Complaints, Daphnaïda and Other Poems, Amoretti and Epithalamion, A View of the Present State of Ireland.* 5 vols. London: The Scholartis Press, 1928–34. A landmark of Spenser editing, full of trenchant comment and useful illustrative material.

Welsford, Enid, ed. *Spenser:* Fowre Hymnes, Epithalamion: *A Study of Edmund Spenser's Doctrine of Love.* New York: Barnes and Noble, 1967. An elaborately annotated edition with an extended introduction relating Spenser's treatment of love to traditions of neoplatonic and Christian thought.

Zitner, Sheldon P., ed. *The Mutabilitie Cantos.* London: Thomas Nelson and Sons, 1968. Especially valuable for its extended introduction and notes.

## SECONDARY WORKS

Listed are the books most likely to help students in their initial work with the texts; I have omitted all articles and many excellent specialized works. I have also emphasized criticism of *The Faerie Queene,* briefly treated in this book. Students of the shorter poems might start by reading the entries in *The Spenser Encyclopedia* and using the bibliographies appended there.

Hamilton, A. C., et al., eds. *The Spenser Encyclopedia*. Toronto: University of Toronto Press, 1990. An invaluable resource, with excellent detailed articles, bibliographies, and a thorough index.

## General Studies

Berger, Harry, Jr. *Revisionary Play: Studies in Spenserian Dynamics*. Berkeley: University of California Press, 1988. Gathers together important essays on the first, third, and sixth books of *The Faerie Queene* and *The Shepheardes Calender*.

Bernard, John. *Ceremonies of Innocence: Pastoralism in the Poetry of Edmund Spenser*. Cambridge, England: Cambridge University Press, 1989. Concerned especially with pastoral as a retreat from the active to the contemplative life. Deals primarily with *The Shepheardes Calender, Colin Clouts Come Home Againe,* and the sixth book of *The Faerie Queene*.

Cheney, Patrick. *Spenser's Famous Flight*. Toronto: University of Toronto Press, 1993. An account of Spenser's works as fulfilling his idea of a literary career.

Helgerson, Richard. *Self-Crowned Laureates: Spenser, Jonson, Milton, and the Literary System*. Berkeley: University of California Press, 1983. Excellent on Spenser's self-definition as a laureate poet, an English Virgil.

Heninger, S. K. *Sidney and Spenser: The Poet as Maker*. University Park: Pennsylvania State University Press, 1989. An excellent account of Spenser emphasizing his platonism, viewing his art as an imitation of an ideal reality.

King, John. *Spenser and the Reformation Tradition*. Princeton, N.J.: Princeton University Press, 1990. Discussions of *The Shepheardes Calender* and *The Faerie Queene* in the light of the native English Protestant tradition.

Nelson, William. *The Poetry of Edmund Spenser*. New York: Columbia University Press, 1963. Shrewd readings of all Spenser's poetic work with attention to intellectual history.

Shore, David. *Spenser and the Poetics of Pastoral: A Study of the World of Colin Clout*. Kingston, Canada: McGill-Queens University Press, 1985. A study of pastoral in *The Shepheardes Calender, Colin Clouts Come Home Againe,* and the sixth book of *The Faerie Queene;* like Bernard, Shore sees the mode as developing a debate about the nature of the poet's commitments.

## Genre Studies

Alpers, Paul. *What Is Pastoral?* Chicago: University of Chicago Press, 1996. Important recent discussion of pastoral with some reference to *The Shepheardes Calender* and book 6 of *The Faerie Queene*.

Cooper, Helen. *Pastoral: Mediaeval into Renaissance*. Totowa, N.J.: Rowman and Littlefield, 1977. Medieval and native traditions of pastoral as they influenced *The Shepheardes Calender*.

Giamatti, A. Bartlett. *The Earthly Paradise and the Renaissance Epic*. Princeton, N.J.: Princeton University Press, 1966. The paradisal garden in European epic tradition with an extended account of the Bower of Bliss.

Greene, Thomas M. *The Descent from Heaven: A Study in Epic Continuity*. New Haven, Conn.: Yale University Press, 1963. Important for its initial chapter on the "Norms of Epic," as well as for individual readings. Has a chapter on Spenser.

Parker, Patricia. *Inescapable Romance: Studies in the Poetics of a Mode.* Princeton, N.J.: Princeton University Press, 1979. A study of the romance genre from Ariosto to Keats, with an extensive chapter on Spenser.

Patterson, Annabelle. *Pastoral and Ideology.* Berkeley: University of California Press, 1987. A study of the political implications of the tradition of pastoral eclogues.

Wofford, Suzanne Lindgren. *The Choice of Achilles: The Ideology of Figure in Epic.* Palo Alto, Calif.: Stanford University Press, 1992. An important account of the ideological work done by epic rhetoric, with an extended chapter on Spenser.


## The Shepheardes Calender

*Note:* See also Bernard, Berger, Cooper, and Shore, above.

Cullen, Patrick. *Spenser, Marvell, and Renaissance Pastoral.* Cambridge, Mass.: Harvard University Press, 1970. An influential study of *The Shepheardes Calender* in relation to classical and Christian traditions of pastoral.

Johnson, Lynn Staley. The Shepheardes Calender: *An Introduction.* University Park: Pennsylvania State University Press, 1990. A richly developed account of *The Shepheardes Calender* in historical context, as a work concerned with reform.


## Amoretti and Epithalamion

Hieatt, A. Kent. *Short Time's Endless Monument.* New York: Columbia University Press, 1960. A seminal numerological reading of the *Epithalamion*.

Johnson, William. *Spenser's* Amoretti: *Analogies of Love.* Lewisburg, Penn.: Bucknell University Press, 1990. An account of the *Amoretti* stressing their relation to the materials of the Bible and the Christian liturgical calender.


## The Faerie Queene

Alpers, Paul. *The Poetry of* The Faerie Queene. Princeton, N.J.: Princeton University Press, 1967. Sensitive analyses of individual parts of *The Faerie Queene,* with special attention to the suggestive surface of Spenser's verse.

Anderson, Judith. *The Growth of a Personal Voice:* Piers Plowman *and* The Faerie Queene. New Haven, Conn.: Yale University Press, 1976. A comparison of the speaker of *Piers Plowman* with that of *The Faerie Queene;* very good on the speaker's emergence during the poem.

Cheney, Donald. *Spenser's Image of Nature: Wild Man and Shepherd in* The Faerie Queene. New Haven, Conn.: Yale University Press, 1966. An account of the uses of pastoral in Spenser's allegory, especially in books 1 and 6.

Evans, Maurice. *Spenser's Anatomy of Heroism.* Cambridge, England: Cambridge University Press, 1970. A fine reading of the whole poem, with emphasis on the first three books.

Fowler, Alastair. *Spenser and the Numbers of Time*. London: Routledge and Kegan Paul, 1964. A numerological and astrological reading of the poem.

Giamatti, A. Bartlett. *Play of the Double Senses*. Englewood Cliffs, N.J.: Prentice-Hall, 1975. Fine brief essays on Spenser's life and literary background and on aspects of *The Faerie Queene*.

Hankins, John Erskine. *Source and Meaning in Spenser's Allegory*. Oxford: Clarendon Press, 1971. An account of Spenser's allegory with special attention to his use of sources. Includes an extended account of the Garden of Adonis.

Heale, Elizabeth. The Faerie Queene: *A Reader's Guide*. Cambridge, England: Cambridge University Press, 1989. A clear, learned, carefully argued introduction to the poem.

Lewis, C[live] S[taples]. *The Allegory of Love*. Oxford: Oxford University Press, 1936. A landmark in the study of allegory and the conventions of medieval love literature, ending with a superb chapter on *The Faerie Queene*.

MacCaffrey, Isabel. *Spenser's Allegory: The Anatomy of Imagination*. Princeton, N.J.: Princeton University Press, 1976. A study of Spenser's treatment of the imagination and of the various kinds of allegory the poem develops.

Meyer, Russell J. The Faerie Queene: *Educating the Reader*. Boston: Twayne Publishers, 1991. A reading that emphasizes the poem's teaching of its audience.

Miller, David. *The Poem's Two Bodies: The Poetics of the 1590 'Faerie Queene.'* Princeton, N.J.: Princeton University Press, 1988. An important Lacanian reading of the first three books.

O'Connell, Michael. *Mirror and Veil: The Historical Dimension of Spenser's* Faerie Queene. Chapel Hill: University of North Carolina Press, 1977. The most thorough and thoughtful account of the poem's treatment of history.

Quilligan, Maureen. *Spenser, Milton, and the Politics of Reading*. Ithaca, N.Y.: Cornell University Press, 1983. The sexual politics of *The Faerie Queene* and *Paradise Lost* and the relation of the poems to one another.

Tonkin, Humphrey. *The Faerie Queene*. London: Unwin Hymen, 1989. A very good introduction to the poem, with particular attention to its patriotic and historical concerns.

Williams, Kathleen. *Spenser's World of Glass: A Reading of* The Faerie Queene. Berkeley: University of California Press, 1966. One of the best books on the poem as a whole.

## Book 1

Rose, Mark. *Spenser's Art: A Companion to Book 1 of* The Faerie Queene. Cambridge, Mass.: Harvard University Press, 1975. A helpful and perceptive canto-by-canto account of the opening book.

## Book 2

Berger, Harry, Jr. *The Allegorical Temper: Vision and Reality in Book 2 of Spenser's* Faerie Queene. New Haven, Conn.: Yale University Press, 1957. A groundbreaking work and still one of the most challenging readings of this book.

**Books 3 and 4**

Goldberg, Jonathan. *Endlesse Worke: Spenser and the Structures of Discourse.* Baltimore: Johns Hopkins University Press, 1981. A structuralist study of book 4 as programmatically refusing closure and conclusive meaning.

Roche, Thomas. *The Kindly Flame: A Study of the Third and Fourth Books of* The Faerie Queene. Princeton, N.J.: Princeton University Press, 1964. Puts forth both a theory of allegory and an influential reading of the two books.

Silberman, Lauren. *Transforming Desire: Erotic Knowledge in Books 3 and 4 of* The Faerie Queene. Berkeley: University of California Press, 1995. An acute, methodologically sophisticated reading of the central books.

**Book 5**

Aptekar, Jane. *Icons of Justice: Iconography and Thematic Imagery in Book 5 of* The Faerie Queene. New York: Columbia University Press, 1967. A reading of the book's ambivalences; works extensively with iconographic traditions.

Dunseath, T. K. *Spenser's Allegory of Justice in Book 5 of* The Faerie Queene. Princeton, N.J.: Princeton University Press, 1968. Treats Artegal's development.

Fletcher, Angus. *The Prophetic Moment: An Essay on Spenser.* Chicago: University of Chicago Press, 1971. Spenser's insistence on the transcendent meanings implicit in the book's historical particulars.

**Book 6**

Tonkin, Humphrey. *Spenser's Courteous Pastoral.* Oxford: Clarendon Press, 1972. An excellent reading of book 6, with particular attention to the vision of courtesy on Mount Acidale.

*Article Collections*

Bloom, Harold, ed. *Modern Critical Views: Edmund Spenser.* New York: Chelsea House, 1986. A good collection of articles; lacks footnotes.

Hamilton, A. C., ed. *Essential Articles for the Study of Edmund Spenser.* Hamden, Conn.: Archon Books, 1972. A fine gathering of criticism up the to early 1970s.

MacLean, Hugh, and Anne Lake Prescott, eds. *Edmund Spenser's Poetry.* 3d ed. New York: Norton, 1993. This edition contains 150 pages of good, representative criticism from the last 30 years.

Miller, David, and Alexander Dunlop, eds. *Approaches to Teaching Spenser's* Faerie Queene. New York: Modern Language Association, 1994. An excellent selection of essays suggesting a range of current approaches to the epic.

# Index

# Character Index:

# The Author

William Allan Oram is Helen Means Professor of English at Smith College. He is coordinating editor of *The Yale Edition of the Shorter Poems of Edmund Spenser* and the author of articles on Spenser, Milton, Drayton, and Herrick. A member of the board of *English Literary Renaissance,* he has served as president of the Spenser Society and chair of the program committee for the Spenser Sessions of the Medieval Institute at Kalamazoo, Michigan.